A
BIOGRAPHICAL DICTIONARY

CONTAINING
A BRIEF ACCOUNT
OF THE
FIRST SETTLERS
AND
OTHER EMINENT CHARACTERS
AMONG THE
MAGISTRATES, MINISTERS,
LITERARY AND WORTHY MEN
IN
NEW ENGLAND

John Eliot, D.D.

Corresponding Secretary of the Massachusetts Historical Society

These were honoured in their generations, and were
the glory of their times.   — *Son of Syrach.*

HERITAGE BOOKS
2025

HERITAGE BOOKS

AN IMPRINT OF HERITAGE BOOKS, INC.

Books, CDs, and more—Worldwide

For our listing of thousands of titles see our website
at
www.HeritageBooks.com

A Facsimile Reprint
Published 2025 by
HERITAGE BOOKS, INC.
Publishing Division
5810 Ruatan Street
Berwyn Heights, MD 20740

— Publisher's Notice —
In reprints such as this, it is often not possible to remove
blemishes from the original. We feel the contents of this
book warrant its reissue despite these blemishes and
hope you will agree and read it with pleasure.

International Standard Book Number
Paperbound: 978-0-7884-0159-6

A
BIOGRAPHICAL DICTIONARY,

CONTAINING

A BRIEF ACCOUNT

OF THE

FIRST SETTLERS,

AND

OTHER EMINENT CHARACTERS

AMONG THE

MAGISTRATES, MINISTERS,

LITERARY AND WORTHY MEN,

IN

NEW-ENGLAND.

BY JOHN ELIOT, D.D.

Corresponding Secretary of the Massachusetts Historical Society.

These were honoured in their generations, and were the glory of their times.   *Son of Syrach.*

PUBLISHED BY CUSHING AND APPLETON, SALEM,

AND EDWARD OLIVER, NO. 70, STATE STREET, BOSTON.

1809.

R. OLIVER, PRINTER.

PREFACE.

FOR the credit of human nature, some men have appeared in every age, who adorned their lives by good actions, or their publick stations by the dignity, virtue, and splendid excellencies of their characters. Memoirs of such persons excite a lively interest, and, from admiring their extraordinary qualities, we desire to see them in various attitudes, and to know the incidents of their private life. Hence encouragement is given to works of biography, which, in some form or other, are daily issuing from the press. Even short sketches of eminent men have been thought instructive, as well as entertaining.

The first discoverers of this quarter of the globe possessed the spirit of enterprise in a very uncommon degree. The fathers of New England were remarkable for their piety and moral worth, and also for their active virtues. They were men of firmness and resolution, ready to endure every suffering, for the sake of civil and religious freedom. They had to level forests where savage beasts, and savage men had roamed for ages, and to make comfortable dwelling places amidst barren deserts. By their sagacity and prudence, their attention to the means of improving their situation, they soon enjoyed the blessings of civilized and cultivated society. Among the first planters, we find men of genius and literary acquirements, who would have been conspicuous as statesmen in the courts of Europe, or as divines of the church of England. It is no wonder that their characters were so highly esteemed by the puritans in their own country, or that they shone as lights in the dark places of this American wilderness. Cotton, Hooker and Davenport might well rank with the Lightfoots and Owens of the age ; they had equal reputation as scholars at the universities. President Chauncy, as professor of Greek, or Hebrew, had no superiour, and might have had any preferment in the national church, if he had become subservient to the views of archbishop Laud. Norton wrote Latin with elegance and purity; his name was celebrated in various nations of Europe. Less is said about Roger Williams before he left his native country. He was young, and perhaps did not preach with the same force as he wrote. All who peruse his works will wonder at the vast expansion of his mind, and lament the eccentricities of his conduct.

The succeeding generation bore a resemblance to their fathers in their character, but were not equal to them in erudition. The writer of the Magnalia divides into three classes the eminent preachers, who emigrated to New England. The first were in the exercise of their ministry when they came over. They were educated either at Oxford, or Cambridge. The second class comprehends those, whose education was unfinished, and had only such advantages to complete it, as they could obtain in the plantations. Mr. John Higginson, Mr. Sherman and Thomas Thacher were the most famous among them. The third consisted of those who were ejected from the ministry, after the restoration of the monarchy, and establishment of the episcopal church. These were pious and good men; but in their literary accomplishments they were not superiour to those who were educated at Harvard College, which was the only seminary in North America for many years. This institution could not vie with the colleges in Europe for endowments; but during the civil wars of England, the universities lost their ablest professors, and less attention was paid to the means of making eminent scholars. We may well suppose that polite literature would fall prostrate with the laws of the realm. Few went to the pure fountains of classical knowledge, though many Greek and Roman authors were read. The works of their theologians, some of whom were great and excellent men, displayed the stores of learning without the skill and graces of composition. The quaint style and manner, which then prevailed in England, was imitated by our American divines. They were as much disgusted with the works of the English writers, who lived in the reign of Charles or of William, as the most famous authors in Great Britain, in those reigns, were disgusted with the writings of the preceding age. Cotton Mather, the most voluminous American author, and a man of immense learning, has very little credit with the present generation, because his narrations are so prolix, and so many strange things occur in so strange a style. He was a man of unbounded fancy, astonishing memory, but of no judgment. With his marvellous stories he has, however, collected many facts, and it would be unpardonable if the author of this work did not pay a tribute to his memory. Every writer of the affairs of Massachusetts is much indebted to him for the use of his materials.

From the date of the new charter we find very few leading characters, who were not born and bred in the colonies. There was no great encouragement for men, who had genius and talents, to come over to New England for the sake of gaining a subsistence. At this time, it has been said, that learning was at a low ebb in our country. A late writer has thus described the college at New Haven : " The students had heard of a certain new and strange philosophy in vogue in England, and the names of Boyle, Locke and Newton had reached them, but they were not suffered to think that any valuable improvements were to be expected from philosophical innovations"* This description is much exaggerated by the prejudices of a party writer. One of the governours of Connecticut had been the intimate friend of Mr. Boyle, and was a principal founder of the royal society. Two of the corporation of Harvard College were fellows of the royal society at this very time, and the mode of instruction was the same in both seminaries. Can we suppose that the Newtonian philosophy was not adopted, or that the first characters in their churches and colleges were sitting so contentedly in the shades of ignorance? From our sketches it will appear, that we had at this period not only students in the new philosophy, but scholars who excelled in polite learning. Philological inquiries grew fashionable, and very excellent productions appeared from the hands of gentlemen in civil life, as well as from the clergy. It is true that these were days of tranquillity, and such times are not favourable to great exertions. If we except the disturbances, which were caused by Indian wars, we can hardly conceive of a more happy state of society, than New England exhibited for the first half of the 18th century. The people were submissive to the laws. There was order in the cities, peace in the villages, and religion in the temples. These are not the times to display great talents any more than great

Chandler's life of Dr. Johnson, president of King's College.

crimes. When occasion called forth the exertions of American citizens, they discovered vigour, abilities, as well as patriotism, strong and manly virtues with political skill, and all that energy of character necessary for raising provinces into an empire. During the course of the war, the officers of the American army showed courage and magnanimity. They were brave, active, with a spirit of enterprise, and would have obtained distinction in the armies of Europe. The members of the first congress were viewed with admiration bordering on enthusiasm. Their abilities as statesmen, and their political integrity, did honour to the United States, and gained them respect from the great men of other nations. They certainly have a claim upon the gratitude of posterity. If more particular attention have been paid to one part of this biographical work, it is in doing justice to the characters of those who lived between the peace of Paris, and the commencement of the American revolution. The age of the writer made every thing impressive. He was acquainted with those who were active in our publick concerns, and has been favoured with written accounts, that are strengthened by the opinion and conversation of those who are still alive. Whenever he has recurred to the publications of the day, he has endeavoured to gain collateral evidence to make the representation just. In writing biography we ought to be very careful about taking the character from newspapers. Facts are not always to be depended upon; characters very seldom. If the deceased had virtues they are exaggerated by his friends; and how often are particular delineations made by those who knew not the man! A pen is employed which is elegant, and if the sketch is done in the best manner, there is no inquiry whether it be true? If we had no other knowledge of men, but what we get from newspapers, would there be a proper discrimination between the good and bad members of society?

A remark of a similar kind may be made upon funeral sermons. If they are not in the style of eulogy they are not printed. What the preacher says he doubtless believes; but how often is his opinion different from that of his audience? How many funeral orators paint nothing? Such performances require a nice and delicate pencil to finish; but, in general, they are the most unstudied compositions of their authors. This is not, however, what first excited the remark. Our objection is, that they are not pure sources of information. A preacher is to say nothing but good of the dead; a writer of lives nothing but the truth; for he exhibits men as they were. The preacher is apt to give a general view of the characters; it is the object of the biographer to enter into the most minute details. All funeral sermons, however, are not liable to the same censure. Those preached upon the death of ministers sometimes bring an obscure clergyman into view, who preferred the shade, as the most agreeable situation, but whose virtues and talents ought to be known, that others might be stimulated by the example. On the other hand, preachers often say better things of their brethren than they deserve; upon no occasion is friendship or flattery more indelicately manifested. The reputation of the deceased depends in some measure upon the orator. If his performance be admired, strangers who read it will think highly of the subject. If the discourse be dull or inelegant, it perhaps is not printed, and no character published. However eminent the deceased was in life, he is not known beyond the line of his near acquaintance, among whom his reputation is long preserved by a most affectionate remembrance.

The author of this work has taken the freedom to mingle his own observations with the documents received from others. His taste always led him to collect curious mss. and ancient books; he was favoured with many letters of the Hutchinson and Oliver families; and had free access to the books and mss. of the Massachusetts Historical Society. He has mostly written from one general mass of information, which he has been many years in collecting; but where he has been indebted for principal facts he has pointed to the main source of his intelligence. The original design was to give a view of eminent men in North America. The difficulty of obtaining documents, or such peculiar notices as are necessary for proper delineations of characters, induced the writer to confine himself to New England. Some articles in its present form are omitted, which would be equally interesting as those which appear. Certain notices, which he expected to receive, did not arrive till it was too late for their insertion. He particularly regrets the omission of judge Trowbridge of Cambridge, gov. Jenks of Rhode Island, Mr. Hobart of Fairfield, Mr. Ellsworth, Mr. Tracy, and several other gentlemen of distinction in Connecticut.

In the beginning of the work, several lives are disproportionate to the general scale, which obliged the author to compress the articles in other parts, and under the last letters of the alphabet to introduce no person who has died since the commencement of the nineteenth century. Among those are several magistrates of this state, president Willard and professor Tappan of Cambridge, and several eminent clergymen. Memoirs of these gentlemen have been published lately, and their characters ably and fully delineated; but with the addition of such names, any work would be materially improved. If the book should ever pass through another edition improvements may be expected.

For the errors which the reader may find in the following pages some apology ought to be made, especially for the transposition of several names and the misplacing of figures in the dates. These are corrected among other typographical *errata*. One name is introduced, page 351, which ought not to appear among persons deceased. Those who thought the information of his death correct, are happy to learn that the gentleman still lives.

In the course of his proceeding the author has been indebted to several friends for their suggestions, encouragement and assistance. Without their kind attentions his labour would have been wearisome. The delicacy and warmth of their friendship have excited sensations which are better felt than expressed; for their literary communications, as well as tokens of their esteem and affection, he begs them to accept his grateful acknowledgements.

A

NEW-ENGLAND

BIOGRAPHICAL DICTIONARY.

————:000:————

ABBOT HULL, minister of the church in Charlestown, was a native of Massachusetts ; graduated at Harvard College in 1720. He was among the first students that were put upon Mr. Hollis's foundation, and recommended by *Mr. Hollis himself*, as a youth meriting the benefit of the fund for indigent and good scholars. In 1723 he was ordained, colleague pastor with the famous Mr. Bradstreet, and continued in the ministry till his death, 1774.

He left a few printed discourses, chiefly occasional, and his character was respectable as a gentleman and divine. *

ADAMS MATTHEW, is worthy of notice in an account of ingenious and literary men of Boston. In the life of Franklin it is said, that he kindled the zeal and encouraged the talents of that philosopher, who had free access to his books; and Dr. Franklin speaks of him with respect and acknowledged his attentions. Mr. Adams was only a mechanick, but with the advantages of a college education would have made considerable progress in scientifick researches, and been very useful at that period. He was one of the writers in the New-England Journal. The essays

* His printed discourses are, Artillery Election Sermon, 8vo. Boston, 1735. A Sermon upon the rebellion in Scotland, 8vo. 1746. A Sermon against profane swearing and cursing, 8vo. 1747.

he contributed were received with marks of publick esteem, and reprinted in periodical miscellanies
of later date. Like many other ingenious men,
Mr. Adams lived in depressed circumstances, and
died with a name and character rather than any
worldly estate. He left several children, who inherited his genius, one of whom was

JOHN ADAMS, minister of the church in Durham, New-Hampshire. His father laboured to give
him a liberal education, and he was graduated at
Harvard College in 1745, and in a few years after
ordained at Durham, where he continued pastor of
the church more than twenty years. No town in
New England was ever more disturbed by fanaticks than Durham. A spirit of opposition to the
order of the churches raged there. Every man
who received a liberal education, who wore a band
or black coat, and held a regular service on the
Lord's day, was called hireling, thief, wolf, and
any thing that would make him odious. They
after this manner insulted this pious minister, who
had not patience to bear it, and was often inveloped
in gloom, or ready to sink into despondency. This
might, in some measure, be owing to the constitution of the man. For he was in his best days, and
when he was not exposed to peculiar trials of his
ministry, very much the sport of his feelings.
Sometimes he was so depressed as to seem like a
being mingling with the dust, and suddenly would
mount up to heaven with a bolder wing than any of
his contemporaries. This would happen frequently in the pulpit, so that when he had been all the
week preparing a sermon which was, according to
his own expression as dull as his feelings, he would
feel an exertion that would give him health, cheerfulness, and new life. It was his method to take a
new text, and give a flow to his sentiments and expressions, which were much better than he was
ever able to utter, with previous consideration. His
delivery then was as lively as his fancy. In these

happy moments he was also a cheerful, instructive and entertaining companion. He could write as well as speak, like one who had cultivated a philological taste. A specimen of his abilities was exhibited in a letter written to a committee of the town of Boston, 1774, when the *Port Bill* had annihilated their commerce.*

Mr. Adams was obliged to leave Durham in the year 1778, in consequence of other disturbances than religious. He had been thought the most proper minister to live with people so enthusiastick as the inhabitants of Durham; for he was himself, from his animal frame and pious sentiments, inclined to enthusiasm; had rather favoured than opposed the *New Lights* in his youth, and preached the gospel according to the strictest *sect* of our forefathers; but as one extreme succeeds another, the most cold indifference to every thing of a religious nature was visible in the inhabitants of Durham during the latter part of Mr. Adams's pastoral relation; and they grew weary of maintaining a minister, in addition to the demands of money, to carry on the war; a contention arose upon the most frivolous pretences, and a council advised to a removal. He was soon invited to settle at Washington, in the county of York, Massachusetts. With this flock he lived in more easy circumstances. He died 1793, aged about 60 years.

ADAMS JOHN Rev. a divine, a poet, a writer of essays, &c. He was the son of the Hon. John Adams, of Nova-Scotia, and was graduated at Harvard College, 1701. He died at Cambridge, 1740. The fellows of the College were his pall-holders, and the first characters in the state attended the funeral. His character was very respectable, though doubtless the eulogy in the Boston newspapers, was from the pen of one strongly prejudiced in his favour—" It deserves to

* There was a committee appointed to receive donations. The letter was accompanied with a present from the inhabitants of Durham.

be written in letters of gold on monuments of marble, or rather to appear and shine forth from some genius of uncommon sublimity and equal to his own, But sufficient are his immortal writings to perpetuate his memory." His literary friends issued proposals for publishing a volume of his sermons, but the subscription failed. They published a volume of poems which discover a good imagination and pure taste. They are equal to any New-England poetry of this date, though not meriting in the encomium passed upon his writings. A second edition was never called for. The book is very scarce, and ought to be preserved among the rare works of *American authors.*

He published during his life, a poem on the love of money, which is ingenious and satirical. It is not contained in the volume.

A DAMS A MOS, minister of the first church in Roxbury, was a very popular preacher, having a voice uncommonly sonorous and plaintive. The energy of his manner in the pulpit is often mentioned by those who sat under his ministry. He was praised in other churches, as a very accomplished preacher, but many were disgusted with his plainness of speech, the length of his discourses, and his very desultory observations. All allowed him to discover some knowledge of human nature, in the addresses he made to his hearers. His preaching was calculated to prick the consciences of sinners, though they wanted correct discrimination and smoothness of period. His memory was tenacious, and his reading very extensive. His publications never appeared to satisfy the expectations of those who heard thm from the pulpit. They want his animated delivery.*

* He printed several ordination sermons. A funeral sermon upon the death of Madam Dudley. A Thanksgiving discourse, 1759.

The discourses which give him the most reputation were two *upon religious liberty*; and *two upon the sufferings of our fathers,* which were re-printed in England, not as sermons, but with the title of a *Concise History of New-England,* The evangelical sen-

Mr. Adams was graduated at Cambridge, 1752, and died at Roxbury, October, 1778, to the inexpressible grief of his family and flock. At this time a putrid dysentery prevailed in the camp at Roxbury and Cambridge, which spread more than twenty miles in the environs of Boston. The people of the first church in Roxbury were very much scattered, but Mr. Adams was assiduous in his labours, and not only visited his own flock, but the soldiers who were stationed among the people of his parochial charge. He himself soon fell a victim to the disease.

ADAMS SAMUEL, a man celebrated in the annals of America, was as remarkable for his piety and puritanism, in younger life, as for his political influence, during the contests of the merican revolution. He was born September, 1722, in Boston. His ancestors were respectable, among the early planters of New-England, but not sufficiently distinguished to be inserted in a genealogical list; and every kind of genealogy he affected to despise, as a thing which gives birth to family pride. His education was liberal, having commenced his studies at the South Grammar School, under the care of Mr. Lovell. He entered Harvard College A. D. 1736. The honours of that seminary he received in the years 1740 and 1743. He made a very considerable progress in classical learning, the art of logic, as it was then taught, as well as the elements of natural philosophy. But his main object was the study of divinity, as he was designed for the ministry.

He was always fond of systematic divinity, and was a Calvinist, of the straitest sect of that denomination. It was the belief of our fathers, and he never spake of them but with the greatest reverence.

timents are curtailed. We see little more then the dry bones of a skeleton, not well hung together. All his printed d scourses are bound in two volumes, 8vo. which he presented to the College Library.

The platform of the New-England churches, in his view, contained every thing necessary or proper for the order and discipline of ecclesiastical bodies, and the Westminster assembly's *shorter catechism*, all the articles of *sound doctrine*.

Why he did not engage in a profession, which was so congenial to his views and habits, does not appear ; but for many years he was uncertain what line of life to pursue.   He only engaged in a petty kind of trafficking ; his business was small, his situation humble, and he seemed to walk in the vales and descents of life, rather than to be formed for conspicuous stations or very active scenes. The same political cast of mind then appeared, which influenced his conduct afterwards. If he spake of men and manners it was freely to canvass them ; his conversation was in praise of old times, his manners were austere, his remarks never favourable to the rising generation ; and he would depreciate the talents and services of those who held offices of honour and public trust.   No man ever despised more those fools of fortune, whom the multitude admire ; and yet he thought the opinion of the common people in most cases to be very correct.

As we have said his employment was humble, it may be proper to mention that his first office in the town was that of tax gatherer ; which the opposite party in politicks often alluded to, and in their controversies would style him Samuel the *Publican.* While the British regiments were in town, the tories enjoyed a kind of triumph, and invented every mode of burlesquing the popular leaders : but where the people tax themselves the office of collector is respectable ; it was at that time given to gentlemen who had seen better days, and needed some pecuniary assistance, having merited the esteem and confidence of their fellow townsmen. Mr. Adams was ill qualified to fill an office which required such constant attention to pecuniary matters ; and, his soul being bent on politicks, he passed more time in talking against Great Britain than in collecting the sums due to the town. He grew embarrassed in his circumstances, and was assisted, not only by private friends, but by many others who knew him only as a spirited partisan in the cause of liberty.

From this time, the whigs were determined to support him to the utmost of their power. He had been always on their side, was firm and sagacious, one of the best writers in the newspapers, ready upon every question, but especially conversant with all matters which related to the dispute between Great Britain and the colonies.

The people in the north section of the town were then more numerous than they have been since; and were by a very large majority on the side of freedom. When Pownal was in the chair, he favoured this party, and lifted several men to office whose merit was rather in their principles and notions, than in their sagacity. It answered his purpose, which was to defeat the schemes of Hutchinson : and it really had a surprising effect upon the transactions of the town.

Mr. S. Adams was well acquainted with every shipwright, and substantial mechanick, and they were his firm friends through all the scenes of the revolution, believing that to him more than any other man in the community we owed our independence. This sentiment prevailed with many who disliked his opinion of federal measures, and who would not vote for him to be governor of the commonwealth. They would often say that he from his age, habits and local prejudices, was not formed to mingle with politicians of a later period, whose views must necessarily be more comprehensive, and whose object was to restrain rather than give a loose to popular feelings. It was their opinion, however, that he did worthily in those times, when instead of building up a government suited to the condition of a people, we had only to pull

down a government becoming every day more ty-
rannical. When the stamp act was the subject of
conversation, of public resentment, and succeeding
tumults, Mr. Adams was one of those important
characters, who appeared to oppose it in every
step. He did not think it amiss to pull down the
office, though he disapproved of the riotous proceedings which the same lawless men were guilty
of afterwards ; for every succeeding night witness-
ed the rage of an infatuated populace, and no man
in any office whatever was safe in his habitation.
If a man had any pique against his neighbour it was
only to call him a few hard names, and his property would certainly be destroyed, his house pulled
down and his life be in jeopardy. The authority of
the town put an end to this savage conduct by
calling out the militia ; and soon after the news of
the repeal of the *stamp act* quieted the minds of all
classes of people.

The *taxes* upon *tea*, *oil* and *colours* were still
more odious to the Americans than the *stamp act ;*
especially to the inhabitants of Boston, where the
board of commissioners was established. The people looked to Mr. Adams, as one of the champions
of liberty, who must stand forth against every claim
of Great Britain, and deny the right of the parent
state to lay a tax ; nor were they disappointed. He
was so strenuous in his exertions to make the people sensible of their charter privileges, that he obtained the appellation of the *patriot Samuel Adams.*

The other members of the general court, from
the town of Boston, were Mr. Otis, Mr. Cushing, and
Mr. Hancock, gentlemen of the same political sentiments, and united in their opposition to the claims
of the British ministry. Mr. Adams had frequently delivered his sentiments in the publick papers ; and being a ready penman was often employed on committees to make reports, addresses, &c.
and to vindicate the acts of the legislature. He assisted in writing most of the letters, which were

sent to the secretary of state. One letter addressed to the earl of Hillsborough was entirely his. His draught was accepted by the house of representatives, and, without any alteration, sent to that nobleman, who was supposed to be most inimical to the colonies of all the king's servants ; and whose name was never mentioned in Massachusetts without reproach.

In the year 1769, the governor removed the general court to Cambridge. The members considered it as an infringement of their rights. Mr. Adams was on the committee to draw up their remonstrances, which were warm and urgent. For several years the governor thus obeyed his instructions, to keep the assembly out of Boston. There were some altercations among the representatives, whether they would proceed or not to business ; and when it was determined to go on, there was a spirited protest, in which our politician took a very conspicuous part. During these sessions at Cambridge, a difference of opinion arose, upon some secondary matters, between Adams and Hancock, which cooled their friendship, and was succeeded by an antipathy, that had an effect upon the minds of the people, many of whom took a warm interest in this personal animosity, though they agreed in political sentiments ; and acted together in the great affairs which arrested the attention of all the whigs. The first impressions were unfavourable to Mr. Adams; for many of the high whigs thought him austere and rigid in his notions, that he was opinionated, and that his object was as much to mortify Hutchinson, and gratify his resentment against the tories, as to serve the cause of freedom. Hancock was the idol of the populace ; his spirit was generous, he enjoyed an affluence of wealth, which he was ready to bestow on all publick occasions : he was affable, condescending, and very engaging in his manners. Mr. Adams preferred to be thought a *Cato* rather than a *Lucullus*. His friends were

lessened in number, but they were the sternest republicans; and those, perhaps, who first dared to
view our independence as *near*. They called themselves the most consistent whigs. Others called
them the restless spirits of their party, who wished
not to have grievances redressed, but to sail upon
troubled waves, as their own political importance
depended upon the tumult of the people. They
mixed in public assemblies; used a coarser style
of speaking in the streets; and calculated upon the
future scenes which would open for the emancipa-
tion of the country.—The period soon arrived:
The battle of Lexington gave the moderate party a
zeal which blazed, and every man became a patriot. Adams and Hancock were proscribed soon after by Gage's proclamation. This was all they wanted to raise their reputation to the highest pitch.
Before they could have known this, they had reason to be satisfied with the triumph of the whigs,
and must have been fully persuaded they were safe
in any part of the country. These gentlemen were
at Lexington the very night the British troops left
Boston, and it was generally supposed that part of
the errand was to take them. They received such
intelligence as to be on their guard. A friend of
Mr. Adams spread a report that he spake with pleasure on the occurrences of the 19th of April. "It
is a fine day," said he, walking in the field after the
day dawned. "Very pleasant answered one of his
companions," supposing him to be contemplating
the beauties of the sky. "I mean," he replied,
"this day is a glorious day for America." So
fearless was he of consequences, so intrepid in the
midst of dangers, so eager to look forward to the
lustre of events that would succeed the gloom which
then involved the minds of the people. Mr. Adams
had been a member of the continental congress the
preceding year. Mr. Hancock from ill health was
not a candidate for the same congress, but was president of the provincial assembly which bore the

name of provincial congress in Massachusetts. They were both members of the congress which sat at Philadelphia, A. D. 1775, 76, &c.

Among the southern whigs the character of Mr. Adams was very high. He was looked upon as an able politician, though less liberal in his views, less informed in great questions of national concern, than several characters from these northern states : but his republican sentiments were congenial to the sentiments of many gentlemen of Pennsylvania and Virginia, who quoted his opinion with respect. There were, however, some southern members of congress who called him an indifferent statesman, a local politician, one whose thoughts were always in Fanieul Hall, and bent upon establishing the customs of the Plymouth settlers ; or introducing the laws of Massachusetts, instead of that enlightened policy which was necessary to animate a great nation ; a nation who had to form their government, to adapt novel opinions to the prudence of old laws, to execute some of the noblest schemes ever designed by man, and which no other state of human affairs had ever given them an opportunity to know and improve.

Mr. Adams was chosen secretary of the state of Massachusetts in the year 1774, while the general court were at Cambridge. The business was performed by a deputy until the year that his seat was vacated in Congress. He was never afterwards a candidate for any office out of Massachusetts government. While he sat in Congress the declaration of Independence was made, which he urged with the utmost zeal. Also the articles of the old confederation to which he was always much attached. It was a favorite expression, which he often gave as a toast in public companies and private circles—"The *states united,* and the *states separate.*" There was also another matter of importance which took place in the autumn of 1777, when the British troops marched to Philadelphia, it was given out that gen. Washington might have prevented them. That, although an excellent and very amiable character, he was too much a *Fabius* in the *field*. He had, however, fought the battle of Brandywine with an army inferiour to the enemy ; and made an attack upon Germantown which only wanted success to make it add much to his military reputation ; it being well planned, and the general discovering great activity and courage in collecting troops, who had been so entirely dispersed a few days before.

An alteration was contemplated in the military arrangements, and the public papers declared that a majority of Congress had determined to advance gen. Gates to a command which would imply a censure upon the commander in chief. Although this did not originate with Mr. Adams, he was known to be unfriendly to Washington, and after this he was not a favourite with certain military gentlemen who had been his most active partizans. Some of these officers had a conference with him in Boston, and he declared that he never meant that Gates, or any other officer who was not born in America, should supercede Washington or be commander in chief. Perhaps he only meant that there should be separate commands, and the generals to be independent of each other, and of the same rank, and to look to the Congress for the chief direction.

Whether he was attached to the General, or thought him the most proper person for the high office of President of the United States, is a subject of opinion, on which his fellow citizens differed. It is certain that president Washington did not speak of him with the highest respect.

It has been said in a European publication, that Mr. Samuel Adams made the motion for Independence, and that he sacrificed a large fortune in the cause of his country. This is not true. But it is true that he contributed to the Independence of America, as much as any man, by his enterprising

spirit at an early period of the contest, by his patri-
otic zeal, by his influence on the minds of the people ; yet no individual ought to be styled the Father
of our Independence. For a nation to be born it
required all the mighty efforts of those bold, wise and
noble-minded statesmen, who adorned this era in
the annals of their country by their presence in
the first Congress.

From being secretary of the commonwealth of
Massachusetts, Mr. Adams was chosen a member of
the senate of the state after the government was
formed in the year 1780, and was placed at the head
of that respectable branch of the legislature.   He
had been one the members of the convention which
formed the government, was a principal leader in
the debates, and eminently useful, from his knowledge and experience, in the committee which made
the first draught; as well as in the great body which
shaped it in its present form ; and styled it the Constitution of *Government* for the *state* of *Massachusetts.*   The address of the convention to the people
was composed by him, and another gentleman who
has since filled several offices of honour and trust in
the commonwealth.

Whilst Mr. Adams was president of the senate,
he was punctual in his attendance upon every part
of duty, and adhered strictly to all the regulations
and forms of proceeding ; till finding the infirmities
of age coming upon him, he was persuaded to resign the chair, a place which required dispatch as
well as constant assiduities in business.   He was
succeeded by Mr. Phillips, who afterwards succeeded him as lieut. governor of the state.

During the time of his influence in the senate,
there was an insurrection, which threatened the
overthrow of the government.   Whoever recollects
the popular phrensy will give due credit to the wise,
spirited and energetic measures which were then
urged, and carried into effect. The most direful
consequences were prevented, the tumult was soon

quelled, and the people as soon convinced of their delusion. In this dark scene of adversity, when even a civil war had commenced, no man was more firm and intrepid than Mr. Adams. It was his constant declaration, that *republicks* could exist only by a due submission to the laws : that the laws ought to be put in force against all opposition, and that a government could be supported by the exertions of a free, virtuous, and enlightened people.

The year after the insurrection the administration was changed ; Mr. Bowdoin was succeeded by gov. Hancock. This was contrary to the opinion of Mr. Adams. No man could have conducted himself in this office better than the former gentleman, yet many people in the commonwealth indulged the idea, that Mr. H. having the confidence of the people more than the other, might serve the commonwealth more effectually at this time. Gen. Lincoln, the officer who had quelled the insurrection, was put into the office of lieut. governor. Perhaps this might also chagrin the good old patriot. It was evident that he disliked this choice, and the opportunity was improved to bring about a reconciliation between two men whose friendship had been broken, and succeeded by personal hatred, but who were now to act like friends, and form a political union in which the sentiments of the heart might have little concern.— Soon after the insurrection, the convention met at Philadelphia to form a new constitution of government for the United States. When the constitution was completed, a convention was assembled in Massachusetts to consider it ; and Mr. Adams was also one of the twelve representatives of Boston. In this body he was almost a silent voter. In former assemblies he had spoken upon every question that became an object of discussion, and as he grew older was remarkable for his garrulity ; yet here he seldom opened his mouth. He had said so much against it in conversation prior to the meeting of this body, that he well knew if he praised it he would be charged with inconsistency, which had been no part of his character through life; and if he spake against it, he was sensible of the odium it would bring upon him; for his constituents were a strong phalanx in defence of it. The trade of the town had been stagnant. The mechanicks were in want of business, and from this they expected golden dreams of prosperity.

Our politician voted for the adoption of the constitution with amendments. He himself proposed one amendment which was not adopted; and which he soon withdrew. It excited a strong resentment at the time, and would have given still greater offence, if he had not declared that it was far from his intention to excite a jealousy that the people's liberty was to be infringed.—There are two different opinions on this part of his conduct: one that it was his design to prejudice the republican party against the constitution: the other that he only wished to have something originating from himself, and therefore proposed an amendment, which he had not well considered, or not at all digested. From this time, however, he was viewed as the leader of that party which disliked the mixture of aristocracy said to exist in that form of government; and looked with pleasure at the things going on in France. It is certain that all those who were styled antifederalists supported his character and influence; and that those who disliked the administration of the government under Washington and Adams, as well as those who first disliked the constitution itself, united their energies to exalt his reputation in his old age; to blazon his name among the first worthies of America, and to give him all the merit that could possibly be due to his services.

Mr. Adams was chosen governor of the state of Massachusetts in 1794, having been second in authority and honour five years. He continued in the chair three years, and then resigned.

The last six years of his life he passed in retirement. At no time did party spirit rage with more violence; but he could only mingle his voice with the friends who visited him. Some mortifications every one must meet with. In public life great men are not without their cares : in the evening of their days when they seek for rest, every want of attention in their old acquaintance is a thorn in their pillow. Many of the old friends of gov. Adams who had gone hand in hand with him during the revolution now forsook him, though he yet received the respect, attentions and caresses of those, who thought him not more venerable for age, than he was for his attachment to republican principles. He was the decided friend of the Jeffersonian administration. Several letters which passed between him and president John Adams discovered his opinion of the politicks of the day, and his general ideas of government. He died in a good old age, and in full belief of those religious principles in which he had been educated, and which he was free to defend even against Thomas Paine himself.

The letter Paine wrote to him in answer to one, which was certainly well meant, discovered *that man* as much a stranger to good manners as to pure sentiments, and moral worth.

His character may be summed up with saying, that he was a respectable politician, though too much influenced by local prejudices. He never appeared to so much advantage in Congress as in Fanieul Hall. He never liked the habits of the people in the southern states. In the latter part of his life he coalesced with their politicks, but the Puritans of New England were the men to set an example to the world. He never swerved from these ideas which imbued his mind at a tender age. His moral sentiments were ever mingled with his politicks, and he perhaps thought too highly of the forms of religion. He was a poor man, who despised riches, and possessed as proud a spirit as those who roll in affluence or command armies. He had three topicks of conversation upon which he always dwelt—*British thraldom*—the *manners, laws* and *customs* of *New-England*—the benefit of publick schools to the rising generation. By publick schools he meant such as there are in every town in Massachusetts, which diffuse knowledge equally among all classes of people ; for he set his face against academies.— In his zeal he often repeated his opinion, and perhaps in his conversation exhibited more the character of a true New England man, than any one of his contemporaries, on which account he was revered still more by his old friends who cease not to mention this, when they describe his worth, his talents, and his exertions in the cause of his country.

ADAMS ZABDIEL, was minister of the church in Lunenburgh and was graduated at Harvard College, 1759.

He was born at Quincy. His father was brother to the father of the late president of the United States, and his mother, whose maiden name was Anne Boylstone, was sister to the president's mother. Mr. Adams was respectable for his abilities. His sermons were sensible and plain, and he delivered them with animation. He also discovered acuteness in managing a controversy upon a question that was agitated in 1774. " *Whether a negative power be allowed to the pastor over the proceedings of the people, in the formation of our churches.*" He took a position which could not be maintained by the platform, or any just sentiments of religious freedom, though many pastors of churches have adopted it, and some reduced it to practice, viz. *That the pastor has a negative, in the proceedings of the church, in the same manner as the governor of Massachusetts negatived acts of the general court.** He was provoked to write this pamphlet from an attack made upon a sermon he had printed, by an anonymous writer, who calls himself *a neighbour.*

* The governors under the crown had a complete negative.

His antagonist answered Mr. Adams' book; and gained the advantage, though he was by no means so fair a disputant. He had the voice of the people, and common sense on his side ; yet he seemed to prefer the glory of a partizan to that of defending the truth. He asserts that a minister is *primus inter pares;* or the moderator of a meeting, which very term explains his power. And he was fortunate enough to find a civil magistrate to answer to this station. The governor of Connecticut has no power of negativing, nor had the governor of Massachusetts till the charter of William and Mary. The old charter had been inhumanly murdered by one of the Stuart race, all of whom were enemies to civil and religious liberty. If ministers or ruling elders, says this anonymous writer, have a negative upon the brethren they must be a distinct branch, or act in distinct bodies and branches, and then the minister or eldership cannot have the moderatorship, according to any acting bodies whatever, or according to the reason and nature of things. The king is not president, nor moderator of the house of lords ; nor the governor of the province president of the council in legislative proceedings, where he is a distinct branch. Several ministers in the county of Worcester adhered to the principles advanced in Mr. Adams' book, and lost their parishes.*

Upon several publick occasions, Mr. Adams was

* From this militant state of the churches arose contentions and contests at our courts of justice. One of the clergy who was dismissed without calling a council, prosecuted for his salary. The question was argued. John Adams defended the minister in the supreme court. The question *of negative* power was not introduced. The people had gone to another extreme in opposition to the platform : more so than the pastor they accused.— They meant to reduce it to a mere piece of parchment, according to the insurgent spirit that was then raging. The ravens of discord were let loose against all form and order. The state of publick affairs prevented a final decision. Since the revolution the question has been revived and urged in a more popular manner; and several ministers lost their salaries when the opinion of the court was unanimous in their favour.

elected to preach discourses, and he always did himself honour, and gratified the hearers. He preached the Dudlean lecture, 1794, upon Presbyterian ordination : which was not printed, but in the opinion of the president of the University, it was one of the very best that had been delivered. He died March 1, 1801, in the 62d year of his age, and 37th of his ministry.

His printed discourses are, the election sermon, 1783. Several at the ordination of young men to the ministry, in some of which subjects of controversy are handled with independence of spirit, acrimony of speech and generous sentiments. He was always highly esteemed by the more liberal part of the clergy.

ADDINGTON ISAAC, an eminent magistrate of Massachusetts. He was one of those worthies who opposed the administration of sir Edmund Andross ; and was appointed secretary of the province, by those who adhered to the old charter. He also received the same appointment from the crown when the charter of William and Mary was brought over. He was chosen for many years one of the council, and was very active as a justice of the peace. He died 1714, leaving a character very respectable for integrity, wisdom and industry.

Judge Dudley, who was then attorney general, and who married one of his daughters, took the seals till Mr. Woodward the next secretary was appointed.

ALDEN JOHN, one of the worthies who first came over to Plymouth in the year 1620. He was then a young man. He settled in Duxbury, on a farm which is now the best in the town, and has been always in possession of one of his descendants. All of the name are descended from him. And many of his posterity have been useful and distinguished members of society. This gentleman lived to the age of 88. For many years he was one of the *assistants* in the old colony. Two of his grand children were living in 1774. Col. Alden who was killed at Cherry valley, was his great grandson. His father was capt. Samuel Alden, who was alive when the revolution commenced.—He saw a new empire peopled with three millions where his grandfather saw nothing but a savage wilderness. *Aldens Cent. Sermon.*

ALLEN THOMAS, minister of the church in Charlestown, was born in the city of Norwich, in 1608; was graduated at Caius College, Cambridge University; and ordained minister of St. Edmunds, in the same city. In 1636, when the clergy were required to read the *book of sports*, he refused, and lost his parish by order from bishop Wren. He sailed from England, and arrived at Boston in 1638. He was invited to settle at Charlestown, and continued their pastor till the year 1651. He then returned to England and spent the remainder of his days at Norwich, where the people highly respected him. Dr. Mather speaks of him as a pious and laborious minister, and a man *greatly beloved;* which he says is the original of the name Allen, or *Alwine,* as it is in the Saxon.

While he was in this country he composed a book entitled an "invitation to thirsty sinners to come unto their saviour," which was printed twice, and prefaced by Mr. Higginson. He also composed another, called "The scripture chronology" which was printed in England, 1659.

Dr. Calamy mentions two other publications— The "way of the Spirit in bringing souls to Christ," and a number of sermons upon "the necessity of faith." He is in the list of ejected ministers, 1662, but he continued to preach till his death, Sept. 1673, etat. 65. *Magnalia, page 215. Calamy's Account of ejected ministers, vol. II.*

ALLEN JOHN, first minister of the gospel in Dedham, Massachusetts, A. D. 1737.

He is styled a courteous man by the author of *Wonder working providences,* who says likewise that

he was full of christian love, while he made such a
bold stand against the errors of the times. He died 1671, etat. 75, having been at Dedham 24 years.

Dr. Mather calls him a diligent student and good
scholar. It is evident that he had good abilities for
a polemical divine from his *Defence of the nine proposition which were so many points of church discipline.* In this work he was assisted by Mr. *Shepherd* of *Cambridge.**

In the synod of 1662, Mr. Allen made a very
conspicuous figure, and he wrote in defence of it
against the celebrated president Chauncy. Besides
these controversial pieces he printed a few discourses which are not now to be met with. His friends
also, published the two last discourses he ever
preached, one from Canticles, viii. 5, and the other from John, xiv. 22. From their account we must
think his epitaph just.

JOHANNES ALLEN,

Vir sincerus, amans pacis ; patiensq ; laboris
Perspicuus, simplex, doctrinæ purus amator.

ALLEN JAMES, one of the silenced ministers who
left England after the act of Uniformity, 1662. He
came to Boston, and was invited to preach at the
first church, as an assistant to Mr. Davenport. Having continued with them six years he was ordained
their teacher, Dec. 9, 1668. He lived in the style
of a gentleman, built a stone house which is now oc-
cupied by his great grandson, the sheriff of Suffolk,
and which is probably the oldest house in the town.
It is said " that he had a farm of forty acres in Boston." He had certainly a very handsome estate, and
was kind and hospitable. He was very strongly
attached to the *order of the churches*, as defended by

* In the history of Cambridge (Hist. Coll. 7th vol.) we find
among the works of Mr. Shepherd, a *discourse to clear up the
old way of Christ*, in the churches of New-England. Mr. Cotton
speaks with respect of these divines. Shephardus cum Allinio
fratre (fratrum dulce par) uti eximia pietate, et conditione non
mediocri, atque etiam mysteriorum pietatis predicatione, &c.
Preface to Norton's sermon.

Dr. Increase Mather, his particular friend, and opposed those attempts to introduce innovations which were made in more than one instance during his ministry. He died Sept. 22, 1710, in the 78th year of his age.*

His posterity have been respectable in Massachusetts. His eldest son James received a liberal education, and Jeremiah his second son, was treasurer of the province. They both filled several offices, with ability and reputation. *Calamy's Account of ejected ministers. Private information.*

ALLEN JAMES, the grandson of the °Rev. Mr. Allen, was elected a member of the house of representatives for Boston, 1739. At this time a pointed opposition was made to the administration of gov. Belcher, and the town of Boston took the lead in it so as to change their representation.†

Mr. Allen continued in opposition to the government while Shirley was in the chair, and was once expelled the house for his freedom of speech. The town immediately rechose him. The house refused him his seat. The altercation lasted till the May succeeding, when another house of representatives was appointed, among whom Mr. Allen's name is enrolled, and to which no objection could be made. He continued a member of the general court till he died, 1755. *Independent Advertiser*, 1749.

ALLEN JOHN, one of the early graduates of Harvard College, having received the honours of that

* The printed works of Mr. Allen are, " Man's reflection, a means to further his recovery of his apostacy from God." 12mo. 2d——The substance of a number of sermons upon the health of the soul. Small quarto. The election sermon, 1679.

† The representatives from Boston, 1738, were Elisha Cooke, esq. Oxenbridge Thacher, esq. Timothy Prout and Thomas Cushing, jun. In 1739, Mr. Thacher and Mr. Prout were left out, because they were Belcher's friends and adhered to his measures—Mr. Allen and Mr. Kilby, who were his most violent opposers, men of zeal in whatever they undertook, were elected in their places. Mr. Bromfield who was likewise on the popular side was a third in the new choice—Mr. Cooke had died previous to the election.

infant seminary in 1643. He was settled in the ministry at Great Yarmouth, in Old England, as a colleague with Mr. John Brinsley ; and was silenced by the act of Uniformity, 1662. He afterwards took a house *at Goulstone* and often preached. He preferred this place because it was out of the jurisdiction of the bishop of Norwich, who was an enemy to Independents. He died, A. D. 1675, after passing the 50th year of his age. *Calamy's continuation, page* 67.

ALLEN JAMES, first minister of the church in Brookline was a native of Roxbury. He was graduated at Harvard College, 1710 ; was ordained 1718, and died 1747, in the 56th year of his age, and 29th of his ministry. " He was a pious and judicious divine." He was one of the ministers who encouraged the revival of religion in 1743, but afterwards, like many other zealous brethren, expressed his disappointment concerning its general effect upon the churches, and on the morals of individuals. He lived and died as a christian, and his publications do equal honour to his head and heart.* *Pierce's Cent. sermon.*

ALLEN ETHAN, was a man born for troublesome times. In a tranquil state of society, and in rural walks he might only have been distinguished for his great bodily strength, or rude, boisterous behaviour. But opportunities were not wanting to display the peculiar genius of the man and his local situation made him a warrior before he was called to fight the battles of his country. The lands granted by the province of New Hampshire to certain settlers, were claimed by the state of New York. If the people who held the lands had made this acknowledgment, they must have purchased what

* He printed seven sermons.—1. Thanksgiving sermon, Nov. 1722.—2. Upon the government of the world by a wise providence, 1727.—3. The doctrine of merit exploded, 1727.—4. Upon the great earthquake, 1727.—5. A sermon to young men, 1731.—6. A funeral sermon upon the death of Mr. Aspinwall, 1733.—7. The election sermon, 1744.

they considered as their own. They disputed the title, and defended themselves by arms. Allen was their leader, and he was declared an outlaw. As soon as hostilities commenced between Great Britain and her colonies, these hardy soldiers of the wilderness, engaged fiercely in the cause of America, and marched directly to Ticonderoga and Crown Point, which places were garrisoned by British troops. These garrisons were surprised and taken May 10th, the former by Allen, and the other by col. Seth Warner, one of the boldest of these mountaneers, who from this time took the name of the *Green mountain boys.*

After this, col. Allen passed the lake with the troops that gen. Montgomery commanded, and was sent to the Canadians to give them information and gain their influence, in which he met with some success. This was during the summer months. He went a second time in November. But attempting to take Montreal, he with his whole party of Canadians, were taken prisoners. He says, that Brown first proposed this, but did not assist him according to his promise. It was thought an imprudent action, and col. Allen, whose fame had been trumpeted through the provinces, was now called a " high flying genius" fearless as a man, but without prudence for a superior officer. His courage did not forsake him when he was taken, but he acted and spake like one conscious of doing well, and deserving applause. He was put in irons and sent over the Atlantick, was in prison in England, and aboard a vessel, in Halifax and New York, and in 1771 exchanged for col. Archibald Campbell, who had been taken with a battalion *of Highlanders* in Boston bay in the summer of 1776. He published a book the next year, which is styled " his narrative" which makes him a hero in suffering as well as action.

We hear but little of him during the last year of the war, the historian not finding so many instances of his prowess as are related in the narrative.—He might perhaps expect a separate command, which some officers had who were inferior to him in the date of their commisions, or had not been so early in the field. He appeared after his exchange to have been more of a politician than a warrior ; and entered fully into all the debates about making the green mountains a separate state ; and amused his mind at the same time with theological enquiries. With these, the publick were favoured. He printed a book called the *Oracles of Reason* in which he thought he had said enough to discard all revelation. But he was not fortunate enough to convince others that religion was a fable ; or that he was able to manage a controversy in which men of much greater ingenuity had failed. The book was equally bad in argument and style ; it was wretchedly printed, very little read, and is now wholly forgotten.

ALLEN EBENEZER, also a green mountain boy, was one of the first soldiers of the revolution. He was in the party that went against Ticonderoga. With forty men he went upon the hill Defiance, and carried the fortress without loss of a man. He also distinguished himself in the battle of Bennington ; taking advantage of a breastwork of rocks, he contended with the front of the enemy, till he caused a temporary retreat. He was among those who exerted themselves in making Vermont a separate state, and lived to see not only the wilderness subdued, where he first ploughed the ground, but the places filled with inhabitants.—The account of his death is mentioned in the newspapers of the year 1805.

ALLERTON JOHN, one of the number who arrived at Plymouth, 1620—he died the first winter.

ALLERTON ISAAC, one of the first settlers, who was employed as their agent in England upon several occasions. In 1620 he went over to treat with the adventurers and to obtain money and articles which were wanted in the plantation. The next year he went again upon a similar errand, and Nov. 6, finished "the bargain with the company at London, delivered his bonds and received their deeds." In 1628 he returned to New England, and was sent in the fall as the agent of those planters, that he might get their Kennebeck patent enlarged, and give some assistance to their friends at Leyden. He returned the next year without accomplishing their object, the enlargement and confirmation of the Plymouth patent. Morton was his clerk in this business, who came over with him, and proved a scourge to the plantation, and also Mr. Rodgers an independent minister, who proved insane, and whom he carried back the year after according to the wishes of his brethren. They also commissioned him to finish the business of the patent. He returned to New England in the spring of 1630, and brought over Ashley and others who had taken a *patent* for Penobscot to trade with the natives in those eastern parts.

We find no further account of his being employed upon publick business. It is most likely he spent the remainder of his days with the people at Plymouth, but the year of his death is not recorded.

AMES DR. NATHANIEL, of Dedham, Massachusetts, was eminent as a physician and mathematician. He published an almanack forty years successively, which was so highly reputed, that no other almanacks were saleable in this and the neighbouring states. When he died, in the year 1765, he had made the calculations for the ensuing year. The almanack was published as his, and so attached were all classes of people to the name, that the demand was great for all that were printed. This worthy man descended in a direct line from the Rev. William Ames, son of the famous Franequer professor, who wrote the *Medulla Theologiæ*.*

*Mr. William Ames was likewise ejected from Wrentham, and the next parish, Frostendon : Having been in the year 1648

AMES FISHER, Esq. the son of the astronomer, one of the most brilliant men this country ever produced, was born at Dedham, and graduated at Harvard College, 1774, when he was only 16 years of age. His compositions at this early period were excellent and original. They discovered not only a rich and glowing fancy, but correct taste and judgment beyond what could be expected from a youth. During the revolutionary war he was engaged in no particular business, but dwelt in the family mansion at Dedham, where he must have adorned and enriched his mind with those stores of knowledge which enabled him to give such delight to his friends, and render such eminent services to the community.

He was afterwards a student at law, and from exercising his profession a few years, he was introduced into a more extensive field of usefulness. In 1788 the convention met in Boston for the purpose of deliberating on the constitution recommended by the grand federal convention. He was sent as a member to this body, from his native town, and made a distinguished figure among the most eloquent speakers. A passage from one speech he

settled as co-pastor with his uncle Phillips, to the church of Christ in Wrentham ; and likewise preaching one part of the Lord's day at Frostendon for many years. And at that time, I suppose Mr. Thomas King, after Mr. Phillips' great decay, supplied at Wrentham. Mr. Ames died in the year 1689, in the 66th year of his age. He was the son of the famous Dr. William Ames, (who after having been twelve years pastor at Franequer, was dismissed from thence, in order to his being professor at Rotterdam, and died not in 1639, as has been represented by some, but in 1633:) and when a child went over with his mother to New England, where he had his education at Harvard College, and became a graduate in 1645, and returned to Old England and came to Wrentham in 1646. He was a very holy man, of the Congregational persuasion, and in all respects an excellent person. He hath a sermon in print entitled the " saints security against seducing spirits ; or, the anointing from the Holy One the best teaching ;" on 1. John, ii. 20 ; preached at Paul's, before the lord mayor, aldermen, &c. Nov. 5, 1651. *Calamy's Continuation, &c. vol. II. pp. 797, 798.*

made early in the session, was quoted with high approbation by a southern orator in their convention,
as being the most forcible and animating description
of the spirit of democracy. The eyes of the people
were turned to him when they elected members of
Congress ; and he represented the Suffolk District
eight years.   Amidst that constellation of worthies
he shone a star of the first magnitude. The latter
part of the time, his health was peculiarly delicate,
and his feeble frame would often sink under the
bold efforts made by a mind of superior native vigour and wonderfully active. But although he was
able to pay less attention to publick concerns than
he was prompted by the ardent desire of his soul,
he delivered some of the best speeches ever heard
in an American assembly. From this publick
sphere he went to the shades of retirement, where
he could enjoy his book, and his friends ; attend to
rural affairs or, as his health permitted, to the business of his profession.

He was chosen into the council in the administration of gov. Sumner, and when the legislature
met after the death of Washington, he was elected
by them to pronounce the publick eulogy.   The
degree of Doctor of Laws he received from New
Jersey, and he was unanimously chosen president of
Harvard College, which honour he declined in a
polite letter to the corporation.   His last days on
earth were painful from his bodily complaints, but
the vigour of his mind never failed ; many admirable productions of a political nature came from his
pen, equally instructive and entertaining, full of virtuous sentiments and true patriotick zeal.   During
every period of his life, his splendid abilities were
guarded by his integrity and religion, and " adorned with the choicest flowers of eloquence :" and
even when the last breath lingered on his trembling
lips the recollection of his past life armed him with
resignation ; and the pure principles of his religious
belief turned the *shadows of death into the light* of
the morning.

His funeral was attended in Boston by all classes of people, and an eulogy was pronounced by the hon. Mr. Dexter. His body was then conveyed to Dedham to be deposited in the family tomb. The publick earnestly desired that a subscription might be brought forward for his works, which are to be collected in a volume ; and with them will be given a more complete biography than has yet appeared.

APPLETON NATHANIEL, D. D. minister of the church in Cambridge was the son of the hon. John Appleton, esq. of Ipswich. He was graduated at Harvard College, 1712 ; ordained, 1717 ; and died Feb. 9, 1784. His manner of preaching was plain, practical and impressive. It is said, that in the younger part of life he excelled as a publick speaker. Many of the present generation remember him as a man venerable for his piety, his prudence and his age. " New England can furnish few instances of more useful talents, and of more exemplary piety, united with a ministry equally long and successful."

There was a cheerfulness mingled with the gravity of his deportment ; such a disposition to make every one happy around him, as rendered his society acceptable to the rising generation ; and he received peculiar tokens of respect from the ingenuous youth of the university. He often preached when ministers were ordained ; and his discourses were calculated to promote harmony, love and peace. There were times when he was obliged to exert all his fortitude, prudence and candour to conduct so, as *not* to give offence.

While Mr. Whitefield was in the zenith of his popularity, the president, and other instructors of the college bore their testimony against him on account of the uncharitable and slanderous reports he made of the state of that seminary. He addressed a letter in reply, which was answered by the professor of divinity. Many pastors of the churches in Massachusetts and Connecticut, also testified against the errors and disorders which then prevailed. Dr. Appleton was censured for his moderation, which was then a very unfashionable virtue, and he was requested by many zealous members of his own church, and by some of his brethren in the ministry, to admit that wonderful preacher into his pulpit. He continued steadfast, however, in supporting the interest and honour of the college. Mr. Whitefield was sensible of his error, when riper years had tempered the fervour of his youthful spirit, and with christian candour he publickly acknowledged his fault. When Harvard Hall was burnt in 1764, he solicited benefactions in England and Scotland, and his kindness met with a grateful return. Every attention was paid him by the president and fellows of the university, on his last visit to America, and Dr. Appleton invited him to preach in his church. The scene was interesting: Mr. Whitefield was uncommonly affectionate in speaking of the aged divine in his prayer, and in his address to the people of his charge. His text was 1. Cor. iii. 11. Several ministers who had always attended Mr. Whitefield's preaching observed, that he never displayed more eloquence, or delivered a more correct discourse.

Dr. Appleton's prudence was exercised in a trial of a different nature some years preceding the revolutionary war. He was as true a Whig in his political, as he was a Calvinist in his religious principles. But several of his hearers were on the other side of the question, and had rendered themselves very unpopular in their publick stations. They had been among his particular friends, and while they blamed him for his opposition to the government, others who were with him in his politicks made severe remarks upon his complaisance to Tories. None, however, could ever accuse him of " speaking unadvisedly with his lips."

Dr. Appleton was fellow of the corporation of Harvard College from the year 1719 to 1779. He then resigned on account of his age. He sat at the board with five presidents. He delivered funeral discourses upon three, Leverett, Wadsworth and Holyoke. Another discourse he also printed when Mr. Flint died, who had been more than 60 years a fellow and tutor of the college.*

ANDROSS EDMUND sir, governor of New-York, New-England and Virginia, came to New-York, anno, 1674, with a commission as governor, having only the title of major Andross, being sent by the duke of York, after he had obtained a grant of the land from the king of England. His administration began with lenient measures, the effect rather of his policy than clemency, or he soon discovered a temper, cruel to individuals and unfriendly to the state. One instance of this was, his quarrelling with Carteret who then exercised jurisdiction over New Jersey. By an exertion of power he threw him into prison for which it is said he was deprived of the government ; but did not lose the favor of the duke, to whom he was a compleat sycophant, making himself subservient to all his arbitrary designs and superstitious devices.

He was appointed governor of New England in 1686, and arrived in Boston on the 29th day of December. The first commission which was granted by James after he came to the throne was to *Dudley*, as president of a council of twenty eight ; of this council Randolph was secretary. But this was of a

* Dr. Holmes has given a list of Dr. Appleton's publications. The wisdom of God in the redemption of man, 1728, 12mo. Discourses on Romans viii. 14, 12mo, 1743. Eight funeral sermons. Six ordination sermons. Two fast sermons. Two thanksgiving sermons. A sermon at the artillery election, 1735 ; general election, 1742 ; convention of ministers, 1743 ; on the difference between legal and evangelical righteousness, 1749 ; at the Boston lecture, 1763 ; against prophane swearing, 1765. He also preached the Dudleian lecture sermon, 1758, upon the validity of Presbyterian ordination.

short duration ; and more extensive powers were
given to Sir Edmund, as he was then styled and every vestige of the old charter was obliterated. His
prejudices were strong against the people of Massachusetts, and the puritanism of New England, these
prejudices he discovered when governor of New
York and they were confimed by Randolph, who is
handed down to us as one of the most despicable
wretches that ever held an office in our government.

· In the year 1688, this governor of Massachusetts,
and of all New England, received another commission, by which New York was added to his jurisdiction. This was said to be done in order to unite
the colonies and make them more formidable to the
French ; but the true reason of it was to abridge
their liberties and to annihilate every idea of their
own importance, and in a particular manner to deprive them of those privileges which were founded
upon former claims, the freedom of the press was
restrained, and no book could be printed without
the license* of Mr. secretary Randolph. This was
an early instance of his ill will to the people and was
followed by a restraint upon marriages. He exact-
ed bonds from all who entered into the matrimonial state, to be forfeited if there should be afterwards
found any lawful impediment. The congregational teachers were considered as laymen, and the fathers of New England considered marriage as a
mere civil contract ; the magistrates also might le-
gally perform the ceremonies. This was not con-
sonant to the ideas of the church of England or of
Rome, an address was therefore sent to the bishop
of London, begging that no marriage should be
deemed lawful unless the ceremony was performed

---

* It has been observed, that a complaint of this kind was rather
inconsistent, as it implied that the press was perfectly free before.
This was not the case, it had been under restraint during former
administrations ; the only change was in the *licenser*—Randolph
prevented every publication which did not suit his own humour
and prejudice.

by a minister of the church of England.* The Congregational societies were to be taxed for the maintenance of the Episcopal clergy. The people were threatened with having their meeting-houses taken from them, or that their mode of worship should not be tolerated. This we have from Hutchinson, who was indeed attached to the forms of the New England churches, though, like Dudley, he often sacrificed his religious prejudices at the shrine of worldly honour.

The people swelled with rage at having their civil and religious liberties trampled upon by an arbitrary governor. The loss of their freeholds was now added to their distresses; and they might well consider whether their lives were to be long secure. They were roused to exertion, and sent Dr. Increase Mather, who was then president of Harvard College, as their agent to England. He was ordered to represent things as they actually were, and to make this rational request—that *the right which they had to their freeholds might be confirmed; and that no laws be made, or monies raised, without an assembly.*

While their civil affairs were thus conducted, sir Edmund was called upon to display his military talents. To stop the incursions of the Indians, who had burnt several of the eastern settlements, he marched a thousand men into their country in the depth of winter; by which he shewed more prowess than judgment. The governor was much blamed; for he might have been informed by the hunters, that the aboriginals always retired into the woods

---

* In one of Randolph's letters he writes, " I press for able and " sober ministers, and we will contribute largely to their mainte- " nance ; but one thing will mainly help, when no marriages shall " hereafter be allowed lawful but such as are made by the minis- " ters of the church of England."

In another letter to gov. Hinckley, quoted by Hutchinson, he says, " perhaps it will be as reasonable to move, that your colony " should be rated to pay our minister of the church of England, " who now preaches in Boston, and you hear him not, as to " make the Quakers pay in your colony.

to spend the winter, where the most alert scouting
parties would hardly find them.   He returned to
Boston with a part of his army, having put the remainder into winter quarters in two forts which he
built, viz. one at Sheepscot and the other at Pejep-
scot falls.   These were the only fruits of his campaign.

The revolution which placed William and Mary
upon the throne proved most fortunate for New England. The friends of this court were the friends of
the colony ; and were also disposed to reverse the
proceedings under the late king, especially where
an attack had been made upon the freedom of the
subject.   As soon as it was rumoured, that the
prince of Orange had prevailed in England, the inhabitants of Boston assembled; sounding the trumpet from the north, every part of the town was in
commotion.   To prevent any extravagance among
the insurgents, the old magistrates put themselves
at their head, and endeavoured to keep things calm
and regular till advices could be received from the
old country.   Sir Edmund retired with his friends,
and several members of the council, to the fort in
Boston. A summons was sent to him upon the
18th of April, 1689, signed by the former governor
Bradstreet, Mr. Stoughton, and others, to whom he
surrendered. The violence of the people, who had
come in from the country, could scarcely be restrained.   They insisted upon his being chained as a
traitor.   It became necessary, in order to gratify
this vindictive spirit, and in fact for his own personal safety, to keep him under confinement in the fort.
When the news came, that William and Mary were
proclaimed king and queen, it was received with joy
by the inhabitants of New England.   Soon after,
sir Edmund demanded his liberty ; but the representatives resolved that he, with several others, could
not be admitted to bail, and they were kept in prison until by orders from the king they were sent to
England.   The king gave assurances that he should

be removed, and promised Mr. agent Mather that he should be made to answer for his mal-conduct. Complaints against him were laid before the privy council; and at the same time he preferred a charge against the colony for rebellion, imprisoning the king's governor, &c. The next day they were all discharged; and upon a report made to his majesty in council, the matter was dismissed by both parties.

Andross was afterwards made governor of Virginia, and arrived there in Feb 1692. He brought over the college charter. Whether he had become more mild by age, more wise by experience, or found it to be more for his interest, there was a change in his measures, and his administration is spoken well of by the historians of the province. He gave encouragement to agriculture, manufactures, and the arts. Fulling mills were erected by act of assembly in his time, the cultivation of cotton he particularly favoured. He loved method and dispatch in all kind of business. During his administration the *state house* was destroyed by fire, together with many of the original patents, records, and deeds of land, &c. He was very assiduous in sorting such as were saved, and caused them to be registered in a better manner than they had been before. He offered to rebuild the state house several times; and it was thought, that much of the expense which attended the rebuilding of it would have been saved if he had continued in the government. But he was removed in 1698, and was succeeded by Francis Nicholson, esq. From that time there was an end of improvement in manufactures, towns and trade. Sir Edmund Andross died in London, Feb. 24, 1713—14.* *Smith's Hist. N. York. Neil. Cook's letter. Beverly's Hist. of Virginia.*

* Beverly relates an anecdote of sir Edmund which deserves to be repeated, as shewing a trait in his character, though we do not vouch for its truth.—Being upon a journey, he stopped at a poor man's house in Stafford county and asked for a drink of water. An ancient woman came out to him, with a brisk lively lad of about 12 years of age. The lad was of a ruddy and fair complexion, and excited the governor's curiosity so much, that he

ASHURST HENRY sir, Massachusetts agent at the court of Great Britain, was the son of Henry Ashurst, esq. who was a member of parliament, and friend to New England. It is said that he had a " great hand in settling the corporation for propagating the gospel among the Indians in New England, and the parts adjacent." The father and son were both favourable to the dissenters ; yet the latter was made a baronet by Charles the 2d, his lady being the daughter of lord Paget, and himself a favourite, which may seem strange, as he was a man more remarkable for his uprightness, his attachment to religion, and friendly propensities, than brilliant parts. He had, however, great influence at court, and yet very often relieved dissenting ministers when they were fined, or sent to prison. Mr. Hutchinson says, that the family of Ashurst had always been favourable to these plantations ; and, therefore, sir Henry was chosen agent. The first addresses that were sent from Massachusetts, after the restoration, went through his hands, as the medium of communication with the king. When Dr. Increase Mather appeared at the British court to obtain redress of grievances, and favour for Massachusetts colony, he engaged sir H. Ashurst to make application, in the character of their agent. He continued in this relation to the colony for several years, and his services were acknowledged with gratitude. At length, a different influence prevailed among the members of our general court ; and as they

proceeded to ask some questions respecting him. To his great surprise he was assured that he was the son of this woman, at 76 years of age. His excellency smiling at this improbable story, enquired what sort of a man had been his father. The good woman made no reply, but ran and led her husband to the door, who was above an hundred years old. He confirmed what the woman had said. Notwithstanding his great age, he was strong in his limbs and voice, but had lost his sight. The woman had no complaint and retained a vigour uncommon at her years. Sir Edmund was pleased at this extraordinary account ; made himself known to her, and offered to take care of the lad ; but the old folks would not part with him. However, he made them a present of twenty pounds.

could not make him subservient to their party zeal, he was dismissed from the agency, without receiving even the pecuniary reward to which he was justly entitled. This excited his honest resentment, and showed how much republicks want gratitude. He died in 1710.

His brother, *sir William Ashurst,* possessed superior talents. The party in opposition to Dudley chose him agent, but he refused the office, " being well acquainted with the slights put upon his brother." He recommended *Jeremiah Dummer,* who was afterwards chosen.

AUCHMUTY ROBERT, an eminent barrister during the administration of Belcher and Shirley. He was one of the directors of the *Land Bank,* and was sent to England, 1741, being joined with Kilby in the agency. His particular business was to settle the Rhode Island dispute concerning the line. While he was in England, he laid the plan of an expedition to Cape Breton. He wrote a letter to the ministry, dated, Cecil street, 1744.

The latter years of his life he was judge advocate of the court of admiralty.

He left two sons, and one daughter, whom Mr. Pratt married, who was afterwards chief justice of New York. The sons were eminent in their profession. Samuel the eldest was graduated at Harvard College, 1742, was minister of the Episcopal church in the city of New York. He received a degree of doctor in divinity from the university of Oxford.

AUCHMUTY ROBERT succeeded his father in his line of business; had not a college education, but was a most agreeable speaker at the bar; his tongue was mellifluous, and his manner very interesting to the jury. In legal knowledge he was doubtless inferior to several of his contemporaries, but in all important causes, where addresses were to be made to the jury, he was applied to, and was generally successful. He was appointed judge of the admi-

ralty, 1768. But, upon one occasion, he appeared after this, as a pleader at the bar.   He was council
with Mr. Adams, for capt. Thomas Preston, and
perhaps no plea was ever more admired, though the
tide of prejudice was much against his cause.   It
has been since handed round in mss. but at this day,
in the reading, it falls far short of the delivery.

Judge Auchmuty was a zealous royalist, and left
America, 1776, and died in England.

AVERY JOHN, of New Sarum, came to New
England in 1635.   The people of Marblehead desired him to be their minister, but he declined ;
because the church was not gathered, and wen to
Newbury, with a view of fixing his habitation in that
town.   In the course of the year he had pressing
solicitations from the inhabitants of Marblehead,
to sit down with them, and Mr. Cotton, with other
eminent men, advising him, he consented to go
there.   He embarked on board a pinnace, August
11, 1635.   The company consisted of twenty
three, among them Mr. Antony Thacher and
family, and Mr William Eliot, who also came
from New Sarum in the same ship.   On the
14th day of the month, they met with a violent gale which overset the pinnace.   Mr. Avery
was washed by a wave upon the island called
Thacher's Woe, from this melancholy circumstance,
several of Mr. Thacher's family being shipwrecked
upon it.   Mr. Thacher also named the rock upon
which they stood, Avery's fall, because he fell
from it, and perished in the waters.   It bears the
name to the present day.

BACKUS ISAAC, pastor of the first Baptist church
in Middleborough, is eminent among the divines,
and historians of New England.

He had not the advantage of a university education, but his reading was extensive, his memory tenacious, his mind strong.   He was a zealous
preacher, an eager disputant, upright in his conduct, though his speech and manners were rough.

Mr. Backus was born at Norwich, Connecticut, 1724; was ordained over a Congregational church in Middleborough, 1748; became a convert to the sentiments of the Antipedobaptists, 1756. He was active in forming a church of that persuasion, and the same year was installed as their pastor, which relation was continued until his death in the year 1806.

The town of Middleborough chose him one of their delegates in the convention which adopted the federal constitution, and he made a speech in favour of it. This speech he read, though he always preached *extempore*. He never missed an opportunity to censure the custom of carrying notes into the pulpit, and the latter part of his life expressed his chagrin, that so many of his own denomination should imitate the common practice.

He was, however, a very industrious man in writing upon many subjects both of theology, and the antiquities of the country.

The history of the Baptists is in three volumes. The two first, he afterwards abridged in one smaller octavo volume.

This work contains many facts, much important information, and would be read with more interest, had it been written with less party spirit. This may give a zest to logical essays; it is always expected in theological controversies, but it tarnishes the pure and serene lustre of the historick page.*

---

* His other works would (if bound together) make several volumes. They consist of pamphlets which are controversial pieces, essays, sermons, and many of them phillipicks against the oppressive acts of the legislature of Massachusetts, and also against the tyranny of the Congregational churches.

Upon this subject he also wrote many fugitive pieces in the newspapers.

The *Historical Society* were benefited by his labours. He wrote a history of Middleborough which is published in a third volume of their collections. He also contributed other communications, being very exact as to dates, and accurate in correcting topographical errors.

There was no funeral sermon printed after his death, but a short sketch of his character is given in the Baptist missionary magazine, Feb. 1807.

BAILEY JOHN, one of the ejected ministers, 1662, went to Limerick in Ireland, and then found it necessary to remove to New England. He was assistant minister of the first church in Boston from the year 1693 to 1697, the year of his death. He was 54 years old when he died. The members of the church were desirous he should settle as colleague pastor with Mr. Allen, but he declined. Mr. Neal mentions his being minister at Watertown, as well as his brother Thomas, who left Ireland at the same time, and who was, afterwards, minister of the church in that place. They both took up their residence in Watertown, but Mr. J. Bailey only preached occasionally there, as in other churches, until he became assistant to Mr. Allen after the death of Mr. Oxenbridge. The author of the Magnalia celebrates his piety in several pages. He was among his greatest favourites. His own works also praise him. His printed *address to the people at Limerick*, which he wrote in 1684, is full of good advice ; it is sensible and pathetick. He says he was not allowed to preach a farewell sermon to *them, and therefore sends a long letter. He* also wrote *a book upon the glory of God ; and the way in which his people may glorify him.*

He was buried in the common burial place, near the old alms-house, and around the spot lie many of his descendants. Of his posterity now living are two grand children ; three great grand children ; and several of the fifth generation. These are in the female line, and bear the name of Willis or Belknap.

BAILEY THOMAS, minister of Watertown, also one of the ejected ministers. He preached chiefly to the people in that town ; but was a man very acecptable to people in other places. A traveller, who was in New England in their time, says he visited the brothers, J. and T. Bailey, in Boston. He calls them ministers of Boston ; which has led some to doubt the correctness of his relation in other parts of his book.

Among the curious mss. in the cabinet of the Historical Society, are a number of Latin odes or poems in different kinds of verse, by Thomas Bailey, all dated, 1668, at Lindsay.

BALCH WILLIAM, minister of the second church in Bradford, was born at Beverly, 1704. He possessed strong powers of mind. Few of our New England divines have surpassed him in clearness of perception, comprehension of understanding or soundness of judgment. The simplicity of his manners was peculiar, and he had a softness and benevolence in his disposition, which he discovered on occasions where most men would have been irritated. He was graduated at Harvard College, 1724, ordained, 1728,.and died, 1792.

The first years of his ministry were spent in peace and harmony with his people and the neighbouring churches. At length a spirit of disorganization prevailed in many places, especially in the towns near the river Merrimack. Nine members of Mr. Balch's church declared themselves dissatisfied with the preaching of their minister, and made a formal complaint to the brethren. The church thought the complaint unreasonable ; and refused to act upon it. Hence the aggrieved party applied to a neighbouring church to *admonish* their pastor and brethren, according to the direction of the platform, *by the third way of communion.* * The church voted to call a council of the neighbouring churches, and the result was signed by the moderator, the venerable *John Barnard, minister of the first church in Andover,* blaming the conduct of those who complained, and approving the *doings* of the church. Mr. Balch published the whole proceedings in a quarto pamphlet, containing the letters that passed between him and the first church in Gloucester, and the transactions of both churches, till the dispute was settled. This was printed 1744. Two years af-

* Chap. 15.

ter the parochial difference, Messrs. Wigglesworth
of Ipswich, and Chipman of Beverly, made a serious attack upon their brother Balch for propagating
Arminian tenets, and wrote an able defence of the
doctrines of Calvin, which were generally the sentiments of the New England planters. It seems the
former controversy began in 1744, by a declaration
of the aggrieved brethren, that "their pastor propagated doctrines, not agreeing with the confession of
faith of these Congregational churches ;" and also
that the church " neglected the proper means of
convicting said pastor of his errors." The gentleman who wrote against him in 1746, had been assisting those who had complained : and they were
not satisfied with the *result of the council.* Their
work, however, had no other effect than to draw
from Mr. B. a most able reply in which he manifested a temper that, with all his meekness, could
feel rebuke. There is much keen satire mingled
with sensible remark and solid argument.

The separatists in Bradford, after this, built a
meeting house for themselves, and the disaffected
members of other churches. Mr. B. lived to a
good old age. His own flock esteemed and loved
him, and when he was advanced in years settled a
colleague. He lived retired and was fond of husbandry ; and the fruit of his orchard was said to be
the best in the county of Essex. He was fond of
the company of young men of talents, and had fine
colloquial powers, especially in discussing theological subjects. Being very desirous to read every
thing new upon ethicks, and metaphysicks, he made
many enquiries which discovered freedom of thought,
and proved the energy of his mind did not fail him
in those years when " our strength is labour and
sorrow."*

* His publications are—a *Discourse upon self righteousness in
which he declares what are false confidences.* from the parable of
the pharisee and publican, 1742.—Election sermon, 1749.—His
account of the proceedings of the council and his reply to Messrs.
W. and C. make two pamphlets of more than fifty pages.

BARNARD JOHN, minister of the first church in Marblehead, was graduated at Harvard College, 1700, and ordained, 1716. He was appointed chaplain of the army sent in 1707 to reduce Port Royal, now Annapolis, and left a particular account of the expedition in mss. Afterwards he went to England with capt. Wentworth, the gentleman, who, in 1717, was appointed lieut. gov. of New Hampshire. He was in habits of intimacy, during his residence in London, with many eminent ministers ; and a curious spectator of those busy scenes, which were opened by the trial of Dr. Sacheverel, in the latter part of queen Anne's reign. When he arrived in Boston he expected to have been fixed in a church then building in North street ; but Dr. Mather's influence in favour of another young man prevented this connexion. This he always felt as a cruel disappointment. He was a member of the old North Church, and the new society proceeded from it ; he looked up to Dr. Increase Mather as his father ; he was therefore wounded by his nearest friends.

Another kind of prejudice prevented his settling at Roxbury, and which shows how unpopular the character of Dudley was in the neighbourhood where he dwelt. He paid some particular attentions to Mr. Barnard, which is the reason given why the people would not have him for their minister. The inhabitants of Marblehead not having any political bias, nor any personal prejudice, gave him the preference of several candidates who were preaching *upon probation*, according to the New England phrase, which perhaps is peculiar to our churches. He was a burning and shining light for many years, and his praise was in all the churches. His own people reverenced him as their father and friend, and he seemed like a high priest among the clergy of the land. He walked erect in his 88th year, retaining the vigour of his imagination and tone of voice, as one sensible of the importance of his character. He spake with energy upon every subject as though he would impress the rising generation that grey hairs were the mark of wisdom, not of weakness. Such instances are rare, where ministers increase their influence in old age; but those who now recollect Mr. B. often mention the dignity of his appearance, and the great respect shown him by all classes of people. His bodily constitution was so strong that, except once, he never was confined by sickness, till the year of his death, 1770, etat. 89. He left no children, and his estate was given for pious and charitable uses.

In a certain mss. with the college catalogue, against his name is Harvardini Collegii benef. munificus.

In his *diary*, certain improvements in the police of the town are said to have arisen from his advice and exertions. He first gave a spring to that commercial enterprise which changed the town of Marblehead from a fishing place, to the second rank of any town in Massachusetts. He even instructed them in ship building, and military tacticks. He certainly had a great mechanical genius, and was as industrious, as he was enterprising. In the year 1745 he was chosen chaplain of the troops that went to Louisbourg, but he declined on account of his age.

He was unfortunate in thinking himself a poet, because, from this mistaken idea, he published a version of the psalms, which was never adopted in any other church than his own. The vanity of this good man appeared in his fondness for his own productions on a variety of subjects. He was willing to publish whatever he wrote, and it seems from his *memoirs* that he was partial to himself in some other respects.

His theological publications do him much honour, and have been very useful in comforting and edifying pious minds. They consist of several octavo volumes bound, and many pamphlets and sermons.*

* The imperfection of the creature, a number of sermons on

BARNARD THOMAS, minister of the first church in Salem, was the son of the rev. John Barnard of Andover, and respected as one of the most profound, liberal, and excellent men of his profession. He was graduated at Harvard College, 1732, ordained at first over a church in Newbury, Jan. 31, 1738, but was disturbed by fanaticks who went about to expose unconverted ministers, and make divisions in societies. A letter addressed to Joseph Adams, one of the most zealous of these eccentrick preachers, by Mr. Barnard, gives a just state of the disorders in the country at that time. Mr. Barnard was the object of peculiar animosity, as he was a man of superior talents and acquirements ; and they had a strong prejudice against human learning, being very ignorant themselves, and owing their importance to the ignorance of the people. He was dismissed from the church at Newbury at his own desire, and many were grieved, not only of his neighbours and friends, but of those who thought losing such a man from the ministry was an injury to the cause of pure, rational, and evangelical piety.

After leaving Newbury, he studied law, and was a practitioner at the bar. He was representative to the general court from Newbury, but his mind was more bent on theological studies than upon affairs of civil life. His abilities were conspicuous in all kinds of business, but his friends were fully persuaded he would be more happy and more useful as a preacher of the gospel. Hence he accepted an invitation from the first church in Salem to be their pastor, upon the death of the rev. John Sparhawk. He was installed, Sept. 18, 1755. It was much to the honour of Mr. Barnard that the gentleman who

Psalm, cxix, 9, 8vo. 1747.—Mercy to sinners by the gospel, a vol. 8vo. on Acts xvi, 30, 1750.—The election sermon, 1734.—Convention sermon.—Dudlean lecture upon the evidences of Christianity, 1756.

His various printed discourses, without those above mentioned, make four octavo volumes in the college library.

first addressed the church in his favour was one, who adorned the supreme bench as chief justice, and would have been an ornament to any profession; his affection for the place of his nativity made him naturally care for their state. More literary characters were members of this church than of any in the province; and their eyes were turned towards a gentleman whose talents were known, as he would have so good an opportunity to exert them This very respectable society had reason to be satisfied with the choice they made. As long as he lived, he was esteemed and beloved by the wisest and best part of the community His manner of preaching was grave, slow and distinct. He had not sufficient animation in his delivery, but his sermons were rational and judicious, calculated for hearers of thoughtful minds, without that *unction*, popular preachers have, and which seems necessary to give a charm to public discourses. It was observed also by men of good sense, that Mr. Barnard's style of preaching was not the most perspicuous. His favourite author was bishop Butler, whose writings are more remarkable for masterly reasoning, than fine turned sentences. In the deistical controversy Mr. B. was superior to most divines, and he often made it the subject of his publick discourses.

In his sentiments he was considered as a follower of Arminius rather than Calvin; he was a semi-Arian of Dr. Clarke's school.

He suffered much from paralytick complaints the last years of his valuable life. His memory left him, and he could only read his notes by close attention to the writing. In 1772, Mr. Dunbar, a young preacher of extraordinary genius, was settled a colleague; but Mr. Barnard continued to preach till within a few weeks of his death. He died, August 15, 1776, aged 60 years. The late Dr. A. Eliot preached the funeral sermon, at the desire of the church. They were long acquainted, and sincerely loved each other, and the discourse spoke the language of the heart, while it gave just conceptions of the character of his friend.*

BARNARD EDWARD, minister of Haverhill, was the younger son of Mr. B. of Andover, and a most accomplished preacher. He was graduated at Harvard College, 1736, and ordained at Haverhill, 1743. His popular talents were not eminent, but his discourses were correct and excellent composition, and highly relished by scholars and men of taste. He was a fine classical scholar, and excelled in poetry as well as prose. It was much regretted that he did not publish more, as what he did publish was so acceptable. His sermon *upon the good man* would do honour to any divine. He preached the election sermon, 1766; the convention sermon, 1773, which was printed, and an ordination sermon when Mr. Cary was settled at Newbury.

The expectations of his friends were excited, when proposals were issued to publish a volume of sermons in 1774, the year of his death; but the revolutionary war commenced before they were committed to the press, and during those years there was no encouragement for any thing, but what bore an aspect upon the times.

Of his poetry nothing is to be found except a poem upon the death of Mr *Abiel Abbot*, his friend, at college, who took his degree, 1737.

BARTLETT JOSIAH, governor of New Hampshire, was born at Amesbury, in the county of Essex, Massachusetts, 21st Nov. 1729. His ancestors, came from the south of England, and fixed at Newbury. The rudiments of his education he received at Amesbury, at the town school; and having a thirst for knowledge he applied himself to books in various languages, in which he was assisted by a neighbouring clergyman, the rev. Mr.

* His publications are, a sermon before the society for promoting industry, 1757; a funeral sermon on rev. P Clark, Danvers, 1768; sermon at the Dudleian lecture, 1768; also, election sermon, artillery election, and three ordination sermons.

Webster, of Salisbury, an excellent scholar as well
as judicious divine.   Mr. Bartlett had the benefit of
his library and conversation, while he studied physick with a gentleman, who was a practitioner in his
native town.   At the age of 21, he began the practice of physick in Kingston, and very soon became
very eminent in the line of his profession.   In 1764,
a field was open for the useful display of his skill.
The *cynanche maligna* became very prevalent in many towns of New Hampshire, and was a fatal disease
among children.   The method of treating it was as
a highly phlogistick complaint ; but he was led
from his own reason and observations to manage it
differently.   He made use of the *Peruvian bark*, as
an antidote and preventative, and his practice was
successful. This afterwards become general among
physicians.

In 1765, Dr. Bartlett was chosen a member of
the legislature, and from this time was annually
elected till the revolution.   He soon after was made
justice of the peace.   In 1770, he was appointed
lieut. col. of the 7th regiment of militia.   These
commissions he was deprived of in 1774, on account of the active part he took in the controversy
with Great Britain.   This was a time when " the
clashing of parties excited strong passions, which
frequently gained the mastery of reason."   The
governor and council of New Hampshire saw
fit to dissolve the house of assembly, supposing that
a new one might become more flexible, or be more
subservient to their wishes.   In the mean while,
col. Bartlett, with several others planned a kind of
authority which was called a committee of safety.
They met at Exeter, and in the course of events,
were obliged to take upon themselves the whole executive government of the state.   When a provincial congress had again organised the government,
col. Bartlett received a new appointment as justice
of the peace, and col. of the 7th regiment.

The first members who were chosen to represent

the state in congress were col. Bartlett and Mr.
Pickering of Portsmouth.   This was in 1774.—
They were both excused from going to Philadelphia ; and Mr. Folsom, and major Sullivan were
elected.   Col. Eartlett was prevented from accepting this honourable trust by the unhappy condition
of his domestic affairs; his house having been burnt,
his family were obliged to seek a shelter without
any thing but the clothes they had upon them. He
was elected member of the second congress which
assembled at Philadelphia the next year, and also
attended his duty in the same station, 1776.   He
was the first that signed the declaration of independence after the president.

In 1777, col. Bartlett and gen. Peabody were appointed agents to provide medical aid and other necessaries for the New Hampshire troops, who went
with gen. Stark, and for this purpose repaired to
Bennington, a spot distinguished by a battle very
important in its consequences.   In April, 1778, he
again went as a delegate to congress with John
Wentworth, esq of Dover.—He returned in November, and would no longer appear as a candidate
for that office.

When the state of New Hampshire was organized,
under a popular government, col. Bartlett was appointed judge of the common pleas ; in June, 1782,
a judge of the supreme court; in 1788, chief justice.

In June, 1790, he was elected president of the
state, which office he held till the Constitution abro-
gated the office of president, and substituted the title of the chief magistrate, governor.   He was then
chosen the first governor of New Hampshire since
the revolution.   He resigned the chair in 1794, on
account of his infirm state of health, and then retired from publick business.

He had been the chief agent in forming the medical society of New Hampshire, which was incorporated in 1791, of which he was president, till his public

H

labours ceased, and when he resigned, he received a warm acknowledgment of his services and patronage, in a letter of thanks which is upon the *records* of the society. He was always a patron of learning and a friend to learned men. Without the advantages of a college education he was an example to stimulate those who have been blessed with every advantage in early life, but cannot exhibit such improvement of their talents, or such exertions in the cause of literature. It was his opinion that republicks cannot exist without knowledge and virtue in the people.

He received an honorary degree of doctor of medicine from Dartmouth University, and was an honorary member of the Agricultural Society.

Gov. Bartlett did not live long after he resigned his publick employments. His health had been declining a number of years. In 1789 he lost his wife, a very amiable lady, with whom he had lived happily; it affected his spirits and increased the lassitude of his frame; paralytick affections followed, and by a paroxysm of this complaint he died suddenly, May, 1795.

BASS EDWARD, bishop of the Episcopal church in Massachusetts, was born at Dorchester, Nov. 23, 1726, and was graduated, 1744; in 1752, he was invited to settle at the episcopal church in Newbury, and was ordained by that great man, Dr. Sherlock, then bishop of London. During the revolutionary war, when most of the episcopal churches were left destitute, he continued to preach, and by his prudence, mildness, peaceable and inoffensive behaviour, he gained the esteem and affection of people who were very different in their politicks. In July, 1789, he received a diploma of Doctor of Divinity from the university of Philadelphia. In 1796 he was elected unanimously, by the convention of the protestant episcopal churches in Massachusetts, to the office of bishop of that church. He was consecrated in Christ church, 7th May, 1797, by the bishops of the episcopal churches in Pennsylvania, New York and Maryland. He was also elected bishop of the churches of the same denomination in Rhode Island, and New Hampshire.

"Bishop Bass was a sound divine, a critical scholar, an accomplished gentleman, an exemplary christian.   On the 10th of September, 1803, after an illness of two days, he died as he had lived, full of piety, resignation and humility." *Historical Collections, vol. IX.*

BEACH JOHN, an eminent writer in defence of the doctrine and government of the church of England, was graduated at Yale College, 1721, and officiated some years as a congregational minister at Newtown, Connecticut. He declared his conformity to the church of England in 1732, and many of his people conformed with him. The same year he went to England for orders, and was appointed their minister. He continued to preach to this people, and the church at Reading, till the revolutionary war. Mr. Beach was well respected among the several denominations for his learning and piety. When Dr. Johnson died, who had been president of the college in New York, it was expected he would deliver the funeral sermon. He was unable, on account of his ill state of health, to attend the funeral, but afterwards preached and printed a discourse, which is said to be a just tribute of respect to his friend, the most zealous supporter of the episcopal claims ever known in New England. Mr. Beach was a very sensible and evangelical preacher. Among other sermons he printed, is one upon "the inquiry of the *young man in the gospel.*" His controversial pieces are--" A vindication of the professors of the church of England against the abusive and fallacious argumentations of *Mr. Noah Hobart,* 1750. To this Mr. B. replied in *a second address to the members of the episcopal separation,* &c.   Mr. Beach then published a continuation of *the calm and dispassionate vindication of the professors of the church of England,* &c. 1756.

The dissenters were ready to acknowledge Mr.

Beach to be the most able of the *episcopal writers*, who engaged in the controversy with Mr Hobart, but against such a *disputant*, their church could not gain the ground they expected : his addresses were read with interest and high estimation by men of all denominations. In England Mr. Hobart was called the *very ablest* controversial writer New England had to boast of. *Chandler's life of president Johnson. Mr. Hollis's letters.*

BELCHER ANDREW, one of his majesty's council for the province of Massachusetts, and father of gov. Belcher, was himself one of the famous men in those times. He is called " an ornament and blessing to his country." He was the most opulent merchant in the town of Boston ; a man of integrity and honour ; a friend to religion and learning. He died, October 31, 1728, aged 71.

BELCHER JONATHAN, governor of Massachusetts and New Jersey, was born in Boston, 1681. His father was desirous he should have the best education the country afforded, and then to travel over Europe. It was a great pleasure to have a son of so promising a genius, upon whom the hopes of the family depended. The youth was an excellent scholar, and was graduated at Harvard College, 1699. The class which he was a member consisted of twelve ; and it is worthy of notice that the four first were as distinguished characters, as New-England has produced.* Three held the highest offices of their country ; and the fourth was a divine who would have been an honour to any age or nation.

Mr. Belcher did not incline to enter upon professional studies, but went into the mercantile line of business. To increase his commercial correspondence, as well as to expand his mind, he spent several years in Great Britain, and upon the continent, and gained testimonies of esteem from some of the greatest and best characters. He was intro-

* Jeremiah Dummer, J. Belcher, Edmund Quincy, and John Buckley.

duced to the princess Sophia, and became acquainted with her son the elector of Hanover, who was afterwards king of England. When he returned to
Boston he enlarged his business as a merchant, and
became a candidate for publick honours. From being a member of the legislature for his native town,
he was chosen one of his majesty's council, where
he was very respectable for his knowledge of mankind, his zeal and activity in serving the interest of
the province. In the year 1728, he was chosen
agent at the court of Great Britain. The circumstances of this election, as related by Mr. Hutchinson, are not so favourable to him, but ought to be
mentioned in a biographical sketch, where we look
not for eulogy, but the just traits of every man's
character. Mr. Belcher had been closely attached
to gov. Shute, and to his measures, the same that
Burnet pursued ; but he suddenly went over to the
other party, and " was thought the most proper person to join with Mr. Wilks, who had been very
friendly to Mr. Cooke in his agency, and upon several occasions had interested himself in favour of *New
England*, and had therefore been the first object of
their choice." They jointly represented the state
of the province, shewing " the people were averse
to a compliance with the instructions given to gov.
Burnet, which he had communicated to the house."
The result of their petition is well known.

Two years after he was appointed agent for the
people, he had a commission from the crown to be
their governor, and he possessed some admirable
qualities for the station. His fine person, engaging
address, urbanity of manners, and splendid mode of
living, made him the most popular man in Massachusetts. The part he had lately acted fixed an
opinion, that he would not perplex the legislature
with those instructions which had produced such
contests with his predecessors When the news of
his appointment reached New England, all classes
of people rejoiced, especially those who had been

in opposition to Shute and Burnet : but as soon as they learned that similar instructions were given, and that no change of measures would follow from having such a man in the chair, most of these popular leaders became his active enemies. He arrived at Boston, August, 1730. New Hampshire was included in his commission. At the first meeting of the general court, he proposed to have his salary fixed according to the instructions he had received. This did not occasion any altercation at first; but when he refused his assent to a bill passed for his support, he found them unmoved by his persuasions, and determined to support the views of former legislatures. He endeavoured to persuade the house of representatives to send word to their agents in England, that he might be permitted to receive the grants, which being obtained, it put an end to the controversy.

There were three events, however in the administration of gov. Belcher which excited an opposition to him, and in the end caused his removal from the government. In 1733, upon application from the court for a new emission of paper bills, when a very large nominal amount was in circulation, he refused his consent ; and urged that the old emissions should be first redeemed. This gave offence to the party whose views were to be answered by the new emission.

It seems that *merchants' notes* had been issued by a confederacy of merchants, who had formed themselves into a company, and these notes were to be redeemed at a certain rate of silver per ounce. The excess of the public bills made silver rise ; and in consequence of it, the notes were hoarded up.

Another thing, which occasioned great uneasiness to the governor was, the dispute between Massachusetts and New-Hampshire, relative to their respective boundaries. This came under consideration of commissioners appointed by the crown. The conduct of the governor towards New-Hampshire was not pleasing to the leading characters of that province ; and they solicited a government of their own, distinct from Massachusetts.

A third event, which happened, while Mr. Belcher was in the chair, was the bringing forward a Land Bank, or scheme of Manufactory. This was not an act of the government ; but a large majority of the court, and some eminent lawyers of Boston, favoured it, and many were subscribers to it. The governor's opposition to it, and his exertions to suppress it, which were successful, brought upon him the ill will of a great part of the people. Some of the politicians of those days took methods to injure him,which would astonish those, who are not much conversant with human artifice and deception. The Land Bank was such an abominable kind of speculation, that honest men in England as well as America, spoke of it with disgust. The enemies of the governor represented him to be the greatest friend to this scheme, which they knew he abhorred ; but there was no bearing up against the poison of the slander. After he had fallen a victim to it, the truth was clearly manifested.

He received another commission, as governor of New Jersey, and he rendered such useful services to that state, that they now speak of him with admiration and love, and his name will be had in everlasting remembrance. There he passed the evening of his life, and the scene around him was gilded with calm and pure lustre. Peaceable days succeeded a troublesome season, and he had an opportunity to do immense service in promoting the cause of religion and learning.

He was the friend and patron of the college at Princetown. Under his fostering care it grew and flourished,and became a rich and extensive blessing to the community.

He lived to the age of 76, and died Aug. 31, 1757. No governor ever died more sincerely lamented. A funeral sermon was preached upon the occasion by president Burr, who in a few days followed his friend to the silent tomb. The discourse was published without the corrections of the author, but is a suitable testimony of respect to a magistrate, whose energies and virtues gave him celebrity among the best characters.

Gov. B. never lost his attachment to his native soil, or the place of his education. He left a request to have a monument erected in the burial ground at Cambridge, with a particular order for defraying the expence. By some neglect it was never finished. It is true of certain gentlemen, that they inherit the fortune without the spirit and industry of their ancestors. And his eldest son did not follow his steps.

In writing an account of gov. B. the religious part of his character ought not to be omitted. He was truly pious, though he might be inclining to enthusiasm. The wits of Massachusetts made sport of this, and suggested that he appeared to greater advantage in Whitefield's journal than in our political annals. He did not want, however, the sagacity of a statesman, and was a man of uncommon industry; he was as strict in his morals, as pious in his walk and conversation. It is a noble kind of enthusiasm which leads a man to promote every literary and religious institution, and to do all the good in his power.

That gov B. loved his country, all were ready to allow. That he had New England prejudices, especially in favour of the churches, is readily granted; and it is as evident that, under his administration, the province enjoyed as much peace and prosperity, as in the same number of years during that century.

The strength of intellect which marked the character and proceedings of Burnet; that extensive knowledge of law and government, and readiness to dispute with a host of representatives, were not so liberally granted to his successor. Mr. Belcher had only an American education, but his talents were above mediocrity, and he exercised them in a manner which secured reputation, esteem and respect.   He felt the lashes of satire from his opponents, who were witty and severe in their remarks ; but he had the support of his integrity ; he possessed a noble, generous disposition ; and might make a demand upon the gratitude of his country for the sacrifice of a large property to serve its best interest.

Gov. Belcher left two sons, who were educated at Harvard College, and made some figure in life. Andrew, the eldest, was graduated, 1724.   He held several publick offices, and was one of his majesty's council.   He possessed a handsome property, without much patriotick zeal, or literary taste. He died before the revolutionary war.*   *Hutch. Hist. vol. II.   Evening Post*, 1740.

JONATHAN BELCHER, chief justice of Nova Scotia, was also the son of gov. Belcher ; was educated at Harvard College, and received the honours of of that seminary, 1728.   He had also a degree of master of arts from the university of Cambridge, and from Dublin.   He applied himself to the study of law, and went to Chebucto among the first settlers.   The spot received the name of Halifax in honour of one of his majesty's principal secretaries of state.   Mr. Belcher was one of their magistrates, and rose to be chief justice of the province, and for some years was lieut. governor.   He was a man of excellent habits, prudent, upright, of great political

* His seat at Milton was consumed, 1776, in the night, by an accident.   His widow, with the old lady, gov. Belcher's widow, who resided with her, hardly escaped the flames.   They were carried into the barn, put into the family coach, and forgotten till all was over.   The barn was near the house but was preserved, there being little or no wind stirring.   The writer of this article recollects taking tea with the ladies in this barn, which was fitted up for a temporary reception   They conversed with cheerfulness upon the *publick* changes, and the changes in their own circumstances.

I

integrity. His prejudices were much in favour of New England, which, in a measure, lessened that respect which the subjects of his British majesty were, otherwise, disposed to pay him during the revolutionary war.

His name and character, however, are held in no small reputation by the people of the present generation.

BELKNAP JEREMY, D. D. holds a distinguished place among the literary men of this country. His publications are as much read, and as likely to attract further notice, as any books of the kind. They have certainly excited a grateful esteem for the author.

He was born in Boston, June 4, 1744, and had the rudiments of his education under the care of the celebrated Lovel, who has been styled the Busby of New England.

He early discovered the marks of genius, and entered Harvard College in 1758. His mind was there cultivated with care; he made considerable progress in classical literature, and was master of a great variety of knowledge, before he took his first degree. At the commencement, A. D. 1762, he received the honours of the college. From this time, till he became a preacher of the gospel, he applied himself closely to his studies, and discovered such talents for composition, so much taste and sentiment, that several of the best scholars among the clergy predicted his future excellence. Some part of this time he employed in instructing youth; and amidst other pursuits, he wrote several fugitive pieces, which were not known to be his, but were read with pleasure, as effusions of a fertile fancy, or the labours of a student, who had more than common parts and learning.

Whilst Mr. Belknap indulged himself in philological inquiries, and studied various branches of science, he had very serious impressions of divine truth; and the more he turned his thoughts to the-

ology, the more he was captivated with the beauties
of religion. He no sooner became a preacher than
his praise was in the churches. His sermons were
excellent ; and his grave manner, just emphasis,
and distinct articulation, were more striking to
well-informed hearers, than those graces of elocution, which render some preachers popular, or
which make the fanatical multitude admire. He
was ordained at Dover, New-Hampshire, when he
was a young man. There he passed several years
of his valuable life, with the esteem and affection of
his flock ; in habits of intimacy with ministers and
other gentlemen of the neighbouring places, all of
whom regretted his departure from the state. He
received marks of attention and respect from the
first characters of the community, who persuaded
and encouraged him to compile a history, which
does much honour to our country, and which has
given the author a name and distinction among the
first literary characters of the age.

The only publications which appear with the
name of Dr. Belknap, while he was a minister in
New Hampshire, beside the first volume of his History, are—a sermon upon military duty, dedicated
to sir John Wentworth, then governor of the province ; a sermon preached before an association of
ministers, which has since been reprinted by the
society for propagating the gospel, &c. and the
election sermon, in the year 1785.

He wrote other pamphlets and several political
speculations in the New Hampshire Gazette, upon
the controversy between Great Britain and the Colonies. He also wrote in the Boston newspapers,
against the African slavery. An ingenious young
man in this town, at the desire of a West India merchant, had written in favour of the African trade,
using all the arguments which can be gathered for
the lawfulness of slavery, from the scriptures and
the practice of nations. He took the signature of
John Marsham, and seemed to court the contro-

versy, as one able to maintain his ground and con-
fute his opponents. These essays being published
in the newspapers, were answered through the same
channel, by several able and ingenious hands.
Among the best pieces were those which proceeded from the pen of Dr. Belknap. When the Co-
lumbian Magazine was published in Philadelphia,
he was solicited to become a writer ; and in that
work may be seen the first sketches of the American Biography.

Dr. Belknap removed to Boston, A. D. 1787.
The church in Federal-street, which had been established upon the Presbyterian model, had agreed
to form themselves upon Congregational principles,
and they invited him to be their pastor. Nothing
could have been more agreeable to the ministers
and people of the other churches, and to all who regarded the interests of the university at Cambridge,
with which he became officially connected ; being
fully confident that he would be a great instrument
in promoting the cause of religion and learning.
As an overseer of the college, he was attentive to
the concerns of the institution ; always taking a
lively interest in every thing that respected its welfare. During the eleven years of his ministry in
this town, the religious society with which he was
connected grew and flourished. The attachment
was strong and mutual. While they admired his
diligence and fidelity, he received from them every
testimony of respect, which marks the character
of a kind and obliging people. He was very active in encouraging those books, which are designed for the use and benefit of children ; for he was
their sincere and affectionate friend ; and very affable and kind with all classes of people. He gave
advice with cheerfulness, and with an attention to
the concerns of his acquaintance, which invited
their confidence.

The friends of Dr. Belknap were numerous.
He became a member of many literary and benevo-

lent societies; and he was active in promoting the good of every association to which he belonged. Wherever he could be of service, he freely devoted his time and talents.

Of the Historical Society he was not only a diligent and laborious member, but may be considered as the founder. While he was in New-Hampshire, he collected a great number of facts, dates and circumstances, and most valuable compilation of manuscripts, which might give information and entertainment to persons who desire to know the history of their own country. The letters which passed between the admiral and general at Louisberg had been copied in a fair hand, to serve for a document of historick information. Col. Sparhawk, who married the daughter of Sir William Pepperell, not only obliged Dr. Belknap with the perusal of them, when he was writing the history of New-Hampshire, but expressed a desire that he would deposite them in some cabinet, where they might be read by others, and be useful in future. This idea led Dr. Belknap to devise a plan for multiplying copies of this and other manuscripts, as the only way to preserve them from fire or any accidents. He was the more impressed with the propriety of this, as he was witness to the destruction of Mr. Prince's valuable collection, which had been deposited in the steeple of the Old-South meeting-house. When he came to Boston, he suggested this to several of his acquaintance. In this town he met with a friend, Mr. Thomas Walcut, a worthy citizen, now living, who had conceived the same idea of multiplying copies of old books, which he himself had of manuscripts, and who had made a great collection to keep them for the service of future generations. Dr. Belknap often mentioned to the writer of this memoir, that what Mr. Walcut suggested, of preserving books, and his own desire to preserve the letters of Sir William Pepperell, were the foundation of the Historical Society : an institution

at first supported by the labours of a few, not sufficiently favoured by the publick ; but now claims a
very considerable reputation among the literary institutions of America.

As an author, Dr. Belknap appears with great
reputation. No one has been more justly celebrated on this side the Atlantick. The *History of
New-Hampshire* is full of good information, well
arranged, and written in a very handsome style.
The Foresters, a work which mingles wit and humour with a representation of the manners of the
American people, he wrote in his leisure hours. It
has passed through a second edition. The *American
Biography* is a monument of his talents, his industry, and his knowledge. He lived to publish one
volume, and to prepare another, which has been
printed since his death ; and it has been well observed, that this event put a stop to the progress of
a useful and interesting work, for which the publick voice pronounced him peculiarly qualified, and
which the world of letters hoped he might extend
through the successive periods of his country's history.

Other publications of Dr. Belknap did much
credit to his character, as a minister of the gospel ;
but it is as a historian, biographer, and promoter of
general knowledge, that he holds so distinguished
a place among eminent characters. As a theologian, he had his equals ; and though his sermons
were well composed, and filled with useful observations, yet we have been used to read such discourses ever since the American wilderness has been cultivated by pious hands, or become a part of the
Lord's vineyard. But very few have excelled as
fine writers, historians, philosophers, poets, like the
scholars of the European schools. We have been
led, therefore, to set no small value upon the lives
of such men as Dr. Belknap and the late Judge Minot, who would have been eminent in any literary
society ; men, who wrote not so much for the love

of fame, as a desire of being useful ; yet who gained a celebrity of character, and will be held in everlasting remembrance.

Dr. Belknap was subject to paralytick complaints, some years before he died. These he considered as indications of a speedy dissolution. He died suddenly with a return of this disorder, in June, 1798.

BELLAMONT earl of, arrived at Boston 26th of May, 1699, being appointed to the government of New York and Massachusetts Bay. He was in the chair fourteen months, and by the urbanity of his manners, and his obliging disposition, he rendered himself as amiable in private life, as he was, in his station, the object of publick esteem. The general court made him grants, for his services, while he remained in this province, to the value of 1875 pounds sterling, a much larger sum than his predecessor, or any of his successors obtained. During his administration, harmony subsisted among all branches of the legislature ; for he knew how to secure the friends of Mr. Cook, and the enemies of Dudley. He died at New York, ten months after he had left Massachusetts, March 5th, 1701.

BELLAMY JOSEPH, D. D. one of the most celebrated divines of New England, was born in the county of New Haven, Connecticut. He was graduated at Yale College, 1735, being then sixteen years old. When he was *eighteen* he became a preacher. He was ordained at Bethlehem in 1740, then an obscure village, but such a retired situation as would suit a person devoted to his studies. In 1742, his zeal blazed in the cause of the great revival of religion, and he could not be confined to one spot of the vineyard, but went from place to place to encourage the work. He preached in different parts of Connecticut, Massachusetts and New York, every day ; and several times a day as occasions offered. Those ministers who were blessed with a good voice, an easy utterance, a sensibility that would glow, and a zeal that would burn, were sure of crouded auditories ; and were followed, by multitudes, for private instruction. Mr Bellamy, with many others, indulged lively hopes of success ; and were ready to think the day of glory dawned upon a dark and deluded world. But the prospect was soon clouded, and all their expectations were frustrated. " Many ignorant and vain pretenders to uncommon attainments in religion, set up for publick teachers ; divisions and separations were multiplied ; the religious awakenings declined fast ; the enemy triumphed ; and the friends of Zion mourned." Satan upon this occasion acted a double, as well as wicked part, according to the sentiments of a pious writer, from whom the sentence above is quoted. He first " attempted to put a stop to this good work by open opposition, and at length transformed himself into an angel of light. This produced a flood of enthusiasm and false religion, under various names." Mr. B. soon retuned to his stated labours at Bethlehem, finding that he could not be useful as an itinerant ; and applied his mind to writing a book, which he called " true religion delineated," which was much read, passed through several editions, and certainly marks the writer as a man of very discriminating judgment, and high theological attainments. The first edition was printed in Boston, 1750.

In his sentiments, he was a supralapsarian Calvinist, one of the first and most eminent divines of the sect, called frequently Edwardians, Hopkintonians, and in some places by his own name. Wherein they differ from the old Calvinists, is not the place of a biographer to point out, but the subject is discussed in the histories of our churches, and controversies which have arisen from Dr. Bellamy's writings.

Besides " true religion delineated," he wrote " dialogues on Theron and Aspasio, by Paulinus," " sermons on the divinity of Christ," " the millenium, and the wisdom of God in the permission of sin," "essay on the gospel," "the great evil of sin," "the law our schoolmaster," "early piety recommended;" these were single sermons.

He also published several pieces on "creeds and confessions; on the "covenant of grace;" and on "church covenanting."

Mr. Bellamy was fond of preaching upon doctrinal subjects, and diffusing the peculiarities of his own belief. His manner of preaching was grave, solemn and impressive. He had not a melodious voice, but it was strong and manly. When he was a young man he was doubtless very popular, which was not the case in his declining years, owing either to less concern upon people's mind about religion, or to his own failure in delivery. He was frequently heard to mark the difference of times and manners, when the aged rose up before him, and when the rising generation would pay little respect to his grey hairs. Serious people always regarded him, especially men of speculative inquiry. Many had profited by his works, and among the ministers of Connecticut, who have a high reputation in their profession, several received their education from him. He kept a school for theological students at his house after they had passed their college exercises, and entered upon the study or profession of divinity.

Among the correspondents of Dr. Bellamy, was Dr. John Erskine, of Edinburgh, a man who has done much honour to the cause of religion, and given of his abundance to pious and charitable uses. This gentleman had a very high opinion of Mr. Bellamy's talents and usefulness, and through his influence, a diploma from Aberdeen of doctor in divinity was presented to him; which at that time must have been honourable as a distinction, it being among the first if not the very first doctorate in the colony. But it was still more honourable to

Mr. Bellamy, as it gave satisfaction to the friends. of learning and religion.

It would be wrong if no particular mention were made of the friendship between president Edwards and Dr. Bellamy. He drank *deeply* of his spirit, and though not so profound a reasoner as that great man, in metaphysical researches, who may be justly called *the Locke of America*, was eminent as a logician ; and an able divine. Their intimacy continued till the death of Mr. Edwards.

Dr. Bellamy died, March 6, 1790, in the 72d year of his age, and 50th of his ministry. *Rev. Noah Benedict's funeral sermon.*

BELLINGHAM RICHARD, governor of Massachusetts Bay, under the first charter, was a lawyer of some celebrity, and a very learned man, compared with his contemporaries in New England. He arrived at Boston, 1635, and was chosen lieut. governor, Mr. Haynes being the same year introduced to the chair. From this year, he was chosen a magistrate (Mr. Winthrop succeeding, 1636, to his place as lieut. governor) till the year 1641, when he was elected governor by a majority of six votes. The inhabitants of the province who lived at a distance from Boston were much displeased at the conduct of Bellingham's friends, and when the general court met, it was voted *not* to make the grant of £100, which had usually been made. The next year gov. Winthrop resumed the place. Mr. Bellingham was continued a magistrate till the year 1666, when he succeeded gov. Endicot.

He was strongly attached to the freedom, civil and religious, which the people of New England enjoyed. The commissioners, who came to inquire into the state of the province when Charles II. was on the throne, looked upon him, therefore, with a jealous eye. By their representation, he, with four other gentlemen, were required to answer for their conduct before the king. The ostensible reason was, that they were best able to give a true account of the province, but it was well known they were odious to the commissioners, and had been presented to the court of Great Britain as men disaffected to his majesty's government. It seems from the history of those times, our general court discovered some political craft upon the occasion. They pretended to be of a doubtful mind concerning the king's letter. But if it were genuine, it expressed only a desire to know the state of the colony ; and every thing appertaining to publick affairs, or their internal state, could be communicated without sending away such a number of useful magistrates. The debates of the house became very earnest. Some thought it necessary to obey the king's order, others said it would be injurious to their privileges. The measure was violently opposed, and the gentlemen never left New England. Mr. Bellingham was elected governor of the province this same year, and continued in the chair till he died, which event took place, Dec. 7, 1672. As a man he was benevolent, upright and active in business; as a christian, he was devout, zealous, attentive to external forms as much as " to the hidden man of the heart." As a governor, he loved the people, and maintained the honour of his station. He leaned rather to the democratick side of politicks, which is not to be wondered at, considering the arbitrary measures of the court when he left England.

By his will, governor Bellingham left his large property at Rumney Marsh for pious and charitable uses. The general court set aside the will. *Hutchinson's History.*

BERNARD FRANCIS, governor of Massachusetts, was descended from a respectable family, educated in the university of Oxford, and was a proctor, or solicitor at doctors commons when chosen to succeed governor Belcher as governor of New Jersey, in 1758. He was removed to Massachusetts in 1760, and arrived at Boston in the month of August. The commencement of his administration

was favourable; but in the course of it was pregnant with evil to the community. In his first
speech to the general court he says, " my duty as
the king's servant, my inclination as an Englishman
conspire together to form the strongest obligation,
that I should be most careful in preserving not only
your general rights, but also those particular privileges which have been granted by your charter."
At this session they granted £1300 as his salary for
the current year; and presented him with an island
called Mount Desert, the title to which was afterwards confirmed by the king. There was no great
subject of altercation between the governor and
house of representatives, until the peace of Paris in
1763. It was a period of glory and triumph for the
British nation of which the remote parts of the empire partook. The people of North America had
made great exertions in the common cause, and
were fully sensible of it. The provincial soldiers
deserved well for their courage and activity; a
pleasing idea was indulged of lasting harmony and
friendly intercourse between the parent country and
her colonies; unfortunately this was soon disturbed, and the governor of Massachusetts was one of
the instruments in bringing on such political debates as caused the most troublesome animosities.
He was always obedient to the mandates of a ministry, unfriendly to the interests of the colonies; and
became the dupe of their crafty policy and ambitious designs. In 1764 restraints were laid upon
the trade of the plantations by certain acts of the
parliament of Great Britain; which were succeeded
by a direct tax upon the colonies. Nothing could
have given greater offence to the people on this side
of the Atlantick, than the stamp act, which Mr.
Grenville introduced into the house of commons
towards the close of this year. It is true, however,
that before the stamp duties were laid, the minister
called a meeting of the agents, and requested them
to propose any other tax as a substitute for the

stamp act, to which he affirmed that he was not particularly attached ; but they remonstrated against this, and every kind of direct tax whatever, as a measure to which the colonists would never submit. When it was known in America that such an act had passed, and was to be put into immediate operation, it arrested the attention of every class of people ; it roused a spirit of resentment which menaced every man in power ; and alienated the affections of the colonists from a country, to which they had hitherto looked with reverence as the land of their fathers. The friends of prerogative became peculiarly obnoxious, and in particular the crown governors. It was natural indeed to suppose that if the agents of the colonies had been consulted, that these immediate servants of the government must have had their share of influence. Bernard was of an arbitrary disposition, and had always been hostile to the freedom which was enjoyed in New England. Upon several occasions he had treated the people with contempt ; the house of representatives with arrogance, and even the council with disrespect, though several of this body were his friends and favourites, and supported his measures, whenever they could do it without risquing the highest resentment of their constituents. The stamp act was repealed in 1766 ; this was a cause of great joy to the people ; but the wiser statesmen in the plantations were still dissatisfied, for the very administration which had repealed this obnoxious act had passed another declaratory of the right of parliament to tax all parts of the empire ; this was designed as a mere declaration and a salvo for the honour of parliament ; but another ministry were not content with this. It was said to be necessary that there should be some acknowledgment or acquiescence at least on the part of America to this effect, or the act was nugatory and lifeless. Charles Townsend was employed to put a soul into it, which he did by bringing forward a duty upon oil and colours, upon tea, &c. These taxes were to be levied in the colonies, and a board was constituted called the commissioners of the customs and placed in Boston : Charles Paxton, a most odious creature of government, was one of the commissioners. He wrote to Great Britain and solicited that troops might be sent over for their protection. The governor also, was favourable to this scheme. Troops soon after arrived in 1768 ; this afforded a subject of controversy between the governor and the inhabitants of Boston, about providing quarters for them. The letters which he wrote to criminate the town, discover his temper, and his views. These were procured by the generous care of William Bollan, esq. through whom they presented their defence, in answer to the slanderous aspersions of the governor, and at the same time acknowledged to Mr. Bollan the grateful sense they had of his services.

From this time the newspapers were filled with sarcastick remarks upon the character and conduct of gov. B. with satirical descriptions of his domestick habits, and with essays upon law and government, in opposition to sentiments delivered by him. In one of his addresses to the council, he complained of a piece in the Boston Gazette, which ended with these lines,

" And if such men are by God appointed,
" The devil may be the Lord's annointed."

Upon which the council resolved, that the piece was scandalous and blasphemous ; which stimulated the writer to explain himself in a still more exceptionable manner.

In Feb. 1769, the house of representatives sent a circular letter to the other American colonies, which gave great offence to the governor. He demanded of the next general court that they should rescind the vote by which their predecessors had authorized this letter to be sent ; this was refused, but 17 members out of 109 voting for it.

In August, following, he dissolved the general

court, finding them not subservient to his will.
Upon which, votes were passed in most of the
towns in the province, which were published in the
newspapers, declaring him a traitor and an enemy
to the country.

His administration had now become so odious,
burdensome, and vexatious; and there were such
constant altercations between him and the general
court, that it seemed necessary he should be removed from the government. A petition to the
king was forwarded, to request this might be done,
but it had no effect. He was in high favour at the
court of Great Britain, where his administration was
the subject of praise, and his services were rewarded with a title. He was now sir Francis Bernard,
baronet of Nettleham, in Lincolnshire. He soon
after obtained leave to return to England, and in
the month of August, 1769, he sailed from Boston
in the Rippon man of war ; and never returned to
the province.

Gov. Bernard left but few friends in the place,
where he passed ten years of his life. He was not
calculated to gain the affections of the people ; and
such as had a political attachment to him, soon
lost their regard, after he had laid down his authority. Such men never have those friendships
which give a charm to social life. It is worthy of
remark, that those of his own household were of
the number who afforded amusement, by furnishing
the most ridiculous representations of his parsimo-
ny, and domestick meanness. There were, however,
some respectable traits in his character, and these
ought to be mentioned. He was sober and temperate ; had fine talents for conversation, if the subject pleased him. He had an extensive knowledge
of books, and memory so strong as to be able to
refer to particular passages, with greater facility
than most men of erudition. He would sometimes
boast that he could repeat the whole of the plays of
Shakespeare. He was a friend to literature, and in-

terested himself greatly in favour of Harvard College, when Harvard Hall with the library and philosophick apparatus, were destroyed by fire.   After
which, he presented to it a considerable part of his
own private library. The building which now bears
the name of Harvard is a specimen of his taste in
architecture ; and while it was building, he would
suffer not the least deviation, from his plan, to be
made.   He was a believer in the principles of
christianity, which was the effect of study as well as
education, and was regular in his attendance upon
publick worship ; attached to the church of England, but no bigot.   When he resided in the country, he seldom rode to Boston upon the sabbath,
but commonly attended service at the nearest congregational church, which was in Brookline, though
his house was within the boundary of Roxbury.
He gave also as a reason for this preference, that the
preacher in Brookline was shorter in his services
than most puritanical divines, and in particular than
the Roxbury minister. After his return to England
he printed several pamphlets, chiefly letters, or such
as had the form of letters, to men in power, which
contained his principles of law and policy while in
America.   He wrote several pieces of the elegiac
kind in greek and latin, which are printed in a collection made at Cambridge after the death of George
II. and the accession of the present monarch to the
British throne. The collection is styled " Pietas et
Gratulatio," &c. which was printed, in 1761, with a
dedication to the king from the pen of lieut. governor Hutchinson.

BLACKMAN ADAM, was a minister in Derby-
shire, but came to New England with the early
planters. He makes one of the first class, as Dr.
Mather calls them ; men who were in the actual exercise of their ministry when they left England. He
was settled first at Guilford, then at Stratford, in
Connecticut, and was so good a preacher, that the
famous Hooker made a speech of this kind, " If he

might have his choice, he would live and die under
Mr. Blackman's ministry.

The epitaph upon Melancton is applied to him
by the author of the Magnalia. *Book III. page 95.*

> Cui *niveus* toto regi..b.t pectore c ndor ;
> Unum cui Cœlum. cura l.borq ; fuit :
> Num Rogitus, quâ sit dictus ra ione Melancton ?
> Scilicet *Kuximum* qua ra'ione vocant

BOLLAN WILLIAM, agent for Massachusetts at
the court of Great Britain, was born in England and
came over to Boston with Shirley, when he was appointed governor. In 1743, he married his excellency's second daughter, who died at the age of 25
years. She was a most amiable and accomplished
lady. Mr. Bollan was a lawyer of eminence in his
profession, and was *advocate general*, when he was
chosen agent for the province, and sent to England
to solicit the reimbursement of the charge in taking
and securing Cape Breton. In obtaining this he
discovered as much address as fidelity ; he acted
like a wise man, who would persevere till he gained
his object. When the other *agent* was willing to
compromise for a sum which would redeem the bills
at their depreciated value, he set the matter in a
clear light, and " made it evident that the depreciation of the bills was as effectually a charge borne by
the people as if the same proportion of bills had
been drawn in by taxes; and refused any accom-
modation without the full value of the bills when issued."*

Of his services in this business, and in all affairs
of the province, the people were fully sensible, but
he was not a man whom the general court of Massachusetts wished to keep in office. His relation
to Shirley, his belonging to the episcopal church,
and being an Englishman, created prejudices in the

---

* Mr. agent Bollan arrived in Boston, Sept. 19, 1740, with
653,000 ounces of silver and ten tons of copper : which makes
175,000 pounds sterling, granted for reimbursement of the Cape
Breton expedition. *Independent Advertiser.*

minds of many in the house of representatives.
These were the men who opposed Shirley, a man
averse from the habits of New England, and who
endeavoured to introduce a more arbitrary system
of government, than his predecessors conceived, or
the body of the people would submit to.　They
were friends to Pownal, who professed himself a
high whig, and afterwards became the pointed enemies of Bernard.　Mr. Bollan even gained so much
influence as to be sent again to England after he had
returned with the money.　Several attempts were
made to displace him when Shirley left the province.
His services, his knowledge of provincial business,
his faithfulness had been a security.　In 1762, he
was dismissed, and Mr. Mauduit succeeded him,
a worthy man, but whose only merit to raise him
to this station was, his being a leading character of
the dissenters.　He soon resigned, confessing himself unequal to the business.　The house of representatives chose Richard Jackson, and then Mr.
Debert; but Mr. Bollan was employed by the council, and in this capacity continued to serve the province.　In 1768, he obtained a copy of the letters
written against the town of Boston by gov. Bernard, gen. Gage, &c and from this time he became
a most popular man amongst those who once could
not view him with any complacency. Mr. Hancock
declared in the house of representatives, that there
was no man to whom the colonies were more indebted, and whose friendship had been more sincere.
In 1775, he was active in promoting the interests,
and honour of the mother country ; by seeking for
conciliatory measures, which he pressed with all his
influence, and much care and concern.　We hear
nothing of his publick character after this year, and
the year of his death is not to be found in any obituary of our American newspapers.*

* His printed works are, Importance and advantage of Cape
Breton truly stated, London, 1746 ; Coloniæ Anglicanæ illustra-
tæ, 4to. London, 1762 ;　Ancient right to the American fishery

BowDOIN JAMES, governor of Massachusetts, was born in Boston, 1727.   His father rose from common life to an eminence among the merchants of the town, and was supposed to leave the greatest estate which ever had been owned by any individual of Massachusetts.   His ancestors were French refugees, who left their country after the revocation of the edict of Nantz   They first went to Ireland, and then came to New-England, 1688.

The subject of this memoir was the youngest son, who, discovering some proof of early genius, was sent to the grammar school of his native town, of which Mr Lovel was preceptor.   He finished his education at Harvard College, where he was graduated, 1745.   He very soon became a distinguished character among the citizens of Boston ; was chosen a representative to the general court, 1756 ; and from this year continued in publick life till the year 1769, when he was negatived by gov. Bernard, on account of his being the most leading whig at the council board.   He was, the next year, sent representative from Boston ; chosen a counsellor ; and accepted by Mr. Hutchinson, because he thought his influence less prejudicial " in the house of representatives, than at the council board."   He was one of the committee that drew the answer to the goverour's speeches where he asserted and endeavoured to prove, by strong arguments, the *right* of Great Britain to tax America.   For this he had the honour of being negatived by gov. Gage, in 1774, who declared that " he had express orders from his majesty to set aside from that board, the hon. Mr. Bowdoin, Mr. Dexter, and Mr. Winthrop."

During this memorable year, delegates were chosen to meet at Philadelphia, which was the first congress of the United States.   Mr. Bowdoin was

examined and stated, 4to. London, 1764 ; Freedom of speech and writing upon publick affairs considered, 4to. London, 1770.

the first member of the Massachusetts delegation. He was prevented from attending his duty by his ill state of health. Mr. Hancock was afterwards chosen in his place. In 1775, when the town of Boston was blockaded, Mr. Bowdoin was moderator of the meeting, when the inhabitants agreed to give up their arms to gen. Gage, on condition of their being permitted to leave the place with their property, and without disturbance. In this business he conducted with great prudence and firmness, and was one of the first who went out of Boston after the agreement. It is well known how shamefully the promises of the British commanders were violated. Mr. Bowdoin took his place as chief of the Massachusetts council at Watertown, and was of the *fifteen*, who by the charter were to act in the room of the governour, when the office was vacated. In 1779—80, the convention for establishing a state government for Massachusetts met at Cambridge, and afterwards at Boston. Of this body, Mr. Bowdoin was president. During the years of 1785 and 1786 he was governor of the state. When the constitution of the United States was planned, and the Massachusetts convention met to consider whether it should be adopted, Mr. Bowdoin was at the head of the Boston delegation, all of whom voted in favour of it. He made a very handsome speech upon the occasion, which may be read in the volume of their debates. From this time, he changed the tumult of publick scenes, for domestick peace, and the satisfactions of study.

He always had been a student. He was an excellent scholar at college, and afterwards pursued philosophical studies, having left his mercantile business, that he might enjoy *otium cum dignitate*. His letters to Dr. Franklin have been published. When the American academy of arts and sciences was instituted, he was appointed the first president, and contributed several papers which were printed in the first volume of their transactions. He also pro.

nounced an oration, " upon the benefits of philosophy," which was printed in a pamphlet, and also in
the volume, with the proceedings of the society.
His literary reputation was not confined to his own
country. He was a member of several foreign societies for the promotion of agriculture, arts and commerce. He was also fellow of the royal society,
London. He received a diploma of doctor of laws
from several universities of Europe, and from Philadelphia, as well as his *Alma Mater* at Cambridge.
It was a great acquisition to this seminary, to have
him connected with their government. As a member of the council he was ex officio, one of the
overseers. And he was elected a fellow of the corporation, which office he executed with great judgment, honour and fidelity, but which he resigned
when he was chosen governor of the Commonwealth.
He was a munificent friend to the college. Beside
his donations to the library, and philosophical apparatus, he left £ 400 Massachusetts currency to
be appropriated to certain purposes, as mentioned
in his will. His large and valuable library was
given to the academy of arts and sciences.

In other walks of life Mr. Bowdoin was conspic-
ous and useful. When the humane society was
instituted he was chosen the first president. He
was always ready to promote every literary, benevolent and religious institution. He exhibited the
virtues of social life in all their engaging lustre, and
he also breathed a christian spirit.

His mind was imbued with religious sentiments,
by his education, and formed to the love of goodness; he was fond of theological inquiries amidst
the course of his other studies. Few men, who are
not of the profession, have studied divinity with more
earnestness, or greater desire to obtain knowledge of
the scriptures. He early in life became a commu-
nicant at the church in Brattle-street. When the
people of this society took down their ancient building, it was the desire of many to rebuild their church

in a more eligible situation. Mr. Bowdoin offered a spot, which is now one of the most valuable estates in the town. The majority preferred the place where their fathers had worshipped. His offer being declined, he contributed largely towards erecting the present noble and superb edifice. That religion which had supported him through various scenes of his life, was the source of consolation, during a long course of sickness, owing to a frame naturally delicate. He recommended to the rising generation to read bishop Butler's analogy, from which he had derived much to strengthen his own principles. He died universally lamented, Nov. 6, 1790. He left one son, the hon. J. Bowdoin, late plenipotentiary at the court of Madrid, and one daughter, the lady of sir John Temple, late consul general of Great Britain in the United States *Pemberton's Mss. Private information. Thacher's Sermon.*

BOYLSTON ZABDIEL, F. R. S was born in Brookline, 1684. He had the advantage of only a common education, but rose to be the most eminent medical practitioner in the town of Boston. What gave him peculiar distinction was, his success in *inoculation for the small pox.* In 1720, he introduced this practice, and is known to be the first physician in the British dominions that dared to do it. It was risquing his reputation and life. The famous Dr. Cotton Mather recommended this method from an account of inoculation at Constantinople, which he had seen in the philosophical transactions. He first communicated it to Douglass, a Scotchman of more learning than true wisdom, who treated the proposal with ill nature, and contempt.*

* Dr. Ramsay, in his Review of Medicine, in the 18th century, gives great credit to the clergy for their exertions at this time. The fact is, a clergyman first recommended it, and that Dr. Boylston was supported by them through all his embarrassments. Dr. Colmam, as well as Dr. Mather wrote in favour of it ; as a body, the *Boston Association* united to stop the torrent of prejudice, which bore down all before it. Some of the

He then made application to Dr. Boylston, a man of more sagacity and moral worth, who gave it to his own children and others; and met with wonderful success. Douglass became a convert, when he had made use of every method to injure his brother physician, whom he called a bold and ignorant quack," many years after this. By this new mode of treating the small pox in Boston, 274 persons were inoculated by Dr. B. 1721, and very few died. The practice was very soon introduced in the Island of Great Britain, and with equal success. Every attention was paid to Dr. Boylston while he was in England; among other honours he was chosen fellow of the Royal Society, which was a reward of merit, sufficient to balance the rough compliments of his professional acquaintance, the canting abuse of persons righteous overmuch, and the coarse epithets which issued from the foul mouths of the vulgar.

He wrote several papers in the philosophical transactions of London. We know not of any other publications, except the pamphlet he printed, on the " benefit of inoculation."

After a long period of eminence and skill in his profession he retired to his patrimonial estate in Brookline to pass the remainder of his days. He died there on the 1st of March, 1766; and was interred in his own tomb, which bears the following plain, appropriate, and just inscription."

" Sacred to the memory of Dr. Z. Boylston, esq.

clergy received personal injury, others were insulted in the street, and were hardly safe in their houses. The people were not willing to hear them on Sunday, till the success of the practice made them think it was the hand of Providence in their favour. The newspapers were filled with arguments for and against it. The *Courant*, printed by the Franklins, was under the influence of the Physicians, who abused the clergy for their interference in the matter. Every bad consequence was painted in lively colours by these learned editors, who thought inoculation unfavourable to the health of people, even if they had the small pox more favourably than common, &c. &c. *New England Courant*, 1721.

physician, and F. R. S. who first introduced the
practice of inoculation into America. Through a
life of extensive beneficence, he was always faithful to his word, just in his dealings, affable in his
manners ; and after a long sickness, in which he
was exemplary for his patience and resignation to
his Maker, he quitted this mortal life, in a just expectation of a happy immortality, March 1, 1766."
Thacher's Memoir. Pierce's Sermon.

BRADFORD WILLIAM, gov. of Plymouth colony, was born in a village called Ansterfield, 1588.
When he was eighteen years old he went over to
Zealand, where he was taken up by an officer, as
a deserter from England, but soon released, having
given a good account of himself. He then proceeded to Amsterdam, and served his time till he
was of age, in " working of silks." He became a
man of industry in his business, converted the estate he had in England into money, and behaved
with great prudence among those religious people
who had left England to enjoy peace of conscience ;
with whom he continued till the church at Leyden
agreed to transport themselves to America. When
they reached Plymouth, he lost his wife, which was
a most melancholy event, and attended with aggra-
vated circumstances of grief, as she accidently fell
from the vessel, and was drowned. After governor
Carver died, he was unanimously chosen governor
of the plantation. No man could discover more
prudence and fortitude than Mr. Bradford. In
those times, when their souls were tried with every
difficulty, he was not cast down with the discouraging state of their affairs, or by the clouds which
covered their future prospects. He found it necessary to manage things differently from what had
been proposed. For, in order to resemble the
primitive church, the planters had a common stock.
He was of opinion that to encourage industry, each
individual should be master of his own property ;
and they all soon perceived the advantage of the
measure.

He was required to exercise his wisdom in another matter, which threatened evil to the plantation, and where the religion they held so dear was wounded in the house of its friends. Every account of the settlement of Plymouth mentions the conduct of Lyford who attempted to disorganize their church, and who was detected by the vigilance of the governor. Mr. B. had afterwards a hard task to exculpate the colony from a charge of dissembling with his majesty in a petition, wherein they declared that their church discipline did agree with the reformed churches in Europe. His answer to this charge is ; that they had kept to their agreement, had been falsely accused, and denied that they were Brownists, or, like those Sectaries, renounced the church of England. Mr. B. was a good writer, compared with others of those times, though his style may seem uncouth to modern ears. He understood several languages ; latin, greek and hebrew ; French and Dutch he spake ; and was conversant with theology. He was in the chair above thirty years, and died, May 9th, 1657, aged 69. Mr. Winslow was elected governor, 1633, 1636, 1644, and Mr. Prince, 1634, 1657. Every other year the old governor was elected. *Magnalia, Book II page 5.*

BRADSTREET SIMON, was of Emanuel College, Cambridge, whence he removed to the family of the earl of Lincoln, as his steward, and afterwards he lived in the same capacity with the countess of Warwick. He married one of Mr. Dudley's daughters, and after her death, a sister of sir George Downing. He lived to be the Nestor of New England ; was born in the beginning of the century, in 1603, and wanted but two or three years of completing it.

This gentleman, one of the fathers of Masschusetts, was a magistrate many years, and, in 1662, was sent to England as agent, at a time of peculiar difficulty, when it required more wisdom than he possessed, though he was a prudent and worthy person, to answer the expectations of the people. Mr. Norton was his assistant. Their business was to represent the colony as his majesty's loyal subjects, when it was well known that they were actuated by republican sentiments, and were puritans of a strict denomination, with no kind of reverence for bishops or nobles. They met with a more favourable reception than their friends in England had anticipated ; and returned with a letter from the king, which caused much joy ; and led the agents to suppose that they had done their duty completely ; and that their business was successful. But when the general court met, and the whole subject of the letter was discussed, it appeared to some of the magistrates, and to the leaders of the populace, that their charter privileges were invaded, for they were required to send their laws to be reviewed in England, and such as might be found contrary to the king's authority to be annulled. There was also a violent attack upon their religious prejudices, and upon the habits and customs of the plantations ; for liberty was given to every man to use the common prayer, and that all of honest lives and conversations should be admitted to the sacrament of the Lord's supper, and their children to baptism.

When the resentment of the people was excited, it did not fall upon Mr. Bradstreet so much as Mr. Norton, who had to defend himself against the religious bigotry of the age. But neither gentleman could retain his popularity, nor resist the publick obloquy. Mr. N. died, it was said of chagrin, while Mr. Bradstreet continued to discharge the duties of his other station, being conscious of rectitude, or feeling a cold indifference towards the opinion and the clamours of the multitude. Every impartial person who now recurs to those transactions will rather wonder, that, at such a court as Charles II. they could obtain so much, than think that they were worthy of blame. In 1679, Mr. B.

was chosen governor. Hutchinson represents him
as the head of the moderate party while he was in
office. The deputy governor, Mr. Danforth, led the
popular side: Stoughton, Dudley and Brown of
Salem were inclined to the royalists. They fell in
with the governor, and were afterwards disposed to
go beyond his measures When Mr. Dudley was
appointed to be the head of administration, Bradstreet was appointed counsellor, and refused the
commission. He opposed with earnestness Andross's arbitrary proceedings. And when the people put down his authority, they made choice of
their old governor for their president; he continued
their first character till the arrival of sir William
Phipps, with the new charter, and then the venerable
old charter governor resigned the chair, which excited the sympathy of many, who remembered ancient times, and beheld the scenes now opening, and
which were to introduce more prosperous days,
with the sigh of regret, and emotions which they
could not express. Governor Bradstreet died at
Salem, March 27, 1697, aged 95. He had been a
magistrate, secretary, agent, commissioner for the
United Colonies, and governor of the province.
Not the most highly esteemed by any party, but
despised by none; upright as well as moderate in
his principles. "*Medium est virtus* quod tenuisse ju-
vat." This is good as a lesson for children, and
agrees well with the christian religion. But it opposes the views of enterprising men, the turbulent
spirit of the ambitious, and the zeal of those who
delight in controversy. *Hutch. vol. I. page* 18.

BRATTLE THOMAS, treasurer of Harvard College, was graduated at that seminary, to which he
was always a munificent friend, 1676. And was
chosen treasurer, 1693; which office he retained till
his death, 1713.

He was an eminent merchant of the town of
Boston, a benefactor to the poor, and a useful, as
well as opulent citizen. From *him*, one of the

streets took its name; and he was the principal
founder of Brattle-street church. He was equally
distinguished for his good sense and good breeding; his liberality of sentiment, his genius and
learning; and his zeal for the publick prosperity.
He was obliged to engage in a controversy with
certain of the clergy and laity, too much attached
to the platform of the New England churches, when
he proposed the plan of the new church; but he
behaved with equal spirit and honour : and having
obtained the consent of Dr. Colman to be pastor,
who was ordained in England, the society grew
and flourished under his care ; and has ever been
considered as one of the most respectable upon the
congregational establishment.

There was another occasion of exerting his talents, when the country was under the strangest delusion, and a number of innocent persons suffered
an ignominious death, from a suspicion of witchcraft. Mr. B. wrote an account of those transactions, which was too plain and just to be published
in those unhappy times, but has been printed since ;
and which cannot be read without feeling sentiments
of esteem for a man who indulged a freedom of
thought becoming a christian and a philosopher.
He, from the beginning, opposed the prejudices of
the people, the proceedings of the court, and the
perverse zeal of those ministers of the gospel, who,
by their preaching and conduct, caused such real
distress to the community. They, who called him
an infidel, were obliged to acknowledge, that his
wisdom shone with uncommon lustre.

Mr. Brattle is recorded among the benefactors of
Harvard College, and when he died they lost one of
their best and most useful officers.

Though Mr. B. was the author of several fugitive pieces, we have have nothing under his name
but the work to which allusion has been made, and
which is styled, " a full and candid account of the
delusion called witchcraft which prevailed in New

England ; and of the judicial trials and executions at Salem, in the county of Essex, for that pretended crime, in 1692. *Hist. Coll. vol. V. page* 61—80.

BRATTLE WILLIAM, minister of the church in Cambridge, was the brother of Thomas, and born at Boston, 1662. Was graduated 1680 ; and chosen tutor and fellow of the corporation.

In the year 1696, he was ordained, and still kept up his connection with the college, though he left the immediate government and instruction. He was active in promoting every thing which would advance the interest and prosperity of that literary society. His benevolent disposition stimulated him to give largely to indigent students, and he bequeathed a handsome legacy, which is now employed for their benefit.

He was himself a very accomplished scholar, a great logician, a philosopher, a writer of philological taste, as well as eminent in theological learning.

As a preacher, he was pathetick, soft, melting and persuasive. A son *of consolation ;* for his spirit dwelt not in *fire*, nor could it ride in the storm. He was the particular friend of pres. Leverett, Dr. Colman, and Mr. Pemberton, three of the most elegant men of New England in their manners, as well as the cultivation of the mind. Mr. Brattle had also an extensive correspondence abroad, and was fellow of the royal society of London.

Mr. Agent Dummer in one of his letters gives an exalted character of the Cambridge minister in a few descriptive lines. " I think the modern sermons which are preached, and printed, are very lean and dry, having little divinity in them or brightness of style ; I am sure they are no way comparable to the solid discourses which Mr. Brattle gives you every week."

This excellent man died Feb. 15, 1717, aged 55. The inscription on his tomb is given by Dr. Holmes in his history of Cambridge. Many particulars of his life and preaching are also recorded.

Dr. Colman preached a funeral sermon upon Mr.
Brattle, which may be read as a most beautiful eulogy from the hand of a wise and judicious friend.

Mr. Brattle published a compendium of logick,
" secundum principia D. Renati cartesii plerumque
efformatum, et cate chistice propositum." This
passed through several editions. It was studied in
college till the year 1765, and is now valued by men
of learning as an excellent compendious system;
but is found only among rare and curious books.

BREWSTER WILLIAM, a distinguished character
among the first planters, was born, 1560. He was
educated at the university of Cambridge. When
queen Elizabeth made a league with the states of
Holland, she sent Davison, as her ambassador, who
carried Mr. Brewster with him, as his secretary, in
whom he placed the greatest confidence, and who
gained the esteem of that people. The keys of
Flushing were committed to him while the negotiation was pending, and when the business was finished, he received from the states a golden chain, as
a reward of merit. The ambassador was afterwards
disgraced, owing to the capricious humour of his
mistress, who always laid her own faults upon her
courtiers. His faithful secretary adhered to him, like
the true friend, in the time of adversity. The same
integrity Mr. B. manifested in all his affairs, and
through all the changing scenes of life; for his pious zeal operated upon the virtuous affections of his
soul. He was so highly respected in the church
of Leyden, as to be chosen their ruling elder; and
he acted like a shepherd in leading the flock through
the paths of the wilderness. He would not accept
the office of pastor, but preached to the people who
came over with him to Plymouth, and performed
most part of a minister's duty. The church were
benefitted by his labours, and would have been happy if he had consented to administer the ordinances,
for he was wise, learned and prudent. By his influence he might have prevented those disorders

which sprang from the gifted brethren, who, were apt to speak; and from those ignorant or designing men, who took upon themselves the pastoral office.

Elder Brewster was as bold in defending the plantation against the Indians, as he was meek and humble when diffusing the light of truth, or describing the offices of love. He lived to be 84 years old, and his usefulness increased with his years. He was able to work in the field and preach to the people till he was called out of the world, April 16, 1644. *Morton, Prince, Belknap.*

BRIDGE THOMAS, pastor of the old or first church, was born at Hackney, in England, 1657; had a liberal education, and, as a man of business, travelled over different parts of Europe ; and from being a merchant of integrity and honour, he became a pious and useful minister of religion. From the Mediterranean sea he made a voyage to the West Indies. He first preached at Jamaica ; from that island he went to New Providence, and while he resided there was the principal man in the place. Thence he proceeded to Bermuda, and was remarkably assiduous in a time of pestilence and great mortality. It is said he preached twenty nine times in one month. His first place of residence in North America was West Jersey, and he came to Boston about the year 1705. He was ordained in May, of the same year, being invited to the pastoral care of a flock, whose famous predecessors were to be succeeded. " The light was now fixed in a candlestick," according to the language of Cotton Mather, " and shone for eleven years together, some of the rays of which we have in his printed composition." He died, Sept. 26, 1715, aged 58.

He has been thus characterised by a writer more elegant, though less learned, than Dr. Mather, as a man upright and conscientious, meek, mild, quiet, gentle; not the brightest and most active of his brethren, but a goodly speaker; his gravity and composure were neither frigid, nor austere ; prayer was his gift, the bible was his library.* *Colman's funeral sermon.*

BUCKMINSTER JOSEPH, minister of the church in Rutland, was educated at Harvard College. He received the honours of the seminary, 1739; was ordained at Rutland, 1742; and continued a faithful and laborious pastor of that church above 50 years. He was highly respected by the neighbouring clergy, for his piety and usefulness, and as much esteemed by his flock. He was in principle a *sublapsarian* Calvinist. In defence of these sentiments he engaged in a controversy, and his writings discover solidity and strength of mind, attention to theology, and an ardent desire that all men should believe what he supposed the doctrines of the scriptures. In 1719, Mr. Foster, of Stafford, printed a sermon, in which he held forth *a twofold justification;* and, "a remedial law, or law of grace, whose precepts are brought down to a level with the fallen sinner's abilities;" according to which they are able to do well, and so ensure their future felicity. This was judged a heretical sentiment by the ministers in Worcester county, and Mr. B. printed a pamphlet on Rom. x. 4, which is an answer to Mr. Foster, and for which he received a vote of thanks from the association, signed by *Nathan Fisk,* scribe. Mr. F. replied, and several pamphlets were written.

Mr. Buckminster also published *dissertations* upon *gospel salvation,* Ephes. ii. 9, 10, 11. In these he holds the *doctrine of election* against the Arminians; but on the other hand in opposition to the supralapsarians, he says, "The decrees have no direct positive influence upon us. We are determined by motives, but act freely and voluntarily. They lie in the foundation of the divine proceedings, and compose his plan of operation. They infer the certain futurition of things, but have no influence ab

* His printed discourses are, 1. The mind at ease. 2. What faith can do. 3. Jethro's counsel. 4. A sermon to the artillery company.

extra to bring them to pass. Whom God chooses, he calls; yet choosing is one thing, and calling another," &c. And although Mr. B. allows "no promises of special favours to the unregenerate;" yet he will grant "that encouragements are given as grounds of hope; and which carry the nature of a promise."

Mr. B. died in the 73d year of his age, Nov. 27, 1792.* He left a son in the ministry, rev. J. Buckminster, D. D. of Portsmouth, whose son, the rev. J. S. Buckminster, is minister of the church in Brattle street. Boston.

BULKLEY PETER, the first minister of Concord, Massachusetts, was the son of Edward Bulkley, D. D. an eminent minister in Bedfordshire, whose name is mentioned with respect in the book of the martyrs. At the age of sixteen years he was admitted a member of St. John's college, Cambridge, and while he was junior bachelor, was chosen *fellow ;* and then proceeded bachelor of divinity. He came to New England, 1635; resided at Cambridge some months, and then preferred a place in the more interior part of the country. The spot was pleasant, and from being one of the towns of the first planters, has since become one of the most flourishing in the *county of Middlesex.* It still bears the name of Concord, which he gave it; and the twelfth church was gathered here, which had been founded in the colony. He possessed a handsome estate; and it is also reported of him that he gave away a number of farms to several persons who became good husbandmen. Some of them had been his servants, and became respectable men among the yeomanry. Dr. Mather says he was a most excellent scholar, a person of extensive reading, who gave advice to young students. He was also a benefactor to Harvard

---

* His publications are, an ordination sermon, a sermon upon family religion, paraphrase on Rom. x. 4, dissertations on Ephes. ii. 9, 10. 11, and a sermon upon the covenant made with Abraham, &c.

N

College at the beginning of that literary institution. Having a handsome library of his own, he endowed the publick library at Cambridge with a considerable part of it.   He was a man of hasty spirit, and quick at shewing resentment ; disposed likewise to make severe remarks in his sermons :   was one of the strictest of the puritans, and had given offence on this account to some of the moderate party in the old country, as well as to the enemies of the dissenting interest.

During his ministry the pastor and ruling elder had a dispute, and it ended in requiring the elder to abdicate his seat.   They called an ecclesiastical council, and this was the advice.   The improvement he made of this unhappy contention may be profitable to ministers in other places, some of whom meet with trials from false brethren ; or those who are wise in their own conceit. Mr Bulkley learned from it, to " know more of God, more of himself, and more of men."

This worthy man died, A. D. 1658, aged 77. He was an author of uncommon reputation, and wrote handsomely in Latin or English. The first settlers of Massachusetts were in general excellent latin scholars, and many of them made a figure in the universities of Europe.   It seems Mr. Bulkley was a poet ;   he wrote poems when he was above 72, which have been praised by scholars of the next age.*

The year before he died he composed the following epigram,

> Pigra senectutis jam venit inutilis etas,
> Nil aliud nunc sum quam fere pondus iners.

---

* He printed several books ; one *upon the covenant ;* several sermons upon Zec. ix. 11. Concerning these, Mr. Shepherd of Cambridge, says, " *The church of God is bound to bless God, for the holy, judicious and learned labours of this aged servant of Christ, who has taken pains to discover, and that, not in words and allegories, but in demonstration and evidence of spirit, the great mystery of godliness wrapt up in the covenant.*

Da tamen, alme Deus, dum vivam, vivere laudi
Eternum sancti nominis usque tui,
Ne vivam (potius moriar!) nil utile agendo
Finiat opto magis, mors properata dies.
Vel doceam in sancto cætu tua verba salutis,
Cælestive canam cantica sacra choro.
Seu vivam, moriarve, tuus sum. Christe, quod uni
Debita vita mea est, debita morsque tibi.

BULKLEY JOHN, minister of Colchester, Connecticut, is mentioned by Dr. Chauncy as one of the greatest men of New England. He knew him when he himself was a young man, and often spake of him in company with his brethren ; relating things astonishing of his memory. In a written account of him, in a letter to Dr. Stiles, he says, "that Mr. Dummer and he, who were classmates at college, were accounted the greatest geniuses of the day. The preference was given to Dummer in regard of quickness, brilliancy and wit; to Bulkley in regard to solidity of judgment and strength of argument."

Mr. Bulkley was the son of the rev. Gershom Bulkley, and grandson of Peter Bulkley of Concord. He was graduated at Harvard College, 1699, and died, suddenly, June, 1731.

In 1729, he printed an account of an impartial debate at Lyme, "upon the subjects of baptism, the mode of baptising, and the maintenance of ministers." No other publication appears with his name.

BURNET WILLIAM, esq. governor of Massachusetts, son of Gilbert Burnet, bishop of Sarum, was born at the Hague in March preceding the revolution, and named William after the illustrious prince of Orange, who was his godfather.

The great part which his father had in the accession of that prince to the British throne, and his steady attachment to the Hanoverian line, brought him early into the notice of the court. In the year 1720, he was in the post of comptroller of the customs, which he exchanged for the government of New York and New Jersey. He arrived at New York, Sept. 19. The first speech he made, discov-

ered the abilities of an elegant scholar, and the manners of a gentleman. " I serve a prince, the best
that ever was, from whom I may expect the most
gracious acceptance of my labours; I succeed a
gentleman who left this province in a flourishing
state, and is still ready to declare for its interests ;
I meet a council and assembly who concurred with
him, and assisted him in those great and good measures, that are now confirmed by his majesty, and
have been so effectual to secure publick credit, and
the peace of the province." His administration was
very acceptable to the people, till an opposition
arose from the merchants of the city, on account of
an act passed against the sale of goods to the French,
which were proper for the Indian trade. This law
was advantageous to the province ; but enterprising
speculators, and the importers of merchandize, did
not regard the general good so much as their own
advantage. They discovered their malevolence
against the governor, and being able to bring some
censure upon him, because, as chancellor, he had
given decrees, in several instances, contrary to a legal process, owing to a quick decision, from the
sensibility of his temper, they were able to do him
considerable injury. Whether it was owing to this,
or what Hutchinson suggests, to gratify a favourite
who wanted the government, he was removed from
this place, to Massachusetts, on the accession of
George II. We are told that with reluctance he
left New York ; he had many friends among the
wise and patriotick, who equally regretted the loss
of such a ruler.

In his first speech to the Massachusetts assembly,
he informed them of his instructions to insist upon
a fixed salary. The assembly voted a sum equal
to 1000 pounds sterling, which was more than any
governor had received ; and also made him several
handsome grants towards his support, and the expences of his journey. These he accepted, but refused the salary. He had now to resist the argu-

ments of the legislature, and the tumult of the people. The people of Boston, from their love of freedom, were against a permanent salary. They discussed the subject at the town meeting; on this account the governor adjourned the court to Salem.

The general court, directed their agent, Francis Wilks, esq. to make application to his majesty to afford them relief. Mr. Belcher was joined with him in the agency, and they procured all the aid in their power. In the mean time the house became importunate for their pay ; but the governor withheld his warrant from the treasury ; not having received any himself, he thought they might as well go without theirs.

The election for counsellors, A. D. 1729, was held at Salem. During this session, the beginning of August, the governor communicated to the house the result of their address to the king, which was unfavourable to their wishes. The same month he adjourned them to Cambridge. This was styled a grievance ; but the death of the governor put an end to all further disputes.

The 31st of August he was taken with a shivering fit after some time spent in fishing on Watertown pond ; he did not confine himself; paroxisms of fever succeeded, which terminated in a coma. He died, Sept. 7, 1729. The pall bearers, at his funeral, were lieut. gov. Dummer, col. Taylor, col. Winslow, col. Hutchinson, col. Brown, and col. Fitch. The rev. Mr. Price preached the funeral sermon, from Eccles. ii. 17.

" Gov. Burnet was large in stature, he had a majestick port and countenance, mixed with a great deal of sweetness ; he was frank and open in his manners ; his sagacity penetrating ; of ready wit, and sound understanding ; his learning, in books and manners, which he had improved by travelling over Europe, enabled him to suit himself to the tempers and conversation of all men. He was a christian upon principle, having studied under such men as his father and sir Isaac Newton. In his youth he had inclined to infidelity, but afterwards become a scholar in sacred as well as profane studies.''

From an account of him in Chandler's life of president Johnson, we should suppose he was an inquirer of some liberality. He persuaded Johnson to read Whiston, and Dr. Clark's works, '' so that he was in danger of becoming an Arian, which the governor wished him to be.'' But according to other accounts there appears an inconsistency. For while he was governor of Jersey he prepared a bill that fixed a penalty upon all who denied the Saviour's divinity, or the truth of the scriptures. This was more pious than judicious. It might have passed in some of the provinces, but here the Quakers had an influence which was exerted against it.

In the year 1724, he printed an '' essay on scripture prophecies,'' which is a work of ingenuity as well as piety, the result, perhaps, of his inquiries when he was under the care of sir Isaac Newton.

While he was governor of Massachusetts, he answered a letter of a popish priest in Canada, which contained a reflection upon the first reformers.

These works praise him, are really curious and worth preserving.

CABOT SEBASTIAN, who first discovered the continent of North America, was the son of John Cabot, an enterprising navigator. a Venetian, was born, 1467. When he was a youth he made several voyages with his father, and brothers. In 1552, he projected the plan of the first voyage of the English to Russia, and laid the foundation of that extensive commerce which has ever since been carried on between the two nations. He was also the first who took notice of the variation of the needle. He died, 1557.*

* This spring, 1496, John Cabota, a Venetian, sails with two ships from England, steers westward, discovers the shore of the

CALEF ROBERT, merchant, in the town of Boston, rendered himself famous by his book against witchcraft, when the people of Massachusetts were under the most strange kind of delusion. The nature of this crime, so opposite to all common sense, has been said to exempt the accusers from observing the rules of common sense. This was evident from the trials of witches at Salem, 1692. Mr. Calef opposed facts in the simple garb of truth to fanciful representations; yet he offended men of the greatest learning and influence. He was obliged to enter into a controversy, which he managed with boldness and address. His letters and defence were printed in a volume in London, 1700. Dr. Increase Mather, was then president of Harvard College; he ordered the wicked book to be burnt in the college yard; and the members of the *old north church* published a defence of their pastors, the rev. Increase and Cotton Mather. The pamphlet printed on this occasion has this title page, " Remarks upon a scandalous book, against the government and ministry of New England, written by Robert Calef," &c. Their motto was, *truth will come off conqueror,* which proved a satire upon themselves, because Calef obtained a complete triumph. The judges of the court, and jury confessed their errors; the people were astonished at their own delusion; reason and common sense were evidently on Calef's side; and even the present generation read his book with mingled sentiments of pleasure and admiration. A new edition was printed at Salem, 1796. It is wor-

new world, in 45 degrees, north latitude, sails along the coast, northward, to 60, and then southward, to 38, some say, to Cape Florida, in 25, and returns to England. *Prince.*

Dr. Belknap, also, supposes J Cabot made the discovery which the European writers generally ascribe to his son Sebastian. He gave a good reason, that Sebastian was only 20 years old; hence it is improbable he should have such a command. Sebastian and two brothers sailed with their father several voyages. It may be that he discovered the coast while aboard of his father's vessel, and hence the credit has been given of making the voyage of discovery.

thy of observation that Hutchinson, who was nearly related to the Mather family, speaks of R. Calef,
as a man of a fair mind, who substantiated his facts.

CALLENDER JOHN, minister of a Baptist church
in Newport, was born in Boston ; educated at Harvard College, where he received his degree, 1723.
He was ordained at Newport, 1731, and continued
a faithful pastor many years ; and still appears with
great lustre among the worthies who have lived in
this country.   His " history of Rhode Island," is
full of information. As a writer he is liberal, candid
and faithful ; christians of all denominations may be
edified by his pious remarks, and all who read, for
the sake of instruction, may gain knowledge and receive entertainment. This work was first preached as
a century sermon, 1738. He then made great addi-
tions, and published it as an " *historical discourse.*"
The book is now very scarce.   He also printed an
excellent " funeral sermon," which he preached after the death of Mr. Clap, the venerable pastor of the
first Congregational church.

Mr. Callender was grandson of Ellis Callender,
who joined the first Baptist church in Boston, 1669 ;
and was a leading character among them when their
meeting was nailed up by authority, 1680. He was
invited to the pastoral office, 1708, and died in 1718.
Elisha Callender his son, uncle to Mr. C. of Newport, who was graduated at Harvard College, 1710, succeeded him, and died, 1737.   He was ordained by
the Congregational ministers of Boston.*   *Church
Records. Backus History.*

---

* In the account of Boston, 4th vol. Historical Collections, the
writer, who is generally very accurate and belonged to this society, has not given an exact statement of the first ministers, if Mr.
Backus' history be correct, which we suppose is the case.—Com-
pare *Backus' abridgement*, &c page 144.   There is however a
considerable mistake in Mr Backus where he saith, Mr Elisha
Callender joined the church in 1713, " after which he went to
Harvard College," &c.   There is no Elisha Callender in the
college catalogue, except, 1710.

CARVER JOHN, *governour of New Plymouth*, was one of the most active, useful and pious men of Mr. Robinson's church while they were at Leyden ; and as praiseworthy while he lived with the pilgrims who first planted this part of North America. Carver and Cushman were the agents to agree with the Virginia company, and make provision for their voyage. The particulars of this voyage and of the settlement of the first colony in New England are preserved in extracts from Bradford's ms. history, which Mr. Prince made, and which have become more valuable as the ms. is lost. Mr. Carver was unanimously elected governour as soon as they reached the shore. The instrument is dated, Nov 11, 1620, at Cape Cod. No man could have conducted more wisely than he did in this office ; he was firm, prudent, zealous for the good of the settlement, and to promote virtue and piety among the planters. Unhappily for those who valued him so highly, and were allured and stimulated by his example, this worthy man and excellent magistrate lived a short time only with them. He finished his pilgrimage state, and entered into his rest. 5th of April, 1630. " He was buried with all the honours which could be shown by a grateful people The men were under arms, and fired several vollies over his grave. His affectionate wife, overcome by her loss, survived him but six weeks. One of his grandsons lived to be 102 years old. In 1755, *he*, his son, his grandson, and great grandson were one day working in the field together." A town in the county of Plymouth has lately had the name of Carver given to it. *Prince. Belknap*.

CHAUNCY CHARLES, president of Harvard College, who is styled in the Magnalia, Cadmus Americanus, was born in Hertfordshire, educated in the school at Westminster, and at the university of Cambridge. He there took the degree of B. D. Being intimately acquainted with archbishop Usher, one of the finest scholars in Europe, he had more

o

than common advantages to expand his mind, and
make improvements in literature. A more learned
man than Mr. Chauncy was not to be found among
the fathers of New England. He had been chosen
Hebrew professor at Cambridge, by the heads of
both houses, and exchanged this branch of instruction to oblige Dr. Williams, *vice chancellor* of the
university. He was well skilled in many oriental
languages, but especially the Hebrew which he knew
by very close study, and by conversing with a Jew,
who resided at the same house.

He was also an accurate Greek scholar, and was
made professor of this language when he left the
other professorship. In Leigh's critica sacra, there
is a latin address to the author by a friend, C. C.
who is called *Vir doctissimus*, &c. It is a commendation of the work in a handsome style. This uncommon scholar became a preacher, and was settled
at *Ware.* He displeased archbishop Laud, by opposing the book of sports, and reflecting upon the discipline of the church. In *Rushforth's* collections,
there is this passage. " Mr. Chauncy using some
expressions in his sermons which were construed to
his disadvantage, ex : g : 'That idolatry was admitted into the church ; that the preaching of the gospel would be suppressed ; that there is as much a-
theism, popery, arminianism and heresy crept in,
&c." This being viewed as a design to raise a fear
among the people, that some alteration of religion
would ensue, he was questioned in the high commission ; and by order of that court, the cause
was referred to the bishop of London, being his ordinary, who ordered him to make a *submission* in
Latin.

This worthy man came over to New England. in
1638, arriving at Plymouth, Jan. 1st.

He was soon after ordained at Scituate.—One
thing is worth mentioning to shew the spirit of the
man, and the quaint manner of expression then in
use. His text was, Prov. ix. 3. *Wisdom hath sent*

forth her maidens, and alluding to his *compliance* with the high commission court, he said with tears, Alas! christians, *I am no maiden, my soul has been defiled with false worship; how wondrous is the free grace of the Lord Jesus Christ, that I should still be employed among the maidens of wisdom!* When a stop was put to the *Laudean* persecution he was invited back by his former people at Ware; and it was his intention to spend the remainder of his life in his native country. At this time, the chair of the president was vacant at Harvard College. He was requested to accept it, and for a number of years performed the duties of that office with honour to himself, and to the reputation of that seminary of learning. "How learnedly he conveyed all the liberal arts to those that sat under his feet, how constantly he expounded the scriptures to them in the College hall, how wittily he moderated their disputations and other exercises, how *fluently* he expressed himself unto them, with Latin of a Terentian phrase, in all his discourses, and how carefully he inspected their manners, will never be forgotten by many of our most *worthy* men, who were made such by their education under him." When he made his oration on his inauguration he concluded it thus, " Doctiorem, certe præsidem, and huic oneri ac stationi multis modis aptiorem, vobis facile licet invenire ; sed amantiorem, et vestri boni studiosiorem, non invenietis."

He was very industrious, and usually employed his morning hours in study or devotion. He constantly rose at 4 o'clock, winter and summer. In the morning he expounded a chapter, in the old testament, unto the students assembled in the chapel; and in the evening expounded a passage in the new testament. Every Sunday he preached a sermon instead of the morning exposition. Yet with all his zeal, attention to his business and to his private studies, with his amazing application to every thing that was before him, he lived to be famous, and preached to much acceptance at an age, to which few reach, and they complain " their strength is labour and sorrow." When his friends advised him to remit his publick labours, he answered, " oportet imperato mori stantem "

At length, on the commencement, of 1771, he made a solemn address, a kind of valedictory oration ; and having lived to some good purpose, he prepared to die in peace, like a good servant who expected his reward. He died the end of this year etat 82, having been about 16 years pastor of the church in Scituate, and 17 years president of Harvard College.

He was a man very hasty in his temper : of this he was sensible and took great pains to govern it.

President Oakes, who was minister of the church in Cambridge and succeeded him as head of the same literary society, preached his funeral sermon, and makes some apology for the quickness of his temper,—" *the mention thereof* was to be wrapped up in Elijah's mantle."

President C. left six sons, all of whom were educated at Harvard College. They were all preachers. Some of them very learned divines. Dr. Mather says, they were all eminent physicians, as their father was before them. In a new country, where there are no physicians, a minister who is a scientifick man, may render himself eminently useful if able to practice physick ; but we are not of the opinion of this gentleman that there ought to be no distinction between physick and divinity. One man had better not be engaged in more than his own profession, he may be learned in one thing, and superficial in another—a learned theologian and a quack doctor, as we have seen in modern times.

The epitaph of president C. upon his tombstone is in the Magnalia.

Conditum
hic est Corpus
Caroli Chauncei
S. S. Theologiæ Baccalaur.
Et
Collegii Harvardini Nov. Angl.
Per XVII Annorum spatium
Præsidis Vigilantissimi,
Viri plane Intergerrimi,
Concionatoris Eximii,
Pietate
Pariter ac Librari Eruditione
Ornatissimi.
Qui obiit in Domino, Feb. xix.
An. Dom. MDCLXXI.
Et Ætatis suæ, LCLXXXII.*

CHAUNCY CHARLES, pastor of the first church in Boston, was a great grandson of president Chauncy, and had much of the genius and spirit of his ancestor. He was born, Jan. 1st, 1705. His father, the youngest son of the rev. Isaac Chauncy, Berry street, settled in Boston, as a merchant. Charles was only seven years old when his father died ; but had friends, who were disposed to give him every advantage of education. At twelve years old he was sent to Har-

* President Chauncy's sons were settled in different parts of the world. Isaac, the eldest, was pastor of the church in Berry street, London. Dr. Watts was chosen his assistant in 1698, and succeeded him in 1701. Ichabod the second son, was chaplain of a regiment at Dunkirk. These sons were graduated, 1651. Nathaniel was minister of Hatfield, and Israel of Stratford. They were graduated, 1661. Also Elnathan who was a preacher, but never settled. It is probable that he and his brother Barnabas who took his degree, 1657, died young. *Israel* lived longer than the others ; he was the youngest son, and died after the commencement of the eighteenth century. His ordination has generally been styled the *leather mitten* ordination, and much ridicule has been thrown upon it by Episcopal writers. The fact was, that when he was settled the laymen of the council insisted upon *their right* " *of laying on hands,*" and one of the brethren forgot to take off his mitten ; hence it has been made to appear as a ludicrous circumstance to lessen the solemnity of the Congregational mode of separating ministers. It was not long after this, that in Connecticut and Massachusetts, the clergy deprived the brethren of this privilege. But could we now refuse them if they insisted upon it?

vard College; was graduated, 1721, and considered as one of the best scholars who had ever received the honours of that seminary. It afforded great pleasure to wise and good men of those times to see a descendant of that president, who had done so much honour to New England, come into life with such high recommendations; and their hopes were highly gratified when he made divinity his study. As soon as Mr. Wadsworth was removed from the first church, to preside at Cambridge, the eyes of that people were fixed upon this young man, and he was associated with Mr. Foxcroft in the work of the ministry. He was ordained, 1727. Mr. Foxcroft and he were colleague pastors for about 40 years. After the death of his colleague, he performed the whole parochial duty nearly ten years. In June, 1778, the rev. Mr. John Clark was settled with him, whom he treated as a son, and who was always sensible of his paternal regards. Dr. Chauncy was one of the greatest divines in New England; no one except president Edwards, and the late Dr. Mayhew, has been so much known among the literati of Europe, or printed more books upon theological subjects. He took great delight in studying the scriptures. Feeling the sacred obligations of morality, he impressed them upon the minds of others in the most rational and evangelical manner. When he preached upon the faith of the gospel, he *reasoned* of righteousness, temperance and a judgment to come. It was said that he wanted the graces of delivery, and taste in composition. But it was his object to exhibit the most sublime truths in simplicity of speech, and he never, therefore, studied to have his periods polished, or his style adorned with rhetorical figures. His favourite authors were, Tillotson of the episcopal church, and Baxter among the puritans. For he preferred the rich vein of sentiment in the sermons of the English divines, to that tinsel of *French* declamation so fashionable in our modern way of preaching. Upon some occasions, however, Dr.

Chauncy could raise his feeble vioce, and manifest a vigour and animation, which would arrest the attention of the most careless hearer, and have a deeper effect, than the oratory which is thought by many to be *irresistibly* persuasive : at all times, he was argumentative and perspicuous, and made an admirable practical use of the sentiments he delivered.

But it is as an author we are chiefly to view Dr. Chauncy in this biographical sketch. His clear head, his quick conception, and comprehensive view of every subject enabled him to write with ease and propriety. However quick, and sudden, and unguarded in his expressions when discussing things in conversation, he reasoned coolly in all his controversial writings. His ideas were so well arranged, and he had such a command of them, that he managed every subject with equal candour, liberality, fairness and skill. In the episcopal controversy he obtained great celebrity. He first began this in a " sermon upon the validity of presbyterian ordination,"preached at the Dudleian lecture, at Cambridge, 1762. In 1767 he wrote his remarks upon a sermon of the bishop of Landaff. In 1771 he printed a complete view of episcopacy, " the two first centuries." Beside these, he had a particular controversy upon the subject of the American episcopate ; he wrote " an appeal to the publick answered in behalf of non episcopal churches" when Dr. Chandler of Elizabethtown, offered his " appeal to the publick," in favour of episcopal churches ; to this Dr. Chandler wrote an answer styled, " the appeal defended," &c. Dr. Chauncy made a reply to the appeal defended, and to this Dr. Chandler also replied in another large pamphlet.

In the *Whitefieldian* controversy, Dr. Chauncy discovered more zeal than in his other works. In 1742 and 1743 he published a " sermon on the various gifts of ministers ;" one upon " enthusiasm," and another on the " outpourings of the Holy Ghost ;"

he also printed an "account of the French prophets," and "seasonable thoughts on the state of religion." At the time of the great revival of religion, there were certain things of a dangerous tendency mingled with it, which the Dr. saw fit to correct It makes an octavo volume in five parts, and by the list of subscribers, we find he was encouraged by many worthy ministers who differed from him in their doctrinal sentiments. His other large works are, "twelve sermons on seasonable and important subjects," chiefly upon justification, in opposition to the opinion of Robert Sandiman, 1765; the "mystery hid from ages, or the salvation of all men;" "dissertations upon the benevolence of the Deity;" these were printed 1784, and the next year he printed a volume "on the fall of man and its consequences."

In 1742, he received his diploma from the university of Edinburgh, the first from that seminary to an American divine. He was also one of the London board of commissioners for propagating the gospel among the Indians; and a corresponding member of the board in Scotland. His health, cheerfulness, activity and the powers of his mind continued to old age. He died, Feb. 10, 1787. Mr. Clarke preached his funeral sermon.*

CHECKLEY JOHN, minister of the Episcopal church in Providence, was born in Boston, of English parentage. He had no brother, and only one sister who died at the age of 17. The early part of his education he received at the grammar school in

---

* In the life of literary men, there are few incidents very remarkable. The notice of them must be an account of their works, the progress of their studies, and the fruits of their labour. Such a memoir of Chauncy would make a volume, and we hope will soon be given to the publick by the pastor of the first church, a gentleman who is very able to delineate the characters of his predecessors. The Dr. printed many occasional sermons. Ten upon funeral occasions: several at the ordination of ministers; a sermon at the annual convention, 1744; the election sermon, 1747. He also left a number of mss. upon theological subjects.

Boston, then under the care of the famous Ezekiel Cheever, but afterwards he was sent to England, and finished his studies at the university of Oxford. He travelled over a great part of Europe, and collected some valuable curiosities, such as paintings, mss. &c. He procured a valuable Hebrew bible, elegantly written on vellum, which, if it could now be obtained, might be of some use, as well as an object of curiosity. When he returned from England he married the sister of the rev. Dr. Miller, episcopal missionary at Braintree, by whom he had two children, John and Rebecca. After this he went to England for orders. The bishop of London refused to ordain him, on account of his being a *non-juror*, and a remonstrance against him, signed by several of the clergy of New England, who represented that he was rather an eccentrick character, than a man of serious deportment. He received ordination some years after, and in the year 1739 was fixed at Providence, having under his care the church in that town, and the small assemblies at Warwick and Attleborough, to whom he preached once a month. He was a very excellent linguist; was well acquainted with four languages besides the vernacular, Hebrew, Greek, Latin and Indian, which rendered him a companion for learned and curious men, all of whom were fond of the company of John Checkley, though some were offended with his opinions; and others thought him too much of a wag, for an intimate acquaintance. Anecdotes concerning him were constantly repeated by people of the last generation, when a company wished to be entertained with witty stories, or ludicrous tricks; many of these were, doubtless without foundation, but they mark the character of the man. One thing is true attested by his own writing. He was tried at the supreme court, held in Boston, Nov. 27, 1724, for " publishing and selling a false and scandalous libel," for which he was fined fifty pounds, to stand committed until sentence be perform-

P

ed.* Upon this trial he made a speech in defence
of himself, which he afterwards published in England. In this pamphlet, he also printed "the jury's verdict; his plea in arrest of judgment and
the sentence of the court." The conclusion of his
plea is these words, "The dissenters are affirmed to
be no *ministers;* to be schismaticks, and *excommu-
nicate* by the laws of *England*, which are part of the
law of the land ; and therefore to say the same things
of them, I humbly hope *shall not be deemed a libel.*"

After Mr. Checkley resided at Providence, his
character was respectable as a divine, as well as a

* The book alluded to, had this title, " A short and easy method with the Deists. To which was added, a discourse concerning
episcopacy, in defence of *christianity*, and the church of *England*, againsts the *Deists* and *Dissenters.*"

The latter part was his own work, in which he made a virulent attack upon the clergy, and people of New England, and
threw some rude glances at the family on the throne of Great
Britain.

In the diary of Mr. Barnard of Marblehead, he says, a letter
was written to Bishop Gibson, declaring the true character of
John Checkley, " that he was a bitter enemy to other denominations, a non-juror, and that he had not a liberal education. He desired Mr. Newman, our province agent, to acquaint the gentleman that he never would ordain a person disagreeable to the people, but would fix at Marblehead a good man, loyal to the
government, and of a catholick temper." The letter was signed by Mr. Barnard, and Mr. Holyoke, ministers of that town,
where Mr. Checkley meant to fix his residence. " The bishop
of London read this letter to gov. Shute, and inquired of him,
concerning the state of New England, who confirmed all which
had been written. The bishop of Exeter afterwards ordained
Mr. Checkley, and he was sent to Narragansett."

A pamphlet was printed, 1727, in Boston, called a modest
" proof of the order of the churches." This gave rise to the
first controversy upon the subject of episcopacy, was anonymous, but supposed to be written by J. Checkley. Dr. Wigglesworth, professor of divinity, answered it by " sober remarks upon modest proof." There was also another answer by Martin
Mar. Prelate.

Besides these pamphlets, Mr. Checkley wrote a small tract
upon *predestination*, against the general ideas of the people of this
country. Mr. Thomas Walter, a young man, an intimate friend
of Checkley, wrote an answer to it, and defended the Calvinistick doctrine. These pamphlets were published in the year 1715.

scholar ; he was, however, bigotted to his own notions, and took pleasure in making puritans of various denominations feel his satirical goads. He was
likewise of the opinion that a prince of the *Hanove-*
rian line ought not to sit upon the British throne ;
and also that no one could be completely virtuous,
if he *were not a high churchman.* He died 1753,
aged 78.

Mr. C. had two children. A son who was graduated at Harvard College, 1738 ; he studied divinity with his father, went to England for orders, and
died of the small pox. His talents were excellent
and he was a most amiable youth. The daughter
married Henry Paget, an Irish gentleman. She left
three children, two of them are living at this time,
united to very respectable connexions.

CHEEVER EZEKIEL, preceptor of the latin grammar school, Boston, came to New England, A. D.
1637. He kept a grammar school in this country
above seventy years. He in the first place fixed at
New Haven ; was then invited to Ipswich, in Massachusetts ; he removed from this place to Charlestown ; and from the year 1670, to his death, was
preceptor of the school in Boston. He died, A. D.
1708, aged 94. Many of the sons of Harvard College received the rudiments of their education from
him. His *accidence* was taught in most of the
schools till the revolution. In 1768, the twentieth
edition was printed. He published also, a book
" upon the scriptures prophecies," which is now
very scarce. His praise was in all the churches ;
he was highly respected by the magistrates of the
colony, and venerated by the people. Dr. Cotton
Mather preached his funeral sermon.

CHEEVER SAMUEL, minister of Marblehead, was
son of the preceptor. He was graduated at Harvard College, 1659 ; ordained at Marblehead, 1684 ;
and died 1724, aged 85. His colleague speaks of
him among the celebrated divines of New England,
" A man furnished with good abilities, both natural and acquired ; a constant and zealous preach-

er."* The family were remarkable for longevity.
Thomas, the second son of the famous preceptor,
lived to the age of 93. He took his degree, 1677,
and was pastor of the church at *Rumney Marsh*,
now called Chelsea, Suffolk county.

There were several other branches of this family,
who arrived at ninety or above four score years.†

CHURCH BENJAMIN, a celebrated commander of
the New England forces, was born at Duxbury,
1639. His father, whose name was Joseph, came
into this country for the sake of religious freedom.
Benjamin was the eldest of three sons, of a vigorous
constitution, brave as a soldier, and a well disposed
member of society. When the country was alarmed with the preparations of Philip of Mount Hope
he was one of the most active and vigilant of those
who opposed his measures, and headed the party
which surrounded that bold sachem when he was
killed.

In his own simple manner he relates the circumstances which led him into the field when he was
appointed to a command. "I was then building
and beginning a plantation at a place called by the
Indians *Sogkonate*, and since by the English, *Little
Compton*. I was the first *Englishman* that built upon that neck, which was full of Indians. My head
and hands were full about settling a new plantation
where nothing was brought to ; no preparation of
dwelling house, or outhouses, or fencing made.
Horses and cattle were to be provided, ground to be
cleared and broken up, and the utmost caution used, to keep myself from offending my Indian neigh-

* Historical Collection, vol. X.

† A daughter of Mr. Cheever, of Chelsea, died in Boston,
1778, at the age of 88. She was the wife of Mr. Benjamin Burt,
goldsmith. They had two sons ; Benjamin, who followed his
father's business, and *John*, who had a college education, was
graduated, 1736, and ordained at Bristol, Rhode Island. He was
sick when that town was burnt by the British men of war, and
attempting to escape the danger, he fell down dead in his field.

bours all around me. While I was thus busily employed, and all my strength laid out in this laborious undertaking, I received a commission from the government to engage in their defence." He kept a journal of his military exploits, which is a very good history of the war, so far as he was engaged in it. This was published afterwards in a quarto pamphlet by his son; a second edition of which appeared in 1772. Hutchinson speaks of colonel Church as a "fortunate officer;" Hubbard had before described him, " both prudent and brave." The account is very entertaining, which is given of his skilful mode of fighting, and the various attacks he made upon the enemy. Philip was a formidable adversary to the New England settlements; he had great address in stirring up the resentment of all the Indian tribes against the white people, and was always ready to expose his life when it could be of any advantage; but he was hunted upon the mountains and through the forests, and was never able to meet the English in a regular battle. He is represented as cruel, treacherous, subtle, full of malice, but his enemies bring this account; he had no friend to give a narrative of his exploits. Could he speak, he might tell of his brave actions, his zeal for his nation whom the white people oppressed, till they drove him to extremity. The last account of him is, " that after a years absence he returned to Mount Hope, where the Indians were gathering to him, but he soon lost his friends, his family were taken prisoners, and he himself escaped by running into a swamp." There he was killed, August 12, 1776. Capt. Church commanded the party, but he was shot by one of his own men whom he had offended, and who had deserted from him. After peace was made with the Indians, capt. Church resided at Bristol, and then settled at Seconet.

In 1692, he was again called into service. He was sent against the eastern Indians, took a number of prisoners, and burned their fort on Kennebeck river. Four years after this he commanded five hundred men, and sailed from Portsmouth for Penobscot, and not finding the enemy, he reconnoitred the coasts, and took a view of Nova Scotia, but upon his coming to Chignecto, the French inhabitants fled, and the English plundered and burnt their houses. This was said to be done without the consent of the commander. It was his object rather to pursue the Indians. He was superseded, and the command given to col. Hawthorne of Salem. This was resented by Church, and Mr. Hutchinson speaks of it as an impolitick measure. In 1704, there was another expedition against Nova Scotia, and the command given to col. Church, the bravest and most experienced officer in Massachusetts colony.

This expedition was a favourite measure of gov. Dudley, and in his speech to the assembly he says, that "it struck a terror to the Indians, and was the means of preserving the frontiers." But he was blamed for it. It is one of the articles of charge against him in a letter to Dr. Mather, wrote to him, 1710.* Col. Church lived the rest of his days in easy circumstances. He died Jan. 17, 1718, having a fall from his horse, which broke a blood vessel. He lies buried in Little Compton. On his tomb stone is this inscription.

Here lies interred the body
of the honourable
Col. BENJAMIN CHURCH, Esq.
who departed this life,
Jan. 17, 1717, 18,
in the 78th year of his age.

His character is thus given by those who knew him well. "A man of integrity, justice and uprightness, of piety and serious religion. He was a member of the church of Bristol at its foundation.

* See 4th vol. Hist. Coll. where the letters to the governor are printed from the original mss. of Dr. Increase and Dr. Cotton Mather.

Constant in family worship, exemplary in observing the sabbath, and attending the ordinances of the sanctuary. He lived regularly, and left an example worthy the imitation of his posterity. He was a friend to the civil and religious liberties of his country, and greatly rejoiced in the revolution. He was col. of the militia in the county of Bristol. The several offices of civil and military trust, with which he was invested from time to time, through a long life, he discharged with fidelity and usefulness." *History of war with Philip. Hutchinson's History of Massachusetts bay.*

CHURCH BENJAMIN, physician in the town of Boston, was graduated at Harvard College, 1754. He rose to eminence in his profession, while he made a figure among the leading whigs, in the years preceding the revolution. He had genius and taste, and was an excellent writer in poetry and prose. Of his poetical pieces there remain some which are now read with pleasure. The " elegy upon Dr. Mahew," who died 1766. And the " elegy upon Mr. Whitefield," 1770, are serious and pathetick. The " elegy upon the times" printed in the year 1765, is rather satirical ; but breathes the spirit which animated the patriots of that day. The poem No. XI. in the collection, styled " Pietas et Gratulatio," in the opinion of the monthly reviewers, had the preference of the others. His prose writings were mostly essays of a witty and philological kind, which are scattered in ephemeral publications, though some of them, perhaps, are known by those who were contemporary with him. The oration on the 5th March, which he pronounced before the town, 1773, discovers a rich fancy ; it is certainly one of the very best of the " Boston orations." When the war commenced in 1775, his character was so high, that he was appointed physician general of the army. This place was first offered to Dr. Warren, but he chose a more active scene, and had a

commission as major general.　Dr, Church was
thought the next meritorious character for that station.　But while he was performing the duties assigned him, he was suspected of a correspondence
with the enemy.　Certain letters in cypher, were
intercepted which he had written to a relation in
Boston.　He was dismissed from his post, imprisoned and tried.　At his trial he made a defence
which required talents to write, but which gave no
satisfaction to the people. *

Nothing indeed could then stem the torrent of
their prejudices.　Individuals, however, were in
doubt whether he meant evil, and nothing very treacherous appeared in the letter.　The crime was in
holding such a secret correspondence.

In the year succeeding, he obtained leave to depart for the West Indies.　No intelligence has ever
been received of the vessel in which he sailed.

CLAP NATHANIEL, minister of the first Congregational church in Newport, a descendant from one
of the first planters of Massachusetts, was born in
Dorchester, 1668.　He was graduated at Harvard
College, 1690, and while he was young, his praise
was in the churches for his piety, learning, and excellent pulpit talents.　He began to preach in Newport, 1695, and in the midst of many discouragements became the pastor of the first Congregational
church, planted in Rhode Island.　Few of this denomination had settled in that colony.　All the leading characters were either Quakers or Baptists; and
their prejudices were strong against the order of the
churches, and the ministers, of Massachusetts.
Mr. Clap had a zeal to do good, and so very little
of a party spirit, that he gained the esteem and affection of the inhabitants of the town, although differing in religious opinions.　The Congregational
church, however, was not formed till the year 1720.
He was ordained their pastor, Nov. 3d, of the same

* This speech is published in the first volume of the collections
of the Massachusetts Historical Society.

year. A few years after, a young man of talents preached among them, who became remarkably popular, so as to draw away the majority of the people. They would have consented that Mr. Clap should remain as the senior pastor; but he chose to leave them rather than to have an associate whom he could not approve. Another church was built in the town, with whom he continued the remainder of his days. The interest the people of Newport took in his favour during his trouble was very lively. The ministers who went from Boston, and caused the separation of the society, met with a cold reception; they were sensible afterwards of their error, and wished the *result of council* had been different. To be sure, there were oddities in the disposition of Mr. Clap, which may be imputed to his state of celibacy. He indulged some peculiarities, which excited remark, and which might be exceptionable, where the character was less prominent for excellent traits. The great Dean Berkeley was very fond of Mr. Clap. He often spoke of his good deeds, and exemplary character. He said he was struck with the gravity of his deportment. In a conversation, while he was in Boston, he said, "Before I saw *father Clap* I thought the bishop of Rome had the most grave aspect of any man I ever saw, but really the minister of Newport has the most venerable appearance. The resemblance is very great." Mr. Clap died October 30, 1745, etat. 78. Mr. Callender, minister of the Baptist church, preached the funeral sermon, in his usual excellent and liberal manner of writing. "There are two things," said he, in which he excelled so much, that I must not omit them; his care about the education of children, and his concern for the instruction of servants. He abounded in contrivances to do good by scattering books of piety and virtue, not such as minister questions and strife, but godly edifying; and put himself to a very considerable expense that he might, in this method, awaken the careless and secure, comfort the feeble minded, succour the tempted, instruct the ignorant, and quicken, animate and encourage all." *Callend. serm. Private information.*

CLAP THOMAS, president of Yale College, was born in Scituate, 1703; graduated at Harvard College, 1722; ordained at Windsor, Connecticut, 1726, and continued a faithful and laborious pastor over that church, about fourteen years. He was then chosen rector of the college at New Haven. Mr. Williams resigned in 1740, and he was immediately elected to the office. The title of rector was soon after changed for that of president. Mr. Clap was one of the most learned men of New England. As a theologian he was well versed in ecclesiastical history, the writings of the fathers, the sermons and controversies of modern divines. He was a Calvinist according to the Westminster confession of faith, attached to the principles of our fathers, and he set his face against every innovation in doctrine, or the discipline of the New England churches. Hence he bore his testimony against Mr. Whitefield, and that itinerant kind of preaching which succeeded his visiting these American provinces. After this, many separations were caused between ministers and their people, and gifted brethren rose up who despised the ministry, and made themselves conspicuous by their boasting. President Clap wrote several pamphlets on this subject. He afterwards wrote a book which he styled *a defence of the New England churches* against the Arminians, who were spreading their doctrines over Connecticut. In 1752, he drew the scheme of the new divinity, as he calls it; or sums up the errors collected from several authors, viz. Chubb, Taylor, Foster, Hutcheson, Campbell and Ramsay. At a general association of the ministers of the county, 1755, this book of president Clap, was approved; and they recommend it to the associations " to insist much on the doctrines contained in this defence, and bear their testimony against prevailing errors ;" it was signed by Jared Eliot, moderator.

Mr. Clap wrote a history of Yale College, which contains many precious documents, and biographical sketches. As the head of that seminary he was indefatigable in his labours, both secular and scientifick, to promote the benefit of the society. This is the language of Dr. Stiles, and to have his commendation is " laudari a vire laudato." The doctor says, likewise, that he studied the higher branches of mathematicks, and was one of the first philosophers America has produced; "that he was equalled by no man, except the most learned professor Winthrop." When Dr. Stiles viewed the character of his predecessor, it must relate to the time he was at the zenith of his reputation. In his latter days, he grew unpopular with the leading characters of the state; and lost the affection of the students at the college. It was said he was hard and unyielding in his temper, opinionated and stiff, as well as contracted in his notions; that he would not suffer any improvement in the means of education, and that the college, though it had produced many of the first characters in the land, did not make that progress in literary reputation which it might, because he would admit of no alteration in the mode of teaching and government, being so much afraid of innovation, and determined that every thing should remain as it had been. One or more pamphlets were written containing pointed remarks; but how easy is it to hurt the reputation of persons by wit and satire! The most eminent men, especially in old age, may be wounded by arrows sharp pointed, or dipped in venom, when young men are in sport, or irritated with or without a cause.

If those things were true in any measure, Mr. Clap differed from his successors. Even since Dr. Stiles was inducted into the office of president, they have made many alterations, and increased their plans of instruction; a high reputation has been given to this ancient seminary, which has thrown a lustre upon its officers.

President Clap resigned the chair, 1764, and died at Scituate, the next year.

CLARKE PETER, pastor of a church in Danvers, was a profound and learned divine, and an author of no small reputation. He was graduated at Harvard College, 1712, and ordained June 5th, 1717 ; died June, 1768. Above half a century he preached to this people ; he was never taken off from his publick labours, till within a few months of his death. He applied diligently to his studies, and was such a redeemer of time, that every hour when he was not in his study, he endeavoured to improve to the good of others, allowing himself very little for his own relaxation. Mr. Barnard of Salem, preached his funeral sermon, and observes, he was well acquainted with ancient and modern learning. " His style was pure, nervous and clear, cool and pathetick, as his subject required ; and by means of his conversing much with the best modern authors, more elegant and pleasing to the politer world than most of his equals in age. His printed works will be evidence of this, which are somewhat numerous upon every public occasion, and will do his memory honour.

His controversial writings have been often quoted by others, who have written on the same side of the question. He wrote several books in defence of original sin,* and in favour of infant bap-

* This gentleman engaged in the controversy of original sin in 1758. What led to it was a pamphlet, called the "winter evening conversation,upon the doctrine of original sin between a minister and three of his neighbours." Mr. Clarke wrote the " summer morning conversation" in answer to it. This was also by way of dialogue. The author of the " winter evening's conversation replied to Mr. Clarke ; and he then wrote a reply in which he took a large view of the doctrine by the disciples of Calvin— 8vo. 200 pages. There were other pamphlets published, and upon opposite states of the question. Such a controversy was very interesting at this time ; but they are little known by the present generation. The same subject has been handled by greater men, such as Taylor, and president Edwards. Mr. Clarke preached the artillery election sermon, 1736 ; convention sermon, 1745 ; Dudleian lecture sermon, 1763.

tism. The famous Dr. Gill entered the lists with him upon the latter subject. To whom Mr. Clarke replied, making some candid observations on his severe remarks. They both understood their subject.

CLARKE JOHN, D. D. pastor of the first church in Boston, was born at Portsmouth, in New-Hampshire, April 13, 1755; graduated at Harvard College, 1774; and was ordained July 8, 1778, as colleague with the late Dr. Chauncy, with whom he lived in the most intimate and respectful friendship about nine years; and afterwards continued, assiduously and faithfully labouring in the service of the church, until the Lord's-day, April 1, 1798; when, in the midst of his afternoon sermon, he was suddenly seized with an apoplexy, fell down in the pulpit, and expired in less than twelve hours, having almost completed the 43d year of his age, and the 20th of his ministry.

Descended from respectable parents, he discovered in early life the signs of genius and industry. At the university, he was distinguished by a close attention to classic and philosophic studies, by a strict obedience to the laws, and by irreproachable morals. In the office of preceptor, he was gentle and persuasive, beloved by his pupils, and esteemed by their friends. As a public preacher, his compositions bore the marks of penetration, judgment, perspicuity and elegance. Faithful to the interest of religion, he deeply examined its foundation and evidence; and persuaded of the truth and importance of the christian system, he recommended, by his publick discourses and private conversation, its sublime doctrines, its wise institutions, and its salutary precepts.

Though fond of polite literature and philosophic researches, yet he considered theology as the proper science of a gospel minister. To this object he principally devoted his time and studies, and was

earnestly desirous of investigating every branch of
it, not merely to gratify his own sacred curiosity,
but that he might impart to his hearers the whole
counsel of God. He was habitually a close student ;
and it is not improbable, that the intenseness of his
mental application proved too severe for the delicate fabric of his nerves.

His devotional addresses were copious and fervent ; and his intercessions strong and affectionate ;
discovering at once the ardor of his piety, and the
warmth of his benevolence. In the private offices
of pastoral friendship, he was truly exemplary and
engaging. His temper was mild and cheerful ; his
manners easy and polite ; and the social virtues of
an honest heart gave a glow to his language, and
enlivened every circle in which he was conversant.*

COBBET THOMAS, pastor of the first church in
Ipswich, was born, 1608, at Newbury, in England,
was a pupil of the famous Dr. Twiss, who was

* This account of Dr. Clarke is in the 6th vol. of Historical
Collections. It was written by the late Dr. Belknap, who requested the compiler of this dictionary to undertake it ; but who
only supplied certain documents, while he preferred to have the
character of his friend delineated by an abler hand.

Dr. Clarke was a member of the American academy of arts
and sciences from the foundation of the society ; also a member
of the historical society, a trustee of the humane society, one of
the first founders of the Boston library, a corresponding member of the board of commissioners in Scotland for propagating
the gospel among the Indians ; and of the Massachusetts society for the like purpose, extending the privileges to others, as
well as the aboriginals.

His publications were four sermons. One upon the death of
N. W. Appleton, an excellent young man, physician of Boston,
who died 1795 ; one upon the death of Dr. Cooper ; one upon
the death of Dr. Chauncy ; a sermon before the humane society,
1793. An answer to the question, " why are you a christian,"
which has gone through several editions in Boston and London.
Letters to a student at the university of Cambridge. Since his
death, a volume of sermons, upon miscellaneous subjects ; and a
volume of sermons to young men. They are written in an elegant, neat and correct style, in which he excelled most other writers, and are filled with pious sentiments.

highly esteemed in this country. His works, though now scarce, were in high estimation with former generations, especially those who were attached to the doctrines of the Geneva school. Mr. Cobbet was sent to Oxford, where he finished his studies, and received his master's degree. He could not be persuaded to conform to the rites and ceremonies of the episcopal church, and on this account, being persecuted by the men in power, he came over to this American wilderness. Mr. Davenport and Mr. Cobbet came over in the same vessel. As soon as he arrived at Boston, he was invited to settle with Mr. Whiting, in Lynn, where he continued from the year 1637 to 1656. Being invited to take charge of the church in Ipswich, he accepted the call, and there passed the rest of his days. He died 1686. It is an evidence that he possessed extraordinary qualifications for the pastoral office, that he was chosen to succeed two such eminent divines as Mr. Norton, and Mr. Rogers, one of whom removed to Boston to stand in the place of the great Cotton, while the other was called to dwell in his everlsting habitation. Mr. Cobbet found his temporal circumstances meliorated by the change in his situation;* and he certainly moved in a more extensive sphere of usefulness. He excited great attention to religion in the people of that town; was fervent in spirit, persevering in duty, while he adorned his profession by his example.

His works which were highly praised in those times have not come down to us of this generation; nor do we know whether they were printed in Old or New England. He published more books than

---

* The town of Lynn, though in a flourishing condition, conceived themselves unable to support two ministers, except they used great economy; and reduced their salary to £ 30 a year. The year this was voted, the town suffered a loss of £ 300 by a disease among their cattle. Dr. Mather observes, that this ought to be considered as a penalty for their parsimonious conduct.

his contemporaries; they are described very minutely in the Magnalia. He first wrote a book " upon the
fifth commandment," then " upon the first," also
" upon the second ;" he also printed upon " toleration and the duties of the civil magistrate ;" to these
tracts he added " a vindication of the government
of New England against their aspersors, who thought
themselves persecuted by it." He also wrote " a
defence of infant baptism," which is commended by
Mr. Norton.

Of all his books, that upon prayer is said to be
most excellent ; hence the inscription on the tomb-
stone.

Sta Viator ; Thesaurus hic jacet
THOMAS COBBETUS
cujus
Nosti preces potentissimas, ac Mores probatissimos,
Si es Nov Anglus.
Mirare, *si pietatem colas ;*
Sequere, *si felicitatem optes.*

CODDINGTON WILLIAM, governour of Rhode-
Island, one of the first planters of Massachus-
setts, was chosen assistant in England, and came
over in the Arabella. He was of Lincolnshire. He
fixed himself at Boston, and was a leading member
of the first church, and every year chosen *assistant*,
as the counsellors were then called. He sometimes
was a popular character in Boston ; at other times
lost his influence. Gov. Winthrop mentions, that
in the year 1634, they met to choose seven men " to
divide the town lands, and contrary to expectation
left out Mr. Coddington, and other of the chief
men." This however was owing to a democratick spirit as Mr. Cotton and gov. Winthrop told
them. They were afraid that the richer men would
not give the poorer sort their proportion. Winthrop
was chosen by one or two votes only and refused to
serve, " telling the people that he was much grieved that Boston should be the first who should shake
off their magistrates, especially Mr. Coddington,
who had always been so forward for their enlargement."

In the controversy with Mrs. Hutchinson, 1637, 8, Winthrop and Coddington took different sides, the one being inclined to support her pretensions to piety, and all her extravagancies of opinion, the other joined in the censure passed upon her at her trial, when the court saw fit to banish her from the colony. The politicks of our little commonwealth were not a little mingled with that spiritual quixotism which disturbed their tranquillity. Vane, Coddington, and others, were opposed to Winthrop and Dudley. The country people were the friends of Winthrop; the inhabitants of Boston were with Vane, whose interest sunk, when the *familists* were banished. Mr. Coddington would not even sit with gov. Winthrop, in the seat provided for the magistrates, but went and took his place with the deacons, and soon after this, he went to Aquetneck, an island in Narraganset. He had a large property in Boston, was a merchant of the first character, and had been treasurer of the colony. He built the first brick house in this metropolis. When the people had incorporated themselves as a body politick, they chose him governour. He continued in this office till the island was incorporated with Providence plantations, seven years after their removal from Boston. In 1647, he assisted in forming their new constitution, and was chosen governour the next year, which office he refused.

In 1651 " he had a commission from the supreme authority in England to be governour of the island, pursuant to a power reserved in the *patent :* but the people being jealous the commission might affect their lands and liberties as secured to them by the patent, he readily laid it down on the first notice from England that he might do so ; and for their further satisfaction and contentment he, by a writing under his hand, obliged himself to make a formal surrender to all right and title to any of the lands more than his proportion, in common with the other inhabitants, whenever it should be demanded."   R

This account is from Mr. Callender's historical discourse, who was prejudiced in his favour from the sacrifices he made, his zeal to promote their interests, especially the general toleration of religious opinions, which was allowed in no other part of New England, and perhaps, we may extend our observation by saying, at that time, no part of Christendom.

He retired from publick business a number of years after this patriotick exertion, but in his latter days was again a candidate for the honours of his country. In 1678, he died governour of the colony. He was then 78 years of age.*

The honourable Mr. Coddington who was a magistrate of the colony, 1738, and highly esteemed for his fidelity and other virtues, was a grandson of the first governour.

COLLINS JOHN, minister of the gospel, was graduated at Harvard College, A. D. 1649. He was elected fellow of the corporation, and continued.

He became a celebrated preacher in London, having a sweet voice and most affectionate manner in the pulpit. He was chaplain to gen. Monk, when he marched out of Scotland into England; was one of the lecturers at Pinner's hall, and died Dec. 3d, 1687, universally lamented.†

---

* On the 24th of March, 1637,8, the Indian sachems signed the deed or grant of Aquetneck, &c. and the English not only paid the gratuities, to the sachems, but many more to the inhabitants to remove off. as appears by receipts still extant.

The settlement began at Pocasset, the east end of the island, since called Portsmouth. In 1644, they called it, Isle of Rhodes, or Rhode Island. When the island was first incorporated, they chose a judge to do justice and judgment and preserve peace. This was Mr. Coddington. In 1740, they voted he should be called governour. W. Brenton was chosen deputy governour; N. Easton, J. Coggeshall, William Boulston and John Porter were chosen assistants.

† In the Magnalia, we are told that when Mr. Collins laid sick, Mr. Mead prayed so affectionately for him that there hardly was a dry eye in the great congregation at Pinner's Hall, where he had been a lecturer. Dr. Mather, in allusion to Mr. Collins's ser-

He had a son who was educated for the ministry at Utrecht, who was afterwards minister of one of the churches in the city of London.

His publications are a *sermon in the morning exercises*, upon this question—How are the religious of a nation the strength of it? a sermon, Jude, 3d v. a prefatory epistle before Mr. Venning's remains, also, one before the *treatise of eternal glory*, written by Mr. Mitchel of Cambridge.

COLLINS NATHANIEL, pastor of the church of Middleton, Connecticut, was the younger brother of John, both were the sons of deacon Collins of Cambridge. The younger brother was graduated, 1660, and he died, Dec. 28, 1684.

He united in his character all the qualities of exemplary piety, extraordinary ingenuity, obliging affability ;" and was a very excellent preacher.

> Ille pius pastor, quo non præstantior unus
> Qui faciendo docet, quæ facienda docet.

COLMAN BENJAMIN, D. D. minister of the church in Brattle street, Boston, was born in Boston, 1674. His parents came from London, not many years before this excellent son of theirs was born. Young Colman received his education at Harvard College, was a studious youth, though of

---

mon in the *M. E.* says, *the nation weakened by his death*, would be a good running title for his funeral sermon.

Of Nathaniel Collins, that there were more wounds given to Connecticut by his death, than Cæsar received in the senate house.

He says likewise that he should have written some verses upon his death, but he recollected the clause in a certain gentleman's *will*, mentioned by Thuanus, that they should not burden his hearse with bad funeral verses ; and because that sacred thing *verse* has been, by the licentious part of mankind, so prostituted, that whatever is now offered, becomes suspected. Nevertheless the merits of Mr. Collins were such, that his life must be written, or at least so much of it as this, that " he deserved highly to have his life written."

The Dr. consoles the colony of Connecticut, lest they should be too much depressed by the loss of a faithful minister, with a saying whereby the mother of Brasides was comforted. Vir bonus est Brasides, et fortis, sed habet multos Sparta similes. So were then living in Connecticut a number of very good preachers!!!

a very infirm constitution. He was graduated, 1692, and commenced preaching, but did not incline to settle in the ministry till he gained wisdom by age and experience. When he arrived at the age of 21, he had a strong inclination to visit the land of his fathers, and his friends supposed that he would fix his abode in England. He suffered during the passage, the voyage being perilous, and the vessel being attacked by an enemy, a French privateer, which captured them after a severe engagement. Mr. Colman was on the vessel's deck during the fight, and received unkind usage from the enemy on account of being a protestant priest. When he was in France, it was a satisfaction to the grinning multitude to insult a man, who was an heretick, and preached against the pope of Rome. But in every place there are humane people, who look with pity upon people in distress ; and among christian nations those who visit the prisoner. They resist the spirit of bigotry, and oppose the demon of persecution, whether clothed in the garb of the saint, or raging with the sword of violence. From having a *wisp of straw* to lie upon, in the gloomy vaults of a prison, Mr. C. received kindness from persons he never knew, and who only considered that he was a stranger. When there was an exchange of prisoners, he went to London, where he had many friends. He preached to great acceptance in that city, became acquainted with Dr. Bates, Dr. Calamy and Mr. Howe, the most famous ministers among the dissenters, and received many marks of their esteem.* He was introduced by them to several

* Dr. Colman was present with the London ministers when they presented their address of condolence to king William upon the death of the queen. Dr. Bates presented it. The composition is beautiful, but when delivered, it had a surprising effect. The courtiers said they never saw the king so moved, and confessed that they never knew the power of eloquence equal to it upon themselves. Dr. Colman in his manner of speaking and writing endeavoured to imitate Bates's excellencies. The same observation was made of the late Dr. Samuel Cooper concerning his method of sermonizing.

churches, and having been so highly recommended, they earnestly requested his continuance. His inclination might have led him to stay in Great Britain, had he not received a more pressing solicitation to return to Boston, and take the pastoral charge of a new church, which some of the principal inhabitants of the town had then erected. The London ministers, with whom he had associated, ordained him, the latter part of the year 1699. He arrived in Boston the next season, where he met with a most cordial reception from the people of his society. There were, however, many hurt by the proceedings of the society in Brattle street. The church was built in opposition to the Cambridge platform. Ministers, venerable for their age and wisdom, such as Mr. Higginson and Mr. Hubbard, bore their testimony to the order of the churches, and one of them in a letter to Dr. Mather, calls it a " presbyterian brat ;" nor would any of the churches hold communion with Mr. Colman for some years. But he continued the faithful, and beloved pastor of this flock, until the summer of 1747, and then died at the age of 73. As a preacher, he obtained great celebrity for his elocution. He had a lively animation without much fiery zeal. He allured men, instead of driving them into right paths. His manners were soft and obliging ; so ready was he to overlook frailties and praise excellencies in others, that he was called a flatterer ; but this was owing to his civility and good breeding. Polite men are not always guilty of simulation, nor duplicity.

Dr. Colman received a diploma of doctor in divinity from the university of Glasgow, 1731. He was elected president of Harvard College, 1724. He was fellow of the corporation during the time, that president Leverett, and his successor, were in the chair. He was at the head of the clergy after the death of Dr. Cotton Mather. One of the best discourses he ever published was, an eulogy upon that great scholar. They had been long at variance, but their friendship was renewed several years before Dr. Mather died, and then they wondered how they could so long disagree.

Dr. Colman had an extensive correspondence, which he made subservient to useful and benevolent purposes. He obtained many donations, for the indian missions, from affluent gentlemen in London. Through him the Hollis family laid their liberal foundations for two professorships at Harvard College. What president Holyoke said of him, in an oration pronounced the commencement after his death, was considered as correct sentiment rather than panegyrick. " Vita ejus utilissima in rebus charitatis, humanitatis, benignitatis, et beneficentiæ. nunquam non occupata est."

Mr. Turell, son in law to Dr. Colman, wrote " memoirs of his life and writings," in an octavo volume. His publications are numerous. They are upon theological subjects, except one in favour of " inoculation for the small pox," in 1721. He printed a volume of excellent sermons, upon " the parable of the ten virgins,"

Cooke Elisha, physician in the town of Boston, was a great politician at the time the charter rights of Massachusetts were disputed ; and agent of the province, when the charter of William and Mary was obtained. He was a popular leader in the general court more than 40 years. In 1681 he was one of the representatives, who were zealous for colonial freedom, and " opposed sending over agents, or submitting to acts of trade," &c. In 1684 he was chosen one of the assistants. When Dr. Mather was sent over as agent, and with Mr. Oakes signed the petition for a new charter, Mr. Cooke refused ; saying, " the old charter or none." He was the opposer of all the governours, but the pointed enemy of Dudley, and never missed the opportunity of speaking against his measures, or declaring his disapprobation of the man. On the other hand, Dudley negatived him as often as he was chosen into the council, till the year 1175, when he approved of his election; the same year, one was deprived of the government, and the other died. Mr. Cooke was this year 78 years old. *Hutchinson.*

COOKE ELISHA, son of the former agent, early bent his mind to politicks, which enabled him to lead the debates in the house of representatives. Before the arrival of gov. Shute he was not distinguished as the head of a party. He was a popular man in the town of Boston, had been one of their representatives to the general court, and was chosen a counsellor; he had the clerkship of the supreme court, which Shute took from him; and from that time he was his open enemy. He commenced a most violent attack upon his administration, and the next year was set aside from the council. There had always been two parties in the general court. Those who were old chartermen; and the governour's friends. The former had all the democratick spirit of ancient times, and were called the patriots of that day. They rested the ground of their opposition against the governour on his application for a fixed salary. Upon this Shute insisted, according to his instructions. And here Mr. Cooke directed his *lethalis arundo*, till he wounded the side of the chief magistrate, and made him quit his place. He went to England to make his complaints against the province; but would never return, though he was offered the government again, and justified in all his proceedings. Mr. Cooke was sent to the court of Great Britain as agent for the people of Massachusetts, but failed in his application, and obtained little of that respect and honour which he had in his own country. He returned to Boston, 1726. At the next election he was appointed counsellor. He was on the side of the controversy, which opposed gov. Burnet, but not so violent as in former days, when his political resentment was stimulated by personal feelings. He was the warm friend of Belcher, who went over to the popular party before Burnet died. And when he was in the chair, appointed his friend a judge of the common pleas. He died in the year 1737. Mr. Hutchinson, though the great friend to Dudley, Burnet, and other governours on the side of prerogative, uniformly gives praise to the Cookes. He says, they were both fair, honest men, open in their conduct, and acted from a love to their country. It is some credit to him as an historian, that he should delineate so fairly the characters of men who certainly were the most zealous republicans, who ever acted their parts in Massachusetts bay.

COOPER WILLIAM, pastor of the church in Brattle street, Boston, was one of the most fervent preachers of the age. In the character given of him, by a brother minister, he was " an interpreter, one among a thousand." He was graduated at Harvard College, 1712. In the year 1715, began to preach, and was invited to settle as colleague pastor with Dr. Colman. At his request, his ordination was deferred a year. But on May 23, 1716, he was separated to the work of the ministry ; and continued to preach to this society with increasing vigour, zeal and activity, till his death, Nov. 13, 1743. He was then in the 50th year of his age. It is said, that he had an uncommon talent at explaining and enforcing the sublimest truths of the gospel, and making them familiar to the meanest capacity. When Dr. Colman preached, the people went away highly gratified, talked of the excellencies of the discourse, and of his charming delivery. But when his colleague had performed the pulpit exercises, he had such a way of addressing the heart, and giving a solemnity to their spirits, that each man had a look of concern, and went home silent as the grave. Death, judgment, and eternity, were the subjects of his preaching.

His character as a learned man was very respectable. In the year 1737, he was chosen president of Harvard College, which honourable trust he declined accepting, in a letter addressed to the over-seers.* *Colman's funeral sermon.*

COOPER SAMUEL, D. D. one of the most cele-brated divines and politicians of New England, was the son of the rev. William Cooper ; and his suc-cessor at Brattle street church.

When he was young he discovered genius and taste, and was a fine classical scholar before he en-tered college. At the seat of the muses he com-posed in poetry and prose in a style beyond his years. He had charming oratorical powers, which he displayed on several occasions before the publick. As his memory was very tenacious he could at any time repeat the orations he then delivered ; the style was rather Virgilian than an imitation of the Roman orator. Horace and Virgil were his favour-ite authors of the ancient classicks ; Addison and Atterbury of latter days. When his father died he was deeply affected; he lost his companion and friend at the time he most needed advice and di-rection. He was graduated at Harvard College, 1743, the year this melancholy event took place. The eyes of the people were fixed on him to take the pastoral care of the church in Brattle street. Dr. Colman was so earnest to have him for a col-

* Works.—Four sermons upon predestination, which were reprinted in London, 1765. Another edition has been lately emitted from the press of E. Lincoln, Boston.

In 1723, Dr Colman and Mr. C, printed two sermons to young people ; in 1736, Mr. C printed a sermon at the ordination of the rev. Robert Breck, which gave rise to a large controversy between him and certain ministers in the county of Hampshire. They printed a " narrative of the proceedings of the council ;" an " an-swer to the Hampshire narrative" was printed in Boston. They published " a reply to this answer," impute it to Mr. Cooper, and make severe remarks upon his conduct. Mr. Cooper engaged in another controversy with Mr. Ashley afterwards on account of a sermon he preached upon charity. The newspapers were fill-ed with this dispute for some months, besides the numerous pam-phlets it occasioned. The other publications of Mr C are a sermon upon the death of gov. Tailor, one upon the death of rev. Peter Thacher, 1739, and two sermons upon the revival of reli-gion, 1741.

R

league, that he urged him to preach at this tender age, and before he had read those books of theology which are thought necessary for preparatory studies.   He gave up his own inclinations to the pressing solicitations of his friends, but requested the same indulgence they had granted to his father, that his ordination might be deferred for some time. This request was complied with.   He preached occasionally, but was not ordained till May 25, 1746. His venerable colleague delivered a discourse upon this occasion, and performed one part of the day, till he was called to receive the reward of his labours. He then dropped his mantle for the benefit of the younger prophet.   Mr. Cooper had from this time the care of a church which was very large, and had been wisely instructed by great and learned divines, who had "the gift and art of preaching;" but he did not frustrate the expectations of the people.   He appeared like the rising light, shining more and more unto his meridian splendor.   The same beauties of style, engaging delivery, and devotional spirit, which they admired in their aged pastor, drew their attention, and allured their affection to Mr. Cooper.   His diction was more chaste and correct, and his gift in prayer peculiar, and very excellent. With a great flow of language, he had an admirable facility of mingling scriptural phrases in their proper places.

His religious sentiments were liberal, and he was a friend to free inquiry.   In discoursing upon religious topics in conversation he discovered the same elegance and propriety of speech which distinguished his pulpit exercises.   He had fine colloquial talents and would have made a great figure in speaking *extempore* had he used himself to it in a publick assembly.   His erudition was rather extensive than deep, but his ready mind, fine brilliant imagination, and quickness of recollection enabled him to shine in company where greater scholars, and much more profound theologians, listened to hear him, to whom, however, he would give up an opinion, when they thought it not correct. If in any thing he was obstinate in his own sentiments it was upon the politicks of the day. His eulogist handsomely describes this part of his character so that no one can object to his becoming a politician. " He well knew that tyranny opposes itself to religious as well as civil liberty ; and being among the first who perceived the injustice and ruinous tendency of the British court, which at length obliged the Americans to defend their rights with the sword, this reverend patriot was among the first who took an early and decided part in the politicks of his country."

He was, however, a political writer earlier in life than any threatening of British thraldom. In the year 1754, he wrote the *Crisis*, a pamphlet against the *excise act*, which our general court contemplated. He certainly was at all times a leading character among the American whigs. And from the time of the stamp act to the revolutionary war, some of the best political pieces in the Boston Gazette were the effusions of his pen. The letters from gov. Hutchinson to Whately which were printed in Boston were sent to Dr. Cooper; whether by Dr. Franklin or Mr. Temple is not ascertained. They were put into his hands to read, to communicate to certain friends, but under a strict injunction not to have them published. They were published by a gentleman to whom they were communicated upon his promise of returning them " uncopied." The Doctor was not to blame, and was much grieved at the consequences of the publication, which were a duel between Mr. Whately and Mr. Temple, and loss of the office of postmaster-general to Dr. Franklin. Mr. Temple was never satisfied with the apology of Dr. Cooper for what he thought a breach of confidence.

In the spring of 1775, Dr. Cooper, with other patriots, was lampooned by the British officers in an oration pronounced in State street. He afterwards met with insults, and it was happy for him that he left the town before Lexington battle, as he was very obnoxious to the authority then in Boston. He was a warm friend to the independence of his country, 1776 ; and joined heartily in promoting the alliance with France. "The great friendship subsisting between him, Dr. Franklin and Mr. Adams was one means of his being known in France ; and the gentlemen coming from that kingdom were generally recommended to him by those ambassadors. When the fleets of his most Christian Majesty adorned our harbours, he was always the confidential friend of the gentlemen who commanded ; and many officers and subjects of that august monarch were received by him with great cordiality that was pleasing, and highly endeared him to them."* It is true that he was much devoted to the French government, more so, than was agreeable to his pious friends, and several, who had been his political friends, blamed him for his sanguine views of their friendship. Franklin, though a great philosopher, was not so great a statesman as the other gentlemen who made the peace in 1783. They saw through the policy of the French court, and prevented the interests of the New England states from being sacrificed.

Dr. Cooper was a member of several societies, for pious and literary purposes ; he promoted them with all his influence. For a number of years he was fellow of Harvard College. In the year 1774, he was chosen president. He was the first vice president of the American academy of arts and sciences, instituted by the general court of Massachusetts, 1780. His diploma of doctor in divinity was presented by the university of Edinburgh.

He enjoyed his vigour of mind, his activity, and his cheerfulness till he was seized with his last ill-

---

* Character written by James Sullivan, esq.

ness ; this was an apoplectick turn, which continued only a few days. He expired, Dec. 23, 1783.* Dr. Clarke preached a sermon at his funeral.

COTTON JOHN, was born at Derby, A. D. 1684. His parents were persons of considerable quality and good reputation. Their condition, as to the good things of this life, competent. They were wise enough to employ their means to good purposes ; and educated their son so as to make him eminent and useful. Their solicitude for this tender plant was well rewarded when they saw him, like a tree of life, feeding thousands with the doctrines of christianity ; and to them also the fruit of his lips was sweet.

After leaving the grammar-school at Derby, he was admitted to Trinity College, Cambridge. His industry was great, and his proficiency uncommon. From Trinity he was admitted to Emanuel, where he was soon made a *Fellow*. When he was elected, he was strictly examined. The portion of scripture, chosen to prove his knowledge of the Hebrew tongue, contains more hard words than any other in the Bible, Isaiah iii. Wherein the prophet declaims against the haughtiness of the daughter of Zion. But so good an Hebrewician could not be at a stand ; it rather gave him an opportunity to show his ability and attention to that language. Being thus advanced, he was in a place for improvement ; he was surrounded with characters, who were proper objects of emulation ; the glow of genius appeared in his manner of giving and receiving instruction, and all his powers and faculties were quickened to attempt a resemblance of those who had the

* His publications, besides those abovementioned, are, artillery election sermon, 1751 ; sermon before the society for encouraging industry, 1753 ; election sermon, 1756 ; sermon at the ordination of Joseph Jackson, 1760 ; thanksgiving sermon on the conquest of Quebec, 1759 ; sermon on the death of George II. 1761 ; at the Dudleian lecture, 1774 ; a sermon before the general court, October, 1780, being the day of the commencement of the constitution and inauguration of the new government.

highest reputations for erudition. He soon rendered himself famous by his funeral oration for Dr.
Some, Master of Peter-House, Cambridge. In this,
he discovered a purity of style with the ornaments
of rhetorick. The fame of his learning increased
from his next publick performance, which was a
University sermon, and he was often invited to
preach in the same place. When he had been at
Boston, in Lincolnshire, some months, he proceeded
bachelor of divinity, and preached a *Concio ad Cle-
rum*, in Latin, which was greatly admired. His
text was Mat. v. 13. He appeared also to great advantage in answering a very acute opponent, Mr.
William Chappel, who disputed with him.

For several years he preached to his people without any opposition, but when he urged his dislike
of the ceremonies, he was brought before the court
of the bishop of Lincoln for his non-conformity ;
from which he was advised to appeal to a higher
court, and employing Mr. Leverett (who was afterwards one of the ruling elders in the church of
Boston, New-England) he was, through his means,
restored to his church, who had much occasion to
rejoice in his labours. He was so much in favour
with Dr. Williams, the bishop of Lincoln, that
when he was *Lord Keeper* of the great seal, he went
to King James, and begged that a man of so much
worth and learning might have liberty of preaching
without interruption, though he was a non-conformist.

The earl of Dorchester, also, being at old Boston, was much affected when he heard him deliver
a discourse upon civil government, and stood his
friend in times of great opposition. These are the
times to try and prove friendship. From men of
urbanity and good nature the civilities of social life
are readily granted ; but how few among the rich
men of the city, and nobles of a kingdom, think of
virtue in distress ! There were some, however, a-
mong the gentlemen and noblemen in England,

who exerted themselves to serve worthy Puritan ministers, and kept them from prison and from penury, while bigots ruled the nation, and the vilest aspersions were cast upon all those who were suspected of non-conformity.

Mr. Cotton was not able to stem the tide of party. He was ordered before the high commission court, who were disposed to pour out the bitterness of their wrath upon his head ; but they were disappointed of their aim, and, through the influence of those who were well disposed, he escaped and came to New-England. It was observed, that he did not fly from the profession of the truth, but unto a more opportune place for the profession of it.

When Mr. Cotton came over to this country, they were busy in settling the affairs of the churches and commonwealth. In both of which he took an active part. Being requested to preach before the general court, his text was Haggai ii. 4. " Yet now be strong, O Zerubbabel, saith the Lord ; and be strong, O Joshua, son of Josedech the high priest ; and be strong, all ye people of the land, saith the Lord, and work ; for I am with you, saith the Lord of hosts."

It was a usual thing for the magistrates to consult with the ministers, and Mr. Cotton was appointed, with gov. Winthrop, to draw an *abstract* of the *judicial* laws of the Mosaick system, so far as they are *moral.* It was his advice to establish a *Theocracy.*

Mr. Cotton began the sabbath on Saturday evening. He gave religious instructions, read the scriptures, and then retired into his study. He spent the sabbath day either in his study or in the pulpit. He was a very accomplished preacher; his voice had melody in it, and was sonorous; his sermons pathetick, and his critical acumen uncommon. This was discovered in his frequent expositions, and dissertations upon passages and whole books of the scripture. He was considered as a great polemick divine ; yet upon two occasions, when his talents were exerted this way, he was under no small disadvantage. In his controversy with Roger Williams, he had an opponent who not only possessed talents which would have made him great in any school, but had bent the force of his strong mind to the very subject which then employed their attention. In England, Mr. Cotton had written in favour of toleration, and against the power of the magistrate in matters of religion. Here he had to oppose the sentiment he had formerly defended, and to write against the principles which the dissenting ministers in England then thought evangelical, and have, ever since, supported; and which are necessary to vindicate their separation.

He was accused of holding a bloody tenet by Williams, and the title of his answer was, *The Bloody Tenet washed in the Blood of the Lamb.*

In the general commotion of the country concerning the Antinomian sentiments, our celebrated divine lost much of the dignity of his character, and his influence in the churches. He did not go to the extreme which would please his friends; some of them compared him to a *light* in a dark lantern. The other side were bitter in their animadversions upon his conduct. At the synod, in 1637, he had to oppose the whole body of ministers, and some of them were disposed to vex him. Once he became so unhappy as to threaten to leave the plantation. The latter part of his ministry was less irksome. He enjoyed some years of rest after being tossed on the troubled sea. His labours were edifying to the people; his abilities and character were equally respected by the magistrates and his clerical brethren, who all lamented his death when he was sixty-eight years old, and mourned for the loss which the country as well as his people had sustained. He died Dec. 23, 1652. His disorder was of a pulmonary nature, owing to his passing a ferry and getting wet, and then preaching in a neighbouring church. He was seized while he was delivering the sermon, and was never afterwards free from the complaint; yet he continued to labour, and a few weeks before his death he took for his subject the four last verses in 2d epistle to Timothy; giving as a reason why he chose several verses, that he should not live to finish them if he were more particular. He dwelt chiefly upon these words, *Grace be with you all.* When he could preach no longer, he was visited by his pious friends, to whom he administered consolation and good instruction. He died in peace, and the last words he uttered were pious and benevolent wishes to a friend who was endeavouring to soften the pillow of death; and which caused others to say of him, that *he was a good man, and full of the Holy Ghost.*

Mr. Cotton married twice, and left a number of children. His descendants have spread over the country, and though no one has appeared equal to him in a rich variety of learning and popular talents, yet several of them have been eminent as preachers, and among the civilians of our country. He published many works; some in Latin. These were printed in London, and they have since been reprinted in New-England. Among them we find *milk for babes,* and *meat for strong men,* according to their power of digesting the *spiritual* food.

Some difference has appeared in the opinions expressed of this celebrated man. It has been suggested, that his character was blazoned beyond its merit; for his biographers were Mr. Norton, his friend, who succeeded him as teacher of the *old church,* and Cotton Mather, his grandson. But his character was high before he came to this country. We have taken our account from books which were not published by any near relation, nor by men who were much prejudiced in his favour. His learning was allowed by all his contemporaries; his piety and zeal none could doubt, for he sacrificed his ease, his interest, and his country, to enjoy the ordinances of religion. His candid spirit was not al-

T

ways in exercise. In the phrenzy of his imagination he blamed worthy men, and censured those who had great claim to his respect and affection; yet governour Winthrop, one opposite in sentiment upon politicks and religion, says of him, that he delivered himself in a gentle manner upon a subject which interested his feelings, and though he censures his opinions, speaks with respect of the man. Others, as strong in their own sentiments, allow him candour and forbearance.

In those instances where he discovered intolerance and the spirit of bigotry, a zeal for ecclesiastical power, he only manifested the inconsistency of human nature. It is a true observation, that when men begin to taste of christian liberty themselves, they forget that other men have an equal title to enjoy it.

Such flagrant instances of inconsistency are so evident among christians, of all denominations, that it cannot be imputed as a reproach peculiar to any sect. Instead of disturbing the ashes of our ancestors, by repeating that the " very men who had fled from persecution became persecutors," we had better imitate their virtues, throw a mantle over their failings, let instruction spring from their graves, and hope to meet them in that better world where just men are made perfect.

CRADOCK MATTHEW, one of the principal undertakers of the New-England settlements, was an opulent merchant in London; they first chose him their governour, May 23, 1628; but afterwards they determined to choose into office only those, who went to America, with the patent. Therefore he resigned the place to Mr. Winthrop. " He was more forward in advancing out of his substance than any other, being the highest in all subscriptions. He continued, divers years, to carry on a trade in the colony, by his servants, but never visited the plantation." *Hutchinson.*

CRANFIELD EDWARD, governour of New Hampshire, was an English gentleman and received his commission, 1682. He exchanged a profitable office at home to better his fortune in New-England. As soon as he came over, he exercised his power in an arbitrary manner, and acted the same part in that province which sir Edmund Andross did in Massachusetts.

He came to Boston the year after his appointment, and pretended a regard to the colony, but led them into measures which hurried the *second warrant* against their charter. He represented to the court of Massachusetts, that 2000 guineas to be given to lord Hyde, " for his majesty's private service," would be of great advantage to the province, and afterwards made sport of their credulity, and his own artifice and deception. In a letter which Dudley wrote to gov. Bradstreet, he tells him, " Truly, sir, we are ridiculed, by our best friends, for the shame Cranfield put upon you. His majesty told my friend, that he represented us as disloyal rogues."

In New Hampshire, Cranfield assumed so much power, that the publick grievances became insupportable. They chose an agent to make their complaints at the court of Great Britain. In the mean while the governour was at a loss how to raise money for himself and the neeessary publick expences. He called an assembly in 1682, and the same year dissolved them. He then ventured upon a project of taxing the people without their consent. But he found " all his efforts ineffectual, and his authority contemptible." The complaint was taken up by the lords of trade, and decided against him. He lost the government after enjoying a kind of honour a few years without the profits he had calculated upon ; and was glad afterwards to be appointed collector of Barbadoes. *Belknap. Hutchinson.*

CUSHING THOMAS, speaker of the house of representatives, 1746, was the son of the hon. Tho-

mas Cushing, one of his majesty's council.   The
father was among the New England worthies, and
the son as much celebrated for his goodness as his
superior abilities.   Mr. Prince speaks of him, as a
man of excellent acquired gifts and natural understanding, well acquainted with affairs of the world,
with men and things, with our civil and ecclesiastical
constitution, with human nature and divinity.   "My
acquaintance," says he, "began with the *table* conversation.   I found, with surprise and pleasure, that
in a small, feeble, relaxed body, there dwelt a great,
a lively, a strong and well composed soul.   Our en-
tertainments were an agreeable variety of divinity,
history, civil and religious matters, or natural philosophy ;   or observations on present occurrences
and transactions, either in town or land, or other
parts of the world ; as various subjects happened to
occur, with a candid freedom ; his genius inclining
him either to unbiassed reasoning, or agreeable observations."

This excellent man was born in Boston, 1693; was
graduated at Harvard College, 1714.   He acquired
considerable property, beside what he received from
his father, to whose business he succeeded.   He very
soon distinguished himself, as one of the best speakers
in the town meeting; and in 1729, was one of their
committee to draw up the instructions for their representatives.   In 1731, he was chosen representative for the town, and continued in this office as
long as he lived.   During Belcher's administration,
when the town saw fit to change three of their representatives, he was the one who claimed their respect, and all the votes were in his favour   He once
was elected treasurer of the province, which trust
he could not accept on account of the multiplicity of
his other business. In 1739 he was appointed agent of
the province to the court of Great Britain, but his infirm state of health prevented him from taking the
voyage.   He was speaker of the house of representatives, A. D. 1742, and was chosen annually till he

died, 1746, in the 53d year of his age. The loss was felt by the publick, as he was in the midst of his usefulness. Mr. Cushing married a daughter of the hon. Edward Bromfield, and left two daughters and one son,*

CUSHING THOMAS, lieut. governour of Massachusetts, was the son of Mr. speaker Cushing, and rose to higher offices in the state than his father or grandfather, each of whom had been distinguished with peculiar honours. He had good talents, and was a very useful man in many departments, though he had not their splendid abilities. He was graduated at Harvard College, 1744; engaged in mercantile business, but his mind was turned much to political affairs. The father enjoyed the affluence of wealth with all the honours his country could bestow upon him : the son was fonder of publick life, and paid too little attention to pecuniary considerations. He was sent representatative from his native town for a number of years, and, A. D. 1763, when the governour negatived Mr. Otis, who had been chosen speaker, he was elected in his place ; and he continued to fill the chair, till he was chosen one of the members of the congress which met at Philadelphia, 1774. He was then commissary general, but the province was in such a state, that there was no great call for a person in this office, nor did any material profit attend it. In 1779 Mr. Cushing declined going to Congress ; and the government of Massa-

---

* Mr. Bromfield, the father of Mrs. Cushing, according to Mr. Prince, was one of the distinguished worthies of New England, whose names will appear in characters of honour in the annals of our church and state. His son, E. Bromfield, esq. who died, 1756, was one of the Boston representatives, 1739. He was on the popular side when the prejudices of the town were so strong against gov. Belcher. In the house he acted in concert with Cushing, Allen, &c. " the firm, uncorrupted patriot, careful to assert the just prerogative of the crown, and to defend the invaluable liberties of the people." He was for many years selectman and overseer of the poor, which offices he discharged. He was a gentleman in high esteem while he lived, and his death was greatly lamented.

chusetts being then organized, he was elected to the second office in the state. He was lieut. governour from the time he was chosen till his death, 1788.

There was a time when Mr. C. was considered in Great Britain as the leader of the whigs in this country. He was not esteemed so in Boston. He had less political zeal than Otis, or Adams, or Hancock ; but by his pleasant temper, his moderation, his conversing with men of different parties, though he sometimes was lashed by their strokes for want of firmness, he obtained more influence than either, except Mr. Hancock. The reason of his being known so much in the mother country was, that his name was signed to all the publick papers, as speaker of the house. Hence he was sometimes exposed to the sarcasms of the ministerial writers. In the pamphlet of Dr. Johnson, called, " Taxation no Tyranny," one object of the Americans is said to be, to adorn the brows of Mr. C——g with a diadem." He had a rank among the patriots, as a sincere friend to the publick good, and he was also a friend to religion, which he manifested by a constant attendance upon all pious institutions. He was also very attentive to the affairs of the college, an example to others of the overseers, being often chairman of committees, and always present at the board ; he was also fellow of the corporation from the year 1785, in which Mr. Bowdoin resigned. He received a diploma of doctor of laws from the university.

Mr. Cushing left a number of children ; one of his daughters married John Avery, esq. who for many years was secretary of the commonwealth. *

* Mr. Avery was graduated at Harvard College. 1759 ; succeeded Samuel Adams as secretary. 1780, and died, June, 1806. He was secretary of the Massachusetts Humane Society He was buried on the day of their semi annual meeting. Their orator, in the midst of his discourse, alludes to the funeral knell which then called them to pay their respects to their worthy officer, an "early, active and important member of the society."

CUSHMAN ROBERT, one of the original planters of New England, was a member of Mr. Robinson's church at Leyden. He was chosen agent, with Mr. Carver, to treat with the Virginia company, when our fathers had fixed their purpose to make a settlement in North America. The object of their mission was to obtain certain privileges, if they lived in the British dominions, especially the rights of conscience. They met with great discouragements, and did not succeed. The next year he was sent upon the same business with Mr. Bradford A letter from Mr. Cushman, May 8, 1619, represents the affairs of the Virginia company as being in great confusion. It was on account of introducing Edward Sandy in the place of secretary, in the room of sir Thomas Smith, of whom there is a minute account in Smith's history of Virginia. In autumn of this same year the Leyden agents procured a patent, confirmed by the company's seal. When these religious adventurers set sail, Mr. Cushman was in the smaller vessel, which proved leaky and was condemned, but afterwards he sailed for New England in the ship Fortune and arrived at Plymouth, Nov. 10, 1621. He returned to England, and died in the year 1626. The news of his death reached the new settlement at the same time they heard of the loss of their venerable pastor, Mr. Robinson. Among the bitter ingredients mingled in their cup, they sorrowed most of all, that they should see *their* faces no more.*

* A sermon of Mr. Cushman which he preached to the Plymouth settlers upon *self-love*, was printed in England, 1622, and reprinted in Boston, 1724. Another edition of it was printed in Plymouth, 1785. Memoirs of Mr. Cushman are annexed, handsomely written by judge Davis, who was then an inhabitant of that town. This account makes one of the lives in the American Biography. The dedication of this sermon is curious. It is, To his loving friends the adventurers for New England, together with all well-willers and well-wishes thereunto, *grace,* peace, &c. He describes New England, " as an island, about the quantity of England, being cut out of the main land in America, as England is of Europe." A parliamentary speaker, in 1774, speaks of the island of New England.

CUTLER TIMOTHY, rector of Yale College and minister of Christ Church, Boston, was graduated at Harvard College, 1701; was ordained at Stratford, (Conn.) 1710, according to the order of the New England churches. He was appointed rector of the college in New Haven, 1719, which was, as has been said, an auspicious event to that institution, for he was a man of profound learning and presided with dignity, usefulness and general approbation. In 1723, he conformed to the church of England. Being joined by several of the tutors and neighbouring clergy, and himself the first scholar in the colony, it was a great shock to the congregational establishment. A church was built for him in Boston of which he was rector from 1723 to 1765, the year of his death. He did not publish any thing except a few single sermons. His powers were rather solid than brilliant, and he was too much of a scholar to allow any thing *superficial* to come from his hand. It was in this language he spake of most publications; those which were written by ministers of the episcopal church, and those whose sentiments and mode of worship might provoke sarcastick remarks. He was haughty and overbearing in his manners; and to a stranger, in the pulpit, appeared as a man fraught with pride. He never could win the rising generation, because he found it so difficult to be condescending : nor had he intimates of his own age and flock. But people of every denomination looked upon him with a kind of veneration, and his extensive learning excited esteem and respect where there was nothing to move, or hold the affections of the heart.

Dr. Stiles calls him the greatest oriental scholar after *Thomas Thacher*, the first minister of the Old South, and the great president Chauncy. No man in New England, he tells us, had such knowledge of the rector and those gentleman. All which may be true. We have sufficient documents to show that they understood Hebrew, and no one who recollects Dr. Cutler will doubt of his being " well skilled in logick, metaphysicks, moral philosophy, theology and ecclesiastical history."

His diploma of doctor in divinity, was presented to him when he was in England. His correspondence with other doctors or with bishops, was never carried on with so much zeal, spirit and perseverance as we find mentioned in the biographical sketches of his brethren ; nor do we read of any production of his, among the controversies between episcopalians and dissenters, during his long ministry. Yet they all looked up to him as a father, and he certainly was more eminent as a scholar than those who served their cause by their writings.

Mr. Hooper of Trinity church preached the funeral discourse and gave the character of this distinguished missionary of their church, with much justice and his usual eloquence.

DANFORTH THOMAS, deputy governour of Massachusetts Bay, was elected a magistrate in 1659. From this year he was assistant till 1679, when Mr. Bradstreet being put into the chair, he succeeded him as deputy. He had a great share of duty upon him, and with resolution and firmness conducted the publick affairs in the most difficult times. Mr. Hutchinson, speaking of three parties during sir Edmund Andross's administration and the times preceding, says, " the head of those on the side of royalty were Dudley, Stoughton, &c. Mr. Bradstreet, the governour, by the voice of the people, was the head of the moderate party. Danforth led the opposition, assisted by Cooke." Though he conducted with prudence, he would yield no privilege which the charter gave them. Hence he was obnoxious to Randolph, Andross, and to the ministry of Great Britain. For the same reason he was the idol of the populace in New England. He acted as president of the council when the people took the government from Andross, and had it not been for his influence, they would have gone to greater ex-

U

travagancics. The extracts of his letters which are preserved show that he had prudence and wisdom in conducting measures, though he was fierce in opposition to arbitrary mandates. When the officers of the old government were restored to their places, Mr. Bradstreet was again governour and Mr. Danforth the deputy.* They held their offices till the charter of William and Mary arrived. He was then deprived of his place, and his name was not suffered to remain as one of the counsellors, although the agents expressed a particular desire to have it. The people received the intelligence with surprise and grief; but it was easy for politicians to account for the omission, as he was against receiving any other charter than that which the fathers of Massachusetts held sacred. We hear nothing more of him in publick life. He passed his days in the town of Cambridge. His only son, Samuel, who died in England, was graduated 1771; was fellow of Harvard College, and a fine scholar. The name of Danforth in another line is preserved, and few names have exhibited more literary characters. *Mather. Hutchinson.*

DANFORTH SAMUEL, minister of Roxbury, came into New England, 1134, with his father, Nathaniel Danforth, was graduated at Harvard College, 1643, was chosen a fellow of the corporation, and instructed a class; he was very respectable for his knowledge of the sciences and theology. Being invited to

---

* The ancient magistrates and elders, although they strenuously advised to further waiting for orders from England, and discouraged any attempts of that nature, " as far as they had opportunity, yet were they now compelled to assist with their presence and councils for the preventing of bloodshed, which had been most certainly the issue, if prudent councils had not been given to both parties." *Danforth's letter to agent Mather.*

When Mr. Danforth was appointed deputy governour, he had likewise another commission, president of the province of Maine, to govern under the Massachusetts, the lords proprietories, and to be accountable to them; thither he repaired, 1779, appointed officers, held courts, &c. In that station also he opposed Andross's usurpation.

settle colleague pastor with Mr. Eliot at Roxbury, he was ordained, 1650. He died, 1674, in the midst of his life and usefulness. Dr. Mather says he wrote as a scholar, yet " was very affectionate in his manner of preaching, and seldom left the pulpit without tears." He married the daughter of Mr. Wilson, the first minister of Boston, and was blessed with twelve children, some of whom died before him. Two of his sons were distinguished among the divines of this state. One of Dorchester, and the other was settled at Taunton. One of his daughters married the hon. Mr. Bromfield, of Boston.*

* When Mr. D. died, old Mr. Eliot wrote verses and Mr. Weld likewise. It was then very common. The Dorchester burial ground is famous for the epitaphs on gravestones. many of which were written by Mr. D. the minister of that town. If we regard the spirit rather than the metre, we might be edified by reading them. But lest the rising generation should " play with the beard of their fathers," which the author of the Magnalia says is a wicked thing, it is best that most of them should be buried with the mouldering stone. A Latin epitaph upon the Roxbury divine may excite pleasure with remarks.

Non dubium, quin eó iverit, quo stellæ eunt
Danforthus, qui stellis semper se associavit.

This epitaph alludes to the studies of Mr. D. " Several of his *astronomical* composures have seen the light of the sun," says Dr. Mather. He published a particular account of the comet, 1664. He observed the motions of it, " from its first appearance in Corvus, whence it crossed the tropick of Capricorn, till it arrived at the maintop sail of the ship, and then it returned through Canis Major, and again crossed the tropick of Capricorn." &c. There is no theological publication of his, except we consider his election sermon as such, which is a recognition of *New England's* errand into the wilderness. It was delivered 1670.

The rev. Samuel Danforth, of Taunton, was born, 1666; graduated, 1683; died, 1727. He preached the election sermon, 1714.

The rev. John Danforth was born, 1664; graduated, 1677; ordained, at Dorchester, 1682; died 1730. " He understood mathematicks; had a taste for poetry and various learning." His printed works are, a sermon on parting with friends; a sermon on contentment; a sermon on Rom. i. 21, 1710; a funeral sermon on Mr. Bromfield; two sermons on the earthquake, 1727; a fast sermon, Exod. ix, 33, 34.

The hon. Samuel Danforth of Cambridge was the son of Mr. Danforth of Dorchester. He was president of his majesty's

DAVENPORT JOHN, minister of the first church in Boston, died suddenly of an apoplexy, March 15, 1670. He was a celebrated divine in England as well as this new region of the earth, where he lived from the year 1637 to the time of his removal to a better world.

Dr. Mather quotes a saying of the learned, concerning Salmasius, and applies it to him, *Vir nunquam satis laudatus, nec temere sine laude nominandus.*"

He was born, A. D. 1597, at a place called Coventry. His parents were respectable and gave him a good education. At the age of fourteen he was a student of Brazen Nose College, Oxford, where he received a degree of B. A. and though a youth, immediately began to preach. He preached constantly in the city of London in the time of the plague, and visited his flock as a faithful minister, which gained him great credit among those who knew how to estimate worth that was then as rare, as it was pure. For what can prayers signify, if a minister does not mingle offices of humanity with his pious walk ; this gives a perfume to the sacrifice. He afterwards received the degrees of A. M. and bachelor of divinity,

About the year 1626, there was a plan devised to make a purchase of impropriations, and with the profits of the same to maintain a number of ministers who would assist in reforming abuses. Mr. Davenport was in connexion with Dr. Sibs, Dr. Gouge, and several laymen, one of whom was lord mayor of London. But archbishop Laud took umbrage at it, as favouring nonconformity and obtained a bill to be exhibited in the *exchequer chamber,* when the court condemned the proceedings, and pronounced the gifts, feoffments and contrivances to be illegal ; and confiscated the money to the king's use.

council several years. In 1774. he was appointed one of the mandamus council. He died 1777, aged 81. He was said to be a great natural philosopher and chymist.

Soon after this Mr. D. became so much of a non-conformist, as to be an object of publick notice, and in consequence of it, he resigned his pastoral office in *Colman street*, and passed over into Holland. This was about the end of the year 1633.

He soon opened a controversy with the Dutch divines upon the subject of baptism, and tried to introduce the practice which he wrote so much in favour of afterwards, and which has been a controversy in New England ever since he came into the country, viz. " Whether the children of communicants only should be admitted to the ordinance ?"

He went back again to England, 1635. He was one of those by whom the patent of the Massachusetts colony was made out, though his name was not among the patentees. He did this before he went to Holland, and there hearing of the progress and prosperity of New England, he resolved to come over and make a settlement, which he did, being considered as one of the fathers of New Haven colony.

He arrived at Boston, 1637, with Mr. Hopkins, two London merchants, and several other worthies, who did not incline to settle within the jurisdiction of Massachusetts. They were offered any spot they might fix upon, and urged to unite with the people of this colony, but they were disposed to form a new plantation. Mr. Davenport was, however, invited to sit with the synod at Cambridge. And Dr. Mather tells us, his learning and wisdom did contribute more than a little to dispel the mist of errors which then overspread the country. While he was minister of New Haven, he was invited to join the Westminster Assembly with Mr. Cotton and Mr. Hooker, and he had an inclination to cross the Atlantick, but the other gentlemen did not suppose it would answer any special purpose, or thought less of the honour; nor were his church willing to part with him. It certainly was more proper for him to lead the few sheep in this American wilderness,

situation was unhappy for himself as well as the churches. It was too late in life to form new connexions; and to leave old friends, whose hearts had been tried by many scenes of adversity, was a wound to his own sensibility, especially as they were hurt by his conduct.

He died, March 15, 1770, of an apoplexy, aged 72 years.* *Magnalia.*

DENISON DANIEL, major general, was an inhabitant of the town of Ipswich. He was the author of a treatise called the *Irenicon*. " His parts and abilities were well known amongst those with whom he lived, and might justly place him among the first three, having indeed many natural advantages above others for the more easy attaining of skill in every science." Mr. Hubbard, from whom this quotation is made, says concerning the *Irenicon*, which was found among his papers " that it would be ingratitude to withhold it from the publick view." It might suit other times. 1st. It takes into consideration the publick maladies. 2d. The occasion of them. 3d. The danger. 4thly. The blameable causes. 5thly. The cure. He died Sept. 20, 1682.†

DIXWELL JOHN, of New Haven, was one of the Regicides, and after the restoration of Charles 2d,

---

* Works.—The saint's anchor hold, a book recommended by Mr. Caryl and Mr. Hook; demonstration of Jesus Christ to be the true Messiah; election sermon, 1669; a treatise of the power of Congregational churches; a discourse upon civil government, in a new plantation, whose end is religion. A volume of sermons upon the Canticles was transcribed for the press but never published.

† The funeral discourse by Mr. H. minister of Ipswich, is from Isaiah, 3 chap. 3 first verses. To which is annexed Irenicon, or a " salve for New England's sore, penned by the said major general, and left behind him as his farewell and last advice to his friends of the Massachusetts."
Mr. Denison pastor of the church in Ipswich died 1679. What relation he bore to the general I have never been able to know, nor when he came into this country. His name is not in the College catalogue and the church records are lost.

came over into America. He went to Hanaw in the first place, and was made a Burgess, but in 1664, he visited Whalley and Goffe at Hadley. He went the same year to New Haven and there he resided till his death.

Though he took the name of John Davids, yet he was known to many; but they were his friends, and would not betray him. It is supposed that Randolph had some suspicion of it, and communicated the thought to sir E. Andross. For that governour once stopped at New Haven on the Sabbath, and attended Mr. Pierpont's meeting. Dixwell was there in the morning, but did not appear in the afternoon. Sir Edmund asked who that venerable old man was? and was told he was a merchant of such a name; he replied, " that he knew he was not a merchant, and became very inquisitive about him."* Col. Dixwell was an officer, who received a commission from the parliament, and was too much of a republican to bow the knee to Cromwell. When he sat among the judges, it was rather by persuasion, than his own wish to condemn the monarch. He died in New Haven, March 18, 1688, in the 82d year of his age. His son took the name of John Dixwell, was one of the founders of the church in North-street, and chosen deacon, afterwards officiated as ruling member. He died 1721. His posterity are chiefly in the female line, but the name is not extinct.—*Ludlow. Stiles.*

* There is a story told which is somewhat characteristick, of New England. When sir Edmund attended worship, the deacon read a psalm which offended him very much, as he thought it pointed. The first verse is,

> Why dost thou tyrant, boast abroad,
> Thy wicked works to praise;
> Dost thou not know there is a God
> Whose mercies lead always?

They told sir Edmund, that it was a psalm in course, but Dr. Stiles thinks if they read psalms in course, it is likely the deacon selected this to touch the feelings of the governour. A question arises concerning the fact; whether they sung the psalms of Sternhold and Hopkins at that time in New-England? They did not in Msssachusetts or the Old Colony. The psalm is 52d of their version.

DOUGLASS WILLIAM, M. D. a native of Scotland, came into America when he was a young
man, fixed himself in the north part of Boston, and
was a writer upon politicks, historical occurrences,
and medicine. When Dr. Mather communicated
to him the success of Timonius in inoculating for
the small pox, he treated the account with contempt,
though recorded in the transactions of the Royal Society of London. When Dr. Boylston, in the year
1721, inoculated many of the inhabitants of Boston,
and met with the greatest success, he still raved a-
gainst Timonius and Mather, as well as this brother
physician. He was a man of great learning, but
wanted judgment and taste; whatever he published
was in a very slovenly style. He wrote many political essays, in the newspapers, which were generally filled with sarcastick remarks upon the magistrates, the clergy, the physicians, and the people of
New England. His "summary," or "historical
account of the British settlements," was published
in 1748, and 1753. This is a collection of things
which came into his head, whether they related to
his family, his private squabbles, or the affairs of
the publick. He would not take pains to arrange
his materials, or to inform himself of particular
facts. He was so opinionated that he never
would correct his mistakes. When Cape Breton
was taken, it frustrated many of his printed de-
clarations. He had ridiculed it, because it was a
measure of Shirley's administration, and called that
place the *Dunkirk*, which *such* forces would
never dare to assail. But though the plan succeeded,
it did not make any difference in his views. Instead of having his pride wounded, he, porcupine
like, wrapped himself in his own down, and darted
his quills at others. He said he was right in his
conjectures, but fortune would always wait upon
blunderers and quacks !
Douglass was a mathematician ; in 1743, 44, he
published an almanack, which was useful at the
W

time, and is now valuable for its list of chronological events ; and also the account of all the sovereigns of Europe and their families. It was called " Mercurius Novanglicanus," by William Nadir, S. X. Q. He also published a dissertation upon " the Cynanche Maligna," when that disorder prevailed in the town, in 1735, 36.*

DOWNING GEORGE, one of the first class of graduates, at Harvard College, was a preacher among the Independents in England, during the usurpation of Oliver Cromwell. He was chaplain to col. Okey's regiment, whom he afterwards betrayed to recommend himself to the court of Charles 2d.

He was ready to serve any master that would employ him, and to commit any act of treachery for the sake of a reward. The protector sent him as his agent into Holland, and gave him this recommendation, "George Downing is a person of eminent quality, and after a long trial of his fidelity, probity, and diligence in various negotiations, well approved and valued by us. Him we have thought fit to send to your lordships," &c.

He was sent likewise by Charles II. as his agent or ambassador to the states, and received the honour of knighthood from his majesty. Here he laid a scheme to seize several of the regicides, at the same time declaring he had no commission to do it, and that they were in perfect safety. Ludlow speaks of it as a thing more flagitious in the Dutch nation than in this renegado politician. For they were under no obligation to deliver them up, and had promised to protect them. About the year 1672 Downing met with some reverse of fortune. The king was displeased with him, and put him in pri-

* Dr. Douglass abuses Cotton Mather very frequently ; one thing in particular he tells makes him an object of ridicule. The Doctor had said, " that cats may have the small pox," or a disorder like it. Now says Douglass this is weak beyond description, because " the small pox is peculiar to mankind." Ought not some writer of the present day to give Cotton Mather due credit. How is it that cows have the small pox ?

son. It is said that he was confined in the same room where col. Okey had been kept before his execution, once his friend and benefactor, but whose death must bring to his conscience accusations of every crime a treacherous courtier could commit. He was again received into favour by Charles, and conducted himself with more prudence and moderation than he had done in former times. Ludlow, and others, who had expressed their surprise that George Downing should succeed such a man as sir William Temple, ambassador to the states, yet allow that he did some things well. And Hutchinson says, that he was a friend to New England, and did every thing in his power to serve this country, when many enemies were active in exciting the resentment of the king against it. He was brother in law of gov. Bradstreet, and held a correspondence with him, and other gentlemen in Massachusetts. He died in the year 1684.

DUDLEY THOMAS, one of the first settlers of Massachusetts, who came over in the Arabella, was the only son of capt. Roger Dudley. In 1597 he was at the siege of Amiens, under Henry IV, having a captain's commission from Queen Elizabeth. Mr. Hutchinson says, he became a sober nonconformist from hearing Dodd, Hildersham, and other puritan divines. He certainly was a zealous man in whatever he undertook as appears from Winthrop's journal; and upon some occasions he discovered very warm passions. That he was a very prudent man appears, however, from his good conduct in the management of the estate of the earl of Northampton, which was committed to his care. He sat under Mr. Cotton's ministry, before the planting of Massachusetts. When he came over in the Arabella, he was 54 years old, but his strength of body, and health of mind, fitted him for any hardships. The company in England chose Mr. Winthrop governour and Mr. Humphries deputy governour of the plantation. Mr. Humphries did not embark as was expected, and Mr. Dudley was chosen in his place. In 1634, he was chosen governour, and also several times afterwards. He was the second in authority seven or eight years, sometimes under Winthrop, and once under ndicot He was appointed major general in 1644 ; this was a new office in the plantation. He was continued in the magistracy from the time of his arrival to his death, which happened, July 31st, 1653, in the 77th year of his age.

He was upright and honest in his disposition, blunt in his manners, and withstood magistrates and ministers when he thought them worthy of reproof. Nor would he yield to any popular opinion to gain honour and authority. A serious dispute took place between him and governour Winthrop, which required the interposition of their friends among the clergy and laity. He was more firm in the *Hutchinsonian*, or Antimonian controversy, than any of the magistrates, and even accused Mr. Cotton of departing from the faith ; and without prejudice or attachment from prior connexions, required an explanation of his principles and conduct. Endicot also found him an opponent that was not to be moved when *he* dissented from the general opinion of the magistrates, or wished to introduce some novel things in their proceedings. Mr. Dudley was not a man of learning equal to Winthrop or Bellingham, but in this respect was not inferior to Endicot. Neither Endicot nor Dudley possessed what, in the present age, would be called liberality of sentiment, or urbanity of manners. Mr. D was such an enemy to toleration that he not only spoke against it, but left a number of lines which the friends of rational religion must wish he had never written, as they are not to the credit of his poetry or his charity, but being written, and handed down, are quoted to give a just view of the character of the man :

Let men of God, in courts and churches watch
O'er such as do a toleration hatch ;

Lest that ill egg bring forth a cockatrice
To poison all with heresy and vice.
If men be left, and otherwise combine,
My epitaph's, *I die no libertine.*

DUDLEY JOSEPH, son of T. Dudley the veteran magistrate of Massachusetts, was educated at Harvard College, and received the honours of that seminary, A. D. 1665.*

He was early made a magistrate, and supposed to be on the side of loyalists, who were willing to give up some charter privileges. It is evident that he loved the principles and practices of the New England planters, though to keep his place he often sacrificed those, and was subservient to men in power. Randolph in one letter speaks of him as a man "opposed to the faction." At other times, he calls him a "man of a base, servile, and antimonarchical principle." In 1686 several gentlemen of the council were appointed to take the administration of the government of Massachusetts; Mr. Dudley received a commission as president. The year before, he had been left out of the magistracy, having rendered himself unpopular by some acts which were thought pleasing to the enemies of New England. His short administration was not grievous to the people. They had expected Kirk to be appointed governour, and were disposed, from dread of his coming, to receive any other man with apparent cordiality. Mr. Dudley, says Hutchinson, considered himself as appointed to preserve the affairs of the colony from confusion until the governour arrived, and a rule of administration should be more fully established.

When sir Edmund Andross was appointed governour of the several colonies, Dudley was president of the council, also chief justice of the province. He was upon the circuit at Narraganset when Andross was made prisoner, and was seized at Provi-

* He is second in the class, Benjamin Eliot, son of the apostle Eliot, being first. As they placed the students according to their parentage, why was not the son of a governour the first?

dence as one of the governour's party. For some time he was confined to his house at Roxbury. He was more obnoxious than any other person, and was treated even with inhumanity during his imprison- ment, reviled by the very soldiers that guarded him, and deprived of the very necessaries of life. He had been so conversant with Andross and Randolph, that he was ranked with them as an enemy to the country, and the resentment was raised the higher because he was born in New England; that which they could bear from a stranger, they thought in- sufferable from an inhabitant of the country. By the order of king William, he embarked for Eng- land in February, 1689. He was the next year ap- pointed chief justice of New York ; but his proper- ty, his friends, and his heart were in Massachusetts. It was said, he made use of all his influence to in- jure gov. Phips, expecting to succeed him in the government if he could be provoked to leave it. For this purpose he went to England, paid court to his majesty's ministers, and was patronized by no- blemen of name and character. The agents oppos- ed the appointment, and obtained their wish, which was to have lord Bellamont sent over. Dudley was not popular enough at New York to have any de- sire to go there, nor were the emoluments of a place on the bench very alluring. He preferred to be lieut. governour of the isle of White, lord Cutts be- ing the governour, a nobleman who had inter- ested himself very much in his favour. When lord Bellamont died, in 1701, he again solicited for the government of Massachusetts. He was then mem- ber of parliament, and lieut. governour of the isle of White, a more splendid, as well as more easy con- dition, than any office in New England; but he had such " a passion for his native country, as would have done honour to the ancient Athenians"—sir Henry Ashurst opposed the appointment. The dis- senters in England, and even Cotton Mather, in New England, joined in promoting his interest and reputation. He came over in 1702, and was received with tokens of respect by men who had always been his political opponents, and some of them his personal enemies. He, however, maintained the side of the prerogative ; he had, therefore, in opposition to him most of the friends of the old charter, and some whose ideas did not glide with the popular stream, were filled with zeal against his administration. The first seven years were spent in debates with the house of representatives, or in private disputes with men who ceased not to accuse him of artifice and deception ; of arbitrary conduct ; of enmity even to those privileges which they had obtained by the new charter. Dr. Increase and Dr. Cotton Mather, wrote him severe letters of reproof, which he answered, copies of which are preserved.* He had many friends, however, who considered him as a great friend to the churches of New England, as well as an excellent governour, among them were president Leverett, Mr. Brattle, and Dr. Colman, who were fellows of the college, to which seminary gov. Dudley ever manifested a very warm attachment.

The last years of his administration were more tranquil, and when his interest and ambition were not thwarted by the opposite party, his polite and engaging deportment, his love for his country, his eminent abilities, and very extensive information, made him a prominent character among the very first men of that generation. He was succeeded by gov. Shute, 1716, and died, 1720, aged 73.

DUDLEY PAUL, F. R. S. chief justice of Massachusetts, was the son of gov. Joseph Dudley. He was born at Roxbury, 1673, graduated at Harvard College, 1690 ; and having read law some years in this country was sent to England to finish his studies at the Temple. In 1702, he came over to Massachusetts with a commission from the queen, as attorney general, which office he held till he was

* Vide Historical Collection, vol. iii.

appointed judge of the superiour court. When he was a young man he was zealous on the side of prerogative, and acted with those who endeavoured to abridge the privileges of the colony. Hence he was very unpopular on this side the water, and provoked the resentment of many who had looked with candour on his father's proceedings, as well as those who had always been in opposition to his measures. Some very severe charges are made against him by Dr. Increase Mather, whose friendship to the governour had been once of service to him. Mr. Dudley, however, grew in the esteem of the people. He conducted so well in the line of his profession, and in every station, that whatever might have been his sentiments when he was in England, he was regarded as one who loved his country, and was active in serving its interest and prosperity. He was chosen representative to the general court for his native town, and was promoted to a seat at the council board. He appeared to great advantage in each situation, but it was on the bench he shone with the greatest lustre. " Here he displayed his admirable talents, his quick apprehension, his uncommon strength of memory, and extensive knowledge ; and at the same time his great abhorrence of vice, together with that impartial justice which neither respected the rich, nor countenanced the poor man in his cause. Thus while with pure hands and an upright heart he administered justice in his circuit through the province, he gained the general esteem and veneration of the people. As his presence always commanded respect, so it might justly be said of him, that he scattered iniquity with his eyes, which struck with awe the most daring offenders. When he spoke, it was with such authority and peculiar energy of expression, as never failed to command attention, and deeply impress the minds of all who heard him ; and his sentiments of law and evidence in all cases before the court, had generally a determining weight with those who were

eharged with the trial of them."* He was first advanced to the supreme bench in 1718, and when
judge Lyndes died he was appointed chief justice.
Judge Dudley was one of the few Americans who
have been honoured by an election to the royal society of London. He wrote several ingenious pieces relative to the natural history of New England,
which were published in "their philosophical transactions, 1720, 1721." He was also a very learned theologian, and wrote a book upon " the merchandize of souls," being an exposition of certain
passages in the book of Revelations. In the latter
part of his life he became a puritan of the straitest
sect of the fathers of Massachusetts. By his *will*
he established a lecture at Harvard College, and
specified four subjects : First, " upon natural religion ;" second, " upon revealed religion ;" third,
" upon the corruptions of the church of Rome ;"
fourth, " upon the validity of Presbyterian ordination." He died the last week in January, 1751.

DUDLEY WILLIAM, Esq. was the youngest son
of gov. Joseph Dudley, and educated at Harvard
College. Having received the honours of that seminary in 1704, he applied himself to the study of
law, but did not incline to enter upon the business
of his profession. In a retired spot of the town of
Roxbury he built an elegant house, and cultivated
his farm. He soon became a candidate, however,
for publick honours. His father sent him to Canada to negotiate an exchange of prisoners. Among
those whom he brought away was the venerable Mr.
Williams of Deerfield, who had been captured with
his family, some of whom never returned. It was
said, young Dudley managed the business with no
small address, and by his manner of negotiating
kept the frontiers from being pillaged. This was
doubtless the policy of his father, but he gained
credit by the execution. Charlevoix speaks of the

* Character by judge Sewal, who succeeded him as chief justice.

X

whole negotiation as a piece of political intrigue. He says the Massachusetts government had no no design of coming to a treaty. Mr. Dudley was afterwards appointed justice of the common pleas and col. of the first regiment in Suffolk. He was also a representative for Roxbury in the general court. He always had great influence in a publick assembly, being an admirable speaker, and possessing strong intellectual powers as well as a brilliant fancy. The opposition to his father's administration felt the weight of his talents. He could render himself very popular, and was for several years speaker of the house of representatives. In 1729 he was chosen one of his majesty's council, and was very serviceable to the community. Douglass says that he was more acquainted with provincial affairs than any other man, especially that he understood landed property better.

Col. Dudley distinguished himself as a military character. He was an active officer in the expedition which was so successful against Port Royal, and deserved the promotion which he received in succeeding years. But he was called off the stage in the midst of his usefulness, and with all his honours thick upon him. He died, August 10, 1743, before his elder brother. His children possessed the fine estate which had always belonged to the family. Judge Dudley leaving no children, it came into possession of col. William's eldest son, being thus entailed to the first male heir. He had two sons, Thomas and William; their mother was the amiable daughter of Addington Davenport, judge of the superiour court, and one of his majesty's council. Thomas was graduated at Cambridge, 1750, and William the year succeeding. The younger, having no prospect of wealth, was educated for the bar. He brought the property into some dispute, and procured a certain part of the inheritance.

These brothers acted differently from what might be expected from their education, and the examples they had to stimulate them. They were very unlike their ancestors. Instead of preserving the honour and dignity of a family which had been illustrious for more than a hundred years, they seemed to prefer the manners of ordinary life, and very soon were mingled with the people who make up the common mass of human society. *Hutchinson. Private information.*

DUMMER RICHARD, one of the fathers of Massachusetts, came into the country, 1635, and was chosen a magistrate. He warmly espoused the cause of sir Henry Vane, and when that gentleman was left out of the government he was no longer chosen assistant. He left the town of Boston, and retired to his own estate in Newbury, where he lived many years highly respected. No man deserved more the praise of doing well. He was very rich, and equally benevolent. When gov. Winthrop lost such immense property by the fraudulent conduct of his bailiff, Mr. Dummer gave 100 pounds towards making up his loss. He contributed greatly to the improvement and growth of that part of Newbury where he dwelt. The lands upon which the academy is built, and were left for the support of this literary institution, were formerly his plantation. He left children, some of whom passed their lives on the estate he possessed. One son came to Boston, was a worthy magistrate of the county of Suffolk, and the father of the famous Jeremy Dummer, the province agent at the court of Great Britain. *Hutch.*

DUMMER JEREMY, was born in Boston, and in 1699 was graduated at Harvard College, and designed for the ministry. The president of the college, when he was student, was the celebrated Dr. I. Mather, who declares in a preface to a publication of Mr. Dummer's, that when he left college, he was by far the best scholar that had been there; which his succeeding reputation evinced to be a just encomium.

His reputation was as high at the university of

Leyden, as it was at Harvard College. *Witsius* was professor of theology when Mr. D. was a student there. This professor spake of the accomplishments of Mr. Dummer, and gave his opinion that he would be useful to the churches, as he was so eminent for his knowledge in divinity as well as philosophy. The university presented him with a degree of doctor philosophiae, which answers to A. M. in other seminaries.

It appears evident that he had a preference for Europe, and perhaps intended to settle as a minister in some part of England. Whether he was so popular as a preacher, as he was excellent for his scholarship, is doubtful. Dr. M. says he did not meet with encouragement to settle in this country, and laments that, for want of it, he was constrained to go away.

While he was in England he turned his mind to jurisprudence and *politicks*, and wrote, in defence of the New England charters, an admirable pamphlet, when their privileges were threatened. He was indefatigable in serving the interests of the colonies, being well qualified by his knowledge, prudence and zeal, as well as by his influence which was considerable, and which he acquired by an intimate acquaintance with many of the best characters, and some of the most brilliant luminaries of the English nation. He was chosen agent for the province, 1710, when sir William Ashurst declined to serve. Contrary to the expectation of his countrymen and constituents, he devoted himself to the persons in power, was employed by lord Bolingbroke in certain secret negotiations, and had assurances of promotion to a place of honour and profit; but the death of the queen blasted all his hopes. His acquaintance with that profligate nobleman not only banished all his religious sentiments, but lessened the effect of his moral principles. He was guilty of much artifice and deception in his publick concerns, and run to excess of licentious manners. His private diary, kept in his youth, shows that he was influenced by pious sentiments in every action; he is the humble suppliant at the divine mercy seat, and every thing wicked touches with horror the devout sensibility of his heart !—It was not without pain, that he overcome the impressions of his education ; he often struggled against their influence. He could only bring his views to a state of forlorn scepticism, and was never able to fix his mind in infidelity. Amidst scenes of dissipation, he had some reflections which prevented him from enjoying what *commonly gives delight to the sons of men*, and confessed to a friend that he wished to feel what he once experienced, when he was a pious man in New England, without any great expectations, and had no other desire than to settle in the ministry of the gospel.   His sentiments on political subjects were always very correct, and he was through all the changes of life a steady consistent friend of his country. But he had not always the happiness to please his constituents, though he speaks of having mens conscia recti for his support.

In 1721 he was dismissed from the agency, the very year in which he *wrote in defence of the charter*. It was sufficient to ruin his popularity that he was friendly to the governour.   In one of his letters, he thus speaks :

" I expect no thanks from the assembly for this service, as I had none for the counterfeit bills sent over last spring, though I thought it an important service.   It is a hard fate, when I am doing the province and the gentlemen in it all the honour and justice in my power, that some persons in the lower house should take equal pains to lessen and expose me. I wish they may not prejudice your minds in the end by it No matter what becomes of me." He was afterwards employed occasionally in the business of the province. He was disgusted that they put no more confidence in him, for even while they held his abilities eminent, the general court of

Massachusetts appointed others to act with him, whose opinions were more democratick, and who were more faithful to their party than to the truth. This great man died in 1739, at Plastow, May, 3d week. His publications have gone through several editions. They are extremely well written.

In 1704 he printed a sermon "upon the *holiness of the sabbath.*" In a latin dissertation printed when he was in Holland, certain expressions dropped which made some think him an Antisabbatarian, but in this sermon he brings proof for the sanctification of the day : and it is so well written, that a new edition of the discourse has been given since his death.

"His letter to a *noble lord* concerning the Canada expedition, was printed in London 1712." It is an able vindication of Massachusetts, against the charges made by the leaders of this romantick expedition under gen. Hill. They were under a necessity of recurring to some cause of blame, or take it upon themselves. Mr. D. makes it evident Massachusetts were great losers, having sunk an immense sum, and performed their part, or more than was required.

These, with extracts from his letters, and "vindication of the New England charters," are all the publications known to be his.

He was skilled in most languages ancient and modern, was a graceful speaker, and polite man. He had a fine memory, a communicative disposition, and was very beneficent, his company was sought after eagerly by all lovers of good sense and humanity. He retired from business a few years before he died, and enjoyed himself with his books and friends. *Daily Advertiser, Lon.* 1719. *Hutchinson and private mss.*

DUMMER WILLIAM, lieutenant governour of Massachusetts, was born in this province, but went over to England, and was at Plymouth holding an office there, as one of the commissioners, when he was appointed, through the interest of sir William Ashurst, to be lieut. governour, in 1716. He was a friend of the Dudley family, and firmly supported the administration of gov. Shute. Hence he was not the favourite of the popular party; nor of those who promoted private banks, but was highly respected by all parties, when their prejudices did not operate. He maintained a most respectable character for virtue and talents, especially during his administration as the chief magistrate. Douglass always styles it, "the wise administration of Mr. Dummer." He was a man of such correct judgment and steady habits, such a firm and temperate conduct, when he supposed himself right, that the vessel of state was secure though exposed to the dangers of a tempestuous sea. For the opposition continued as the adherents of Mr. Shute, and the minds of people were agitated by the subjects of dispute, continually brought forward in the house of representatives.

There was only one part of his conduct which gave offence to the British administration; but this was a matter no way worthy of reproof, and it tended to give him popularity in this country. Had he not assented to it, he certainly would have lost the favour of a very pious and respectable part of the community. In the year 1726, the convention of the clergy passed a vote to hold a synod. As this is a subject purely ecclesiastical, the lieut. governour fell in with it; or granted his consent. But the jealousy of the episcopal party was excited, and such representations made to the bishop of London, that an instruction came from the ministry to stop all proceedings. Douglass has preserved the copy of the reprimand sent to the chief magistrate for not sending the "account of such a remarkable transaction." Lieut. gov. Dummer was in the chair, from Nov. 1722, to July 19, 1728. Upon gov. Burnet's death, Sept. 7, 1729, he was again in the chair, till the arrival of gov. Belcher, April 8, 1730.

Mr. Tailer who had been in the office, before Mr. Dummer, but was afterwards collector, was then appointed lieut. governour. And Mr. Dummer retired to a more private station. He lived to old age enjoying *otium cum dignitate.* It is true that for some years he held his seat at the council board, and took his rank as the first; but upon some popular question, where he acted with his usual independent spirit, he gave offence, and he was left out of the number at the succeeding election. His house was in Nassau-street, afterwards owned by Mr. Powell. He was one who contributed to build the church in Hollis-street. For many years that part of the town, now so populous, was very sparingly settled. When Mr. D. died, the funeral sermon was preached by Dr. Byles the minister of this church from its foundation to the revolution. *Hutchinson. Douglass.*

DUNSTER HENRY, president of Harvard College, came over in 1640 to Massachusetts; he was a man of an excellent spirit, as well as famous for his literary acquirements. He is recorded as the first president of the college, though Dr. Eaton was placed at the head of the institution before him. This man was set aside, by order of the general court, on account of his severity; he, indeed, wanted every qualification, except learning, for the office. The same man afterwards went over to the old country, conformed to the church of England, and was a bitter enemy to Massachusetts, during the reign of Charles 2d; but his power and influence were small, compared with his malicious humour. Mr. Dunster was mild and amiable in his temper. His faculty of governing the students, and mode of instruction, gave him a great share in the esteem and affection of all who were interested in the reputation of the college. He continued in the chair from the year 1640 to 1654; and then resigned on account of a difference of opinion, between him and the other governours of the college, upon the subjects of baptism. Mr. Dunster was persuaded in his own mind that infants ought not to be baptized, though he would not separate himself from the churches who baptized their children. He thought liberally, but allowed others the same freedom of opinion without any interruption of church fellowship. He died at Scituate, A. D. 1657. And left tokens of his affection to those friends who had advised him to leave Cambridge. The ministers and magistrates of the colony were very desirous of his continuing in the station, if he could be persuaded not to propagate his peculiar opinion, but he was equally conscientious and candid, and preferred retirement to a situation where he might give offence.

The New England psalms were revised by president Dunster who was a great Hebrewician, and had more taste for poetry, than the divines who first undertook to make the version. It is said that till they were corrected by him, they were not fitted to be sung in the churches. These psalms passed through many editions, and till very lately were sung in some of the churches.* *Magnalia.*

EATON THEOPHILUS, governour of New Haven colony, was the eldest son of the Rev. Mr. Eaton, minister of Stratford in Oxfordshire, who afterwards removed to Coventry, and there also performed the duties of a parish minister. Mr. Daven-

* In "New England's first fruits" a scarce and curious book 4to. London, 1643. It is said, over the college is master Dunster placed as president, a learned considerable and industrious man, who has so trained up his pupils in the tongues and arts, and so seasoned them with the principles of divinity and christianity, that we have to our great comfort (and in truth) beyond our hopes, beheld their progressive in learning and godliness also. The former of these has appeared in their publick declamations in latin and greek disputations logical and philosophical, which they have been wonted (besides their daily exercises in the college hall) in the audience of the magistrates, ministers and other scholars for the probation of their youth in learning, upon set days constantly once every month to make and uphold: the latter hath been manifested in sundry of them by the savoury breathings of their spirits in their godly conversation, &c.

than to display his gifts amidst so much wisdom, as was collected in that part of the kingdom. If he had gone to England he might have been as zealous as Hugh Peters, who went over as agent for Massachusetts about this time; In this country he acted a part which made him almost as obnoxious to Charles II. He concealed two of the regicides in his own house, and instigated the people of that government by his publick preaching,* to protect these unfortunate men, and not suffer the king's commissioners to execute their purpose.

Mr. Davenport was threatened with the vengeance of regal authority for concealing traitors, and had reason to dread the consequences of his democratick zeal, mingled as it was with motives of humanity. Upon this gen. Whaley and Goffe offered to surrender, and appeared publickly in several places. It is supposed they would have done this rather than Mr. D. should suffer on their account. But when he was no longer exposed to any particular danger, and the commissioners had manifested their resentment otherwise, they again concealed themselves.

In 1667, Mr. D. left the people at New Haven and came to Boston to succeed Mr. Norton, the minister of the first church. This caused great grief to his own people, and divided the Boston church. Dr. Mather quotes an observation that " it is ill transplanting a tree that thrives in the soil." He might have said that a tree should never be transplanted which has past its growth. It will die before it will yield much fruit, however rich the soil in which it is fixed. His making this exchange of

---

* " About the time the pursuers came to New Haven, or a little before, and to prepare the minds of the people for their reception, Mr. Davenport preached publickly from this text, Isaiah, xvi. 3, 4. Take counsel, execute judgment, make thy shadow as the night in the midst of the noon day, bewray not him that wandereth ; let mine outcasts dwell with thee. Moab, be thou a covert for them, from the face of the spoiler. This doubtless had its effect," &c. *Stiles's history of the judges.*

port, the father of the famous preacher of that name, was mayor of that city. The families became intimately acquainted. Young Mr. Eaton pursued the mercantile line of business, and his friend studied divinity. The one was diligent, and grew rich, and the other made a shining figure in his profession. Their friendship, which began in the old country, was increased by the circumstances which led them both over to the American wilderness ; and was uninterrupted till death parted them. Mr. Eaton was among the most opulent men who came into this country. He arrived at Boston in the year 1637. He had been a patentee of Massachusetts colony, but had no idea of leaving England, until Mr. Davenport was compelled " to seek a refuge from the storm in these cold and rude corners of the earth."

This company preferred to be a distinct colony, and purchased a large territory, where they built a town, and called it New Haven. It has ever since been considered among the fairest places in the plantations. Mr. Eaton was chosen governour of this new colony, and continued in the office, being annually chosen, until his death, A. D. 1657.

" It was the admiration," saith Dr. Mather, " of all spectators to behold the discretion, the gravity, and equity with which he managed all publick affairs. He carried in his countenance a majesty which cannot be described, and in his dispensations of justice he was a mirror for the most imitable partiality." He also quotes a saying of his which evinces the correctness of his mind. " Some account it a great matter to *die well*, but I am sure it is a great matter to live well. All our care should be while we have our life to use it well, and so when death puts an end to *that*, it will put an end to all our cares.

Dr. Trumbull, author of the history of Connecticut, speaks highly of gov. Eaton's character. " There was no man, among the first planters of

New England, who had a more general acquaintance with publick business, or who sustained a
fairer character." He says likewise that his monu-
ument is in good preservation at this time, with lines
upon it, expressive of his worth and usefulness.

Gov. Eaton was one who signed the confederation of the united colonies in 1643. And his name
appears to all their acts and proceedings till the latter end of the year 1657. In this assembly he had
an opportunity to exert himself for the good of New
England, which he failed not to improve. In these
records, which make the chief part of the 2d vol. of
Hazard's Collections, are precious documents for
historians, and very great displays of wisdom. The
first characters of each colony were honoured with
this commission.

Gov. Eaton was twice married, his first wife died young; she left two children. The second was
the daughter of the bishop of Chester. She left
New England after the death of her husband. He
educated one son at Harvard College, who was graduated 1649, and died a few years before his excellent father. *Magnalia. Trumbull. Hazard.*

E DWARDS JONATHAN, president of Princetown
College, in New Jersey, was the son of the rev.
Timothy Edwards, pastor of the church in Windsor, Connecticut. He was born, 1702; graduated
at Yale College, 1720; he was soon chosen tutor,
for which office he was well qualified; being then
distinguished for his abilities and learning. While
he resided at college, he applied his mind closely
to the study of divinity; and very soon after he began to preach, he was invited to settle at Northampton. Mr. Stoddard, who was then minister of the
church, was his grandfather, and had lived to old
age. It gave the highest satisfaction to that venerable man, to have one for his colleague and successor, whose gifts and graces were so extraordinary; and for whom he must naturally care more than
any other candidate whom the people might

call. Mr. Edwards was, indeed, as a son with a father, the staff of his age, as well as a blessing to the people. Mr. Stoddard died, 1729. The church had been in peace and harmony. Both their ministers were highly esteemed at home and abroad. The practice of baptising children of persons making a profession of religion, who did not join in full communion, had not been called in question. Unhappily for the town of Northampton, a difference of opinion arose upon this subject; Mr. Edwards was fully persuaded in his own mind, that none but the children of communicants have a right to baptism; and it was his desire to bring the church over to the same way of thinking. He had thought much upon the subject, and in 1748 he published a quarto pamphlet, entitled, " an humble inquiry into the rules of the word of God concerning the qualifications for a full communion in the visible christian church." The rev. Solomon Williams wrote an answer to this; to which Mr. Edwards replied. The dispute occasioned many divisions in churches, and the contention was so great in the church at Northampton that it issued in a separation. A council was called, which advised to a dismission. He resigned the pastoral office in 1750, and had an " honourable quietus." He was then invited to settle in the church at Stockbridge. The minister of that town was supported from the funds of the London society. Mr. Sargeant had been their missionary to the Indians; they elected Mr. Edwards to succeed him, and the inhabitants of the town joined heartily in the invitation. In this retired situation he made himself useful to the people both Indians and English, who sat under his ministry; and he had a fine opportunity to indulge his mind in those profound speculations, which had given him a distinction among the greatest men of the age.

When president Burr died, he was chosen to succeed him. He had good reasons for not accept-

ing the place, but a sense of duty prevailed over
every other consideration, and he removed to Princetown in New Jersey. In this station, which he
adorned by his reputation, and where he might have
been very useful if it had pleased Heaven to spare
his life, he continued but a short time. He died
of the small pox, Feb. 23, 1758. His death was
universally lamented. Though many differed from
him in theological opinions, yet all respected his
piety and learning. As a preacher he was pathetick, serious, experimental; he had a small voice,
and therefore was not popular among that class of
people who think that to be zealous, and to cry
aloud, is the same thing. But his performances in
the pulpit were peculiarly acceptable to persons of
serious views. They were plain, practical and
adapted to the various capacities of his hearers;
which is very remarkable, considering how much
he wrote and thought upon doctrinal subjects. He
was certainly a great controversial writer; most of
his writings discover this turn of mind, and he has
written very largely and ably upon many theological subjects. His book upon the "freedom of the
will" is the most celebrated; this gives him a name
among the greatest metaphysicians. "Several professors of divinity in the Dutch universities sent
him their thanks for the assistance he had given
them in their inquiry into some doctrinal points,
having carried his own further than any author they
had ever seen." This book is written in opposition
"to Arminian principles;" and the "Pelagian heresy;" Dr. Priestly, however, speaks highly of it,
and says he should suppose an Arminian wrote it.
The doctor is well known to be a high Supralapsarian, or Necessarian, which he will not allow to be
a sentiment exclusively confined to Calvinistick divines. President Edwards' book is not so clear
upon the subject as some others upon that side the
question. The style is somewhat intricate, but it
is a book of deep research; it discovers great appli-

cation of mind, with uncommon strength of intellectual powers. This has been said of it, that it not only proves him a man of great genius, but " the superiour force of argument has baffled all opposition." His " treatise upon the affections" is another work of great celebrity, and has been read more than his " essay on the freedom of the will " He published many works, and left many in mss. Since his death have been printed, " his defence of the doctrine of original sin ;" a volume upon the " nature of virtue ;" the " history of redemption," &c. All his works have been collected lately, in eight volumes, of which there is a very good American edition, with " memoirs of his life."

President Edwards left ten children. Of his posterity there are now several who are very conspicuous among the literary and famous men of New England.

EDWARDS JONATHAN, D. D president of Schenectady College, was the son of the rev. president Edwards of New Jersey. He was educated at Jersey College, and graduated in 1765. He was settled at New Haven, and continued a number of years in the ministry ; but left the place some years before he was chosen president of Union College, in which office he died. He was an author of very considerable reputation. His most celebrated publications were, an answer to Dr. Chauncy's book entitled, " salvation for all men," which proved him to be a critick and a scholar ; and a reply to the " essays upon liberty and necessity," written by Dr. Samuel West, of New Bedford, which shows much logical acuteness, and is more luminous than what his father wrote upon the subject.

ELIOT JOHN, commonly called the apostle to the Indians, exhibited more lively traits of an extraordinary character than we find in most ages of the church, or in most christian countries. He, who could prefer the American wilderness to the pleasant fields of Europe, was ready to wander through this wilderness for the sake of doing good. To be active was the delight of his soul; and he went to the hovels which could not keep out the wind and rain, where he laboured incessantly among the aboriginals of America, though his popular talents gave him a distinction among the first divines of Massachusetts, at a time that the magistrates and all the people held the clergy in peculiar honour.

We know but little of his connections before he left his native country. He was born in England, A. D. 1604. There is nothing related of his parents, except that they gave him a liberal education, and were exemplary for their piety;—for this their memory is precious.

" I do see," says this excellent man, " that it was a great favour of God to me that my first years were seasoned with the fear of God, the word and prayer." Is there not sufficient encouragement to educate ingenuous youth, and impress the tender heart with lessons of wisdom, to think they will shed tears of grateful sensibility on our sepulchres?

When Mr. Eliot left the university of Cambridge, he himself became a teacher; and while he led children and youth into the paths of virtue, acquired also an acquaintance with the human heart. At this time he had an opportunity of hearing the venerable Hooker, and never lost the serious impressions which he received under his preaching; to him he was always attached, as well as to his mode of administering the order of the churches.

In the year 1631, Mr. Eliot arrived at Boston; and the succeeding year, Nov. 5, 1632, was settled as teacher of the church in Roxbury. Gov. Winthrop says, " Mr. John Eliot, a member of Boston congregation, whom the company intended presently to call to the office of teacher, was called to be a teacher to the company at Roxbury; and though Boston laboured all they could, both with the congregation at Roxbury and with Mr. Eliot himself, alledging their want of him, and the covenant between them, yet he could not be diverted from accepting the call at Roxbury; so he was dismissed."

When Mr. Eliot came to Boston, the preceding year, there was no minister at the first church. Mr. Wilson had gone to England, and the religious service was carried on by gov. Winthrop, Mr. Dudley and Mr. Nowel, the ruling elder. Mr. Hubbard says these men accepted the charge, " knowing well that the princes of Judah, in king Hezekiah's reign, were appointed to teach the people out of the law of God."

Mr. Wilson left Boston the latter end of March, 1631. Mr. Eliot arrived November following, with the governour's lady and sixty other persons, in the ship Lyon. He immediately joined the first church, and preached with them till he settled at Roxbury. Had he accepted the call from the first church, it might have been happy for the people; but most probably the great work which he afterwards undertook, would not have been devised, and for this he was very peculiarly qualified. But had the connexion taken place, those animosities might have been prevented, which afterwards divided the church, banished the christian spirit from their councils, and disturbed the whole community. Mr. Cotton, who was called to be their teacher, was a learned and excellent man, but opinionated; he countenanced Wheelwright, Mrs. Hutchinson, and others, who were spreading antimonian errors through all the churches. The pastor, Mr. Wilson, gov. Winthrop and Mr. Dudley, supported and defended the principles and practices of the churches, before this fanatical woman, Mrs. Hutchinson, came into the country. With them were the ministers and people of the other congregations; but Vane was governour, a hot-brained enthusiast, and under his wing Mr. Cotton carried on the opposition against the pastor; the church was divided; mutual censures passed between the brethren, and every thing, especially their ecclesiastical affairs,

wore a most gloomy aspect.   Amidst this melancholy kind of embarrassment, the prudence and
good sense of gov. Winthrop were conspicuous.

Such abilities and so much candour as he possessed were absolutely necessary for the times.

The prior engagement of Mr. Eliot to settle with
the people at Roxbury, who came over with him in
the same ship, and to whom he was warmly attached, was sufficient to satisfy his friends of the church
in Boston, and they gave him a regular dismission.
He was accordingly united with the church at Roxbury as their teacher, and Mr. Welde was called the
next year to be their pastor.   They lived in much
harmony ; and under their ministry the town grew
and flourished ;—it still retains a rank of distinction
among the best places in the environs of the metropolis.

He certainly was the most successful missionary
that ever preached the gospel to the Indians.   His
prudence and zeal, his patience, resolution, activity
and knowledge of mankind, were equally conspicuous.   Many have done worthily in this benevolent
work ; but if we unite an *apt method* of applying the
truths of christianity to the minds of the heathen
with the success of his labours, he far excelled them
all.   He likewise claims a very peculiar character,
as being the first Protestant minister who diffused
the beams of evangelical truth among the wild nations of this benighted part of the globe.   The tribes
that roamed through the desarts become dear to
him, like his own people, and he often forsook the
charms of civilized and cultivated society, to reside
with men, who were not only unacquainted with
every thing called *urbanity*, but who wanted comfortable means of subsistence ; with whom he would
associate days and weeks to instruct them in divine things—and also acquaint them how they could
improve their condition upon the earth. He partook
with them their hard fare, with *locks* wet with the
dews of the night, and exposed to attacks from the

beasts of the forests ; or to *their* spears and arrows who were fiercer than wolves, and more terrible in their howling. None of these things moved him, but he was more collected as he was in the face of danger ; like a brave soldier, he fought the good fight of faith, bearing every suffering with cheerfulness, and every pain with resignation.

When our Indian apostle began his mission, there were about seventeen or twenty tribes within the limits of the English planters. But these tribes were not large, and hardly to be distinguished ; for their manners, language and religion were the same.

The *Massachusetts* language, in which he translated the bible and several practical treatises, would serve the purpose of a missionary. The first thing he did was to learn this language of the people, and then he could preach without the medium of an interpreter, which is likely to cause mistakes—and sometimes in material points. An old Indian, who could speak English, was taken into his family, and by conversing freely with him he learnt to talk it, and soon was able to reduce it to some method, and became at last so much master of it, as to publish a grammar, which is printed in some editions of the Indian bibles.

From his contemporaries, and from his writings, we learn, that he always preached in a plain manner, but had a happy facility of communicating his ideas upon subjects adapted for his people. He was warm and diffusive, tender and pathetic, rather copious than correct in his language ; but though his style was not varied with much art, his publick performances were acceptable in all the churches. His method was natural, his expression easy, his voice audible, and his manner very interesting. Out of the abundance of his heart his mouth spake, in preaching and praying ; and no pastor of New England saw more of the fruit of his labours. His discourses are without those quibbles, gingling words, and quaint turns, which mark the false taste of the age ; but were as common in English, as in American sermons. This strain of preaching was introduced here by scholars educated in European seminaries, and too successfully imitated by the sons of our college. The author of the Magnalia abounds even with puerile conceits, and on this account has not received that tribute of respect from literary men of this generation, which he deserves, for preserving many facts, or such minute circumstances of events, as are entertaining to read, without his peculiarities of style ; and are of infinite service to all who would know the affairs of their own country. To this author, who was intimately acquainted with Mr. Eliot, we are indebted for an extract of a sermon upon the heavenly conversation, which exhibits the preacher in his common attitude ; for the words were taken as they dropped from his mouth, without his supposing that they would ever appear in print. We certainly can form a more correct opinion of the preacher's talents than from the description in his biography, where he tells us, that " lambs might wade into his discourses, on those texts and themes wherein elephants might swim."

As to his moral and christian character, it was as exemplary as his ministerial qualifications were excellent. His mind was governed by a sense of duty, and not a mere ease and complacency of humour, which makes a man good-natured when he is pleased, and patient when he has nothing to vex him. He brought his religion into all his actions. A stranger to artifice and deceit, he disliked the appearance of them in others. He felt equal obligations to perform the duties of piety, virtue and benevolence. Such was the man. He clothed himself with humility as with a *robe*. Literally speaking, he wore a leathern girdle about his lions. Perhaps this might show too strong a prejudice against dress ; but all his actions discovered a temper free from vanity, and a desire to *be* humble, rather than to gain the praise of men. He was very temperate :

one dish was his homely repast. When he dined abroad, he would not indulge himself in the luxuries of the table. He drank water, and said of wine, " it is a noble, generous liquor, and we should be humbly thankful for it, but, as I remember, water was made before it." His maintenance was a free contribution, or raised upon pews, and the people of Roxbury cheerfully supported two ministers. It was his request, to give up his salary when he could no longer preach. " I do here," said he, " give up my salary to the Lord Jesus Christ; and now, brethren, you may fix that upon any man that God shall make a pastor." But the society, in their answer, told him, that they accounted his presence worth any sum granted for his support, even if he were superannuated so as to do no further service for them. The youth of the congregation called him their father and their *friend*, and their affection chased away the gloom so apt to hover around the evening of life. Such attentions from the rising generation, are like medicine to the spirit of a man sinking within him. The reflection of a life well spent, and the kindness of his friends, made his old age pleasant.

In domestick life, Mr. Eliot was peculiarly happy. His lady was an excellent economist, and by her prudent management enabled him to be generous to his friends, and hospitable to strangers. It ought to be mentioned to the credit of this excellent woman, that with a moderate stipend and her prudence, he educated four sons at Cambridge, who were among the best preachers of that generation. A small salary, where a proper arrangement is made of the expenses, and the wife *looks well to the ways of her household*, may answer generous as well as necessary purposes : But when frugality is despised, and prudence called a nigardly virtue ; when the fragments which might be gathered are lost, it is not the income of the most lucrative stations, much less the salaries of pastors of churches, that will maintain people in ease and independence.

By the influence of Mr. Boyle, his honorable friend, Mr. Eliot was allowed fifty pounds, annually, from the society *de propagand fide.* This enabled him to gratify his benevolent propensities ; the poor Indians, to whom the gospel was preached, shared the most of the donation. His character is thus celebrated by one of his biographers :—" .t was a brilliant star in the constellation of his virtues, and the rays of it were various and extensive. He gave largely from his own income to the poor, and promoted all kinds of useful distributions, especially if he could serve the cause of religion. When his age unfitted him for publick employment, he reflected that he did good as he had opportunity. " Alas !" said he, " I have lost every thing.—My understanding leaves me, my memory fails me, but I thank God my charity holds out still *

It becomes necessary to mark the minute circumstances of a person's character, if we would obtain just views of his temper and actions. Hence biography differs from history, whose province is to describe great events which elevate the mind of the reader ; and which require a dignity of manner with the glow of sentiment. But in the narrative of private life, we survey the man in all his various atti-

---

* So great was Mr. Eliot's charity, that his salary was often distributed for the relief of his needy neighbours, so soon after the period at which he received it, that before another period arrived his own family were straitened for the comforts of life. One day the parish treasurer on paying the money for salary due, which he put into a handkerchief, in order to prevent Mr. Eliot from giving away his money before he got home, tied the ends of the handkerchief in as many hard knots as he could. The good man received his handkerchief, and took leave of the treasurer. He immediately went to the house of a sick and necessitous family. On entering, he gave them his blessing, and told them God had sent them some relief. The sufferers with tears of gratitude welcomed their pious benefactor, who with moistened eyes began to untie the knots in his handkerchief. After many efforts to get at his money, and impatient at the perplexity and delay, he gave the handkerchief and all the money to the mother of the family, saying with a trembling accent : " Here, my dear, take it ; I believe the Lord designs it all for you."

tudes, frequently without a design to *point* a moral :
We follow him through the vales and descents of
his situation, and feel interested in every thing which
concerns him, till, by dwelling upon *kindred* ima-
ges, he grows into a familiar acquaintance.

Most men have their oddities and strange humours. Among the prejudices of Mr. Eliot was
one very strong against *wearing wigs.* He preached against it ; he prayed against it ; he thought all
the calamities of the country, even Indian wars,
might be traced to this absurd fashion. Many
things have been told by the people of Roxbury,
which were handed down to them by their ancestors, that seem only like amusing stories, of the
good man's resentment. And in the written account by Cotton Mather, it is said that he thought
it a " luxurious, feminine protexity for men to wear
their hair long." Especially, a shame for ministers of the gospel to " ruffle their heads in excesses
of this kind." The doctor touches lightly upon
this subject, *for he himself wore a wig ;* and he
makes a judicious observation—" Doubtless," said
he, " it may be lawful in us to accommodate our
hair to the modest customs which vary in the
cuurch of God ; and it may be lawful for them,
who have not hair of their own, enough for their
health, to supply themselves according to the sober
modes of the places where they live. Mr. Eliot
lived to see the prevalence of the fashion, to see many an orthodox minister wear a great white wig,
and it is reported that he gave over the utterance
of his grieved spirit, saying only as a *last word* of
complaint that the " lust was insuperable."

His prejudices were as strong against the use of
tobacco. He thought it was a sacrifice of precious
time—a silly amusement, disgusting in itself ; that
christians ought not to become slaves to such a pernicious weed, and besotted by its influence. But
he might as well have preached to the moon, as to
resist the tide of fashion ; or fought with the stars

in their courses, as to struggle with the pride of o-
pinion, or the appetites of sense ; and try to persuade men not to use a weed which carries a charm
with it for its intoxicating quality ;—which equally
tends to exhilarate their spirits and amuse their leisure hours.

The use of ardent spirits was then hardly known.
Hugh Peters, a friend of his, and contemporary
writer, says : He never saw a man, woman, or child,
drunk in the streets of Boston—nor recollects hearing an *oath*. Stern virtue had a dominion or authority which she has lost since, and it may be long
before we recur to the practices or principles of
the New England planters.

Our Roxbury divine has been accused by some
of versatility in his opinions and conduct : By
others, of being too set and rigid in his notions. If
there is an inconsistency in this, it is what we see
every day. Persons think themselves right and are
warm in defending a sentiment.—The same sensibility of mind may be manifested after they have altered
their way of thinking. Hutchinson quotes a letter
of Hooker, where he says : " A copy of Mr. Vane's
expressions at Roxbury, I desire to see and receive
by the next messenger. I have heard that my brother Eliot is come about to this opinion : I have
writ to him—I would fain come to a bandy with
him, where I might be a little rude in the business,
for I do as verily believe it to be false, as I do believe any article of my faith to be true." From his
behaviour at the trial of Mrs. Hutchinson, we rather
think Mr. Hooker was misinformed. He never was
a partizan of Vane, but always adhered to gov.
Winthrop.

His setness of opinion was also manifested in
controverting with the great Dr. Owen the proper
observation of the sabbath, but he thought the doctor's name and character, might carry more weight
than his arguments had intrinsic excellency.

His political opinions more than once brought

him into trouble. He spake with freedom against the Indian treaty, and was obliged to recant before the magistrates. Roger Williams and he were of the same opinion, but the one was convinced, and confessed *his error; the other was not so easily moved or convinced.*

This was in the year 1636. Afterwards he discovered more of a democratic spirit, by writing against monarchy, when it was not safe for puritan divines to speak of the ruling power, and the republicans in the mother country had their tongues locked in silence. Hutchinson tells us, in the first book of his history, that the governour and council, in the year 1660, took notice of a book published by Mr. Eliot not long before, intitled, the *Christian Commonwealth,* full of seditious principles and notions, in relation to all established governments in the christian world, especially against the government established in their native country. Upon consultation with the elders, their censure was deferred until the next general court, that Mr. Eliot might have an opportunity, in the mean time, of making a publick recantation. At the next session, Mr. Eliot gave in his acknowledgment to the court:

" Understanding, by an act of the honoured council, that there is offence taken at a book published in England by others, the copy whereof was sent over by myself about ten years since, and that the further consideration thereof is commended to this honourable general court, now sitting in Boston. Upon perusal thereof, I do judge myself to have offended; and, in a way of satisfaction, not only to the authority of this jurisdiction, but also to any others that shall take notice thereof, I do hereby acknowledge to this general court, that such expressions as do manifestly scandalize the government of England by king, lords, and commons, as antichristian, and justify the late innovator, I do sincerely bear testimony against, and acknowledge it to be true, not only a lawful, but eminent, form of government.

" 2.   All form of civil government deduced from scripture, I acknowledge to be of God, and to be subjected to, for conscience' sake ; and whatsoever is in the whole epistle or book inconsistent here-with, I do at once most cordially disown." JOHN ELIOT."

The books were ordered by the court to be call-ed in, and this acknowledgment to be posted up in the principal towns of the colony.

During the war with the sachem Philip, 1675, our Roxbury divine appears in a character very in-teresting to the community.   The traces of war are blood and slaughter.   The people of Massachu-setts, in their phrenzy, would have destroyed the *praying* Indians with the savages whose feet were swift to spread destruction in every path.   Mr. El-iot was their advocate and friend.   They were put under a kind of duress, which was injurious to them if they were innocent, but which was more aggra-vating because they took a decided part against their own nation ; *this* they bore with patience, or a ve-ry faint expression of complacency.   Mr. Eliot was not only persuaded that they were friendly, but that they were of great service to the English, with whom they would live or die, rather than mingle with *heathens.*   Being assisted by gen. Gookin, he defended their cause, and protected them against those men of violence who were less in the *image of God* than those poor *outcasts* of human society ; *men*, who lost their reputation, as christians, be-cause they gave way to the fury of their passions. Every thing was said against the minister and ma-gistrate which could be uttered by the foul mouth of the vulgar, or from the lips of some whose edu-cation was liberal, and whose religion ought to have made more candid ; but who stimulated the bitter sarcasms of the multitude.   Nothing could shake the resolution of such men, conscious of rectitude :

and we never behold the *subject of these memoirs* to more advantage than he appears when he pleads the cause of these poor, friendless beings. It is no wonder, therefore, that having shown his abilities and firmness, he acquired such an influence over the various tribes as no other missionary to the Indians could ever obtain. We can overlook a multitude of errors, where such divine charity throws the purest lustre upon the character. We can excuse such prejudices, which by themselves seem like *effusions of human weakness*, when, in the same life, we see the *charms of virtue ;* nor let us blame even an obstinacy of humour if mingled with a firmness that gives dignity to human nature. Having mentioned certain oddities in his disposition, or a few singularities, or puerile antipathies against new customs, which in the present day would cause a smile of ridicule, let these be balanced by the honesty and frankness of his manners He was as tenacious of truth and justice as of his own opinion. He must also have possessed some of those rare qualities which conciliate popularity an uncommon affability to gain an influence in society which could never be acquired by ministerial gifts and graces, although these might make him an ornament to the pulpit.

There is a story which perhaps should not be omitted. It is related by *one* fond of the marvellous, (Cotton Mather.) Mr. Eliot was in a boat, that was overset by a vessel running against it. A profane wretch, one who clamoured for the extirpation of the *praying Indians* said, he wished the man of God had been drowned. In a few days this man was drowned in the very place where Mr. Eliot had received his deliverance.

After living eighty-six years in this world of trial, the *spirit* of this excellent divine took its flight to a better world. For many years he *had his conversation in heaven ;* his faith seemed to be swallowed up in vision, and his hopes in fruition. He lost his most amiable companion two years before. He was then sick and expected and longed for his own departure. Their children they had followed to the *grave*, and had comforted each other as they drank the bitter ingredients from the cup of adversity. He died in the year 1690.

Few of his family were alive to lament his death; but he was lamented by the whole family of virtue, and by all the sincere friends of religion. The poor *church at Natick* not only joined with those who dropped a tear upon his dust, but streams of sorrow flowed from the heart. Though he lived many years they were filled with usefulness; succeeding generations mentioned his name with uncommon respect; his labours were applauded in Europe and America; and all who now contemplate his active services, his benevolent zeal, his prudence, his upright conduct, his charity, are ready to declare his memory precious. Such a man will be handed down to future times, an object of admiration and love; and appear conspicuous in the historick page when distant ages celebrate the *Worthies of New England.* *

* Works —The true commonwealth; tears of repentance, &c. harmony of the gospels; an Indian grammar; Indian psalter; the whole bible in the same language.

Of Mr. Eliot's four sons, the eldest, John Eliot, was graduated at Cambridge in 1656; was settled at Newton, the spot where the first assembly of praying Indians were assembled. He was a preacher to the aboriginals, and probably assisted his father in translating the scriptures. Mr. Homer in his history of Newton has given a very interesting view of the character of this excellent divine. He died. 1668. in the 33d year of his age.

Joseph, the second son, was graduated at Harvard College, 1653. He was minister of the church at Guildford, in Connecticut, above 30 years. He died. 1694

Samuel, the third son, was graduated, 1660; was a tutor and fellow of Harvard College; a candidate for the ministry. He died early in life, " a young man eminent for learning and goodness."

Benjamin, the fourth son, was graduated, 1665; was ordained colleague with his father, but died before him : upon which the author of the Magnalia makes this reflection, after G Nazianzen. " The father having laid up in a better world a rich inheritance for his children sent a son of his before to take possession of it."

ELIOT JARED, pastor of the church at Killingworth, Connecticut, was the son of the rev Joseph Eliot, of Guildford, and born, Nov. 7, 1685; he was graduated at Yale College, 1706. He proceeded master of arts; and had the degree also presented from Harvard College. He was minister of Killingworth till his death, April, 1763. In Chandler's life of president Johnson, we are told, that Mr. Eliot once doubted of the validity of presbyterian ordination. He afterwards acknowledged that he had been too precipitate in forming and communicating his opinion. From the account of the episcopal writers one would suppose that the clergy and people of Connecticut, at that period, were very illiterate; or that none but the rector of Yale, and those young gentlemen who had declared in favour of the episcopal church were conversant with books, or had any reputation for knowledge. By other accounts, especially by certain letters sent to the ministers of Boston, it appears, that there were other men of talents in the government of the college; and that, in this very controversy with the rector, they were able to convince *three*, who made a great figure in their profession, that their ordination had been valid. Mr. E. had been among those who were the most strenuous. He, and Mr. Johnson had not only expressed doubts, but a full persuasion, that there was no ordination except from the hands of bishops in a line from the apostles. It is agreed on all sides that the six young gentlemen who signed the declaration, were excellent scholars, and of irreproachable morals; but the opinion which some had of the rector was very different from what his friends have represented. " He was an episcopalian many years while minister at Stratford;" he accepted the chair of Yale College when " he knew he was guilty of dissimulation;" he acted a jesuitical part in seducing young men of talents from the paths they and their fathers had walked; and was such a bigot as to declare before the trustees, that he believed " there was no salvation out of the *episcopal* church." These things were said by the trustees of the college; perhaps their prejudices might give a tone of severity to their censure of his conduct when he first delivered his sentiments in publick.*

Mr. Eliot was a member of the corporation of Yale College from the year 1730 to 1762.

In 1752, president Clap wrote his defence of the New England churches. At a general association of the ministers of the county this book was approved, and signed by Jared Eliot, moderator.

Whether he ever published any sermons or theological treatise, we have not been able to ascertain, except a " sermon upon the taking of Louisburg, 1745." He was distinguished for his skill in natural philosophy, and made some physical experiments which were useful as well as ingenious. As a botanist he was certainly the first in New England, and his " agricultural essays" have passed through several editions.†

ELIOT ANDREW, D. D. was born in Boston; had the rudiments of his education at the south gram-

---

* How is the gold become dim, and the silver become dross, and the wine mixt with water! our school gloried and flourished under the first rector, the rev. Mr. Pearson, a pattern of piety, a man of modest worth, of solid learning, and sound principles, free from the least arminian or episcopal taint; but it suffered a decay for some years, because of the want of a resident rector. But who could have conjectured, that its name being raised to Collegium Yalense from a Gymnasium Saybrookense, it should groan out Ichabod in about three years and a half, under its second rector, so unlike the first, by an unhappy election set over it, into whose election or confirmation, or any act relating to him, the senior subscriber hereof (though not for some reason through malice bruited about) never came.—Extract of a letter to the Boston ministers, signed, John Davenport, Stamford S. Buckingham, &c.

† By the kindness of gov. Trumbull, part of the information concerning Mr. Eliot was obtained from his son George Eliot, esq. of Killingworth —Concerning the family of the apostle, he differs from the author of the Magnalia—Benjamin was not the fourth son—there was one named Aaron, next to Samuel, who died young. Mr. E. also relates that his great grand father, the apostle Eliot, was born at Nasin, Essex county.

mar school under Dr. Williams and Mr. Lovel; was graduated at Harvard College in 1737; and ordained pastor of the church in North street, April 14, 1742. To delineate his character may not be proper for the compiler of this work; such facts will be mentioned only, as are necessarily connected with the notices of his life. He had a strong attachment to the constitution of the New England churches; was zealous in promoting the interest and reputation of the college, and active in serving the purposes of all humane and pious as well as literary institutions. He was a member of the London society for propagating the gospel among the Indians, and when a board from Scotland was constituted in Boston, he was appointed one of the first members. He joined with others in getting an act through the general court to establish a similar society in Massachusetts, which was negatived by gov. Bernard; and a large subscription lost, that was designed as a fund for the institution. If he ever manifested enthusiasm, it was in the persuasion of the great good which would arise from the missions to the various tribes of the aboriginals. The result, however, did not answer his expectations; and the latter part of his life he often expressed his concern that such lively hopes were defeated, and vast sums expended to so little purpose.*

* The circumstances preceding the war might occasion this disappointment. The Indians were wrought up to a different temper by other persons, from what the preachers of the gospel of peace effected. Sir William Johnson it is supposed had an influence over them, who was prejudiced in favour of the church of England and the measures of the British administration. By certain letters which passed between gov. Hutchinson and this gentleman, it seems the society desired the governour to write, and remonstrate against his conduct, which he very highly resented. Another thing ought to be considered as the great hindrance of the success of the missionaries. That they did not first civilize them. It was generally believed that the first object should be to convert them; and civilization would follow of course. This was a favourite sentiment of the board in Scotland. It met the opinion also of Dr. Chauncy, and several gentlemen in Bos-

In 1765, Dr. E. was chosen fellow of the corporation of Harvard College. He had been some years
secretary of the board of overseers ; and was one of
the committee to obtain donations after the old college was burnt.   Many of the present generation
remember his exertions to procure the present library and apparatus.   He did not confine his application to gentlemen in the provinces.   Several valuable presents were made to the library at his particular request by his correspondents in England.
When that venerable man, president Holyoke, rested from his labours, it was the publick expectation
that he would succeed him, but as he could not
think of breaking the connection with his people,
who were unwilling to part with him, he declined
standing a candidate for the office.   Afterwards,
when the chair was again vacant by the resignation
of another president, he was one of three fellows of
the college, elected by the corporation.   This he
opposed, but his opinion was overruled.   It appeared to him, as to many other persons in the province,
a deviation from the line of decorum for gentlemen
of the same body to choose each other into office,
for the sake of the honour, when it was well understood they would not accept it.

There were other events in his life, which are
worthy of a relation, as they manifest how much his
aim was to be useful. When lieut. gov. Hutchinson's
house was pillaged, and pulled to pieces by an infuri-
ated mob, his books and mss. were thrown into the
streets, and were in danger of being completely
destroyed.   Dr. E. made every exertion to save
them.   Several trunks of mss. among them the second volume of the history of Massachusetts Bay,

ton.   The method the societies now practice is, to teach them
the arts of life ; and some tribes feel the necessity of cultivating
their lands, of acquiring manual employments, are sensible of
the benefit of early instruction for their children, so that the prospect is fair of their improving the means of religion while they
enjoy the blessings of social life.

were preserved by 'his care and attention, and he spent much time in assisting to arrange them.

Another thing may be mentioned as manifesting how much he was influenced by a sense of duty. He remained in Boston during the blockade from April 19, 1775, to the March of the succeeding year. His friends, his family, and most of his congregation had left the town, but the inhabitants who could not leave their dwellings were many, and they constituted a very large religious society. He shared with them in their affliction, preached every Sabbath, and paid every attention which is ever expected from a pastor to his flock. He often observed, that although he never passed a season, when his own feelings were more tried, yet he never had an opportunity to be more useful. Others have said, his preaching was uncommonly impressive. For several months Dr. Mather and he attended the Thursday lecture, but finding it inconvenient, they agreed to bring it to a close, and a farewell sermon was preached upon an occasion which many circumstances concurred to render very solemn and affecting. When the people of the town returned, this lecture was again opened; gen. Washington and the officers of the American army attended; a fuller assembly has been seldom known; Dr. E. preached from Isaiah xxxiii. 20, and gave a very interesting view of the state of the town. The latter years of his life, he appeared to enjoy a good degree of health, had the same animation in the pulpit, and vivacity in his conversation, but he was subject to bodily complaints which he supposed to be indications of a speedy dissolution. In the summer of 1778, he complained more than usual, but did not confine himself to the house till the first week of September, and died the 30th day of the month. He had been 36 years in the ministry and was in the 60th year of his age.*

* Works.—He was never fond of printing sermons. When he was desired to publish any single discourse which had gratified

Endicot John, governour of Massachusetts, was from Dorchester in England, and one who purchased of the council of Plymouth that part of New England three miles to the south of Charles river, and three miles north of Merrimack from the Atlantick to the South sea. In the summer of 1628, he was sent over to Naumkeake with a company who considered him as governour of the plantation, because all the affairs of this infant settlement were committed to his care. He was a man peculiar in his notions, rigid in his religious principles, eager and ardent in all his views. One of his odd opinions was, that women ought to wear veils that their faces may never be seen in the church;

his people; his answer was, that he intended to collect a number, which he would publish in a volume after some years. This volume of twenty sermons was printed in the year 1774. The other discourses which appeared at different times, were five "ordination sermons;" one upon the "inordinate love of the world;" a sermon after " the death of Mr. Webb;" a fast sermon, 1754; one upon the thanksgiving, 1759; the election sermon, 1765; a sermon at the Dudleian lecture, 1771; also, a sermon " upon the thief on the cross." He wrote several pieces in the episcopal controversy, particularly " remarks upon the bishop of Oxford's sermons," extracts of which were published in England, by Dr. Blackburn; his friends there also printed an edition of his election sermon. In the memoirs of T. Hollis, esq. of London, there are several pages filled with the letters he wrote to that gentleman. A letter from a friend of his will close the account of his writings. " I well remember two (I believe there were three pieces) of your father's, which I copied at his desire and carried for publication, saying nothing, save that they were written by a worthy friend. To say they were excellent would be superfluous. One of them on prelatical ordination was much spoken of and admired. Old justice Dana in particular was abundant; I need not say that he was loud in his praises. How many others he wrote, of which he was willing to be known as the writer, I am not able to say." The gentleman who wrote the above, was his particular friend.* Their intimacy, which began in youth, and was founded on mutual esteem, increased with their years; death separated them for a while, but a most affectionate remembrance of the good qualities of his deceased friend is still lively in the breast of the survivor.

* Hon. Samuel Dexter.

and this matter he disputed with Mr. Cotton at a lecture in Boston. He acted so violent a part in executing his plan of church government, that we are told, the "friends of the colony in England wrote a reproof to him, and that he never recovered his reputation in England."* He also gave great offence to the civil power in the plantation, by cutting the cross out of the colours. He considered this as a piece of Romish superstition, being influenced by the opinion of his minister, Mr. Williams, who, with many prominent traits of a great character, was very zealous and opinionated. They, however, carried their point. For though the militia first refused to train with colours that were so defaced, the cross was very soon left out by the general expression of the publick sentiment. Mr. Endicot was, at the time, censured by the people, as well as the government, and the succeeding year, 1635, left out of the magistracy. "They adjudged him worthy of admonition, and to be disabled for one year from bearing any publick office; declining any heavier sentence, because they were persuaded he did it out of tenderness of conscience and not of evil intent."

Mr. E. was chosen afterwards an officer to command fourscore men, against the Pequods; but not succeeding in making an attack upon them, he was much blamed. According to the best accounts he acted with prudence; for winter was approaching, and he must have followed them through the woods wherever they fled; his object likewise was to make a bolder attempt to subdue them the next season. He soon acquired more ascendency in the civil affairs of the colony; and in 1641 was chosen deputy governour, which office he held the two succeeding years, and was placed in the chair of government in 1644, Winthrop being the deputy. A new office was created the same year, that of major gene-

* Bentley's description of Salem.

.ral, and given to Mr. Dudley. He had the sole command of the militia, as the governour was at the head of the civil department. In 1645, Mr. Dudley was chosen governour, and Mr. Endicot appointed major general. After gov. Winthrop died, Dudley and Endicot were the candidates for the chief seats. In 1649, Mr. E. was in the chair, at the head of the magistrates, and signed a declaration against wearing wigs, " as a thing uncivil and un. manly, whereby men do deform themselves, and offend sober and modest men, and do corrupt good manners." He was chosen governour every year from 1655 to 1660. No governour since the set- tlement of the country has been for so many years chief magistrate. He was 16 years governour of the colony, and in the office when he died, 15th of March, 1665.

Though he was more rigid in his notions, and bigotted in his religious principles than any other of the magistrates, yet he was very acceptable to the people when they had advanced him to the chief places. The opposition he made to gov. Winthrop, and the discordant proceedings attending it, might arise in some measure from jealousy and envy. He had been a kind of sub-governour in the plantation before the gentlemen came over in the Arabella. They were his superiors in property, character and influence. Though he was one of the assistants, it did not satisfy him. There was another ground of rivalship between the settlement at Naumkeake, and the towns that were situated upon the banks of Charles river, which place should be the capital. This caused bitter altercations, and had a political influence, especially upon the choice of magistrates. Boston being such a convenient mart for business, and other circumstances concurring to increase its population, soon obtained the preference; and has. continued unto this day to be the metropolis.

Mr. Endicot being in the chair of government, and having moved to Boston, had every inducement to promote the general harmony and peace of the community. The change of government in England, when Charles II. came to the throne was grievous to all the people of New England, but to no individual more than to Mr. Endicot. He had every thing to try his fortitude and his prudence. Several of the regicides had been protected under his government, who fled from Massachusetts when the proclamation issued against them, reached these shores. He afterwards made exertions to secure them. His duty, as a publick officer, stimulated him to act thus, whatever might have been his friendship for the persons. The commissioners sent over by the court of Great Britain, to inquire into the state of the colonies, always gave unfavourable accounts of Massachusetts and their governour. Such was their representation of his conduct that the secretary of state wrote, " The king would take it well, if the people would leave out Mr. Endicot from the place of governour." But no other power than death removed him ; his body was buried in peace, and his name is mentioned among those who did honour to their country.

FANEUIL PETER, esq. presented the market-house, to the town of Boston.—At a meeting of the inhabitants, it was unanimously voted, that the town do with the utmost gratitude receive and accept his most generous and noble benefaction, and that a committee of 21 gentlemen be appointed to wait on him in the name of the town to render him their most hearty thanks for so bountiful a gift, with their prayers that this and other expressions of his bounty and charity may be abundantly recompensed by the divine blessing.

In testimony of their gratitude they named it Faneuil Hall. They also voted that the picture of the said Peter Faneuil, esq. be drawn at full length, and placed in the hall at the expence of the town. He died, 1742.

FIRMIN GYLES, physician in New England, preacher at Stratford, in Great Britain, was born in Suffolk, 1614, 15, educated at Cambridge university, and is mentioned by Dr. Calamy among the ejected ministers, 1662. He was in Boston early in life, being of the puritan stamp, and not finding religious freedom in his native country. Soon after he came to New England, he was chosen deacon of the church in Boston. He was one of the synod at Cambridge, 1637, and a great opposer of the Antinomians. In Hutchinson's collection of papers there is a letter of his, addressed to gov. Winthrop, in 1642, soon after the treachery of the governour's servant, who defrauded him of his property. He expressed his sympathy upon this occasion, and then proposes a settlement for himself and others upon Shawsin river.

At the end of the civil wars he returned to England, left the profession, though not altogether the practice of physick, and settled at Stratford, or Strawford. He was 40 years of age when he was ordained. He continued to preach as long as they would suffer him ; and when ejected by that arbitrary mandate which threw so many excellent men into straits and misery, he retired to Redgwell, a little village, where he continued till his death, April, 1697.

It is said he continued longer preaching than most dissenting ministers, on account of the favour of the neighbouring gentry and justices of the peace, who applied to him as a physician, and saw how much the poor were benefited by him, whom he was ready to serve gratis. He lived to be above fourscore, and enjoyed a fine state of health, to which change of climate, and active life in subduing the wilderness doubtless contributed. He was eminent for his parts and learning. His skill in physick and surgery was uncommon. He understood the oriental tongues ; had read the fathers, schoolmen and church history ; had a logical acumen which he discovered in disputing with Papists, Socinians, Arminians, &c. but especially with Episcopalians. His own sentiments brought him to a middle way between the Presbyterians and Independents. He states in his book, " the conformist and non-conformist compared," that there ought to be several elders in each church, of which the teaching elder is president. This was the opinion of many of our fathers, and was practised in a large proportion of the churches, but is now set aside for very good reasons, which were not so forcible in early times of the plantation. His most famous work, " the real christian or a treatise on effectual calling," has been printed several times in Boston, and few works were read more by serious people of the last generation. As a man he was not rigid nor morose, but peaceable, quiet and inoffensive ; he let his moderation be known, and was a lover of good men of all denominations.*

FISK JOHN, educated at Emanuel College, Cambridge, came to New England, 1637, preached three years at Salem, then removed to Wenham, where he resided fourteen years. In 1656, he, with the greatest part of his church, removed to Chelmsford. He died, Jan. 14, 1676, aged 75.

He was an able physician as well, as a useful preacher. When he was silenced in England on account of his nonconformity, he studied physick,

* His publications were numerous. He printed, 1651, Questions whether baptism should be administered to the children of persons notoriously wicked. In 1658, a treatise upon the schism of parochial congregations in England. In 1673, his most famous work, the real christian or a treatise upon effectual calling. In 1681, Questions between a conformist and non-conformist truly stated, &c. Beside these, he published Presbyterian ordination vindicated ; the plea of children of believing parents for their interest in Abraham's covenant, their right to church membership, and several other treatises upon infant baptism ; remarks on Dr. Crisp's writings ; weighty questions discussed, 1. About the interposition of hands, 2. About teaching _elders and the members meeting in one place, 4to. 1692.

and after a proper examination, he obtained a *license* for publick practice. While he was at Salem he was an instructor of youth ; among his scholars was the famous sir George Downing, whose father had made his settlement in that town.

Mr. Fisk published a catechism which he entitled, " the olive branch watered," which was said to be a useful work ; yet he chose the *assembly's catechism* for his publick expositions, which he went over in discourses before his afternoon sermons on the Sabbath. He died of a complication of ails, and is compared on this account to Calvin, who was troubled with as many infirmities, as in different subjects might have supplied a hospital.

Mr. Fisk left several children. One was settled in the ministry at Braintree. This gentleman was graduated at Harvard College, 1662 ; he had a son who was graduated, 1708, who was invited to settle in the new church, Summer street, Boston, but the division was so great, that he declined their call. The ministers of Boston were very desirous Mr. F. should be fixed in the town. He afterwards was minister of the first church in Salem ; ordained, 1718 ; was dismissed from the ministry, 1745, and died, 1770, aged 81. He was father of the late gen. Fisk. *Magnalia. Bentley's description of Salem.*

FISK NATHAN, D. D. was born at Weston, Sept. 6, 1733; graduated at Harvard College, 1754 ; and ordained pastor of the third church in Brookfield, May 28, 1758. He received his diploma of D. D. 1792. He was a critical and learned divine ; his discourses were calculated to give instruction, and allure men to the love of religion. They are among the best that have been published in this country. Though he was not a popular preacher, yet his manner was pathetick, and he gained the affections of his people while he grew in their esteem. He was an example of the virtues he preached to others, and all who knew him loved him. In simplicity and godly sincerity he had his conversation in the world. Had he not been so modest and unassuming, he would have made a greater figure among the celebrated characters of the age. In the circle where he moved he had great influence; all the neighbouring clergy looked up to him as a father and a friend. Among the stars of the churches he appeared with a pure and serene lustre. His path was that of the "rising light which shineth more and more unto the perfect day." This text was chosen by him for the last discourse he ever preached, and it must be peculiarly impressive to those who knew the character of the man. After preaching on the Lord's day, Nov. 24, 1799, he passed the evening in company, appeared cheerful and in good health, went to bed apparently well, but during his sleep, death came as a friend to remove him to the mansions of eternal rest.

Dr. Fisk did not confine himself to theological publications; he wrote a number of essays in the Massachusetts Spy under the title of the " Worcester speculator," and also under the signature of a " Neighbour ;" and in the Massachusetts Magazine under the title of the " General Observer ;" also, the philanthropist in twenty numbers.*

FRANKLIN BENJAMIN, L L. D. F. R. S. was born in Boston, January 27, 1706. His father was in a humble occupation, but industrious, sober and very respectable among his fellow citizens. The newspaper which announces his death, represents him as modest and unassuming. " Though he courted not the admiration of men, yet all who knew him admired him." He constantly attended

---

* His other printed works are, an historical sermon on the settlement and growth of Brookfield, 1775 ; a fast sermon, 1776 ; a funeral sermon on Mr. Joshua Spencer, 1778 ; an oration on the capture of lord Cornwallis, 1781 ; a sermon at the funeral of Mr. Josiah Hobbes, who was killed by lightning, April 24, 1774 ; a volume of sermons on various subjects, 1794 ; the Dudleian lecture sermon, 1796. All his essays were collected and published in two volumes, styled, the Moral Monitor, 1801.

publick worship, and brought up his children in
the ways of piety. He had a particular desire to
give Benjamin a college education, but wanted the
means. He therefore put him as an apprentice to
the elder brother, J. Franklin, who then published
the *Boston Gazette*. B. Green had printed the Boston *Newsletter* from April 24, 1704. Franklin
printed the first No. of the Gazette, Dec. 21,
1719. The very next week Bradford published
the Mercury at Philadelphia. These were the first
newspapers printed in America. Soon after this,
Franklin delivered over to S. Kneeland the Gazette,
and emitted another paper, called the *Courant*, which
became famous from the literary effusions of his
brother Benjamin. When he was only a lad, he
wrote essays which were sprightly and satirical, and
of a tendency to gain subscribers. Young Franklin was fond of books, and acquired more knowledge than is common at that age; and according
to the account which he gives of himself, was as
wise in his own conceit, as he was in the estimation of others. The life of an author written by
himself generally displays more vanity than wisdom.
Such talents, however, as Franklin possessed could
not be concealed, had he not been disposed to
trumpet his own fame. He not only brought himself into notice by his writings, but distinguished
himself among the wits, free thinkers, and merry
wags of the town. By this conduct he forfeited
the friendship of several gentlemen who were disposed to serve him; who loved his family, but
were the friends of virtue and religion. He was always the head of every deistical club, with whom
he associated. His zeal against the religious part
of the community, as well as his superiour genius,
gave him a claim to the first place of distinction.
While he remained in this country, his chief companion was *Ralph*, who afterward went to England,
and became a celebrated political writer. Pope
gives him a rank among dunces; but lord Melcombe

speaks of him, as holding the best pen among the opposers of the administration. The literary reputation of Ralph is buried with him; but Franklin shines among the most brilliant characters of the age. His works have given his name uncommon celebrity; and his publick services will never be forgotten in his own country. While he shines with such a peculiar lustre, we regret that his principles and moral sentiments in early life were not more worthy of praise. One lesson is to be learned from his memoirs: never to put great confidence in a man's friendship and promises, who is destitute of religious principles. The conduct of his bosom friends, who were libertines and without religion, almost persuaded Franklin to be a christian. In every instance, where he trusted them, they deceived him, and he gives a warning to others from his own sad experience. He left Boston when he was only 17 years of age. He went to Philadelphia, and was introduced to gov. Keith, who seemed disposed to patronise him. By his advice he took a voyage to England, that he might complete himself in every part of his business. The governour assured him of his assistance, which the young man vainly hoped would be greatly to his profit; but in this he was disappointed. The governour was a man of the world, obliging in his manners, but without fidelity in his dealings. Finding therefore that he must depend upon his own exertions, young Mr. Franklin would not be idle, nor had he a disposition to sink under misfortune. His mind was always active, and with such a spirit of industry and capacity for every kind of work, it is no wonder that he met with success, if not equal to his wishes, yet beyond what common men would expect. He deserves the greater credit when we view him a youth, in a strange land, fond of pleasure, and exposed to every kind of temptation. In 1726, he returned to Philadelphia. He soon obtained employment, and by his prudence and economy, as well as habitual industry, gained a subsistence, and in a very few years increased his property. In this city, he instituted a club for the discussion of political and philosophical questions, which were well calculated to try and improve their minds. These are printed in his works. In 1732, he published " poor Richard's almanack." This is full of prudential maxims, economical hints, and good advice. We see in every page something congenial to the humour of the man. How far such maxims influence the generality of readers, is not easy to say. If they prevent youth from being extravagant or idle, they are useful; but they hang on the lips of some, as an excuse for their avarice. Profusion is not generosity, nor should a prudent man be parsimonious. The wise sayings of " poor Richard," have been repeated, and copied, and printed in many works. They appear in another form, from their author, in a book entitled, " The way to wealth."

Mr. Franklin was chosen master of the post office in Philadelphia in 1737. The year before he had been clerk to the general court. He was employed in much publick business, and in many useful projects. In 1731, he founded the famous library of Philadelphia. In 1738, he improved the police of the city, by organizing companies to secure their property against fire. It is said this was the origin of all the fire clubs which are now in every city. His patriotick zeal was also discovered in the year 1744, when a very serious dispute happened between the proprietary interest, and that of the people, concerning the forces which were to be raised for their common defence. He proposed a method which seemed well calculated to end the dispute. It was a voluntary association; and ten thousand joined in it as subscribers. Other remarkable services might be mentioned which gave Dr. Franklin a high character among philanthropists. But as a philosopher he gained the most notice,

and applause from mankind. He began his " elec-
trical experiments" about the year 1747. These
manifested an inventive genius, and he had all the
activity and perseverance necessary for any investi-
gation. From studying the properties of nature he
discovered a resemblance between lightning and
the electrick fluid. He placed pointed metallick
conductors upon the tops of houses with rods that
went into the ground, that the passing clouds might
discharge their fire, and do no injury to the building. Some physical reasons, and certain réligious
scruples, were at first raised against their use ; but
soon the metallick conductors became common in
North America, and were adopted in other countries.

His other meteorological observations are also
valuable, and are proofs of industry, as well as genius. He could readily turn his mind to any thing
useful, and delighted to make his philosophical experiments subservient to the convenience of common life ; in which he is as much to be praised, as
for enlarging the bounds of science.

Among the writers upon politicks, and the persons who have acted an important part in the revolution of their country, Dr. Franklin has been highly esteemed, and conspicuously distinguished. He
preferred the busy tumult of the world to the " calm
delights of mild philosophy." In 1747, he was chos-
en representative for the city of Philadelphia. In
that assembly he exerted all his influence in opposing the proprietary claims. In 1754, he proposed
a plan for the general government of the colonies,
which did not meet the approbation of the British
court ; nor of several eminent characters on this
side the Atlantick. In 1757, he was sent to England as agent for the province of Pennsylvania, and
he succeeded in his application to the British court,
that the proprietary lands should be taxed for the
publick service. He was also employed in the a-
gency for Jersey, Maryland and Georgia. At this

time he was elected a fellow of the royal society of
London; and received the degree of L L. D. from
several universities. He was a member of all the
celebrated academies of arts and sciences in Europe,
and was also elected president of the philosophical
society in Philadelphia. In 1762, he returned home,
and received thanks for his services; but was again
appointed agent. We read of his conversation with
Mr. Grenville concerning the stamp act, and his
exertions to prevent any act passing in the parliament of Great Britain to raise a revenue from the
colonies. When the stamp act was repealed, he
had more leisure than he had enjoyed for many
years, and spent the time in travelling over several
parts of Europe.

In 1774, Dr. F. was employed by the house
of Massachusetts to present a petition, that the
governour and lieutenant governour might be removed from their offices. According to his own
account, the privy council were not disposed to do
justice to himself, or his cause. Mr. Bollan, who
was agent for the council of Massachusetts, and had
been a lawyer of eminence in this country, desired
to be heard; but was silenced because he was only
agent for the branch which did not join in this prosecution. Finding that Mr. Wedderburne appeared for the governours, he desired to have council;
but at the same time, was willing their lordships
should give a decision merely from the papers without having a word said upon the subject. The business was deferred till another day, and he then appeared with Mr. Dunning and Mr. Lee, who did
all in their power to support the petition. Mr.
Wedderburne on the other hand, threw every kind
of abuse on the house of representatives, and their
agent, mingled with encomiums upon their governours. "The favourite part of his invective,"
says the Dr. "was levelled at your agent, who
stood there the butt of his ribaldry and invective
for near an hour, not a single lord adverting to the

indecency or impropriety of treating a publick mes- senger in so ignominious a manner, who was only as the person delivering your petition, with the con- sideration of which no part of *his* conduct had any concern."* After his return to America, he was chosen a member of Congress. In this body he did not make any great figure. But he was sent in a publick capacity to France, and signed two treaties of alliance and commerce with that nation, one dated Jan. 30, the other Feb. 6, 1778.

He was one of the commissioners who signed the provisional articles of peace in 1783. It was fortu- nate for New England that Mr. Adams and Mr. Jay were with him. Their talents as statesmen, and their particular services at this time saved these parts of the union from poverty and humiliation. This, the best friends of the old sage were obliged to acknowledge.

In 1785, Dr. Franklin returned to Philadelphia, and was appointed president of the supreme execu- tive council.

He was one of the members of the convention who framed the constitution of the United States. He mingled not in the debates, but made a speech at the close of the business, which did not discover his talents as a statesman. It was time for him to retire from publick business. He had arrived at an age when human infirmities increase, and the " ve- ry strength is labour and sorrow." He died, April, 1790, aged 84.

Dr. Franklin never professed any religion. His friend president Stiles pressed him upon the sub- ject, and wished to have him say he was a believer in christianity, but the philosopher evaded the ques- tion. He said that he had been led to think favoura- bly of the sentiments of Dr. Kippis, Dr. Priestley,

---

* Letter to Thomas Cushing, esq. speaker of the house of re- presentatives, Feb. 15, 1774, in Historical Collections, volume iii. See also Dr. Priestley's letter, giving a particular account of Wedderburne's speech, of which he was a hearer.

and others, with whom he had been acquainted in England. Their opinions did not bear the puritanick stamp, and he doubtless respected them more as philosophers than ministers of the gospel.

Dr. Franklin never published any large work; but his various tracts make up three large octavo volumes. It is said that in society he was sententious, but not fluent; a listener rather than a talker; an informing rather than a pleasing companion; impatient of interruption. He often mentioned the custom of the Indians, who remain sometime silent before they give an answer to a question they have heard attentively, unlike some of the politest societies in Europe where a sentence can scarcely be finished without interruption.

He made certain bequests and donations by his will, which discover his peculiarity of temper, and a mind swayed by vanity, as well as under the influence of minute calculation.

His epitaph is an instance of oddity, but is ingenious. He made it to be put on his tombstone.

The body of
BENJAMIN FRANKLIN, printer,
(like the cover of an old book,
its contents torn out,
and stript of its lettering and gilding)
lies here food for worms:
yet the work itself shall not be lost,
but will, as he believed, appear once more
in a new
and more beautiful edition,
corrected and amended
by
THE AUTHOR.

FULLER SAMUEL, one of the worthies who came over to New Plymouth. He was chosen deacon of Mr. Robinson's church, with Mr. Carver, who was afterwards governour of the plantation. As it was determined that the pastor should remain at Leyden, they sent Mr. Brewster, their elder, with the two deacons, who were qualified to instruct the people, and lead in the publick services. Mr. Ful-

ler sailed from Holland, July 21, 1620. He took a
servant boy with him, who died on the passage,
Nov. 6, a few days before they made the land of
Cape Cod.   When gov. Carver died, they chose
another deacon, but Mr. Fuller's services were in
very special demand, both for the souls and bodies
of the people. Beside his duty in the church, which
he was active in performing, he was eminently useful as a surgeon and physician. Nor did he confine his benevolent offices to the inhabitants of New
Plymouth, and to the aboriginals of the country, but
readily gave his assistance to the people of Naumkeake after Mr. Endicot came to that part of Massachusetts Bay. Several of the people died of " scur-
vys and other distempers," and many were subjected to diseases arising from unwholsome diet and
want of proper accommodations.   Having no physician among themselves, it was happy for those
planters that Plymouth could supply them with one
so able as Mr. Fuller, who visited them at the request of Mr. Endicot, and met with great success
in his practice. According to Mr. Prince, he went
there more than once. He says, " gov. Bradford and
Mr. Morton from him, seem to mistake in blend-
ing the several sicknesses at Naumkeake of 1628 and
1629 together, and writing as if Dr. Fuller first
went thither to help in the sickness introduced
there by the ships in 1629 ; whereas by gov. Endicot's letter of May 11, 1629, it appears that Dr.
Fuller had been there to help them, which was
above a month before the ship arrived in 29."
    When he returned from Salem to Plymouth Mr.
Endicot wrote to gov. Bradford a letter of thanks,
speaking highly in praise of the physician, and also
his hearty concurrence with their church in its form
and discipline.   From which it is evident that the
conversation of Dr. Fuller had some effect upon his
religious opinions, for there was a difference of sentiment before this interview, and a jealousy lest the
Plymouth church should exercise a jurisdiction
over the church in Salem.

GAGE THOMAS, governour of Massachusetts, 1774 and 1775, was brother of lord viscount Gage, and an officer of distinction in the British army. He came into America as a lieut. col. of Braddock's forces, and when that unfortunate general was wounded, he, with another officer, carried him off the field. He acquired some credit by this action, because the confusion was so general, and the flight so disorderly, that the body might have been mangled by a savage enemy, or exposed to every kind of indignity. In 1758, Mr. Gage had a colonel's commission. In 1760, after the reduction of Canada, he was governour of Montreal; and the ten succeeding years was commander in chief of the British forces in North America. The greater part of the time, he resided in the city of New York. He paid a visit to Boston in the autumn of 1768, where the 14th and 29th regiments were stationed, with a view to know the state of the town, and to see that proper accommodations were made for the troops. A handsome address from the members of the council was presented to him, in which they say, " it affords a general satisfaction that your excellency has visited the province. Your own inquiries will satisfy you, that though there have been disorders in the town of Boston, some of them did not merit notice, and that such as did, have been magnified beyond the truth." To this address he gave a polite answer; but at the same time wrote to the ministry a bitter invective against the council, the people of the town, and province. His answer to the address of the council is dated Oct. 28; the letter to the ministry, Oct. 30. This letter is totally destitute of that candour, which the people had always connected with the general's character. At the date of it, he had been in town about a fortnight; at which time from his own knowledge and observation, he could not gain such an acquaintance with the character and disposition of the council, and of the people in general, as to authorize him to say so many harsh things concerning them, which at the same time are as unjust, as they are rash and precipitate. The similitude of sentiment in this letter, and the letters of Bernard, leaves no room to doubt whence the matter of it was furnished.

Such are the remarks made by our whig politicians on the general's letter.* It was also observed that, as the general thought proper to step out of his line, and give characters, a regard for the public, and especially for himself should have induced him to give such as were consistent with truth.

In the year 1774, it was his fortune to succeed Hutchinson in the government of Massachusetts; and to command the troops quartered in the province, to force the people into a compliance with unconstitutional and oppressive acts of parliament. If there had been no prejudice imbibed against the man, they could not but feel resentment at having a governour appointed with such authority over them. It is no wonder therefore that their opposition to his administration was so fixed and violent. His polite address and easy manners, however, gained him friends; and it was frequently observed that in good times, he would have made a worthy governour. This might be the case; but the opinion could not be formed by observations upon his managing the affairs of the province. He acted with the advice of men who wished to deprive the people of all their civil privileges, and to make the governour of Massachusetts as despotick as the Dey of one of the Barbary powers. The port bill was under consideration of the Boston town meeting when governour Gage arrived; and it was more particularly the province of the admiral to put this into execution.

But what were the prominent traits of his administration?

* Letters of gov. Bernard, gen. Gage, his majesty's council to the earl of Hillsborough, with an appendix, containing diverse proceedings referred to in said letters.

" He negatived thirteen provincial counsellors chosen at the first election after his arrival.

" Adjourned the court to Salem, that he might reduce them more easily to his arbitrary measures.

" He summoned the mandamus council to their seats, in violation of the provincial charters.

" He attempted to put in execution an act of parliament "for regulating the government," which entirely altered the charter constitution of the province ; and another act, authorizing the governour, in case any person is indicted for murder or any other capital offence in aid of magistracy, &c. to send such person (if the governour approves not of their having a trial in Boston) to any other colony, or to Great Britain to be tried.

" He issued a proclamation, forbidding any of the inhabitants of the province from signing a paper called a solemn league and covenant for the purposes of non-importation and non-consumption of British goods.

" He sent troops to seize the provincial powder in the magazine at Charlestown.

" He tried to prevent the Essex county meeting at Salem ; and ordered troops from the village to assist in dispersing said meeting.

" He broke up the ground on Boston neck, for entrenchments and fortifications, which was an impediment to passengers going to, and coming from, the country towns.

" By a proclamation he discharged the members of the general court, to deprive the province of a representative body.

" He sent troops to Marshfield and Salem ; and attempted to seize cannon and other military stores.

" The several avenues to the town of Boston he ordered to be guarded by centinels from his troops, and reduced the town to the state of a garrison.

" He altered the terms of agreement with the town, as a condition of the citizens removing out of it, after they had complied with their part of the condition; and detained articles he had previously promised should be removed by the owners, and caused many impediments in the manner of their removal.

" In the month of June, 1775, he proclaimed Massachusetts to be in a state of rebellion, the provincial congress having in the month preceding *renounced* the government of gen. Gage. In his proclamation he proscribed the patriots, S. Adams and Hancock.

" Under his orders Bunker Hill battle was fought, and Charlestown burnt," &c. &c.

All these transactions took place during his short administration.

Having obtained leave to depart from America, he sailed from Boston, October 10th, 1775, and passed the remainder of his days in retirement. We hear of no peculiar honours conferred upon him in his own country; and here, if men did not feel an abhorrence of his conduct, it was because they viewed him with contempt.

GAY EBENEZER, D. D. pastor of the first church in Hingham, was born in Dedham, of parents, who descended from the first settlers of that ancient town. He made early progress in literature, and was sent from the town school to Harvard College, where he was graduated, 1714. He was ordained over the church in Hingham, 1718. When he was a young man he obtained the notice of gov. Burnet, who was a good judge of characters, and particularly fond of men of letters. It is a saying of his, handed down from the last generation, that among the clergy of Massachusetts, Mr. Bradstreet of Charlestown, and Mr. Gay of Hingham had the most erudition. One of these left no publication as evidence of his talents. The other printed many sermons, chiefly occasional. During the long life he passed on earth, very few works, except sermons, were emitted from the presses of New England. What encouragement could be given to talents in a country just rising into notice? Many a flower has dropped its leaves in this American wilderness, which, transplanted in some fair garden, would have grown and flourished. The clergy of this country were formerly very dependent, though treated with great respect by their people. They had to labour hard in the fields of this world, as well as to do their duty to God's husbandry, that souls " might not wither, but have their fruit in love and good works." They were, however, happy and contented with their lot : though not in easy or affluent circumstances they were above want. If they had a thirst for knowledge, they suffered, because few men had libraries, nor were many books imported upon any subject but law, physick and divinity. If no professional men were in their parishes, they could not gain much information. Dr. Gay was as well situated as most of his brethren ; and he had great resources in his own mind. Among his parochial connections were several gentlemen in conspicuous stations, and capable of improving the minds of each other. When he was 85 years old, he preached upon this text, Joshua, xiv. 10, marking the number of his years—" I am this day fourscore and five years old." He says, sixty three years have I spent in the work of the ministry among you. One hundred and forty six years ago, your forefathers came with their pastor and settled in this place. I am the third in the pastorate of this church which has not been two years vacant. Scarce any parish but hath had more in the office in the same space of time. The people of this town have been steady to their own ministers living to old age ; have not been given to change, nor with itching ears have heaped to themselves teachers. I bless God who disposed my lot among a people, with whom I have lived in great peace eleven years longer than either of my predecessors. I have only to wish that my labours had been as profitable as they have been acceptable to them. I retain a grateful sense of the kindnesses (injuries I remember none) I have received from them. While I have reaped of their carnal things to my comfortable subsistence, it has been my great concern to sow unto them spiritual things, which might spring up in a harvest of eternal blessings. That their affections to me, as their pastor, have continued from fathers to children, and children's children, hath been thankfully observed by me; and should have been improved as an advantage and incentive to do them (in return of love for love) all possible good. It is but little I can do now in the work to which I am kept up so late in the evening of my days," &c. This sermon is styled the " old man's calender ;" and is a very interesting discourse, though not equal in composition to those he printed in younger life. " His election sermon, 1745 ;" the sermon " before the convention of ministers, 1746," and at " Dudleian lecture, 1759," have been much celebrated. The funeral sermon " upon Mr. Hancock," father of the late governour, and two upon " the death of Dr. Mayhew" are among the best occasional discourses.

Mr. Gay received his diploma of doctor in divinity, in 1785, from the university where he had his education.

This great and good man died, Sabbath day, March 8, 1787, in the 91st year of his age, and 69th of his ministry. The vigour of his mind continued to this remarkable age. He was preparing to go through the labours of the day when he died. " His indulgent Lord, as it has been well expressed, " when he was about to enter upon the service of his sanctuary here below, called him to the more sublime enjoyments of his temple above."*

* His publications, beside those mentioned above were, a sermon at the ordination of Mr. Joseph Green, May 12, 1725.; there was a high encomium upon this sermon by Mr. Foxcroft of Boston; a sermon upon the arrival of gov. Belcher, 1730; a sermon at the ordination of Ebenezer Gay, jun. at Suffield, 1742;

GEE JOSHUA, rev. minister of the second church in Boston, was colleague with the famous Cotton Mather. He was born in Boston, the son of a reputable tradesman, and graduated at Harvard College, A. D. 1717; ordained in November, 1723. His talents were not of the popular kind, though he was fervent in spirit, zealous in promoting the great revival of religion in 1742, 3. His genius was profound; his learning considerable; his theological attainments very superiour. His sermons are well composed and argumentative, and they, who were intimate with him, speak of his talents for conversation as very uncommon. He indulged a kind of literary indolence, and preferred to converse rather than to write. Yet he never delivered in the pulpit any thing like an extemporaneous address; and was reluctant to print his discourses, when urged, because he must finish them with some labour. He was bigotted in his opinions, which were in favour of high *supralapsarian* doctrines. He was somewhat bitter in controversy. This appears by his attack upon the convention, which gave a testimony against the errors prevailing in 1745, and the spirit which had been too much encouraged, when itinerant preachers and fanatical priests disturbed the churches. His passions led him to imprudence in his ministerial conduct. During his ministry a divi-

of Dr. Mayhew at Boston, 1747; Mr. Derby at Scituate, 1751; Mr Carpenter at Swanzey, 1753; Mr. Rawson at Yarmouth, 1755; Mr. Bunker Gay at Hinsdale, 1763; Mr. Gannet, Cumberland, Nova Scotia, 1768; a sermon at the annual thanksgiving, 1770.

In a note of Dr. Shute's sermon at his funeral, is an account of the ministers of Hingham.—Rev. Peter Hobart, who came from England with his church, was the first minister, and settled, 1635, and died, January 20, 1679. Rev. John Norton, ordained, Nov 27, 1678; died, October 3, 1716. Vacant one year and six months. (During this time the church invited Mr. Samuel Fiske to be their pastor, who gave an answer in the negative, expecting then to be settled in the New South, Boston.) June 11, 1718, Dr. Gay was ordained. Three ministers in 152 years, and through the whole of the time, vacant hardly a year and six months.

sion was made in the church : nearly one half separated with his colleague, (Mr. Samuel Mather,)
and built a church in the neighbourhood, where the
latter continued till his death in 1785. Mr. Gee
died, 1748, May 22, having been consumptive several years.

His printed discourses were, a small volume upon Luke xiii. 24 ; a funeral sermon on Dr. C. Mather, &c. He also printed observations on the convention of ministers, beside several political pamphlets.

Mr. Gee married the daughter of the rev. Mr.
Rogers of Portsmouth. She was a most amiable
and accomplished woman, She died, 1730, aged
29. A beautiful sermon was printed upon the occasion by rev. P. Thacher, the only discourse that
great man ever published, except the election sermon, 1726.*

GIBBONS EDWARD, major general, was one of
the first planters of Massachusetts Bay. He was
one of those enterprising young men, who settled
at Mount Wollaston, but whether he joined with
Morton in all his mad pranks, we are not able to
say. Most probably he went to Salem for the sake
of better company. He was at the ordination of
Mr. Higginson, and it affected him so much to see
a church formed, and a whole congregation wor-
shipping God in the beauties of holiness, that he expressed a desire to join with them. They chose to
have some evidence of his sincerity, but encouraged
his good intentions. He went afterwards to Bos-

* This biographical sketch of Mr. Gee was written before Dr.
Chauncy's list of famous men was published. The Dr. shows
much candour to a man who in his writings and conversation endeavoured to injure his character,and was bitter against every one
who had liberal views of christianity. One observation ought
perhaps to be mentioned, which the late Dr. Chauncy often made,
and which is to be found in a letter to an eminent correspondent,
"that it was happy Mr. Gee had an indolent turn ; for with such
fiery zeal and such talents, he would have made continual contention in the churches.

ton, joined Mr. Wilson's church, and became one of the most useful, active and worthy men in the colony. In the year 1644, when the militia was organized, he was chosen commanding officer of the regiment in Suffolk. There was a regiment for every county; one in Suffolk, one in Middlesex, one in Essex, and one in Northfolk, which included the towns of Haverhill, Salisbury, Hampton, &c. on the banks of the Merrimack, or beyond it. The chief officer instead of having a colonel's commission, was styled only sergeant major. A major general, was appointed over the whole, as related in the life of Mr. Dudley, who was the first in the office; then, Mr. Endicot, and the third was major Gibbons. In Johnson's annals of Massachusetts for 1644, after mentioning the several regiments, over each of which " the commander is only a sergeant major," the first chosen to the office, says he, was major Gibbons, now major general, a man of resolute spirit, bold as a lion, being wholly tutored up in New England discipline, very generous and forward to promote all military matters, his forts are well contrived, and batteries strong and in good repair, &c.*

* Johnson's annals, are continued to the year 1652. The book is called " wonder working providences of Sion's Saviour in New England." Mr. Prince discovered their author to be Mr. Johnson of Woburn. The book contains much valuable information of the early settlement of Massachusetts. And he is very particular in narrating the organization of the militia in 1644. As the book is scarce and curious it may gratify some persons to know, who were officers in the first regiment in Suffolk, which shall be given in his style and manner.

After speaking of major Gibbons having his forts in good repair, his artillery well mounted and cleanly kept, half cannon, culverins and sakers, as also field pieces of brass very ready for service, he says, " his own company, led by capt lieut. Sarag, are very complete in arms, and many of them disciplined in the military garden, beside their ordinary trainings ; the captains under him are capt. Humphry Atherton of the band in Dorchester ; a very lively courageous man, with his stout and valiant lieut. Clap, strong for the truth ; of the band of Roxbury, capt. Pritchard and ensign Johnson ; of the band of Weymouth, capt. Perkins, and

Gen. Gibbons was not only high in military rank, but was also one of the assistants ; to which place he was elected in 1644, and continued many years. In 1645, he was sent, at the head of the New England forces, against the sons of Canonicus, who did not inherit their father's prudence, but were oppressive and arbitrary, and caused contentions among the neighbouring tribes. They were, however, so frightened at the preparations of war, when they found the white people in hostile array, that they sent a certain number of their chief nobility to the commissioners of the united colonies, who were then sitting at Boston, to treat concerning a peace. The commissioners took advantage of their situation, and made them pay a part of the charges which such preparations had occasioned ; and to give four of their sons, for hostages, till they had paid what was demanded.

Major general Gibbons was in the office till he died, and was succeeded by major Sedgwick. We would observe, however, that this high commander was chosen annually by the freemen, while the other military officers were chosen for life. The

his proper and active lieut. Torrey ; of the band of Hingham, capt. Allen ; of the band of Dedham, capt. Eleazer Lusher, one of a nimble and active spirit, strongly affected to the ways of truth ; of the band of Braintree, capt. William Tyng ; these belong to the regiment of Suffolk." He then goes on to describe the regiment of Essex under sergeant major Robert Sedgwick, stout and active in all the feats of war, nursed up in London's artillery, and furthered with sixteen years experience in New England's exact theory, besides the help of a very good head piece, being a frequent instructor of our artillery men, &c. He says likewise, " that surveyor general Johnson, one well qualified for the work, overlooked the whole, and often reminded the general court to keep a good supply ;" that several persons contributed largely to provide ammunition ; the rev. Dr. Wilson gave generously a thousand pounds, &c. that a castle was built on an island upon a passage into the bay ; as the country had no lime, but what is burnt with oyster shells, it fell to decay a few years after. It was built again at the expence of the six towns, the rest of the country furnishing a small matter towards it. The first commander was one capt. Davenport, &c.

people assembled once a year to elect a governour, lieut. governour, assistants and major general. Very few alterations were made in their arrangements till officers were appointed by the crown, and the old charter taken away.

GOOKIN DANIEL, major general, was at first a planter in Virginia, but preferred to spend his days in New England, where he found a people more congenial to his views, principles and manners. He became a freeman of Massachusetts in 1644, and had a captain's commission in the regiment of Middlesex. "He had formerly been a Kentish soldier, and a very forward man to advance marshal discipline, and withal the truths of Christ."*

In 1652, he was chosen assistant, and was as ready to execute justice and maintain peace in the province, as to fight the enemies of his country. In 1656, he left New England, and visited Cromwell's court, who employed him to persuade the inhabitants of Masssachusetts to remove and settle Jamaica, which had lately been taken from the crown of Spain. In this he met with no success. In 1662, he was appointed one of the licensers of the printing press in Cambridge. He was of the high republican party in politicks, and stood firm to the old charter, unwilling to yield the rights and liberties of the people, when they were required to do it, by the arbitrary measures of king Charles II. He would rather face the storm and risque every danger. He gave his reasons in writing, which were lodged in the publick records. Mr. Gookin was as conspicuous for his piety as his morals. He set a high value upon the religious freedom, which the first settlers enjoyed, and for which they had left their own country to dwell in an American wilderness. Perhaps, he was too rigid in his notions; perhaps, his religious and political sentiments were tinctured with party spirit; but his lively and active turn stimulated him to noble and generous ac-

* Johnson.

tions. We ought always to distinguish between enthusiasm and fanaticism. The one will stimulate a warrior to destroy villages, and even the lives of men; the other will rouse the patriot, and excite the philanthropist or christian to do benevolent actions. Such a zealous, such an upright magistrate was gen. Gookin. In 1675, he boldly stepped forward to support the cause of the praying Indians, whom the people hated and despised, merely because they were Indians; and whom the magistrates were ready to persecute even unto death. Major Gookin endeavoured to calm the ebullition of their passions. He was assisted by Mr. Eliot; and they both suffered every thing from the obloquy and scorn of those, who ought to have respected their good intentions, and who were convinced afterwards that they acted a wise and honest part.

Major Gookin had been superintendant of all the Indians, who had submitted to the provincial government. He knew more about them than all the other magistrates. So far from joining in the war against the English, many of them were objects of pity, and some were brought into distress by their friendship for them, and attachment to christianity.

Mr. Gookin was the last major general under the old charter. This post of honour was continued under the charter of William and Mary; but the officer was not chosen by the freemen. After Dudley, Endicott and Gibbons had adorned the station, major Sedgwick was chosen. Major Atherton succeeded him; then Daniel Dennison, John Leverett and Daniel Gookin.

Our worthy magistrate appears very respectable as an author. A considerable work of his is published in the first volume of the collections of the Massachusetts historical society. It is a very particular account of the Indians in New England, with a biographical sketch of the writer from an accurate pen, to which we are indebted for several facts. He had prepared a much larger work, the history of New England, which was left in mss. but which probably is lost.

Gen. Gookin died in 1687, an old man, whose days were filled with usefulness. He left no estate ; his widow was in such indigent circumstances, that Mr. Eliot solicited the hon. Mr. Boyle to bestow upon her ten pounds.* He left a number of children. His eldest son, Daniel, who graduated in 1669, was minister at Sherburne, and a preacher to the Indians at Natick. His second son, Nathaniel, who graduated, 1675, was minister of Cambridge, and fellow of Harvard College. He died, August 7, 1692, in the 34th year of his age, and tenth of his ministry. Mr. G. minister of Hampton, was the son of the minister of Cambridge. He was graduated, 1703. He also had a son, Nathaniel, who graduated, 1731, who was settled in the same town, in a parish called North Hill. And a grandson capt. Daniel Gookin, who was an officer in the American army during the revolutionary war. *Collections of Historical Society. Hutchinson.*

GORGES SIR FERDINANDO, governour of the fort and island of Plymouth in Devonshire, and one

---

* The following extract from the " Journal of the commissioners of the united colonies," shows Mr. G. received something during his life from the corporation de propag. fide. It is a letter dated, London, March 7, 1663, 4.

" We do much rejoice that captaine Gookin has proued soe usefull an instrument amongst the Indians as in gouerning theire children in learning ; and as many other thinges of like nature which wee highly approve off as alsoe of youer allowance of 15 pounds made to him towards his expences the yeare past ; and wee are uery willing that you should make the same unto him another yeare ; and wee are glad to heare that the Indian youthes at Cambridge have made so good proficiency in learning and wee are not without hopes but that the Lord will use them as instruments in his hand to preach and promote the gospel of Christ amongst their own countrymen. To this end and for the better carrying on thereof wee desire that care may be taken that they retaine theire native language ; and as for those five Indian youthes att inferior schooles wee desire that all incouragement may be given them according to theire capassities and attainments in learning, &c. Hazard's Collections, vol. ii. page 492.

of the first and chief promoters of the New England plantations. He was the intimate friend of sir Walter Raleigh. They were both men of enterprizing genius, with a similar turn for adventure, and promoted some of the most important voyages, which never would have been undertaken without their assistance. In 1604, Gorges was appointed governour of Plymouth. Obtaining a patent from king James, of making settlements in America, he fitted out a ship, August, 1606, for discovery, which was seized and carried to Spain. The next year he, and sir John Popham, sent over two ships, with 100 men, who landed at the mouth of Kennebeck river on a peninsula, where they built a fort. When the ships departed, only 45 persons were left. It was the month of December, and they had to bear the cold of a North American winter. They had but a poor shelter from the storm, and to add to their misfortune, their store house was burnt, with a large part of their provisions. Other melancholy circumstances concurred to make them sick of the place, and they left it with disgust. This was the first settlement in New England. It was begun and ended in less than a year. Gorges was not discouraged ; but with other associates, after the death of sir John Popham, who contributed the most to help the first adventure, he planned several voyages to New England, which were executed with more or less success. He probably would have been discouraged, if the church at Leyden had not formed a settlement at New Plymouth ; but this gave a new animation to his spirits, and strengthened him in his schemes. In 1623, a settlement was begun at Piscataqua, in which sir Ferdinando Gorges was concerned, and this led him into speculations that were afterwards injurious to the people of Massachusetts ; for he joined with Mason in certain projects, equally detrimental to their freedom and interest. They endeavoured to bring the whole country, from St. Croix to Maryland, under one form of government, and because Massachusetts charter stood in their way they tried to get it revoked. This was about the year 1635. A quo warranto was issued against the charter and order for the establishment of the general government, but the commotions in Great Britain prevented it being completed. Gorges obtained in 1639 a confirmation of his own grant, which was styled the province of Maine, of which he was made lord palatine. He was on the royal side in the civil war, but died soon after it commenced. *Belknap.*

GORGES ROBERT, son of sir Ferdinando, was active and enterprising, but had not the perseverance of his father. He obtained of the council a patent of a tract of land in the north east of Massachusetts, 30 miles long, and 10 in breadth, and had a commission to be lieut. general and governour of New England. He came to Plymouth, 1623. This was the first essay for a general government; but he met with so little assistance that he returned to England in the course of the year. Hutchinson says he conveyed his title to sir William Brierton, who afterwards became an adventurer in the Massachusetts corporation.

GORGES FERDINANDO, esq. son of John Gorges, and grandson of the governor of Plymouth, was heir to the estate and title of his grandfather. He says, that he was appointed by his grandfather with col. Norton and others to settle a plantation upon " the river Agamentico ;" and that they obtained a patent of 12000 acres on the east side, and then 12000 to the west, and that " they had hopes of a happy success." His controversy with the government of Massachusetts is rather a subject for the history of the country, than a biographical sketch of the man. When Charles II. came to the throne, he expected to have no more dispute about his claim, calculating upon the friendship of the family to the royal cause, and the enmity of the king to the New England puritans. But while he met with

court favour, he found himself involved in difficulties with the settlers of Agamenticus, and that instead of receiving large profits from the possessions
of these lands, they were a bill of cost continually,
beside other discouragement from the depredations
of the savages. He was glad therefore to sell his
whole interest in the province of Maine, which he
did for 1250 pound sterling. It included the counties of York, Cumberland and Oxford.

Mr. Gorges published a book concerning New
England. His grandfather compiled it, but it was
much enlarged by him : it is entitled, " *America
painted to the life ;* a true history of the original
undertakings, of the advancement of plantations into those parts, with a perfect relation of our English discoveries, shewing their beginning, progress
and continuance from the year 1628 to 1658, declaring the forms of their government, policies, religion, manners, customs, military discipline, wars
with Indians, commodities of the countries, a description of their towns, havens, the increase of their
trading, with the names of their governours and
magistrates, written by sir Ferdinando Gorges,
knight, governour of the fort and island of Plymouth, in Devonshire ; and published by his grand-
child, F. Gorges, esq. who hath much enlarged it
and added several curious descriptions of his own."
small 4to, Lond. 1658. This is a curious and
scarce book. Hutchinson and Belknap have made
great use of it.

GORHAM NATHANIEL, esq. was born in Charlestown, May 27, 1738. He had the advantage of a
good school education, and possessing uncommon
talents, he always appeared to advantage in company with literary men. He settled in business at the
place of his nativity, but seemed to be formed more
for publick life than to succeed in mercantile pursuits. He was chosen representative for Charlestown in 1771, and every year till the commencement of the revolutionary war. He was a very

assiduous attendant on the house of representa‑
tives, was a leader in all their debates, and pre‑
served independence enough openly to dissent
from measures, which he disapproved. On this
account he did not escape the obloquy of some
ignorant, narrow‑minded persons, whose zeal was
only the ebullition of their passions, and who con‑
founded all who had any moderation, with those
who were unfriendly to the cause of liberty. He
spent some years in retirement; but returned to
Charlestown in 1779, and was again sent to the gen‑
eral court. The same year he was elected a dele‑
gate of the convention, which formed the present
constitution of this commonwealth. In 1788, he
was chosen a senator for Middlesex county. He
also served his country with diligence and respec‑
tability as a magistrate, and was several years judge
of the court of common pleas. In 1784, he was ap‑
pointed one of the house of representatives, and being
delegated by this state to be a member of congress,
was elected president of that honourable body.

He was one of the convention which formed the
present constitution of the United States, and he ob‑
tained a high reputation among the southern mem‑
bers for his knowledge and integrity. He stood high
with all parties for his wisdom and prudence as well
as skill in managing debates. He was on this ac‑
count one of the most influential members of the
state convention which adopted it. He died, June
11, 1796. Dr. Thatcher preached a funeral ser‑
mon; the town also appointed an orator to deliver
an eulogy upon their deceased friend, and most use‑
ful fellow citizen. In compliance with their request,
Dr. Welch paid this tribute to his remains; and
the town testified their acknowledgments, by a vote
of thanks, and by publishing the discourses.

GORTON SAMUEL, the head of a sect who made
much noise in New England, came to Boston in
1636. He had been a citizen of London, but was
too unsteady to remain in one place, or was stimu‑

lated to change his situation for the sake of spreading his wild fantastick notions of religion. He did
not give any particular offence while he remained in
Boston, or was artful in explaining his sentiments ; for those who inquired could not determine
whether they were heretical or not. But he soon
went to Plymouth where he acted the same part, as
Wheelwright and Mrs. Hutchinson did in Massachusetts. Not being permitted to stay in the old
colony, he went to Rhode Island in 1638: but even
in this land of freedom, he rendered himself obnoxious, and, by order of the governour, Mr. Coddington, was imprisoned and whipped. In 1640, he
went to Providence, where he was treated by Roger Williams with the greatest humanity, though
he disliked his principles, and blamed his conduct. He set down in this section of the country, and mixing with others, who were fond of
novelty, they fixed at Patuxet, where they not only
indulged their spiritual Quixotism, but were very
troublesome as neighbours. A charge was brought
against them that they seized the estates of people,
who held them in quiet possession. The governour
of Massachusetts ordered Gorton to answer to the
complaint, and he refused to obey the summons because he was out of their jurisdiction. He treated
the message in the most contemptuous manner ;
upon which he was apprehended and brought to
Boston. It is said he had a fair trial, and that he
was then banished the colony. But he thought
othewise about the trial. And Mr. Hutchinson
says the sentence was cruel. Gorton was ordered to be confined to Charlestown ; there to be
kept at work, and wear such bolts and irons as
might prevent his escape.

After being confined one winter, he, with others,
was banished the jurisdiction. They obtained an order
from the king, August 19, 1644, that they should
peaceably enjoy their lands, which were incorporated by the name of Providence plantations in Narra-

ganset bay. They named the chief town Warwick, in honour to the earl of Warwick, who was a great friend to them. Gorton was again in Boston, 1648, and threatened with punishment; but he soon after returned to his plantation, where he lived to a great age. He wrote a letter, June 30, 1669, to Mr. Morton, author of New England's memorial, accusing him of the grossest slanders in the account which he gives of him and his followers, which is printed by Mr. Hutchinson. It is evident that he was not so bad a man as his enemies represented; that his principles of religion were different from those notions generally ascribed to this sect; and that so far from being illiterate he was able to write well. From this letter it appears, that he was a preacher, and that he understood the scriptures in their original language. We ought never to judge any man's opinions from the consequences we draw from them. This was the case wherever the Gortonists were described. But they were able to give their reasons, which we should hear before we condemn them.

GOSNOLD BARTHOLOMEW, an Englishman, discovered a promontory on the American coast, in lat. 42, to which he gave the name of Cape Cod, from the multitude of fishes he caught. He landed on several islands, and named them Elizabeth isles. He built a small fort; but the same year returned to England. This was in the year 1602. It was the first voyage to this part of America, since called New England. Josselyn speaks of the first colony of Plymouth in 1602. He must mean this attempt to settle the islands in the bay, upon which Gosnold landed, but could not persuade his men to stay.

GREEN SAMUEL, the first printer in New England, was an inhabitant of Cambridge, and kept his press in that town above forty years, and then moved to Boston. We are indebted to the rev. Mr. Joseph Glover for this great blessing to the country, a printing press. It is not likely our fathers would have been so soon favoured with it, had he not exerted himself to serve them. In the year 1638, he took his voyage to these plantations, but died on his passage. He brought out with him one Daye, a printer, and every thing necessary in the typographical art. The first thing which was printed was the freeman's oath; the next was Pierce's almanack; and then the New England psalms. Great pains have been taken to procure one of the first edition of these psalms, but without success.* It is not probable that one remains. We know but little about Daye; but we know that Mr. Green had this press in 1639, and every book that was published had his name in the title page. When he was employed to print the Indian bible by the society for propagating the gospel, they sent over Marmeduke Johnson as his assistant, whose character was very much against him, being an idle, dissipated youth, though he afterwards set up for himself, and did very well in his business.† Mr. Green was a printer in Boston the latter end of the century, and lived only a few years after his removal. He was a man of piety, the strictest probity, of good abilities in his profession, and considerable of a literary character.

Green Bartholomew, the son of Samuel Green, who succeeded him in his line of business,

* These psalms have gone through twenty three editions.

† It pleased the honored corporation to send over one Marmeduke Johnson a printer to attend the worke on condition as they will enform you; whoe hath carryed heer unworthyly of which hee hath bine openly convicted and sencured in some of our courts although as yett noe execution of sentence against him; peculiar favour haueing been showed him with respect to the corporation that sent him ouer; but notwithstanding all patience and lenitie used towards him, he hath proued himself very idle and nought and absented himself from the worke more than half a yeare at one tyme; for want of whose assistance the printer by his agreement with us was to have the allowance of 21 pound, the which is to be defalcated out of his sallary in England by the honoured corporation there," &c.—Letter from the commissioners in Boston to the hon. Robert Boyle, Sept. 10, 1662. Hazard's Collections.

emitted from his press the first newspaper in America. Several of the first numbers are on the files of the historical society. It was called the Boston Newsletter. The first number is dated, April 24, 1704. It was continued by him during life. Mr. Green also published another paper, called the Weekly Newsletter, which was afterward combined with the other, and then it was styled the Boston Weekly Newsletter. He died in December, 1733, in the 65th year of his age. " He was one of the deacons of the old south church; printer to his excellency the governour and council, and to the honourable house of representatives; and generally known and esteemed as a humble and exemplary christian, one who had much of that primitive christianity in him, which has always been the distinguishing glory of New England."

His descendants were printers in Boston till the revolution. The present printers of that name in Connecticut are of his posterity. Daye's press is said to be still in use in Vermont. A printer now in Boston says he has worked at it. This seems incredible; perhaps a certain part is kept as a curiosity.

GREEN JOSEPH was born in Boston, 1706; received the rudiments of learning under Mr. Williams, the preceptor of the south grammar school; and was graduated at Harvard College in 1726.

He was a man of wit and humour, a celebrated poet, classical scholar, and writer of fugitive pieces. When he left college he turned his attention to mercantile affairs, and, by his diligence in business, acquired a handsome property. He was respectable for a very comprehensive knowledge of things relating to commerce, and for his integrity, punctuality, humanity and generosity. To these virtues he added good breeding, politeness and elegance. He was not fond of high life, nor of large companies; but among a few friends would indulge in social mirth, and by his original strokes of humour, and pleasant vein of satire, afford peculiar gratification to those who enjoyed his society. His wit, taste, and learning might have connected him with persons eminent for their influence in the community, or given him any distinction an ambitious man would seek after; but he never would accept of any publick office, preferring a retired situation, and the happiness of domestic scenes. In 1774, when an act passed in the parliament, depriving Massachusetts of their charter, a new list of counsellors was appointed by mandamus, among the most respectable of whom was the hon. Joseph Green, esq. but he declined accepting the place. As soon as he received the summons from gov. Gage, he went to Salem and gave in his resignation.

Of the poetical pieces he published, the "elegy on Mr. Old Tenor," and the "satire upon the procession of Free Masons," have passed through many editions, and are still read with keen sensations of delight. During the *Whitefieldian* controversy, there was a club of sentimentalists who spake what they thought, and wrote what they pleased: though the authors were not always distinguished, as the pamphlets were emitted from the press, it was easy to conjecture what parts Mr. Green composed, especially if a line of poetry was introduced. The same circle of literary friends took a zealous part in politicks. They began by attacking the administration of gov. Belcher. Every speech he made was put into rhyme; and many parts of his conduct exposed to ridicule. They could joke in prose and verse.*

During the administration of Shirley, they engaged in a more serious opposition, not so much against the governour, as the general court who introduced the *excise* bills, which was very obnoxious

* Siste Viator, here lies one,
Whose life was whim, whose soul was pun;
And if you go too near his herse
He'll joke you both in prose and verse.
　　　　　Epitaph made for Mr. Green, 1743.

to the people. But Shirley did not sign it. In the controversy with Great Britain previous to the revolution, most of these gentlemen, who had written so freely against arbitrary measures in their own government, joined the party of loyalists, conceiving that the high toned conduct of the whigs would bring ruin upon their country. Mr. Green left Boston in the year 1775; passed the rest of his days in England, and there died.

It is the wish of many that his poems and prose writings, which are now scattered, might be collected, and put into a volume.

GREEN NATHANIEL, major general, was a native of Warwick, in the government of Rhode Island, where he lived and was engaged in commercial pursuits till the commencement of the American war. He was proprietor of the iron works in that town, where the manufacture of this article was carried on to much advantage. He had not a college education, but was highly esteemed among the sensible men of that colony. He was a man of more than common sagacity in business, early famed for political wisdom, and inclined to the study of military tacticks. Having arrived at considerable proficiency in this science, and being a good parade officer, the governour selected him to command the first troops which were raised to resist Great Britain after the battle of Lexington. While the army was at Cambridge he commanded a brigade, stationed on Winter Hill. He led part of the army to New York, when head quarters were moved in 1776, and made a conspicuous figure in all the succeeding campaigns. His actions make some splendid pages in the history of the American revolution. In 1776, he was appointed major general. The American army met with a series of defeats, and were in a manner driven through the Jersies by lord Cornwallis, who was as superiour in numbers, as in discipline. At this time gen. Lee was taken, which struck the people with the greatest sorrow, as they had placed great

confidence in his military skill; but it answered one
good purpose at the time, for it brought our own
officers into more notice, and whatever credit they
obtained was undivided.   The battle of Trenton
was gained by the American generals, Washington,
Sullivan and Green.   They succeeded also in
gaining advantage of the British forces by making
a rapid march to Princeton, which gained them immortal honour, while it appeared the only way of
saving the army.   " When we lay at Trenton, after
the crossing the Delaware a second time, the enemy advanced from Princeton with a force nearly
double to ours.   Our outguards were repulsed, and
the enemy entered one part of the town, while we
remained in possession of the other.   There was
now only a small branch of a river between us over
which there was a bridge; this, though well secured, would have been of little advantage to us, as the
stream was fordable in every part.   Our army was
drawn up in order of battle, waiting their approach.
But the day being far spent, a stop was put to their
making the attack that night.   This was the most
critical moment our bleeding country ever beheld.
The fate of this extensive continent was suspended
by a single thread.   Happy for us, and for unborn
millions that we had a general who knew how to
take advantage of every thing, and by a masterly
manœuvre frustrated the designs of the enemy.   A
general battle would have ruined us.   But the
march to Princeton proved the salvation of the
country."* In both these engagements gen. Green
distinguished himself; as he did afterwards in the
battle of Brandywine and Germantown in the fall
of 1777.   In 1778, he commanded the right wing
of the army at the battle of Monmouth.   His conduct that day gave much pleasure to gen. Washington, who had been very much chagrined at the
misbehaviour of gen. Lee.   That famous officer had
been exchanged; he had received every honour this
country could bestow upon him; but from this day

* Major Shaw's mss.

he lost their confidence and esteem. He demanded a court martial, and was disgraced. Gen. Green was one of the court, whose attachment to him, previously to this, had been very strong.

It shows the consequence of gen. Green in the army of the United States, that, while he acted as quarter master general, he did every kind of military service. He was better qualified, on account of his activity and mercantile ideas, to provide for the army, than any other man; but such an officer could not be spared from the field. And he would not accept of the place of quarter master general, except he retained his right to command in action. His military skill and prudence were manifested in drawing off the American army from Rhode Island, when the French fleet left the harbour. This happened, August, 1778. It was a time of great expectation : but the hopes of the people were cut off, and the military sensibility of the soldiers much wounded. Had the army been supported according to promise ; had the French fleet, or our militia remained with them, they would in all probability have taken the island.

When major Andre was taken, October, 1780, gen. Green was president of the court martial which tried and condemned him.

We are in the next place to view our general as commander of the southern section of the army. He there reaped the greatest laurels, and reflected as much lustre upon his country as upon himself. The success of our arms from January, 1781, when the battle of Cowpens gave a new turn to affairs in South Carolina, to the conclusion of the war, may, in a great measure, be imputed to his wise measures for removing difficulties among the people, conciliating their affections, and stimulating their exertions against the common foe. Great credit is due to Morgan, who fought at Cowpens. This victory was of infinite advantage to the commander in chief. But he discovered his own wisdom and virtue in

making use of the best talents in his army. And
when he had made preparations for a general engagement, he boldly met lord Cornwallis, fought a
regular battle, near Guildford court house, and was
near gaining a victory. Had the militia stood firm,
like the soldiers of the army, the British troops must
have retreated. Lord Cornwallis acknowledged it
was a " hard fought action," and that the American
army behaved admirably well. They lost one of
their best officers, col. Webster of the guards, and
many of their officers as well as soldiers fell. The
wounded were left to the care of the humane. Neither Green nor Cornwallis could remain upon the
spot, but were under the necessity of abandoning the
hospital. These unfortunate men found friends. A
body of quakers were in the neighbourhood : to
them gen. Green recommended the sick and the
wounded, acquainting them that he also was of their
religion, which required them to perform every
kind office, especially to strangers. To the honour
of these men be it spoken, that they did every thing
necessary for their ease and comfort. Gen. Green
afterwards attempted to reduce the fort at Camden,
where lord Rawdon commanded. His lordship was
brave, sallied out, and a battle was fought, 25th
April ; but Green saw fit to retreat. He lost in the
action about the same number as fell on the side of
the British troops. It had this effect to make lord
Rawdon quit his post.

In May our general began a siege of fort Ninety
six. He made an attack upon the garrison, and
was repulsed with the loss of 150 men ; in consequence of which he retreated over the Saluda. In
this gloomy situation, when he was advised to leave
the state, and retire with the remaining forces to
Virginia, he replied, I will recover the country, or
die in the attempt. We learn this from Dr. Ramsay's history of the revolution in South Carolina,
one of the first and best works of that distingushed
writer. He enters into a minute description of the

battles fought in that state, and gives a just account
of all the proceedings of the southern army.   On
the 19th of September Green made an attack upon
the enemy at Eutaw springs.   In this engagement,
as we are informed by the author above mentioned,
the American army lost 500, the British 1100 men.
The congress presented gen. Green with a British
standard, and a gold medal emblematical of his success, " for his wise, decisive and magnanimous conduct in the action at Eutaw springs ; in which, with
an inferior force, he obtained a most signal victory." The historian informs us that during this time,
there was a plot laid by certain mutinous characters,
among his own troops, to deliver up to the enemy
this brave and fortunate commander, which was
providentially discovered.   All the very active operations of the army were over in the beginning of
1782.   In October, 1781, lord Cornwallis, with
his army at Yorktown, surrendered.   The rumour
was, that the city of Charleston was to be evacuated, which would end the disturbances in South
Carolina.   It was officially announced, August 7th.
The olive branch was soon displayed in the hand
of Britannia, and peace was established the next
year.   Among the warriors who left the field to
retire to their own habitations, we may now look at
gen. Green, and behold him one of the best of citizens, as he was in his military character one of the
best of our generals.

In 1785, he removed his family to Georgia, and
he there cultivated a large plantation, which the general assembly of that state had granted him, as a reward for his publick services.   He died suddenly,
it was supposed by a coup de soleil, June 19th,
1786.   Every honour was paid to his remains by
the citizens of Savannah, where his body was carried that the funeral procession might be more respectable.   The congress voted to have a monument erected at the seat of the federal government,
with the following inscription,

SACRED
to the memory of
NATHANIEL GREEN, esq.
who departed this life
the nineteenth of June, MDCLXXXVI.
Late major general
in the service of the United States,
and commander of their army
in the southern department.
The United States, in congress assembled,
in honour of his
patriotism, valour and ability,
have erected this
MONUMENT.

GREENWOOD ISAAC, a mathematician, was graduated at Harvard College, 1721 ; elected professor of mathematicks, and natural philosophy, 1728 ; he continued in the professorship ten years, and was then dismissed.

Mr Greenwood was the first professor in these branches on this side the Atlantick ocean. Mr. Thomas Hollis, of London, a man famous for his munificence, laid the foundation of it, and the officer is styled, Hollis professor of mathematicks and natural philosophy. When the news of Mr. Hollis's death reached America, Mr. Greenwood published " a philosophical discourse concerning the mutability and changes in the material world," in which great respect is paid to their benefactor. It was read, April 7, 1731, and concludes in the following manner :

" As in the vegetable kingdom, it is with a superiour pleasure and expectation, that we consider the revival of such plants as have always been distinguished by the delicacy or plenty of their fruit, so with the earnest desires and hopes we should wait for the day when we shall behold the *resurrection* of *such*, as have distinguished themselves by acts of charity and bounty."

GRIDLEY JEREMIAH, attorney general of the province of Massachusetts Bay, member of the general court, colonel of the first regiment of militia, president of the marine society, and grand mas-

ter of freemasons, died at Boston, Sept. 7, 1767.
In 1725, he took his degree at Cambridge; was assistant in the grammar school in Boston, and a
preacher of the gospel. But soon turned his attention to the law, and became one of the most eminent of the profession. In 1732, he was editor of
a newspaper, called the Rehearsal, and filled the first
page with an essay, either moral or critical, besides
writing political paragraphs. His manner of writing is handsome, and his speculations ingenious:
at the bar his speech was rough, his manner
hesitating, but energetic, and his words forcible by
a peculiar emphasis. His opinion was always given
even to the judges with a magisterial air; his legal knowledge was unquestionable.

He was on the side of the whigs; and in the house
of representatives, where he was a member some
years, from Brookline, he opposed the measures of
Great Britain; but in a question on search war-
rants, his speech as attorney general, contains sentiments, incompatible with freedom, which was
confuted by Otis. Both speeches are preserved in
Minot's history. When Trowbridge was promoted
to the bench of Judges, Gridley was appointed attorney general. He died poor, because he despised
wealth.

HAKLUYT RICHARD, one of the corporation of
adventurers for the prosecution of discoveries in
North America, was born in London, 1553, and
educated at Westminster School. In 1582, he published a " collection of voyages;" and in 1587
translated into English a French account of Florida
by capt. Loudonnier, which he dedicated to sir
Walter Raleigh. In the same year he published an
improved edition of Peter Martyr's book " de novo
orbe." He was nominated by Raleigh, and chosen
one of the corporation of counsellors and assistant
adventurers; and was very active in collecting accounts, and prosecuting voyages. In 1589, he published " the principal navigations, voyages and discoveries of the English nation made by sea or over

land," folio, three volumes. These books contain the narratives of two hundred and twenty voyages. The last volume was printed in 1600. He also published a translation from the Portuguese of " Antonio Galvino's history of discoveries," 4to.

In 1605, he was appointed a prebend in Westminster ; with this he had a rectory in Suffolk. He was in more easy circumstances than he had been ; and in 1609 published a translation of " Ferdinand de Soto's description of Florida." He died, 1609.

Purchas made great use of his papers, mss. as well as books that were printed.

That famous navigator Hudson, named a promontory on the continent of Greenland, Hakluyt's Headland. *Biog. Dict.*

HANCOCK THOMAS, merchant in the town of Boston, was the son of the rev. Mr. Hancock of Lexington,* was born, July 3d, 1703 ; and died suddenly, August, 1764.

He left 1000 pounds for founding a professorship of the Hebrew and other Oriental languages ; 1000 pounds for the society for propagating the gospel

* The rev. John Hancock, of Lexington, was venerable for his character, and great abilities in his profession ; he had such an influence among the ministers, that he was called bishop. He was graduated at Cambridge, 1689, and in the year 1698, ordained over a society,which then made part of the town of Cambridge, called the Farms. It is now Lexington, being incorporated in 1711. Mr. H. died, 1752.

This worthy minister left three sons; John, Thomas and Ebenezer. The eldest son was graduated at Harvard College, 1719. He died, 1744, etat. 42. He was minister of the church at Braintree, a very elegant and accomplished preacher. He published several volumes, and a pamphlet in the controversy concerning the proceedings of the convention of ministers in the year 1748. It is entitled, " a reply to Mr. Gee's remarks on the printed testimony of pastors in Boston against several errors and disorders in the land." Mr. Hancock was one of the committee that formed this testimony. Thomas, the second son, served his time with col. Henchman, a stationer in Boston; but having a turn for more extensive business, became one of the principal merchants in New England. Ebenezer was graduated, 1728 ; was settled with his father six years, and died, January 28, 1739, 40, etat. 29.

among the Indians. Upon this his heart was very much set ; but the design was frustrated. Such a society was instituted by the general court, but the act was negatived by the governour. He also left 600 pounds towards a hospital for the reception of persons deprived of their reason ; and two hundred for carrying on the linen manufacture.

While he lived he was a most useful member of society ; active in every office, a patriot full of publick spirit. He was often employed in the service of the town, and for many years a member of his majesty's council. As a merchant he exhibited the strictest probity. "He never fell short of his engagements to any, and his humanity often prompted him to go beyond them."

"His house was the seat of hospitality, where all his numerous acquaintance, and strangers of distinction, met with an open and elegant reception."

The procession at his funeral was very great, and the mourning of the inhabitants sincere. They felt the magnitude of the loss, especially vast numbers of industrious men whom he constantly employed.

HANCOCK JOHN, governour of Massachusetts, was the son of the rev. John Hancock, of Braintree. He lost his excellent father when he was young, but had every advantage of a virtuous and liberal education from the care and kindness of his uncle, the hon. Thomas Hancock, esq. He was graduated at Harvard College, 1754, and went into the mercantile line, serving an apprenticeship with his uncle, who then was in the midst of his prosperity, and did more business than any other man in Boston. He was regarded by his friends as an amiable young man ; but discovered no prominent traits of character which should lead his acquaintance to prognosticate the conspicuous figure he was afterwards to make in society. The hon. Thomas Hancock died suddenly in 1764. The property he left was very great. In the imagination of the people it was immense. It was the subject of conversation in every street, and by every fire side, while all lamented the loss the publick had sustained. But they soon turned their attention to him who was the heir of his fortune, and appeared disposed to imitate his virtues. He was promoted to every office which a man fond of publick life could expect or desire. His manners were pleasing. He was polite, affable, easy and condescending, and what was greatly in his favour did not appear to be lifted up with pride. Such an elevation to prosperous circumstances would make some men giddy, and cause others to despise the neighbour, poorer than themselves. He was, for several years, selectman of the town; and in 1766, representative to the general court. He there blazed a whig of the first magnitude. Otis, Cushing, and S. Adams were the other three, who represented the capital, men of name in the revolution of their country. Being fond of publick notice, he was flattered by the approbation of the people, with their marks of confidence, and the distinction he had in the general court. He was generally chosen on committees, and was chairman upon some occasions, when the most important concerns of the country were the subjects of the *report*. How far he was engaged in drawing these reports is not to be ascertained ; but they contained his sentiments upon publick affairs. He often gave his opinion when questions were before the house, and mingled in the debates, but possessed no great powers as a parliamentary speaker. He never made a long speech, either in the style of declamatory eloquence, or the masterly reasoning of a great statesman. The vivid and energetick orations of Otis were the theme of admiration. The political sagacity of Adams, the publick spirit and patriotick zeal of Hancock, also gave a lustre to the Boston seat. Perhaps there never was a time when the representatives of the capital had such an influence in the affairs of the province. There was a collision of sentiment among the leading whigs about the removal of the court to Boston. Hutchinson offered this upon certain conditions, which the majority of members saw fit to comply with. Mr. H. voted with them. Adams was against the measure, and expressed his sentiments in opposition to his friend and colleague. Mr. Hancock was a man impatient of contradiction, and, upon some occasions, indulged a petulant humour. He could not bear the opposition of Mr. Adams on this question. It was one cause of the alienation between them. That gentleman was cool and determined, hard and unyielding, as well as bold in his argument. He sometimes was sarcastick in his replies ; but upon the subject which then divided the house, he observed the utmost delicacy, and seemed to dread the consequence of this political difference. These gentlemen had different views, though equally zealous in their opposition to the mother country. Or else one looked further than the other. Mr. H. was not against a reconciliation, if Great Britain would repeal all her unjust acts, and pay due respect to the rights of the colonies. Adams did not wish the ancient friendship should be renewed. From the time of the stamp act, he saw that hostilities would commence, and the American colonies become a nation by themselves. He was desirous of being an actor in the most important scenes, and have his name handed down to posterity among the patriots, who were to form a new era in the revolution of empires.

The division of these two leading characters made parties among the whigs, especially in the town of Boston. Mr. Hancock was the idol of the people. His generosity upon all publick occasions, and kindness to individuals, were the theme of continual and loud applause. It was said that his heart was open as the day to acts of beneficence : that he sunk his fortune in the cause of his country. This was the prevailing idea, and it gave a perfume to the sacrifice. What bounds could be given to the people's affection to a man, who preferred " their loving favour to great riches !"

He was certainly the most popular man in the community. Nor was his popularity a transient thing. At future periods of our revolution, when attempts were made to depreciate him ; when other characters were brought forward whose merit was conspicuous ; and even when he was accused, in the publications of the day, of wanting qualifications for administering the government, he still retained his influence in the community. It is well known, that some of our greatest and wisest and best men have solicited his concurrence in their measures, from the full persuasion that the popular voice was so much in his favour.

In the year 1774, Mr. H. was chosen to deliver the publick oration in Boston on the 5th of March, to commemorate the massacre of 1770. It is a very handsome composition, and was very well delivered. During the course of this year his health declined. When the general assembly of the province elected members of the first congress, he was so ill, as to be unable to attend publick business. The ensuing winter was favourable to his health ; he recruited his spirits and activity. He was one of the provincial congress, and, for a time, their president. He was then elected a member of the general congress, that was to meet at Philadelphia in 1775. This year was the most remarkable of any in the annals of the British nation. The revolutionary war commenced, April 19. The battle of Lexington was succeeded by a proclamation from the governour, declaring the country in a state of rebellion, and proscribing Hancock and Adams, as the chief leaders, whose behaviour was too flagitious to be forgiven. This only served to give importance to their characters ; to fix them in the esteem and affection of their country. There were men in these states who coveted such a mark of distinction ; many, who would have given all their wealth, and run any risk of consequences.

This year Mr. Hancock married Miss Dorothy Quincy, the daughter of one of the magistrates of Boston, and descended from one of the most ancient families in New England.

In 1776, July 4th, his name appears as president of the congress which declared the colonies independent of the crown of Great Britain. The name of the president alone was published with the declaration, though every member signed it. It was a mark of respect due to Massachusetts, to have one of their members in the chair, which had been filled with a member from South Carolina and Virginia. Mr. H. had those talents which were calculated to make him appear to more advantage as chairman, than in the debates of a publick body. He excelled as moderator of the Boston town meetings, as president of the provincial congress, and state convention; and, as head of the great council of our nation, he was much respected. He discovered a fine address, great impartiality, sufficient spirit to command attention, and preserve order. His voice and manner were much in his favour, and his experience, in publick business, gave him ease and dignity.

In 1779, Mr. Hancock resigned his place in congress. He was chosen a member of the convention that formed the constitution for this commonwealth. He was not one of the committee to draw up the plan. Many were earnest to have him president; but the majority were for Mr. Bowdoin. He attended his duty, however, very regularly, and sometimes expressed his sentiments. He dissented from those, who would have given more power to the governour, and more energy to the constitution.

From 1780 to 1785, Mr. Hancock was annually chosen governour of the commonwealth of Massachusetts. He declined being a candidate for the office the ensuing year, and was succeeded by the hon. James Bowdoin, esq. During the administration of Mr. B. there was an insurrection in the state, which was happily quelled. Every thing was done in the most judicious manner by the governour, and the legislature, yet a part of the community appeared to be discontented with the administration, and, in the year 1787, Mr. Hancock was again placed in the chair. The friends of Mr. Bowdoin were disappointed. They consisted of a large number of respectable characters in the commonwealth; men of property and wisdom, who felt the injury that gentleman had received, as a deep wound given to the body politick. The present governour could not escape their censure, and his administration was attacked by certain political writers, who exposed his faults with the keenest satire, and excited prejudices against him. A more friendly disposition was excited towards him, when the constitution of the United States was offered to the people. His conduct in the state convention during the discussion of it, gained him honour. The opposition to this excellent form of government was great. It was said that the majority of the convention would be against the adoption; and that the governour was with the opposers. He was chosen president of the convention, but did not attend the debates till the latter weeks of the session. Certain amendments were proposed to remove the objections of those, who thought some of the articles deprived the people of their rights. He introduced these amendments with great propriety, and voted for the adoption of the constitution. His name and influence doubtless turned many in favour of the federal government. When the president of the United States visited Boston, there was some obliquity or peculiarity in his behaviour, which renewed the old prejudices against him. It was thought he failed in certain attentions to that illustrious character, and he was in some danger of losing his popularity; for all classes of people looked upon Washington as the first of men.

The latter years of his administration were easy to him, on account of the publick tranquillity. The federal government became the source of so much prosperity that the people were easy and happy. The two patriots, Hancock and Adams, were reconciled. When lieut. gov. Cushing died, gen. Lincoln was chosen, as his successor. This gave great offence to Mr. Adams, and it was very disagreable to the governour. They joined their strength to support the same measures, as well as renewed their friendship. The next year, Lincoln was left out of office, and Mr. Adams chosen lieut. governour. This gentleman succeeded Mr. Hancock, as governour of the commonwealth, after his death. He died, October 8, 1793.

The death of such a man was interesting to the people at large. The procession at his funeral was very great. Dr. Thacher the minister of Brattle street church, preached his funeral sermon the next Sabbath. To this society, he had been a great benefactor; he subscribed very largely for the building of this superb edifice, and was always liberal in his contributions upon other occasions. He was very friendly to the clergy of all denominations. Born and educated among them, he was never weary of assisting them. He did a great deal also to promote the cause of learning as well as religion. The library of Harvard College will give an exhibition of his munificence. His uncle expressed his intention of subscribing 500 pounds sterling towards furnishing a new library and philosophical apparatus, when Harvard Hall was burnt in 1764, but died suddenly and this was not expressed in his will. The heir made no hesitation about granting it; and the name of Hancock, in golden letters, now adorns one of the alcoves of the library room, and is upon the records of the university among her greatest benefactors.

HARVARD JOHN, pastor of the church at Charlestown, came over to America in the year 1636, 7.

He died of a consumptive complaint soon after his arrival, greatly lamented, being a very excellent man, and worthy minister. By his will, he bequeathed about 800 pounds to promote the cause of literature in New England. The general court had given 400 pounds towards a publick school at Newtown; and the institution found encouragement from several other benefactors. But because the memorable John Harvard led the way, by a generosity exceeding the most of them, his name was justly eternised, says the author of the Magnalia, by its having the name of Harvard College imposed upon it.

HAWTHORNE WILLIAM, one of the fathers of Massachusetts, came over to Dorchester; but when Hugh Peters was minister of Salem, he removed to that place. He became one of their most useful citizens, and their representative to the general court. Johnson says, that he was the most eloquent man in the assembly. He was a friend of Winthrop, and often opposed to Endicot, who glided with the popular stream. It was Mr. Hawthorne's opinion, which he publickly advanced and supported, that none but men of property were qualified for civil offices. He was also of opinion that the council ought to be permanent. This political tenet was the subject of a treatise, which Mr. Saltonstall wrote, in 1642. His book was highly censured. Mr. Norris, the minister of the church in Salem, answered it. The reply is handsomely commended by gov. Winthrop. In 1650, Mr. Hawthorne was chosen speaker of the house of representatives, and is the first upon record. He certainly was very influential in all the affairs of the province for many years, and whatever his former opinions had been, he drank deeply of the republican spirit of New Eng-in his latter days. For he was one of the obnoxious characters, which king Charles II. required to be sent to England. He mentioned five gentleman who were to answer for the conduct of the colony. And the letter expressed two of their names, Mr.

Bellingham and Mr. Hawthorne. The court of Massachusetts did not send them. It was the opinion, however, of many of the first characters in the province, that it would be best to comply with the order of the king. But their conduct was censured. The governour called the court together, and desired that the elders might be present, who gave their advice against it.*

Mr. H. was as reputable for his piety as for his political integrity. He was a friend to the constitution of the New England churches, and, whenever occasion required, was ready to defend the privileges of the brethren against the encroachments of the elders. Major Hawthorne was a magistrate in 1676. He died the latter end of the century. Several families of the name are in the state ; and some of his descendants are respectable inhabitants of the town, where their ancestor was so well esteemed and made such a conspicuous figure. *Hutch. Bentley.*

HAYNES JOHN arrived at Boston, A. D. 1633. The next year he was chosen assistant, and in 1635 advanced to the chair of government. He removed from Massachusetts to Connecticut, and was, for many years, their most distinguished character. Had he continued in Massachusetts, he would have been a rival to gov. Winthrop. His property, which, combined with any considerable qualifications, will always give a man influence, was equal to a thou-

* Among the magistrates, some are good men and well affected to his majesty, and would be well satisfied to have his authority in a better manner established ; but the major part are of different principles, having been in the government from the time they formed themselves into a commonwealth. These direct and manage all affairs as they please ; of which number are Mr. Leverett, governour, Mr. Symonds, deputy governour, Mr. Danforth, Mr. Tyng, major Clarke, major Hawthorne, who still continued a magistrate, though commanded by his majesty upon his allegiance to come into England, yet refused, being encouraged in his disobedience by a vote of the court, not to appear, upon some reasons best known to themselves. These, with some few others of the same faction, keep the country in subjection and slavery, backed with the authority of a pretended charter. Randolph's letter to the lords of the privy council.

sand pounds a year in his own country ; but when Mr. Hooker came over to New England, he joined the company. They resided at Newtown, with a number of families from the county of Essex. They were, most of them, farmers, and wanted more extent of land to cultivate. Dr. Trumbull says, " that the growing popularity of Mr. Haynes, and the fame of Mr. Hooker, who, as to strength of genius, and his lively, powerful manner of preaching, rivalled Cotton, were supposed to have had no small influence upon the general court in giving liberty to this company to remove to Connecticut. There, it was judged, they would not so much eclipse the fame, nor stand in the way of the promotion and honour of themselves and friends. Mr. Haynes was chosen governour of Connecticut ; and his great integrity and wise management of all affairs so raised and fixed his character in the esteem of the people, that they always, when the constitution would permit, placed him in the chief seat of government, and continued him in it until his death.

The fathers of Connecticut, according to the historian above mentioned, were Mr. Haynes, Mr. Ludlow, Mr. Hooker, Mr. Warham, Mr. Hopkins, Mr. Welles, Mr. Willis, Mr. Whiting, Mr. Wolcott, Mr. Phelps and Mr. Webster. These were the first class of settlers ; and all, except the ministers, were chosen magistrates, or governours of the colony.

Dr. Trumbull says, the name of Haynes has become extinct in this country. There are several families of Haynes' in Massachusetts ; but whether they came from the same parts of old England cannot be ascertained.

Gov. Haynes died in the year 1654.

HIGGINSON FRANCIS was educated at Emanuel College, Cambridge ; proceeded master of arts, and was settled in the ministry at Lancaster. He had a very pleasant voice ; was very courteous and obliging in his behaviour, and so popular, that the people flocked from all the neighbouring towns to hear him preach. For some years he continued in his conformity to the rites and ceremonies of the episcopal church, but afterwards became a sincere convert to the doctrines and manners of the puritans. His acquaintance with the famous Hildersham, and Mr. Thomas Hooker, brought about this alteration of his opinions. They had studied the controversies, which then divided the churches of the reformation, and persuaded him to indulge the same spirit of free inquiry. He acknowledged, that he could find no foundation for many things, which had been introduced by the church of Rome, and still continued in the church of England; and he was a man of too much simplicity and godly sincerity to practise them after he was convinced from what source they came. Hence he offended the ruling party, and was not allowed to exercise his ministry in his own parish church. The people, however, procured the privilege of his preaching a lecture one part of the Sabbath for them; and the other part he preached for an aged minister, who needed his assistance.

He was maintained by a voluntary contribution, which came easily from his hearers, because he was so well beloved. The ministers of the episcopal church were also so fond of him, that they opened their churches to him, as long as they could do it with any safety. Happily for them, they were in the diocese of one of the most exemplary and sweet tempered bishops that ever filled an episcopal see. This was Dr. Williams, whom bishop Laud, with the fierce spirit of bigotry, hated, because he had so much evangelical charity. The rods of his wrath were shaken against Mr. Higginson, among the other favourites of the good bishop of Lincoln. He could not, however, destroy the work which Mr. Higginson had done. It pleased God to give lustre to his character, and success to his ministry.

Before Mr. H. became a non-conformist, he appeared to manifest more regard to discipline in his church than was common, though nothing more than the rubricks required. He publickly declared that ignorant and scandalous persons were not to be admitted to the Lord's supper. After preaching upon this text, " Give not that which is holy unto dogs," a man, who was a common drunkard and swearer, approached the chancel. He said to him, before the whole assembly, that he was not willing to give the Lord's supper to him, until he had professed his repentance, to the satisfaction of the congregation. The man was full of resentment, but could not resist the commanding influence the man of God had, as much by the virtue of his character, as the sacredness of his office. Another instance is mentioned in the Magnalia, which may be related in the words of the author, as it is less accompanied with marvellous circumstances, than are generally combined with *his* biographical sketches. " A famous doctor of divinity, prebend of a cathedral, and chaplain to his majesty, then lived at Leicester. This gentleman preached but very seldom ; and when he did at all, it was after that fashion, which has sometimes been called gentleman-preaching ; after a flaunting manner and with such a vain ostentation of learning, and affectation of language as ill became the oracles of God ; the people generally flocking more to the edifying preaching of Mr. H. than to these vain harangues. Our doctor so extremely resented it, that both publickly and privately, on all opportunities, he expressed his indignation against Mr. H. and vowed that he would certainly drive him out of town. Now it so fell out, that the sheriff appointed this doctor to preach at the general assizes there, and gave him a quarter of a year's time to prepare a sermon upon that occasion. But in all this time he could not provide a sermon to his own satisfaction, insomuch that a fortnight before the time was expired, he expressed to some of his friends a despair of being well provided. Wherefore his friends persuaded him to try, telling him that if it came to the worst, Mr. H. might be procured to preach in his room ; he was always ready. The Dr. was wonderfully averse to this last proposal, and therefore studied with all his might for an agreeable sermon ; but he had such a blast from heaven upon his poor studies, that the very night before the assizes began, he sent his wife to the devout lady Cave, who prevailed with Mr. H. to supply his place the day ensuing ; which he did with a most suitable, profitable and acceptable sermon ; and unto the great satisfaction of the auditory. When the lady Cave had let this matter be known, how this thing, which was much wondered at, came about, the common discourse of the town so confounded the doctor, that he vowed he would never come into it again. Thus Mr. Higginson was left in the town, but, I pray, who was driven out ?"

The high reputation of Mr. Higginson procured him the offer of some of the best livings in the island, but his principles of non-conformity operating upon a mind imbued with the love of truth, he sacrificed every worldly consideration, and trusted in providence for the means of support. He educated a number of youths, who were afterwards good scholars at the universities, and shone as lights in the christian church. From the benevolence of his disposition, he forwarded every pious, useful and charitable work ; but his generous sympathy was peculiarly remarkable towards the protestant exiles, who came from Bohemia and the Palatinate, when the French had burned their cities, and they had beheld their dulcia arva changed to fields of blood.

In the year 1628, the company of Massachusetts bay in New England began a plantation. It was their decree, that none but honest and godly men should go over to settle. Mr. Higginson was a man admirably calculated to manage their design of propagating what they styled reformed christianity. He complied with their request ; for he thought their invitation a call from heaven to which he must listen. They set sail from the isle of Wight, May, 1629, and when they come to the land's end, Mr. Higginson calling up his children and other passengers of the ship, said, "We will not say as the separatists were wont to say at their leaving of England, Farewell Babylon! Farewell Rome! But we will say, Farewell dear England! Farewell the church of God in England, and all christian friends there! We do not go to New England as separatists from the church of England, though we cannot but separate from the corruptions in it, but we go to practise the positive part of church reformation, and propagate the gospel in America."

This company arrived at Salem harbour 29th of June. There were only six houses, beside Mr. Endicot's. The same voice was then heard in this American wilderness, which had charmed the crowded cities of Europe. Mr. Skelton being associated with Mr. Higginson, in the work of the ministry, a day of religious preparation was observed. Mr. Higginson's church considered the two articles, which had been agreed upon between Mr. Endicot and Mr. Fuller, of Plymouth, who, though laymen, were deeply interested in the ecclesiastical affairs of the plantations, viz. "That the church of Salem would not acknowledge any ecclesiastical jurisdiction in the church at Plymouth. And that the authority of ordination should not exist in the clergy, as in the protestant churches, but, as the unqualified sense of the reformed churches, should entirely depend upon the free election of the members of the church, and that there should be a representative of this power continually in the church." We are told that Mr. Endicot had explained his views to the church at Plymouth; and that Mr. Higginson consented. He drew up likewise a "confession of faith," with a scriptural representation of the "covenant of grace," applied to their purpose, whereof thirty copies were taken for the thirty persons, who gathered the church.

This ancient church was organized, August 6th, 1629. Mr. Skelton was chosen pastor, Mr. Higginson teacher, and other officers, according to the regulations they had adopted.

After this, many others joined, whose good conversation and conduct were amply testified. The first winter our fathers were exercised with many trials, and more than one hundred of the inhabitants of Salem died. Mr. Higginson also fell into a hectic fever, but continued preaching for some time. The last sermon he preached was upon this text, " What went ye out in the wilderness to see." Matt. xi. 7. It was occasioned by the arrival of many persons from Europe to settle in different places of New England. Finding himself near his dissolution, he conversed freely upon it. He said " that although the Lord called him away, he was persuaded God would raise up others, to carry on the work that was begun, and that there would be many churches in this wilderness." He died August, 1630, leaving a widow and eight children.*

He lived long enough, however, to secure the foundation of his church, to deserve the esteem of the colony, and to provide himself a name among the worthies of New England.

Mr. Higginson wrote an account of New England, which is printed in the first volume of the collections of the historical society. It is styled, " A short and true description of the discoveries and commodities of the country. Written in the year 1629, by Mr. Higginson, a reverend divine, now resident there. London, 1630, third edition."

Higginson Francis, eldest son of Mr. H. of Salem, was educated by his father in England, and was an excellent scholar. He kept a school in this country; but having a desire to visit some European univer-

* This is the time mentioned in the Magnalia. Mr. Bentley in his history of Salem, says it was 15th March.

sity, he went to Leyden, where he finished his studies. He settled in his native country, and was minister for many years at Kerby-Stephen, in Westmore-
land. In this place, the quakers early made their
appearance. He wrote a book against them. It
was entitled, " the irreligion of northern quakers,"
which is said to be the first thing written against
the people of that persuasion. He also published a
treatise, " De quinque maximis Luminibus; De
luce increata; De luce creata; De lumine naturæ,
Gratiæ et Gloriæ."

He died, in 1660, in the 55th year of his age.

HIGGINSON JOHN, was born in England, 1616,
and came over with his father to this new world.
When his father died, he, like his brother Francis,
had no other means of support but the fruit of his
knowledge. By his diligence and industry, he
was able to acquire learning, and to assist the family in their destitute state. He kept school at Hartford in Connecticut, and afterwards accepted an invitation to be chaplain of the fort at Saybrook. He
must have been there in 1639 : for we find his
name as witness to the articles of agreement between the settlers at Guilford in Connecticut, and
the Indians concerning the lands, which were then
purchased.* That excellent and upright man
George Fenwick was then at the fort. He gave to
the planters a large tract of land, on condition they
would accommodate Mr. Whitfield, his particular
friend, according to his mind.

This Mr. Henry Whitfield was the first pastor
of the church in Guilford, and he led this little flock
into the wilderness. He was also a wealthy man, having considerable possessions in the old country; and
at Guilford, he built, at his own expense, a large stone
house, which was a defence against the Indians.
He was " a well bred gentleman, a good scholar, a
great divine, and excellent preacher." When he

---

* Ruggles account of Guilford, vol. iii. of historical collections.

had continued with his people about twelve years, he went to England, leaving the care of his flock to Mr. Higginson, who was his son in law. This gentleman had preached at Guilford some years. He removed from Saybrook about the year 1643, was one of the seven pillars of the church of Guilford, and assisted Mr. Whitfield in the pulpit. He never was ordained at Guilford, but took care of the flock till the year 1659, when he purposed to go with his family to England. The vessel in which he sailed, put into Salem harbour on account of the weather, and he was persuaded to settle in the church, which his father had planted. He was ordained their pastor, August, 1660. "Major Hawthorne, with the deacons, imposed hands upon him in the presence of the neighbouring churches and elders."

As a minister, Mr. Higginson was highly respected. That he was very popular in all the country appears from a paper which Chalmers published in his political annals. It is supposed to have been written by Randolph who, being employed as a spy, sent a minute account of the state of Massachusetts. One question was, Who are the most popular clergymen? Answer. Thacher, Oxenbridge and Higginson. Dr. Cotton Mather says, likewise, that even when he was eighty years old, he preached with such a manly, judicious, pertinent vigour, and with so little decay of his intellectual abilities, as was a matter of just admiration. After speaking thus highly of him, he says, that he should praise him still more, did he not recollect the saying of a German divine, Auferte ignem, &c. i. e. "Oh, bring not the sparks of your praises near me, as long as I have any chaff left in me." He is afraid of receiving such a check from his reverend father of Salem; but he comforts the good man by telling him that he must soon die, and then complete justice would be done him in all the churches. This was written in 1696; but Mr. Higginson lived a number of years after: he died in 1708, aged 93.

He preached the election sermon in 1663. He also published other occasional discourses, and several prefaces to devotional books. His name, with Mr. Thacher's, is affixed to the commendation of " Morton's memorial." He also wrote the attestation to the church history of New England, Magnalia Americana, &c. wherein he gives a particular narrative of the *Mathers.* Of the author of that work he thus speaks, " As I behold this exemplary son of New England, while thus young and tender, at such a rate building the temple of God, and in a few months dispatching such a piece of temple work as this is, a work so notably adjusted and adorned, it brings to mind an epigram upon young Borellus ;

Cum juveni tantam dedit experientia lucem,
Tale ut promat opus, quam dabit illa seni ?

As to myself, having been, by the mercy of God, now above 68 years in New England, and served the Lord and his people in my weak measure, 60 years in the ministry of the gospel, I may now in my old age, say *I have seen all that the Lord hath done for his people,* and have known the beginning and progress of these churches unto this day ; and having read over much of this history I cannot but in the love and fear of God, bear witness to the truth of it."

The last work which appears with Mr. Higginson's name is, the " Testimony to the order of the gospel in the churches of New England, left in the hands of the churches. By the two most aged ministers of the country, Mr. H. of Salem, and Mr. H. of Ipswich."

HOAR LEONARD, M. D. president of Harvard College, was elected into that office, July 13, 1672, and inaugurated the 10th of September.

This gentleman was graduated at the college, over which he afterwards presided, in 1650. He went to England, and was a preacher of the gospel ; he also studied physick, and received from the university of Cambridge, the degree of doctor of medicine. He returned to New England to accept of an invitation he received from the Old South church in Boston to be their pastor. Upon his arrival he was chosen to succeed president Chauncy at the college; but though possessed of sufficient learning, he wanted a proper spirit of government, and some other qualifications, to make himself respectable in the office. Prejudices were excited against him. The students all left the college, and the doctor resigned the chair, March 15, 1675, which had been truly a thorny seat. "Sceptrum illum scholasticum plus habet solicitudinis quam pulchritudinis, plus curæ quam auri, plus impedimenti quam argenti."*

His mind was much affected by this alteration in his situation, and he died a broken-hearted man, Nov. 24, the same year.

Dr. Hoar married a daughter of Lord Lisle, who came over the Atlantick to share his troubles. She exhibited, in her life, the charms of virtue, and the practice of piety. *Magnalia.*

HOLYOKE EDWARD, president of Harvard College, was born in Boston, had the rudiments of his education at the north grammar school, and graduated at Cambridge, A. D. 1705. He was chosen tutor, 1712, and the next year a fellow of the corporation. "These stations he filled with reputation to himself, and advantage to the society with whose interests he was so nearly concerned." He was invited to the pastoral office in Marblehead, 1716. That ancient church divided, and made two distinct societies. Mr. Barnard and Mr. Holyoke were the preachers: the one was settled at the first church, the other in a church built for him. Here Mr. Holyoke officiated till the year 1737, and he was then elected president of the college.

Father Barnard says,† "that he went to gov. Belcher, and asked him why they chose one Boston minister after another, and neglected the man who was most qualified to fill the chair of that seminary,

---

* Melchior Adam, as quoted by Cotton Mather.
† Mss. penesme.

K k

his worthy brother Holyoke.   His excellency answered, that it would be agreeable to him if he were
assured of his orthodoxy, but suspicions had been
spread of his being liberal in his sentiments.   He
told him, that he was more acquainted with him
than any other person, and he knew him to be sound
in the faith." Mr. Holyoke continued in the chair
above thirty years.   The college flourished under
his government.   He mingled prudence with a just
and noble spirit, and was a gentleman in his manners.   His erudition was considerable ; but he
chiefly excelled as a mathematician and classical
scholar.   It was seldom he could be persuaded to
commit any thing he wrote to the press.   The convention sermon, which he printed in 1741, is an admirable discourse. He preached the first discourse
at the Dudleian lecture, soon after the death of the
founder ; but would not publish it.   Nor would he
often appear in the pulpit upon publick occasions.
President Holyoke died the first week in June,
1769, in the 80th year of his age.   He was buried
with every mark of distinction due to such a respectable character.   Gov. Hutchinson, treasurer
Hubbard, two members of the corporation, and two
ministers of the board of overseers, who were not
of that body, supported the pall.   Professor Sewall
delivered a funeral oration in latin ; and the next
Lord's day a sermon upon the occasion was preached by the rev. Dr. Appleton, which was printed,
with a character of the president annexed, drawn by
one of the gentlemen in the immediate government
of the college.

HOOKER THOMAS, the renowned pastor of the
church in Hartford, Connecticut, was born at Mar-
field, Leicestershire, in 1586, educated at the
university of Cambridge, and elected a fellow of
Emanuel College.   He was, in 1626, a lecturer in
Chelmsford, Essex street, but not being willing to
conform to all the rites of the church of England,
he was obliged to lay down the ministry.   He af-

terwards kept school, and had for his usher, John
Eliot, who, in America, was afterwards styled the
Indian apostle. Finding himself still prosecuted by
the spiritual court, in 1630, he went over to
Holland. He there became intimately acquainted
with the celebrated Dr. Ames, who declared, that
although he had been acquainted with many scholars of divers nations, yet he never met with Mr.
Hooker's equal for preaching, or for disputing.
Dr. Mather says, that Mr. Hooker and Mr. Cotton
were the Luther and Melancton of New England :
he meant to describe their different genius. It is
difficult for us, at this day, to know which was Melancton, or how either resembled him.

Mr. Hooker arrived at Boston, Sept. 4, 1633, in
the Griffin, gov. Haynes, Mr. Cotton and Mr. Stone
being his fellow passengers. In October Mr. H.
was ordained pastor of the church in Newtown. In
June, 1636, he went with his church above a hundred miles, and settled upon the banks of the river
Connecticut. Here he was the chief instrument of beginning another colony. Had this divine been called to the church in Boston, and Mr. Haynes had no
rival in gov. Winthrop, it is most probable they
would have continued with their people in Massachusetts. He often visited Boston ; and whenever
he preached, his great fame drew crowded assemblies. This great man died, July 7, 1647. Mr.
Cotton said, that he did "Agmen ducere et
dominari in concionibus, gratia spiritus sancti et
virtute plenis ;" and that he was "vir solertis et
acerrimi judicii." A very full memoir of Mr.
Hooker has been written by the grandson of Mr.
Cotton, who calls him the light of the western churches. It makes part of the Magnalia, and is also
printed in a separate volume.

Many volumes of Mr. Hooker's sermons were printed ; most of them are now out of print. One volume
on John xvii. is yet preserved among us, and certain
of his polemical writings. His most famous work is

the survey of *church discipline:* the first copy was sent to England in a vessel which was lost. The copy which we now have, wants the finishing hand of the author, but is a work of great merit and research. He was a friend to the consociation of churches. He also gives more authority to the elders than was ever allowed by our fathers of the Massachusetts colony.

HOOPER WILLIAM was born and educated in Scotland. After he arrived at Boston, he was employed as a private tutor in a gentleman's family a few miles from the town. His oratory at his first setting out as a preacher gained him vast applause. A number having engaged him to settle with them as their minister, built a house for publick worship at New or West Boston, and ordained him the pastor of it. But upon a vacancy happening in Trinity Church in Boston, he disgusted his parishioners by accepting an invitation from that church, and asking a dismission from his own : they however granted it. He embarked for England, and having received episcopal ordination he returned to Boston, and officiated as minister of Trinity Church till his death in 1767.

HOPKINS EDWARD, governour of Connecticut, born at Shrewsbury, A. D. 1600, was brought up a merchant in London, and lived in that city in a handsome style, with the esteem and affection of the people. He married the daughter of Theophilus Eaton, esq. with whom he removed to New England ; and when the company went from Massachusetts bay to Connecticut river, he was one who fixed at Hartford, and became a pillar and ruler of that colony.

He was exemplary for his piety, integrity and charity. In his publick character he did every thing to maintain peace, as well as to execute justice. He had to combat with many evils, not only in subduing the wilderness, but with others, which gave a wound to the spirit ; an incurable dementia had seized the brain of his wife, at the same time that he was subject to pulmonary complaints. The latter he could bear with resignation; for what are the infirmities of the body compared with the trials of the heart! "I promised myself," said he, "too much content in this relation and enjoyment; and the Lord will make me to know, that this world shall not afford it me."

Upon the death of his elder brother it was necessary that he should return to England, and he was there a favourite of the ruling power. He was soon appointed warden of the fleet, commissioner of the admiralty, and also chosen member of parliament. His friends in New England were unwilling to lose such a man from their plantation; but they derived much benefit from his services in the mother country. He was eminently qualified for every publick employment; was the friend of learning and religion; and having enjoyed the luxury of doing good while he lived, his virtues blossomed on his sepulchre. He died in the month of March, 1657, leaving a large estate in New England for pious and charitable uses. After mentioning certain legacies in his will, he bequeathed the remainder to "encourage hopeful youths in a way of learning, both at the grammar school, and at college, for the publick service of the country in future times."

He also gave 500 pounds out of his estate in England "for the promoting the kingdom of the Lord Jesus Christ in these remote parts of the earth." This donation was, by a decree of chancery, 1710, paid to Harvard College. The interest given in New England was estimated at 1000 pounds sterling, and has been appropriated to the support of the grammar schools in New Haven, Hartford and Hadley. A certain part of the income at the disposal of the corporation of Harvard College is given to the master of the schools in Cambridge, according to the number of grammar scholars; a certain part in books to the best scholars of the university ; but the greatest part of it to students in divinity, who reside at the college, bachelors of arts, upon this condition, that each one should read four theological dissertations in the course of the year.

Mr. Hopkins was elected governour of Connecticut while he was in England. He was in the office the year he died. He was also one that formed the union of the New England colonies, 1643. His name is signed to the articles of the confederation. Gov. Winthrop was the first president. In 1644, the hon. Edward Hopkins of Connecticut. *Hazard's Collection.*

HOPKINS SAMUEL, D. D. was born at Waterbury, Connecticut, educated at Yale College, which he entered in the year 1737, being then 16 years old. Having received the honours of that seminary, he was settled at a place on the Housatonick river, since called Great Barrington, the 28th of December, 1743. He continued the pastor of the church in this place 25 years, and was afterwards invited to Newport by the people of the first congregational church ; was ordained their minister, 1770, but was obliged to leave the place in 1776, when the British troops took possession of Rhode Island. From this time to the year 1780, he travelled over Connecticut and Massachusetts, preaching to destitute flocks, as his local situation admitted. When his flock returned to Newport, he also returned with them, and preached to their edification even to old age. He died the latter end of the year 1803.

Dr. Hopkins was a man of great abilities in his profession, a profound metaphysician, eminent as a writer of polemick divinity, but more eminent as the head of a denomination of christian professors, which have greatly increased in New England. From his own account of them, " they are the most sound, consistent, thorough Calvinists, who in general sustain as good a character, as to their morality, preaching and personal religion, as any set of clergymen whatever, and are most popular where there appears to be the most attention to religion : and at the same time are the most hated, opposed and spoken against, by arminians, deists and persons who have no religion." We may allow something, perhaps, for his own prejudice as well as the prejudices that have gone out against them. They certainly may reckon in their number some of the most ingenious and celebrated divines of our country.*

HOWARD SIMEON, D. D. was graduated at Harvard College, A. D. 1753. Soon after receiving the honours of that seminary, he was elected to the tutorship, for which place he had peculiar qualifications. He was an excellent scholar, had a pleasant manner of giving instruction, and mingled condescending manners with a proper spirit of government. He was invited to take charge of the west church in Boston, after the death of the great Dr. Mayhew. His ordination was 6th of May, 1768, and for a course of years he diffused his light for the edification of a people, who gave him lively tokens of their affection, and to whom his memory is dear. He was an example of that simplicity and godly sincerity which his preaching made essential to the life of a christian. His sermons were methodical, full of good sentiments and judicious remarks ; perspicuous and evangelical. He had not

* His various publications are three sermons, Rom. iii. 5, 6, " sin an advantage to the universe, and yet this no excuse for sin, or encouragement to it," 1759 ; " an inquiry concerning the promises of the gospel," 1765, 8vo. ; a sermon upon " the high and glorious character of Christ," Heb. iii. 1, 1768 ; a sermon Rom. vii. 7 ; ditto John i. 13, same year. The true state and character of the unregenerate, &c. 1769, 8vo. ; animadversions on Mr. Hart's dialogue, &c. 1770, pamphlet, 31 pages ; " an inquiry into the nature of true holiness, with an appendix containing replies to Mr. Hart, Mr. Mather, Mr. Hemmenway," 1773 ; " a dialogue concerning the African slavery," 1776 ; " an inquiry concerning the future state of the wicked," 1783 ; " Body of divinity, 2 vols. 8vo. 1793.

Sketches of Dr. Hopkins' life. Hart's sermon.

the striking talents which draw crowded auditories, nor an ease and grace in delivery, but he had weight and dignity in his composition, and "spoke as to wise men." Upon certain occasions he could manifest spirit and animation, or an energy which made the subject interesting and arrested attention. He grew in reputation as he advanced in years, which is a remark not often made upon ministers in the decline of life, but applies to the character of this worthy man.

Dr. Howard was a member of many societies for the promotion of learning, piety and humanity. Of several he was an active and useful officer. He was fellow of Harvard College, from the year 1780 to 1804; and secretary to the board of overseers. A member of the American academy of arts and sciences; of the society for propagating the gospel among Indians, and others, in North America; vice president of the humane society; also one of the counsellors of the congregational society for minister's widows. Whatever he undertook he performed with fidelity; wherever he was known he was highly esteemed. He died August 12, 1804. President Willard, his particular friend, preached a discourse the afternoon of his funeral.*

HOWE SIR WILLIAM. arrived in Boston in May, 1775, with Generals Burgoyne and Clinton, to take an active part in the war. The British troops, by order of Gen. Gage, had fought Lexington battle, April 19. He began HIS military exploits, the next month after his arrival, with the battle of Bunker hill. He never made any further progress in Massachusetts. In March 1776, he departed for Halifax, with all his forces; thence he went to New-York, and for several years conducted the American war.

---

* His publications were few. Though often solicited to print his discourses, he was prevailed upon only in certain instances; an artillery election sermon, 1773; the election sermon, 1779; a sermon after the death of his wife; one upon the death of Dr. Winthrop of Cambridge; and a discourse addressed to the free-masons

having obtained a temporary possession of Philadelphia, he embarked for England, in the spring of 1778, leaving the further prosecution of the war to Sir Henry Clinton.

Gen. Howe succeeded to the chief command of the British army in America, on the departure of gen. Gage, and had a commission to be governour of the province of Massachusetts.

A letter from gen. Lee, while he was a prisoner at New-York gives the following account of this officer.

" From my first acquaintance with Mr. Howe I liked him. I thought him friendly, candid, good natured, brave and rather sensible than otherwise ; but a corrupt, or more properly no education, the reigning idolatry of the English, especially the soldiery, for every sceptred calf, wolf, hog or ass, have totally perverted his understanding and heart, that private friendship has not force sufficient to keep the door open for the admittance of mercy towards political heretics.—He is the most indolent of mortals, never took further pains to examine the merits or demerits of the cause in which he had engaged, than merely to recollect that Great Britain was said to be the mother country, George the third, king of Great Britain ; that the Parliament was called the representative of Great Britain ; that the king and parliament formed the supreme power ; that a supreme power is absolute and uncontroulable ; that all resistance must consequently be rebellion ; but above all he was a soldier and bound to obey in all cases whatever ;— these were his notions, and this his logic.—Never poor mortal thrust into station, was surrounded by such fools and scoundrels. McKenzie, Balfour, Galloway, were his counsellors, they urged him to all his acts of harshness, they were his scribes. All the vile stuff which was issued to the astonished world were theirs. I believe he scarcely ever read the letters he signed. I can assure you

as a fact, that he never read the curious proclamation issued at the head of Elk, till three days after
it was published. He is naturally good humoured,
complaisant, but illiterate, indolent to the last degree, except as an executive soldier, in which
capacity he is all fire and activity ; and brave and
cool as Julius Cæsar. His understanding is rather
good than otherwise, but was utterly confounded
and stupified by the immensity of the task imposed
on him. He shut his eyes, fought his battles, drank
his bottle, &c. advised with his counsellors, received his orders from North and Germaine, one more
absurd than the other, took Galloway's opinion,
shut his eyes, fought again, and I suppose is now to
be called to account for acting according to his instructions. I believe his eyes are now opened, and
he sees he has been an instrument of wickedness
and folly.*

HUBBARD WILLIAM, was in the first class of
graduates at Harvard College, 1642. In the book
of " Wonder-working providences" mention is
made of William Hubbard, one of the representa-

* How just this observation,when we consider the reception he
met with in Great Britain ! Lord Germaine laid all the ill success
of the campaign in 1777 upon him ; and his friend Galloway was
the chief evidence against him. Israel Mauduit, the secretary of
Germaine, was also employed to write virulent pamphlets to render the general's character odious. Howe had advocates in the
house of commons ; his old friends in the minority, who blamed
him for serving in America, took his part against the minister ;
lord Germaine's orders and instructions were the subject of their
philippick, and they were powerful enough to make that minister
retire. In the examination before the house of commons, however, the general's conduct did not appear much to his credit. A
man may make an excellent captain of grenadiers, who has no
talents to command an army. If one half of Galloway's evidence
were true, he was the most unfit man to bring America into subjection they could have chosen. What is a little remarkable, a
private letter of a British officer when the army was in Boston,
has this expression, " Gen. Howe don't seem as if he wanted to
conquer America." This agrees with Galloway's account,
though nothing can excuse the perfidy of that man, the satellite
of the minister of war, whose own ignorance and gross absurdi-
ties, were more glaring than gen. Howe's.

tives in the general court, from the town of Ipswich. It is said, he was among the most able speakers in the assembly 1637. One gentleman from Salem was allowed to be more fluent, but none more solid and argumentative. This gentleman is supposed to have been father to the subject of this article, who was teacher of the church in Ipswich till his death. The year of his ordination I have never been able to obtain; the records of the church of Ipswich not being preserved. His gravestone is not to be found, and none of the present generation can recollect much about him. The oldest men in the town, who tell of those former divines that were contemporary, such as Rogers, Norton, Cobbet, &c. whose manner of preaching they have heard their fathers describe, have no impressions made upon their minds of the character of Mr. Hubbard, who certainly was for many years the most eminent minister in the county of Essex; equal to any in the province for learning and candour, and superiour to all his contemporaries as a writer. Perhaps he was not so fervent a preacher as some. He might want a voice and manner, or that animation in the pulpit which some preachers have, and which will be more talked of, than the still sound of wisdom. Or perhaps he lived too long for his reputation. When a man's life is cut short in the midst of his days and usefulness, the excellencies of his name and character are the subjects of remark for many generations. If another continues to old age, and mental imbecilities succeed the more vigorous intellect, he is remembered only in the last stage of life, and he drops into the grave without emotions of sorrow. His name is seldom mentioned in the neighbourhood where he dwelt; but those at a distance, who have heard of his fame when he appeared upon the stage with engaging virtue, or read his works with delight, wish to know what were the more minute parts of his character.

Whether these observations apply generally or not, they certainly apply to the subject of this memoir. He has been quoted by all who give accounts of New-England, but few, very few notices of him are in the records of the town, where he spent his days.*

In the year 1676 Mr. Hubbard preached the election sermon, which is among the very good ones published during that century. He was one of the seventeen ministers who bore testimony against the old church in Boston, when they settled Mr. Davenport; also, when the general assembly approved of the act of the first church, and censured the proceedings of the third church, commonly called the Old South. The division excited upon this occasion interested the passions of the people at large, so as to give a new complexion to publick affairs. Most of the deputies, who had so severely censured the brethren who built the Old South church, *for their spirit of innovation, and leaving the good old path of their fathers*, were left out, and new members chosen. The town of Ipswich took an active part in this matter; and Mr. Hubbard's influence had considerable effect upon their proceedings.

In 1682, Mr. Hubbard is brought to view as the historian of Massachusetts. He received some reward from the publick for his useful work. The following vote is copied from the records of the general court, October 11.

" Whereas it hath been thought necessary and a duty incumbent upon us, to take due notice of all occurrences and passages of God's providence towards the people of this jurisdiction, since their first arrival in these parts, which may remain to posterity, and that the rev. Mr. William Hubbard hath taken pains to compile a history of this nature, which the court doth with thankfulness acknowledge, and as a manifestation thereof, do hereby order the

* See Mr. Frisbie's letters, Hist. Coll. vol. x. page 35.

treasurer to pay unto him the sum of fifty pounds in money, he transcribing it fairly into a book, that it may be the more easily perused, in order to the satisfaction of this court."

In 1684 Mr. Hubbard presided at the commencement. This was after the death of president Rogers. But though Dr. Increase Mather was in the neighbourhood, the Senatus Academicus saw fit to send for a minister from the county of Essex ; so respectable was his character among the literary men of his profession.

The publications of Mr. Hubbard were not very numerous. They consist of several volumes in duodecimo; of which are a narrative of the Indian wars ; Memoirs of major gen. Dennison, &c. But his chief attention was paid to his ms. history, which was composed upon the plan of Winthrop's journal. For some reason or other neither of these mss. were permitted to be seen by the publick, till lately the journal has been printed. In all his histories Mr. Hubbard appears a steady friend to the constitution of the churches. He expressed indignant feelings at the erection of the church in Brattle-street, upon a more liberal plan than our fathers were willing to adopt.

There is nothing of this said in his ms. history, which only comes down to 1680, but he speaks pointedly in his private letters to several gentlemen, and in the last thing he published, his Dying testimony to the order of the churches, which he wrote jointly with Mr. Higginson of Salem. He died Sept. 24th, 1704, aged 83.

HUNTINGTON SAMUEL, governour of Connecticut, was the son of Nathaniel Huntington, esq. of Windham, and descended from an honourable and respectable family. His early years were distinguished by indications of an excellent understanding and a taste for mental improvement. Without the advantage of an education at any university, or the assistance of professional studies, he acquired a competent knowledge of law, and having fixed at Norwich, he in a few years became eminent in his profession. In 1764, he was a representative to the general assembly, and the year following attorney-general. In 1774, he was appointed assistant judge in the superiour court. In 1775, he was elected a counsellor and a delegate to congress. In 1779, he was president of that illustrious body. When the time expired for which he was chosen into the national councils, he resumed his seat upon the bench. In 1784 he was appointed chief justice of the state and lieut. governour. He succeeded gov. Griswold as chief magistrate in 1786, and was annually re-elected until his death, Jan. 8. 1796.

" His natural disposition was mild and amiable, the whole tenor of his conversation ingratiating and exemplary. The prosperity of the state during his administration, the flourishing condition of its civil and military interests, are unequivocal testimonies of the wisdom and fidelity with which he presided.

As a professor of religion, a constant attendant upon the institutions of christianity, he manifested an unvarying faith in its doctrines and joyful hopes in its promises."

The governour left no children. Mrs. H. died, June 4, 1794, in the 56th year of her age. She was the daughter of the rev. Ebenezer Devotion of Windham. *Strong's sermon.*

HUMPHREY JOHN was early engaged in the settlement of the New England plantations. He was one of the original patentees from the council of Plymouth. He married the lady Susan, daughter to the earl of Lincoln, and brought her with their children to Massachusetts bay in 1632; and was immediately chosen assistant. He fixed his habitation at Lynn, or Saugus. The spot of ground which he cultivated lies on the old road between Boston and Salem. In 1640, he was about removing to the Bahama islands, but altered his purpose upon hearing that New Providence was taken by

the Spaniards. Having met with some losses by
fire, and his estate being otherwise impaired, he returned to England. Lady Moody purchased his
plantation at Saugus.* *Hutchinson.*

HUTCHINSON THOMAS, governour of Massachusetts Bay, was a descendant from one of the most
ancient and honourable families in New England.
Several of the name held offices of honour and trust
under the old charter; others were of his majesty's
council under the charter of William and Mary.
The hon. Thomas Hutchinson, esq. father of the
governour, a distinguished merchant of Boston, was
colonel of the first regiment in Suffolk, and a counsellor from 1714 to 1739, the year of his death. He
was the man who seized the famous capt. Kidd
when he resisted the officers of justice sent to arrest
him. His son gives a brief delineation of his character in saying " I wish that many of his posterity
may so justly deserve the character of true friends
to their country. Regardless of the frowns of a
governour, or the threats of the people, he spoke
and voted according to his judgment, attaching
himself to no party any further than he found their
measures tend to the publick interest." Col. Hutchinson left several children. Neither of them discovered talents or ambition except the eldest, who
is the subject of this memoir. This gentleman
passed through strange vicissitudes; at one time
he was the most popular character in Massachusetts,
at another the object of publick abhorrence.

Mr. H. received the rudiments of his education
at the north grammar school, and was admitted into
Harvard College when he was only 12 years of age.
His progress in literature was the subject of notice
and applause. In 1727 he was graduated; but in-

* This lady made herself notorious in the early settlement of
the country. She was member of the church in Salem, but very soon renounced infant baptism. She was admonished, and
still persisted in her opinion. To avoid further trouble she removed to one of the Dutch plantations.

stead of following his studies and entering one of the professions, as was expected, he applied himself to merchandize. It seemed to be the most ardent desire of his soul to acquire property. Ambition and avarice frequently agitate the same breast ; and he might attach an importance of character to wealth, which would enable him to gain any distinction he wanted as he advanced in life. He did not succeed in his commercial pursuits, but rather diminished than augmented to his patrimony. His fellow townsmen regarded him more for his probity and honour than for his mercantile skill ; they thought him capable of transacting publick business, and by their favour he was stimulated to bend his mind wholly to the study of history and political constitutions. He was chosen a selectman of Boston in 1738, and conducted with so much prudence and fidelity, that he was appointed by the town their agent to manage very important business in Great Britain, which he undertook, and settled to their satisfaction. When he returned from London, he was chosen one of the representatives of Boston for the general court, and was annually elected to the same office, till he was advanced to the council board. In the house of representatives he acquired great reputation. He had the charms of oratory beyond any man in the assembly. There was equal fluency and pathos in his manner ; he could be argumentative and smooth. He was active, diligent, plausible, and upon all occasions seemed to be influenced by public spirit more than selfish considerations. Some who admired him for his good qualities were afterwards of a different opinion, and wondered how he could conceal his views under the veil of hypocrisy, or with the mask of dissimulation. In 1747 he was chosen speaker of the house ; but had the same influence among the members as when he led in their debates. At this period the country was much embarrassed by the publick debt. The nominal value of which was above 2,000,000 pounds, and the provision made for redeeming it less than 200,000 pounds. All classes of people, except speculators, suffered beyond description. Especially the clergy, and widows, or orphans, whose paternal inheritance had been sunk by the depreciation of current money. All complained, but none could suggest a method to do justice, till Mr. H. pointed out a way of serving the publick, which made him conceive himself to be the prince of politicians. The "abolition of old tenor," and "introduction of a fixed currency," he relates in his history without sparing any account of his own exertions. *He* proposed the plan to gov. Shirley, who approved it! *He* then offered the same to the members of the house, who were too shortsighted to comprehend it! Out of respect to the speaker, they appointed a committee to examine what it might be! The plan, however, which their most experienced members were disposed to reject, which the most politick thought ridiculous, which seemed impracticable by men engaged in commerce, was at last by his exertions adopted, and found upon trial to be wise and judicious. The monster of frightful mein was soon changed to the fair form of benevolence, holding in her hands the fruits of industry; or riches to individuals, and honour to the community. The bill passed in the year 1749. At the succeeding election, Mr. H. was chosen a member of his majesty's council; but was still an advocate for the cause of the people on some occasions, though generally on the side of prerogative. When the excise act passed the house of representatives, and was confirmed by the council, Mr. Hutchinson, with that excellent man, chief justice Sewall, opposed it with all their influence. In the pamphlet called "the monster of monsters," which was a satirical description of the speeches made upon the excise act in the general court, Hutchinson is characterised as the friend of liberty. He is styled Madame Gracchia: for the assembly is supposed to consist of ladies, old and young, orators fair faced and fair spoken, with a goodly number of scolds. The act was so unpopular that Shirley negatived it, though it was well known that in his heart he approved the thing. Mr. H. maintained his popularity some years after this. He was then judge of probate, having succeeded his uncle Edward Hutchinson, who died in 1752. His conduct in this office had endeared him to many. He was tender and compassionate, had a generous sympathy with the children of affliction, and often wiped the tear from the eye of the mourner. In 1758, he was appointed lieut. governour, which gave pleasure to all classes of people : his deportment gave him a further interest in their affections. He was affable and condescending in his manners, yet upon publick occasions he appeared with great dignity, and stepped with majesty and grace. In 1760, he was appointed chief justice. This raised a popular clamour : it gave offence especially to one of the most brilliant families of the province, who had merited a large share of the publick esteem. The branches of this family were high whigs; one of them had been promised a seat on the bench the first vacancy, and now saw his expectations frustrated. They shook the rods of their wrath against all who were in the government, and threatened the man who was the instrument of their disappointment.*

---

* The 29th day of April, 1775, the writer of this memoir passed the afternoon with the late venerable judge Trowbridge at his house in Cambridge. It was a time of very earnest and anxious expectation. The judge made this observation after a very solemn pause : "It was a most unhappy thing that Mr. H. was ever chief justice of our court. What O——— said, ' that he would set the province in flames, if he perished by the fire,' has come to pass. He, poor man! suffers ; and what are we coming to ? I thought little of it at the time. I made every exertion in favour of Mr. H. and think now he was the best man to be there, if the people had been satisfied, and he had never looked beyond it. But I now think it was unhappy for us all. And I fully believe this war would have been put off many years, if gov. H. had not been

In 1760, Pownall left the province, and Hutchinson presided as chief magistrate. His ambition was gratified. His influence was used to advance his relations to places of profit, some of them to honourable stations, for which they were not qualified. His ruling passions often biassed his judgment, and stimulated him to act a part injurious to himself, as well as prejudicial to the province. At one time he held the places of lieut. governour, counsellor, judge of probate, chief justice, &c. These offices, with his own property, would enable him to live handsomely in the style of a gentleman. But he wanted to be rich. High life has its charms, and he wished to give a splendour to his station. This will account for certain peculiarities in his conduct, which brought upon him the charge of profusion and meanness.

The friends of gov. Pownall were enemies to Hutchinson. The patriots of Boston hailed Pownall as their friend, because he was a whig. A club of sturdy whigs, who met at the battery in the northern section of the town, endeavoured to render the administration of his predecessor odious. It was said the governour was sometimes seen amidst this merry association. It is certain that they were frequently visited by friends of a higher order, when certain points were to be carried in town meeting. At other times they admitted into their company many of the lower class, whose tongues had no bridle, when Hutchinson and Shirley were to be aspersed.

While Mr. Hutchinson was on the bench of judges he performed his duty so well, that his manner of getting the place was forgotten. He was so much a favourite with the house of representatives,

made chief justice !" He spoke of Hutchinson as a man of great abilities, who could fit himself in a very little time for any business ; and told likewise how their friendship was broken off, which manifested that gov. H. could be guilty of mean resentment, and sordid ingratitude.

in the year 1763, that they chose him agent to the court of Great Britain. In this election he had all the votes of both houses except eight.

The state of our affairs, at that period, was critical. Jasper Mauduit was unequal to the business assigned him. Bollan was left out of the agency, though every way capable and assiduous, because he was an episcopalian; Mauduit was a dissenter, but more pious than judicious; he looked upon the most important concerns of Massachusetts with frigid indifference, except his zeal was excited to convert Indians; his brother was also the tool of the ministry. Mr. Hutchinson was prevented going, by the advice of Bernard, till he could obtain permission to leave the province, of which he was lieut. governour. He wrote to lord Halifax, who complied with his request. But then the tide of his influence had turned, the popular gale was changed, and the general court voted not to send an agent. He was sorely mortified, but his friends could not help him; and his enemies rejoiced at the effect it had upon him. They had exerted themselves, totis viribus, to persuade the general court, that he was a man of arbitrary notions, and would seek his own aggrandizement more than the advantage of his constituents.

The next year the stamp act passed the British parliament. Secretary Oliver was stamp master in Boston. His office was pulled down, August 14, 1765, the day the act was to be in force. Mr. H. being his brother in law, was also the object of political animosity; riots increased till the town was completely under the influence of a mob, whose fierce spirits were let loose to do mischief.

The house of the lieut. governour was torn to pieces within a fortnight of the first lawless attack upon the secretary. This excited the attention of the friends of order. The militia were called out the next evening, and they put a stop to all riotous proceedings. But those who were active in doing the mischief were never called to account by the civil authority. There was a publick grant to Mr. H. of £.3194 17s. 6d. and to other sufferers in proportion.

Mr. Hutchinson grew still more unpopular the ensuing years. He had many friends, however, who never could harbour an ill thought of him till his letters were published, which he sent to England, wherein he advised, that " colonial privileges should be abridged." He always declared to these friends that his sentiments were contrary. Among them were clergymen of great respectability, and many sober-minded citizens. They believed him a friend to the province, as well as to the New England churches. He read to them letters, which he wrote in favour of the people, and against the arbitrary measures of the British court. But this was a mere artifice, and made his character more odious after it was fully discovered.

On the evening of the 5th of March, 1770, when a party of British soldiers fired upon the inhabitants of Boston, he had a most difficult business to manage ; but he behaved with so much discretion in his advice to the commanding officer of the troops, and his address to the people, that his enemies could not speak a word against him, with all their violence against the soldiers. His prudence calmed the tumult of the people.

In 1771, Mr. H. received his commission, as governour of Massachusetts bay, and from this time he became completely subservient to the views of the British ministry. He entered into a controversy with the general court, in which he asserted and endeavoured to prove the right of the British parliament to tax America. In this he did not succeed as he expected. It was evident that the management of the argument was superiour on the other side, and it was said the ministry, instead of being pleased, were rather disgusted, that he should make it a subject of controversy. It was a thing to be

taken for granted; not to be discussed. Whoever
reads the newspapers, from 1771 to the commencement of the war, may get a good idea of Hutchinson's character. He had his eulogists in the Gazette or Newsletter; and the writings on the other
side of the most respectable class were in the Boston Gazette, signed *Marchmont Nedham*, or *Novanglus*. The first were supposed to flow from the
pen of Mr. Quincy, a lawyer of great abilities and
eloquence, who unhappily for his country lived but
a short time after. The letters from Novanglus
were written by one of the greatest statesmen this
or any country has produced.* Gov. Hutchinson
was superseded by gen. Gage, in 1774, and on his

---

* Novanglus, who knew Hutchinson completely, thus describes
him (Boston Gazette, Feb. 20, 1775.) "That Hutchinson was
amiable and exemplary in some respects, and very unamiable
and unexemplary in others, is certain truth, otherwise he never
would have retained so much popularity on the one hand, nor
made so pernicious a use of it on the other. His behaviour in
several important offices was with fidelity and integrity in cases
which did not affect his political system, but he bent all his offices
to that. Had he continued steadfast to those principles in religion
and government which he professed in former life, and which
alone had secured him the confidence of the people, and all his
importance, he would have lived and died respected and beloved,
and done honour to his native country. But by renouncing those
principles and that conduct which had made him and all his ancestors respectable, his character is now considered by all America, and the best part of the three kingdoms (notwithstanding the
countenance he has received from the ministry) as a man who
by all his actions aimed at making himself great at the expense of
the liberties of his native country. He was open to flattery to
such a remarkable degree that any who would flatter him were
sure of his friendship; and every one who would not was sure of
his enmity. He was credulous in a ridiculous degree of every
thing which favoured his own plans, and equally incredulous of
every thing which made against him. His natural and acquired
abilities were certainly above the common standard, but were
greatly exaggerated by persons whom he had admitted to power.
His industry was prodigious, and his knowledge lay chiefly in the
laws, politicks and history of this province, of which he had long
experience, yet with all his advantages, he never was master of
the true character of his native country, nor even of New England,
and the Massachusetts Bay.

arrival at Boston, he embarked for England. He
was called to give an account of his administration,
or to describe the state of the colonies, which he
did in such a manner as met the views and designs
of the British cabinet, who took him into high favour, and made him giddy with vain expectation.
Two instances, which show the imbecility of a mind
once strong and vigorous, and also how ignorant
a wise man may become, who neglects pure sources
of information, shall be here related.   The writer
of this article vouches for their authenticity.

The governours Hutchinson, Carlton and Tryon
were called upon for their opinion upon the question about going to war with America. Mr. H.
said that the people would not, with their armies, resist the authority and power of Great Britain. " That
a few troops would be sufficient to quell them if
they did make opposition. "   Gen. Carlton spake
to this purpose, " that America might easily be con-
quered, but they would want a considerable army
for their purpose.   That he would not pretend to
march to New York or Boston without 10,000
men."   Tryon, said, " it would take large armies
and much time to bring America to their feet. The
power of Great Britain was equal to any thing ; but
all that power must be exerted before they put the
monster in chains."

Another thing is a proof of the vanity of his mind.
He wrote to a friend in Boston that his services
were so acceptable to his majesty's ministers, that
he was to have a peerage. He observed on his own
part how small his estate was, that he could never
appear in the character of a peer of the realm. But
was told the honour would be accompanied with
such lucrative appendages as would banish all concern of this kind from his mind.   His advice was
followed at the beginning of the war.   The battle
of Bunker hill convinced the army of Britain, that
the Americans would fight, and the capture of Burgoyne opened the eyes of the ministry as well as of

the nation. Hutchinson lived retired at Bromp-ton. He received no mark of honour from the court; his literary friends visited him; he often made dinners at which were assembled the American loyalists and others attached to the same cause. In the spring of the year, 1780, he was taken ill after returning from a journey. His feelings had been deeply wounded by the death of a most amiable daughter, and of his youngest son. Each had pulmonary complaints, to which he was also subject. The daughter died, Sept. 21, 1771; his son William, Feb. 20, 1780. The father soon followed; he was very sick from the beginning of April, and died June 3d of the same year. He was buried on the 9th at Croyden; Charles Paxton, Mr. Clarke, and the rev. Dr. Chandler were three of his bearers. He left no other works than those which he published in America. His history of Massachusetts is a most valuable collection of facts, but wants the style of an historian. It is sufficiently known to excuse our saying any thing more of it.

JAMES, REV. Mr. pastor of the church in Charlestown, arrived in New England in 1632. He was of Lincolnshire, Great Britain. He was invited to take the pastoral care of the church in Charlestown in the place of Mr. Wilson. Soon after his settlement, Mr. Zachary Symmes was chosen teacher of this church. He came over, in 1634, with Mr. Lathrop, and has left a name recorded among the worthies of the land. Mr. James' reputation is more clouded. He was involved in some disputes with the people of his society, which ended in his separation. Different accounts are given of his conduct, and perhaps blame may be attached to both parties. Johnson says, "seeds of prejudice were sown against him by the enemies of the work of the Lord." Governour Winthrop relates the affair differently: "The teacher, Mr. Symmes, and most of the brethren had taken offence at divers speeches of his, he being a melancholy man, and full of causeless jealousies,

&c. for which they had dealt with him both in publick and private. But receiving no satisfaction, they
wrote to all the neighbouring churches for advice
and help in this case, who sending chosen men
(most elders) they met on the 4th day of the first
month, 1635 ; and finding the pastor very faulty,
yet because they had not dealt with him in due order, (for of two witnesses adduced one was the
accuser) they advised, that if they could not com-
fortably close, himself, and such as stood on his
part (if they would) should desire dismission, which
should be granted them, for awarding extremities ;
but if he persisted, &c. the church should cast him
out ! ! He went to New-Haven, and there spent
the remainder of his days.

JOHNSON ISAAC, was the son of Abraham Johnson, esq. of Clipsham, in the county of Rutland,
Great Britain. He may be called the father of Boston, as it was he who persuaded gov. Winthrop and
the company to cross over the south side of the
river Charles. He was the richest man of all the
planters, and was filled with pious zeal to encourage
the plantation. The affairs of the company were
committed to five persons in England, and five who
were going over to the new settlement. Those
last mentioned, were Winthrop, Dudley, Johnson,
Saltonstall, and Revel. The confidence, which
the whole corporation had in Mr. Johnson, is evident from their electing him one of the referees in
the dispute between J. and S. Brown, and capt.
Endicot 1629. The Browns complained of the
abuse they had received at Naumkeake, and demanded damages. It does not appear how the dispute was settled ; but it appears, that John Winthrop, and Isaac Johnson, together with two clergymen, the rev. Mr. White, and J. Davenport,
were chosen to meet with four on the other side,
who were to finish the business. Mr. J. built
his house upon a hill in Boston. Tremont street
passes by it. He was a man greatly beloved,

Had he lived he would have been among the most distinguished characters of Massachusetts; but he died, September 20, 1630, about two in the morning. The death of such a man spread a melancholy paleness upon every countenance. "He was a holy man and wise," says gov. Winthrop, "and died in sweet peace, leaving a part of his substance to the colony." Before his death, he expressed his joy to see a church of Christ gathered in America, and was buried, at his own request, in part of the ground on Tremontane, which is between school street and court street. The people manifested their attachment, by ordering their bodies to be buried near him, as they died. It has continued a burial ground ever since. He died without children. He married the lady Arabella, daughter of the earl of Lincoln. This virtuous woman died a short time before her husband. She was taken sick at Salem. Among others that were seized with mortal sickness, says Mr. Hubbard, was the lady Arabella, wife of Mr. Isaac Johnson, who possibly had not taken the counsel of our saviour, "to set down and consider what the cost would be after she began to build. For coming from a paradise of plenty and pleasure, which she enjoyed in the family of a noble earldome, into a wilderness of wants, it proved too strong a temptation for her, so as the virtues of her mind were not able to stem the tide of the many adversities of her outward condition, which she soon saw after her arrival, she was surrounded with, for which she in a short time after ended her days at Salem, where she first landed, and was soon after solemnly interred, as the condition of those times would bear, leaving her husband (a worthy gentleman of note for piety and wisdom) a sorrowful mourner, and so overwhelmed in a flood of tears and grief, that about a month after, they carried him after her into another world."

In his will, which he made in England, he left a great number of legacies to his friends, and to pious and charitable uses. To Mr. Cotton from whom, to the praise of God's grace, he acknowledges he had received much comfort and help in his spiritual estate, he gave 30 pounds and a gown cloth. The advowson and right of patronage of the parish church of Clipsham, he gave to Mr. Dudley and Mr. Cotton. He limited his funeral charges to 250 pounds. A small part of this charge sufficed to bury him in Boston. Here many scattered blessings upon his grave, and bedewed it with tears of friendship, while their minds were soothed with the sweet remembrance of his virtues. *Hutchinson. Hubbard's mss.*

JOHNSON SAMUEL, president of King's College, New York, was born at Guilford, Connecticut, of very worthy parents. In his puerile years he discovered a lively fancy, a thirst for knowledge, and improved every opportunity to cultivate his mind. The rudiments of his education he received from Jared Eliot, who then kept school at Guilford. It is a very great advantage to youth to receive early impressions from an able hand. Many of the teachers in country villages, and we may extend our observations to larger towns, are not the men to disseminate virtue, or promote knowledge. The subject of our notice was fortunate in having Mr. E. for his instructor, but suffered from the ignorance of others. He had talents and resolution to overcome every difficulty; but how many ingenious youth sink under discouragement, where the master shakes his iron rods, but has no faculty of winning the souls of his pupils or giving instruction ! Mr. J. entered Yale College, 1710, was graduated at the usual time, and very soon was chosen tutor, being considered as the best scholar in his class. In 1724, he was ordained at West Haven, being then in the 24th year of his age.

While he was tutor of the college, valuable presents of modern books were made to the library. Mr. agent Dummer's donation was 800 vols. A fondness for the new library brought together a number of young gentlemen of literary taste, who mutually assisted each other in studying the philosophers, as well as the divines. The result of the study and consultation was, that ordinations in the New England churches were not valid; that the New England divines were very ignorant, and their preaching contemptible. The knowledge acquired by reading the works of Barrow, Patrick, South, Tillotson, &c. was "like a flood of light breaking in upon the mind." Few, however, Mr. Johnson observed, discovered an inclination or curiosity to consult any of the abovementioned writers, except Messrs. Cutler, Eliot, Hart, Whittelsey, Wetmore, Brown, and himself. All these men, from drinking deeply of these streams, became converts to the church of England.

Dr. Johnson went to England for orders, in company with Dr. Cutler, and Mr. Brown; Mr. Wetmore followed. Three of the gentlemen, Messrs. Hart, Eliot and Whittlesey, upon further consideration, did not enter into the views of those, who embraced episcopacy. They lived to an old age, ministers of the churches where they first settled, and were among the most eminent and useful men in New England. Mr. Johnson was appointed missionary of the London Society for Stratford, where he arrived Nov. 4, 1723. He was the only episcopal clergyman in the colony. His society consisted of 30 families in the place of his mission, and about 40 more in the neighbouring towns, to whom he officiated as often as he could make it convenient. When Burnet was governour of New York, he cultivated Mr. Johnson's acquaintance, and esteemed him for his talents as well as relation to the episcopal church. But this led the clergyman into some difficulty, as the governour was from the liberal school of theology, and Mr. Johnson inclined rather to the high church. Gov. Burnet persuaded him to read Clarke, Hoadley, Whiston,

&c. and it was feared by some of his friends that he would be borne down by the weight of their reasonings. But in this case he would have lost the friendship and patronage of the bishops and divines, to whom he had been introduced in England, who were all on the opposite side, in the great Bangorian controversy.

Among the friends of Mr. Johnson, Dean Berkley was the most useful and affectionate. He came to America in 1729, and resided two years at Rhode Island. These years were very interesting to a man, who had a thirst for knowledge. Mr. Johnson did not fail to cultivate his acquaintance, and improve every advantage arising from such exalted friendship. Berkley was capable of improving the human race. His virtue was equal to his genius and learning. What a luxury for those, who were intimate with him! After he left New England he kept up his correspondence with Mr. Johnson, presented him with many books for his own use, and gave to Yale College by his advice, above 1000 volumes, besides his farm on Rhode Island, the income of which was appropriated to the three best classical scholars.

In 1725, Mr. Johnson engaged in a controversy with Mr. Dickenson of Elizabethtown, New Jersey, a gentleman of whom the ministers of the church of England speak with the highest respect. Mr. Dickenson's book was printed in Boston with a preface written by Mr. Foxcroft, to which Dr. Johnson replied.

In 1723, Mr. Graham, of Woodbury, published "a ballad," in which he was satirical on several episcopal ministers in Connecticut. This led to another publication, from the pen of Dr. Johnson, styled, " plain reasons for conforming to the church." To this Mr. Graham wrote an answer; Mr. Johnson replied, and the controversy was kept up, each of them writing another tract, the last of which was in 1736, from Mr. Johnson. These defences of the church gained Mr. Johnson so much reputation, that he was, in the year 1743, presented, by the university of Oxford, with a degree of *Doctor in Divinity*.

In 1746, Dr. Johnson printed a work, which he called, a " *system of morality*," containing the "*first principles of moral philosophy, or ethicks in a chain of necessary consequences from important facts*."

He also prepared another work, 1752, " *a compendium of logic*," &c. which issued from the press of Franklin, and had a high recommendation from that philosophick gentleman.

Mr. Johnson was so distinguished a scholar, that the trustees of King's College, New York, elected him their first president. He continued in this office from 1754 to 1763, and then retired from his station at New York to the town of Stratford in Connecticut, where he had passed his youthful days in laborious and active services for the church of England ; nor was his ardour in that cause cooled by age. Amidst many bodily infirmities, he had a lively, vigorous exercise of his mind. He employed his time and pen in making proselytes to the church of England. He wrote an *appendix* to the pamphlet, which first appeared against Dr. Mayhew's considerations of the conduct of the society for propagating the gospel. The vindication of the society, to which Dr. Johnson's appendix is annexed, is anonymous. It is said to be the production of Dr. Caner, minister of the king's chapel, Boston, who was supposed, at the time, to be only the editor ; but the report comes from good authority, that he was the writer. In 1765, he published an English grammar and catechism. Also another edition of his logick, and also a Hebrew grammar, in which he undertakes to prove the " Hebrew to be the mother of all languages, and that it would be proper to begin a learned education with that language, which tends to all other languages, and borrows from none."

No man could enjoy a more happy old age than Dr. Johnson. He had resources in his own mind, was fond of books, was able to correspond with his friends at a distance, and to give pleasure to those with whom he conversed at home. Beside this general tranquillity, he had the consolations of religion, looking beyond this world to that place where the virtues of the rational mind will be improved, and the christian's hope be turned into fruition.

He died January 6, 1772, aged 76. Mr. Leaming preached at his funeral: Mr. Beach also printed a sermon in which he endeavoured to do justice to his character. *Private letters. Chandler's life of president Johnson.*

JOLYFE JOHN, esq. died at a great age, Nov. 1701, " a man who had been very useful in former days, and a member of the council in latter days." *T. M. H. mss.*

JOSSELYN JOHN, gentleman, is better known by his writings, than by any biographical sketches given of him. A person of the name is mentioned among the commissioners that came over in the reign of Charles II. to put F. Gorges into possession of his lands. He was justice of the peace in England. Mr. Hutchinson says, that John Josselyn was his brother. He discovered upon all occasions a prejudice against the people of the Massachusetts colony. He published, in 1672, a book called, " *New England's rarities* discovered, in *birds, beasts, fishes, serpents* and *plants* of that country. Together with the *physical* and *chirurgical remedies* wherewith the *natives* constantly use to cure their *distempers, wounds* and *sores,* also, a *description* of an *Indian squa,* in all her bravery, with a *poem* not improperly conferred upon her, also, a *chronological table,*" &c. Mr. Josselyn says, he came into New England, 1663. On the 28th of July, he arrived at Boston.

In 1674, Josselyn printed " an account of two voyages to New England, with a dedication to the president and fellows of the royal society."

KNOLLYS HANSERD came over to America in 1638. He had been, nine years, a minister of the church of England, and then became a nonconformist. In Boston, he was accused of Antinomianism, and meeting with trouble on this account, he went to Dover, in New Hampshire, where he preached four years, and then returned to the old country. While he was at Dover, he wrote a letter, full of resentment, against the Massachusetts colony. He declared, "they were more arbitrary than the high commission court, and that there was no real religion in the country." A copy of this letter was sent to gov. Winthrop. Mr. Knollys being much affected with the discovery, went to Boston, and at the publick lecture made a humble confession of his faults, and wrote a retraction to his friends, in England, which he left with the governour to send. According to Dr. Belknap he was an eccentrick character. In their political altercations he joined with capt. Underhill, and, upon one occasion, was armed with a pistol to defend him; another had a bible mounted on a halbert for an ensign, and with this ridiculous parade threatened the other party to the combat. He gathered a Baptist church in London, and, it is said, often preached to a thousand hearers. Mr. Henry Jessy, who was in the church, with Mr. Lathrop, was baptised by him. He was one of those who signed the Baptist confession of faith, in 1643, a copy of which is preserved. He continued many years a minister of the church in London, which he had exerted himself to establish; and died, Sept. 19, 1691, aged 93 years, "a very respectable old man."

KNOX HENRY, major general in the American army, was born in Boston, July 25, 1750. He was the sixth of 12 children, most of whom died in infancy. He had only a common school education; but when he was a youth discovered fine talents, and a desire to obtain information of the great characters of antiquity, warriors, patriots and eminent statesmen. From love of the science, he studied military tacticks before there was any appearance of a war with Great Britain. He was an officer of the Boston grenadiers, a company formed and commanded by major Dowes, who exerted himself to make the militia respectable, and was an officer of great activity and fine address. Knox was also active and enterprising, fond of applause; a distinguished character among those ardent sons of liberty, who blazed in the cause of their country; and continually gave presages of his future eminence.

He entered the army under honourable and flattering circumstances. As soon as hostilities commenced, he was appointed colonel of the battalion of artillery. There were several very excellent officers, who had been educated under major Adino Paddock in his military school; but they were young, not equal to the command, and were willing to serve under col. Knox. Paddock was a loyalist. It is true, that capt. Mason, who had raised the artillery company, to whom major Paddock succeeded as captain, was on the spot. But he, instead of seeking for the command, offered to serve as lieut. colonel, if Mr. Knox might be appointed colonel. The regiment of artillery was soon enlarged to a brigade, and Mr. Knox appointed brigadier general. He was the idol of his brigade, and highly respectable through the whole army. He was the soldier's friend, and the companion of Washington. The accounts of the several campaigns, in every history of the American war, make his services appear prominent. In 1781, after the British army surrendered at Yorktown, he had a commission of major general granted to him by congress. As his rank in the line of the army did not entitle him to this distinction, it gave offence to some of the brigadier generals, who were older on the list; but it was the desire of the army as a decent tribute of respect to the artillery, to whose efforts and skill the success of the campaign was so much owing.

The capture of lord Cornwallis and his army is certainly the most splendid event of those times, and the name of gen. Knox ought therefore to be handed down to posterity among the heroes of the revolution.

In an excellent discourse, delivered after the death of the general, by Alden Bradford, esq. it is well observed, "that his exertions were united with that illustrious patriot, gen. Washington, in composing the discontented and mutinous spirit which appeared in some part of the army, at the close of the war, and which threatened the country with the most calamitous events. And, by the same exalted character, he was selected as one well qualified to fill a responsible and important office in the federal government, which, under providence, has been the instrument of our political welfare and happiness."

After gen. Knox had resigned his office as minister of war, he employed his time in the district of Maine, and made every exertion to promote its settlement and cultivation. Here he possessed a large landed estate, and had the pleasure of beholding the wilderness subdued, and a vast extent of country, which had only exhibited the gloominess of the forest, filled with inhabitants, enjoying the blessings and improvements of social life. He did not, however, wholly seclude himself from publick cares, nor from the circles of the gay world. A part of the year he generally passed in the metropolis of old Massachusetts; and he was called to fill very respectable and honourable posts in the government. No man was ever more decided in his opinions, or undisguised in his conduct. His political sentiments were correct. His talents, his publick spirit, zeal to promote literary, humane and religious institutions, and his philanthropy, ought never to be forgotten.

Gen. Knox had a very robust constitution, enjoyed fine health and spirits, and his friends indulged the hope of his living many years; but he died suddenly, October 25th, 1806, ætat. 56.

LANGDON SAMUEL, D. D. A. A. S. was born in Boston of poor, but respectable, parents. He acquired the rudiments of knowledge at the north grammar school, and being an amiable youth, very studious, with uncommon talents, he found friends, who made every exertion to give him a liberal education. Having entered Harvard College, in 1736, he was graduated at the usual time, and went to Portsmouth, New Hampshire, to take charge of the grammar school in that town. His reputation for learning and piety was very high, and, in 1745, he was invited to preach in the first church at Portsmouth, as assistant to Mr. Fitch. He was ordained pastor, 1747. His first publication was a sermon preached at the ordination of the late Dr. M'Clintock, 1756. In 1759, he printed a thanksgiving discourse, which is one of the best occasional discourses extant; in 1761, he assisted col. Blanchard in delineating a map of New Hampshire. This was published, as their joint production, and inscribed to Charles Townsend, secretary at war. That gentleman obtained a diploma of doctor in divinity, from Aberdeen, for Mr. Langdon. In 1765, the doctor published " an examination of Sandiman's letters," in 8vo. ; this was followed by a " summary of christian faith and practice." By his manner of expressing himself upon the person of Christ, he was charged with Arianism ; but he always declared to the contrary, and professed himself a Trinitarian, and also a Calvinist, in those points which were discussed at the synod of Dort. In the year 1774, Dr. Langdon was chosen president of Harvard College. His character, as a very zealous whig, was of more advantage to him, at this time, than his reputation in the republick of letters. Mr. Hancock was in the corporation, and it was suggested to him, that prejudices were spreading against several in the government of the society, who were on the side of the tories ; and that the interest and honour of the college were likely to suffer.

When president Langdon took the chair, it gave great delight to the sons of liberty. He warmly espoused their measures, and was chosen to preach the election sermon, 1775, a month after the commencement of the war. Many things, however, concurred to make his situation very unpleasant at Cambridge. He wanted judgment, and had no spirit of government. He did not receive all that kindness from the students and officers, or legislature of the college, which his character, as a scholar and a christian, merited. He therefore, in 1780, resigned the presidency of that institution, and once more entered on the " milder task of teaching a church of Christ." He was installed at Hampton falls, 18th January, 1781; and was one of the most useful ministers in the state. In 1788, he preached the election sermon at Concord: he was also a distinguished member of the convention of New Hampshire, which adopted the federal constitution. He often, in that assembly, led their debates; and he used all his influence to convince people of their error, who indulged prejudices against it. He lived to see his expectations realized, to enjoy the political blessings this constitution afforded to the country, and was himself a blessing to his flock. It has been well observed, " that his extensive knowledge, hospitality, patriotism and piety, secured to him, in his calm retreat, the respect and affection of the people of his charge, and of his numerous acquaintance."*

He published, beside the works above mentioned, observations on the Revelations, 8vo. 1791; several sermons on particular occasions; a pamphlet, showing the mistakes of J. Ogden, rector of St. John's church, Portsmouth, 1792; also, remarks on Dr. Hopkins' scheme of divinity, 1794.

LATHROP JOHN, one of the fathers of New England, was educated at Oxford, as appears from A.

* Alden's account of Portsmouth.

Wood, who mentions his name in Athenæ Oxoni-
enses. He was afterwards an independent minister
in London. Mr. Jacob was the first minister of the
independents, who went to Virginia in 1624, and
was succeeded by Mr. Lathrop. About 40 of this
religious society were imprisoned in 1632. The
crime alledged was their assembling unlawfully.
Many of them were afterwards released, but no favour could be obtained for Mr. Lathrop. He requested that he might have liberty to depart the
kingdom. The petition was presented to king
Charles. Laud had discovered the most virulent
prejudice against him. He hated puritans of every
denomination, and felt the more resentment against
a man, who was a leader of their straitest sect, a
minister of a church in the city, which made themselves independent of all ecclesiastical rule or power, except what was exercised by the *brethren.*
Having obtained liberty of the king, Mr. Lathrop
sailed from England in the year 1634, and arrived
at Boston the 18th day of September. Being
there on the sacrament day, the first week in October, he desired liberty to be present at the administration of the ordinance, but said, " that he durst
not desire to partake in it, because he was not then
in order (being dismissed from his former congregation) and he thought it not fit suddenly to be admitted into any other for example's sake, and because of the deceitfulness of man's heart." He met
the ideas of our fathers upon this subject, for which
they are censured in a letter, supposed to be written
by Mr. Cotton, before he came over to America:
" I am constrained to bear witness against your
judgment and practice, that you think no man may
be admitted to the sacrament, though a member of
the catholick church, except he be a member of
some particular church. "

Mr. Lathrop and his people went to Scituate.
But in the year 1639, there was some difference of
opinion, which caused a division; and a considerable

number, with their pastor, removed to Barnstable. Several letters upon the subject of their removal are preserved in the hands of the family. It was a matter of surprise ; and excited many observations at the time. The church at Barnstable, however, grew and flourished under his fruitful ministry; the town increased in numbers, and remains, to this day, conspicuous in the county for numbers, wealth, trade, social order, and religious character. Mr. Lathrop died in 1653. His character was that of a learned, pious, meek christian minister, who was in season and out of season, ready to every labour of his office, and to promote the good of the settlement. He left a numerous posterity. The late Isaac Lothrop, esq. a gentleman of Plymouth, and member of the historical society, was one of his descendants. In Connecticut and Massachusetts several are magistrates, and others very respectable in private life ; two aged clergymen, also, among the most worthy and distinguished of the profession in this state are his great grandsons, the rev. Dr. Joseph Lathrop of West Springfield, and rev. Dr. John Lathrop of Boston.

LEE SAMUEL, M. A. fellow of Wadham College, was proctor of the university of Oxford, A. D. 1651. He possessed a strong and brilliant imagination, and his learning was very extensive. He printed a large book in Latin de excidio Antichristi, and also a description of Solomon's temple, folio, 1659. He came into New England the latter part of the reign of Charles 2d, and was pastor of the church at Bristol, in Rhode Island, which was then part of the colony of Plymouth. Two reasons are assigned for his leaving Great Britain. One, that he was afraid of the growth of popery ; another, that he was invited to be president of Harvard College. He was never pleased with the manners of the people, nor with the state of things in New England. Being eccentric in his genius and extravagant in speech, he disgusted many, who admired his talents, and read his books with delight. He was rich, haughty, and overbearing. Many anecdotes are related of him, which served as a kind of entertainment to the generation which succeeded those who *knew* him. He was returning to his native country, after the revolution, and was taken prisoner by a French privateer and carried into St. Maloes. After suffering every thing which the prejudices of bigots could add to what national antipathies prompted, he died a victim to their cruelty.

He published a book, which has been much read in New England. "The triumph of mercy in the chariot of praise." He also published the "joy of faith," and a discourse upon the "ten tribes, 8 vo. and a number of single sermons."

LEETE WILLIAM, governour of Connecticut, came into New England, A. D. 1638. He was bred a lawyer in the old country, and was clerk in the bishop's court, but gave up his office on account of the spiritual tyranny which was exercised in those courts. He sailed in the vessel with Eaton and Hopkins, and joined Mr. Whitfield's company, who laid the foundation of the town of Guilford. His name is among the six planters who signed the deeds and writings at New Haven, in Newman's barn, Sept. 1639, when they purchased the lands of the squaw Sachem; and afterwards 31st of January the same year when they confirmed the agreement; as appears from the records of that colony. He was also one of the seven pillars of Mr. Whitfield's church. When Mr. W. went to England, several of the first planters went with him, but Mr. Leete remained at Guilford, where he lived much esteemed by the people of that town, and highly respected by the colony. He was chosen a magistrate in 1643. In 1658, he was elected deputy governour of New Haven; and in 1661, placed in the chair of government. He was a rigid puritan and stern republican. In 1660, he contrived to evade the mandates of Charles 2d, concerning the regicides, though urged by the authority of the governour of Massachusetts. Whaley and Goffe had taken refuge in Connecticut. They made themselves known to Mr. Leete, and he was charged with concealing them; but he was not intimidated by the wrath of their pursuers. Even when the regicides would have given themselves up, as victims to publick justice, rather than expose their friends to a prosecution, he prevented them, and assisted in every measure for their comfort and safety. In 1665, when the colonies united, he was chosen one of the magistrates of Connecticut; in 1669, deputy governour; and annually received this honour from the people, till in 1676, they chose him their first magistrate. After he was chosen governour of Connecticut, he removed to Hartford, where he lived to a good old age, and in 1683 finished his course. In both colonies, says Dr. Trumbull, "he presided in times of the greatest difficulty; yet always conducted with such integrity and wisdom as to meet the publick approbation." That excellent historian mentions an instance where, in his latter days, he departed from those rigid principles of opposition to royalty, which once influenced him. "The acts of trade and navigation were exceedingly grievous to the colonies. They viewed them as utterly inconsistent with their chartered rights. This made them extremely unwilling to submit to them. Massachusetts never would fully submit; but as it was matter of great and continual complaint against the colonies, and as his majesty insisted on the respective governours taking the oath respecting trade and navigation, it was judged expedient that gov. Leete should take it, in presence of the assembly. It was accordingly administered to him at the session in May, 1680."

LEVERETT THOMAS, one of the first inhabitants of Boston. He was ruling elder of the old church and ordained to that office, October 17th, 1633, the same day that Mr. Cotton was ordained teacher.

LEVERETT JOHN, governour of the Massachusetts colony, had been a soldier, and distinguished himself in several actions abroad. The first notice we have of him, in our annals, is, in 1642, when the Narraganset Indians were preparing to make war upon the English. He was sent, with Mr. Edward Hutchinson, to Miantinomo, to make complaint of his duplicity, and to require their sachem to come to Boston, or send two of his chief counsellors, that complete satisfaction might be obtained concerning his conduct. He was, in the year 1653, one of the commissioners of Oliver Cromwell to raise five hundred volunteers to assist in the war against the Dutch, at Manhadoes. They were required to do this, by the lord Protector, at the request of the New Haven colony, who had reason to dread every thing from their Dutch neighbours, and the Indians, who were instigated, by that people, to fall upon the nearest English settlements. Mr. L. was after this employed in places of trust. He was in England at the restoration, and an advocate for the colony. Upon his return, he was chosen a member of the general assembly for Boston ; in 1664, he was appointed major general, and assistant in 1665 ; in 1671, he was promoted to be deputy governour. He succeeded Willoughby, a man of two much liberality for his brethren ; for he opposed all the persecutions against the Baptists. In 1673, gov. Bellingham died, the only surviving patentee of the charter, and Mr. Leverett was introduced to the chair. He was so beloved by the colony, that his election was never contested ; and he descended with honour to the grave, March 16, 1678. Mr. Nowel preached at the funeral, and Mr. Allen an occasional sermon the Sabbath after.

LEVERETT JOHN, F. R. S. president of Harvard College, was a grandson of gov. Leverett. He was born in Boston, and graduated, A. D. 1680. He soon made a figure among gentlemen of the civil order, was chosen representative for Boston at the general court, and, for a number of years, was speaker of the assembly. He was advanced to his majesty's council, and appointed judge of the superiour court. All these honourable posts he sustained with dignity, integrity, and the applause of the people. He was also appointed one of the three commissioners with power of controlling the army, sent against Port Royal.

In 1707, this honourable gentleman was chosen president of Harvard College, which station he adorned by his learning, and excellent character. He was one of gov. Dudley's particular friends, and did all in his power to serve him, when he was in the civil line, and was very instrumental in making his administration acceptable to the people. In Dr. Cotton Mather's diary, he says, " I received a visit from gov. Dudley, June 16, 1702." With other observations of a familiar nature, he said to his excellency, " I am humbly of opinion, that it will be your wisdom to carry an indifferent hand towards all parties, if I may use so coarse a word as parties, and give occasion to none to say that any have monopolized you, or that you take your measures from them alone. I should approve it, if any other should say, by no means let the people have cause to say, that you take all your measures from the two Mr. Mathers. By the same rule I may say without offence, by no means let any people say, that you go by no measures in your conduct but Mr. Byefield's and Mr. Leverett's." This conversation was related to these gentlemen, and tended to increase their prejudices against the good doctors. While president Leverett was in the chair, they seldom or ever attended the overseers' board. It also prevented Dr. Cotton Mather from being " fellow of the corporation ;" but he had the mortification to see Dr. Colman and Mr. Brattle, men, who were not even on friendly terms with him, members of the corporation, and all college affairs under their influence. He complained bitterly of this thing in his diaries.

President Leverett received honours from abroad, as well as from his own country. From a sense of his literary merit, he was elected fellow of the royal society, London.

In the character given of him after his death, written at Cambridge, it is observed, " that for more than forty years, he shone with near a *meridian lustre*; the morning of his life being so bright, that it shone like noon, and both the college and country rejoiced greatly in his early and uncommon light, and now his sun yet seems to us to have gone down at noon, such being his vigour and brightness to the age of sixty two."

His death was very sudden, on the Lord's day morning, 3d of May, 1724, dying, as is supposed, in his sleep, without a groan or struggle.

Mr. Welsteed, one of the tutors, had an eloquent, and a very pathetick, oration in the hall upon the sorrowful occasion.

Locke Samuel, D. D. president of Harvard College, was a man of very uncommon powers of mind, a very accomplished preacher, with a most extraordinary gift in prayer. He was graduated in 1755, and ordained minister of Sherburne two years after, where he continued till he was invited to Cambridge. He was installed president of the college, March 21, 1770, and resigned his office, December 1, 1773.

Lovell John, a celebrated preceptor in Boston, was graduated at Harvard College, A. D. 1728. Two years after he had received the honours of that seminary, the selectmen of Boston chose him assistant to Dr. Nathaniel Williams, for many years master of the south grammar school. In this office he succeeded the famous Jeremy Gridley, who then entered upon his professional pursuits. Upon the death of master Williams, in 1738, he was advanced to the chief place, and continued to discharge the duties of that important station with great diligence and skill, above forty years. Most of our

first characters, in church and state, during that period, had been under his tuition.   He was an excellent critick and classical scholar ; his learning
was extensive, and he had a clear understanding,
and solid judgment. Though a rigid disciplinarian
in his school, yet he was an agreeable companion,
and very humourous.   He wrote many fugitive
pieces, and several political and theological pamphlets.   In 1742, when Mr. Faneuil died, he was
chosen to deliver a funeral oration, which he pronounced in Faneuil hall, March 14, the day of the
annual town meeting.   This was printed, and is an
elegant composition, in which the virtues of that munificent friend of the town are celebrated,

   In the controversy between Great Britain and
the colonies, master Lovell took a very decided
part.   He joined the loyalists, and went away with
the fleet and army, which left Boston, March 17,
1776, and passed the rest of his days in Halifax.

   LOWELL JOHN, minister of the first church in
Newburyport, was born in Boston, March 14, 1703
—4, was graduated at Harvard College, 1721 ; ordained January 19, 1725—6, and died, May 15,
1767, in the 64th year of his age, and 42d of his
ministry He was distinguished among his brethren,
as a scholar and a gentleman ; as a lover of good men,
though of different denominations, and differing sentiments ; amiable in his domestick and social connections, and happily furnished with that kind of
knowledge which enabled him to be very useful
as a minister of religion. . *Tucker's funeral sermon.*

   LOWELL JOHN, L L. D, and A. A. S. son of
the rev. Mr. L. was born at Newbury, 1744, was
graduated at Harvard College, 1756, and applied himself to the study of law.   He very soon
rose to great eminence in the profession, and he
grew in publick esteem, and the affections of his
acquaintance, as he advanced into life.   The integrity of his character always secured him the confidence of those, who admired his abilities.   In the

year 1761, he removed from Newburyport to Boston ; was chosen representative for the town at the general court, and one of their twelve delegates to the convention, which formed the constitution for the commonwealth. In that assembly, he was very much distinguished by his knowledge and eloquence. Being one of the committee, who drew the plan, he was fully acquainted with the subject whenever he took a part in the debates ; his speeches were perspicuous, while the energy of his expression and glow of manner made them very interesting and entertaining. In 1781, he was chosen member of congress, and, in December, 1782, he was appointed, by that body, one of the three judges of the court of appeals, a tribunal established by congress in the year 1780, for the trial of all appeals from the courts of admiralty of the several states. When the federal government was established, he was appointed, by president Washington, judge of the district court in Massachusetts. He remained in that office, till the new organization of the federal judiciary in 1801, when he was appointed chief justice of the circuit court for the first circuit, comprehending the District of Maine, New Hampshire, Massachusetts and Rhode Island. In the discharge of that office he continued until the repeal of the act in 1802.

On the bench judge Lowell appeared with peculiar and engaging lustre. With the most condescending and obliging manners he maintained the dignity of his station. In critical causes, he was mature and deliberate in making up a judgment, and his quick apprehension and faculty for discrimination, enabled him to give despatch to ordinary business. People of different political sentiments, had the same persuasion of his knowledge, and impartiality ; and those against whom judgment was given, were disposed to confide in the equity and legality of it. Had the act been continued, which established the circuit courts, he would have had a greater sphere of usefulness, and for the display of his talents.

When he left publick business and retired to private life, his mind was active in promoting benevolent associations, and literary improvements. He had a fondness for agriculture, gardening, botany, and other branches of natural history. He first originated the subscription for a professorship of natural history at the university, and was among the most generous subscribers.

Judge Lowell was always a great friend to Harvard College ; his mind was constantly employed in devising means for its prosperity. When there was a vacancy in the corporation in 1784, he was elected one of that board, and was, for eighteen years, a very attentive, firm and judicious member. The critical state of the publick funds during this period caused some doubtful and anxious expectations, and required of the members of the corporation peculiar watchfulness over the property they had in trust. Mr. L. acquainted himself with the interest and circumstances of the college, and its treasury was specially benefitted by his discreet and active exertions. He was one of the most active of our publick characters, in forwarding the plan in 1780, for establishing an academy of arts and sciences ; and the society elected him one of their counsellors. They had also such a sense of his literary merits that they chose him, with an unanimous vote, to deliver an oration when president Bowdoin died. The service was performed in Brattle-street church, January 26, 1791. The oration was published in one of the volumes of the academy. His other publications are without his name, but are specimens of elegant composition. He died, greatly lamented, May 6, 1802.

LUDLOW ROGER, came with Mr. Warham and his company to Dorchester, in 1630, was chosen a magistrate, and was deputy governour of Massachusetts in 1634. He succeeded Thomas Dudley, who was promoted to the chief place in the room of gov. Winthrop, whom the freemen left out, for the sake of making a rotine in the office.* The next year, Mr. Ludlow was set aside even from the magistracy. It seems, he aimed at the governour's place, and was disappointed. For some reason or other, he protested against the choice, which offended the freemen. Instead of advancing him, therefore, they gave him an opportunity to enjoy private life. He soon after removed to Connecticut. He fixed his abode in Fairfield, and, being clerk of that town, had the care of all their records, which he carried off when he left New England, 1654. He was a magistrate of Connecticut, or deputy governour from the time of his coming into the colony to his departure. In 1648, he was one of the commissioners of the United colonies. He was chosen again in 1650, and several years after. At their meeting, 1653, they voted to carry on the war against the Dutch. He was full of resentment at the conduct of the people, who opposed the determinations of the commissioners. He was rash enough to head a party, who were ready to go from Fairfield to Manhadoes, and begin the war. Men of warm sanguine tempers are not apt to weigh consequences till it is too late. He gave so much offence as to make it best for him to leave the country. The least he could expect was to lose his offices. And the neglect of the people is apt to chill the frame of politicians, as much as their ingratitude can wound

---

* " Mr. Cotton preached before the General Court this month, and delivered this doctrine, that the magistrate ought not to be hurried into the condition of a private man without just cause, and to be publickly convicted ; no more than the magistrate may now turn a private man out of his household, &c. without like publick trial. This falling in question in the court, and the opinion of the rest of the ministers being asked, it was referred for further consideration." *Winthrop's Journal.*

This would be strange policy in some states of society. So far from being adopted by the *sovereign* people, at this time, that they let the ministers know, that all magistrates were only the creatures of their power, and should be shifted at their pleasure.

the spirit. Dr. Trumbull gives Ludlow a high character. He says, he rendered very essential services to the commonwealth; was a principal in forming its original constitution, and the compiler of the first Connecticut code, printed at Cambridge, 1672. For jurisprudence he appears to have been second to none, who came into New England at that time. Had he possessed a happier temper he would, probably, have been the idol of the people.

MANNING JAMES, D. D. president of Brown College, Rhode Island, was born in New Jersey, Oct. 22, 1738; was graduated at the college of Princetown, 1761. He was ordained a preacher of the gospel, and acquired as much fame by his abilities and learning, as by his very fine voice and delivery. As soon as they erected a college in Rhode Island and Providence plantations, he was invited to preside over that seminary. In 1764, Mr. Manning removed to Warren, where the legislature contemplated fixing the college. But a spacious building being erected in the town of Providence, through the influence of some leading characters, the college was established in that town. President Manning removed in 1770, and continued to discharge the duties of his station to the great advantage of the institution, as long as he lived. The same year he was chosen pastor of the Baptist church, and was able to discharge the duties of president, and to preach to a very large parish. In 1786, he was elected a delegate to congress. He was a strong federalist when the constitution was the subject of debate. He attended very frequently the convention, which met in Boston, for the sake of hearing the arguments on both sides, that he might acquire greater strength to combat those, who opposed the constitution in the state of Rhode Island.

He received his diploma of doctor in divinity from the university of Philadelphia.

Finding it inconsistent with his other offices to attend congress, he resigned his place, and gave his whole attention to college duties, and no man was better calculated to make the institution flourish. He was suddenly called off the stage of action, by a fit of the apoplexy, and died, 24th July, 1791, in the 53d year of his age.

MATHER RICHARD, minister of Dorchester, was the first of the family, who came over to New England ; and from him are descended many worthy and learned men, who have been celebrated in England, as well as in these new plantations. He was called a great man in his day by others, besides his descendants, who were never backward in celebrating the talents and literary accomplishments, on eminent christian virtues of their ancestors. Perhaps many men, among the wisest and best of their generation, have not been mentioned in a succeeding age, having no friend to flatter, and no children to bear up the name.

For more than a century the name of Mather was known and celebrated in every part of the land ; many branches are now cut off, and we must go out of the state of Massachusetts to find one engaged in the work of the ministry, though formerly so many of them were distinguished among the angels of the churches. "In all ages, there have been stars to lead men to the knowledge of the Lord Jesus Christ. Angelical men, employed in the ministry of our Lord, have been those happy stars. And we in the west have been so happy, as to see some of the first magnitude, among which was Mr. Richard Mather." *Magnalia.*

He was born in the county of Lancaster, A. D. 1596. His parents were respectable, and gave him a liberal education. He was educated at the university of Oxford, became a preacher in early life, was eminent for his pious discourses in the pulpit, and for conversation, but was suspended for his nonconformity, in 1633. He was again restored, and again suspended, and after some inquiry and debate, in his own mind, he resolved to leave the fair fields of his own country for the obscure *places of the wilderness.* In May, 1635, he sailed from Bristol, and arrived in Boston harbour, August 17. Two days previous to his arrival there was a tremenduous storm, of which he has given a printed account.

He was ordained pastor of the church at Dorchester, August 23, 1636, and was a distinguished ornament of the churches of New England. In the year 1669, he had a violent fit of the stone, to which he had been subject many years, and died 22d day of April. Though an old man, yet his death was a great loss, because his talents and industy enabled him to be useful, and, at this very time, he was moderator of a council, which had met in Boston to settle a dispute, and which led one of his brethren to write this *epitaph,* Vixerat in synodis, moritur moderator in illis. He had been a leading character in every synod, which had met in New England, from his arrival to the time of his death. In 1639, there were 32 questions printed *concerning church government.* These were answered by the ministers of New England. Mr. R. Mather is said to have written the answer; and, also, that the platform of church government, which was held in so much veneration for so many years, though now only resorted to upon convenient occasions, was chiefly composed by him. He prepared for the press a book entitled, a plea for the churches in New England, a large work. Besides these, he wrote several pamphlets to mark the difference between the Congregational mode of government and the Presbyterian establishment.

In 1662, the famous synod was appointed by the general court to settle the controversy concerning the subjects of baptism, and also the consociation of churches. Certain propositions were drawn up, and presented to the general court, which were accepted. One of these excited no small controversy, which has been kept up even to the present day. It is not likely that our *general court* will again meddle with it; but there will be disputants among those, who have the spirit of religious controversy. It was the fifth proposition discussed by the synod, " Whether those, who make a profession of religion, whereby *they give themselves up to God in a solemn covenant, and subject themselves to the discipline of the church, shall have the privilege of baptism for their children.*"

There were several, who opposed the voice of the synod, among them president Chauncy, Mr. Davenport, of New Haven, and Mr. Increase Mather, minister of the second church in Boston.

Three very eminent divines were elected to manage the controversy with them. Mr. Allen of Dedham, to answer president Chauncy, *Mr. Richard Mather* to write against *Mr. Davenport,* and Mr. Mitchel of Cambridge a younger divine, but Vir, *claro nomine,* to discuss the subject with Mather the younger. The books were well written, but the manner of writing, which Mr. R. Mather adopted, pleased old Mr. Higginson of Salem so much, that he said, " *he was a pattern to all the answerers in the world.*"

From the general account of this eminent divine, his talents were adapted for controversy, and his knowledge of ecclesiastical affairs made him more qualified to write, than many of his brethren. As a preacher, he was plain and practical, solid and judicious; but less popular, than several of his sons, whose sermons and pulpit eloquence have been more applauded.

He printed a treatise upon justification, and several small treatises, which were well spoken of; and prepared several sermons for the press, which were never published.

Mr. Mather was blessed with a number of children. He left four sons, all of whom were distinguished preachers of the gospel, and of whom mention should undoubtedly be made in these biographical sketches.

MATHER SAMUEL, preached the first sermon which was delivered in the church at North Boston. He was afterwards settled at Dublin, where he died, A. D. 1671, having been laborious in his business, serviceable in his generation, and respectable among men of worth and talents. He was the author of a number of publications.

MATHER NATHANIEL, who succeeded Samuel at Dublin, and was afterwards pastor of a church in London, was graduated at Harvard College, 1647.

MATHER ELEAZER, was graduated 1656, and was settled at Northampton 1661. He died at the age of 32.

Of the fourth son, we are prepared to give a more circumstantial narrative.

MATHER INCREASE, D. D. president of Harvard College. was graduated the same year with his brother Eleazer, and was invited to preach at the north church in Boston, rendered vacant by the resignation of Mr. *Mayo.* He was ordained pastor, May 27, 1699. In 1681, he was invited to take charge of the college, and, at the commencement of this year, he moderated at the master's disputations, and conferred the degrees. But, upon consulting with his church, they refused to part with him, and Mr. Rogers was chosen president of the college. In 168?; Mr Rogers died, and Mr. Mather was again honoured by an election to that office, and accepted it upon certain conditions, by which he could comply with the request of the corporation, and satisfy the objections of his own church. He was allowed to preach every Sabbath in Boston, and attend his duty as president of the college on week days. His great industry and application to business enabled him to do this. He excelled likewise in extemporaneous performances, which rendered his ministerial duties more easy to him. He governed the college with great reputation till the year 1701, when his age required relaxation from a multiplicity of cares, and he resigned his place at Cambridge.

While he was at the head of the college, he was presented by the fellows of the corporation and board of overseers, with a diploma of doctor in divinity.*

Dr. Mather was eminent for his services both to the church and commonwealth. He must have possessed talents and influence, or he never would have been chosen agent to the court of Great Britain. He used all his influence to persuade the people never to surrender their charter, and published his reasons. He found in Randolph, therefore, a bitter enemy, who contrived the most base methods to ruin him. A letter was sent to sir Lionel Jenkins, with the signature of Dr. Mather, which contained reflections upon him, and praises of Oates, lord Shaftesbury, &c. men, who were obnoxious to the king. There was such appearance of forgery,

---

* By Mr. Mather's influence the general court passed an act, bearing date June 27. 1692, for a new college charter, and sent it over to Great Britain for the royal assent ; but the king negatived it, because it did not reserve to him, by his governour, the power of a royal visitation. Upon this, the general assembly of New England after some time revised the act, and sent it back, with an amendment, admitting the king by his governour and council in New England, to be visitors of the college ; but the court not accepting the amendment, the affair was dropped, and the college left to act upon the foot of the old charter, which they had by George Dudley, in 1650. But it being proved by the new charter of the province, that when the general court passes the act, and sends it over to England for the royal assent, it continues in force for three years, if it be not sooner repealed, the governours of the college took advantage of this clause, and presented the president with a diploma of doctor of divinity, under the seal of the college, with the hands of the fellows annexed to it, bearing date from Cambridge in New England, Nov. 17, 1692. Mr. M. accepted the diploma, but was never installed, nor did he assume the title for several years ; but the great services he had done his country, his universal learning and goodness, together with his venerable old age, at length supplied the defects of the title, and confirmed him in this honour with the universal consent and approbation of his country. *Neal's history*, vol. ii. page 115.

The expression " continuing in force three years" is not quite correct. The laws were perpetually in force, or for the term therein mentioned, unless the king, within three years, disallow them.

that sir Lionel treated it with contempt. When this was told Dr. Mather, some years after, he explained the business to that gentleman with his opinion, that Randolph wrote it. Upon this, Randolph brought an action against him for defamation; but the case was given in favour of the defendant. Randolph was not satisfied; and it being the triumph of his power, he determined to bring another action, if it were only to vex and torment him. About this time the general assembly had fixed their eyes upon him, as a proper person to send to England to represent their grievances, and remonstrate against the arbitrary conduct of sir Edmund Andross. Randolph's writ would have prevented his voyage; but he went on board the vessel in the night, April, 1688, and sailed immediately for London. When he arrived, he presented himself to king James, and described the situation of the colony, and his majesty made a promise to redress grievances. He was afterwards introduced to the prince of Orange, and when king William and Mary were on the throne, all the New England agents addressed their majesties for the restoration of their charters. Their applications were deferred on account of the affairs of Europe, which drew the king to Holland. In one audience, which they obtained of his majesty, April 28, 1691, Mr. Mather humbly prayed his majesty's favour to New England. "Your subjects," said he, "have been willing to venture their lives to enlarge your dominions: the expedition to Canada was a great and noble undertaking. May it please your majesty, in your great wisdom, also, to consider the circumstances of that people, as in your wisdom you have considered the circumstances of England and Scotland. In New England, they differ from other plantations: they are called congregational and presbyterian; so that such a government will not suit with the people of New England, as may be proper for people in the other plantations."

The several applications, which were made to the king; the difference of opinion among the agents of New England; the various conferences with the ministers, lawyers, and noblemen, who were friends to the colonies, are all related very minutely in the history of Massachusetts bay, and in the memoirs of Dr. Increase Mather, which his son published after his death.

The new charter arrived, 14th May, 1691, and the general court appointed a day of thanksgiving for the safe arrival of his excellency the governour, and the rev. Mr. Increase Mather, who (say they) have industriously endeavoured the service of this people, and have brought over with them a settlement of government, in which their majesties have graciously given a distinguished mark of their royal favour and goodness.

There were many, however, who disliked the abridgment of their privileges, and censured their agents, who accepted the new charter; some of Mr. Mather's old friends forsook him; and he often complains of the ingratitude of those whom he wished to serve. He was, to be sure, covered with many honours, which it was rare for a minister of the gospel to receive; but he was troubled with many cares, which those are freed from, who confine themselves to their professional duties. He doubtless thought full enough of his services, and many, on the other hand, were disposed unreasonably to take from him part of the credit, which he deserved. The dissenting ministers in London were his friends; but they knew better how to estimate his piety than his policy. He had testimonies from some eminent statesmen of his abilities, probity and industry, particularly from lord Somers; but if praises were bestowed upon him because he acted by their advice, the compliment is more to themselves than to him.

As the pastor of a church, Dr. Mather was highly esteemed by all classes of people. His gifts, his preaching, and his writings were accounted excellent. He was the father of the New England clergy, and his name and character were held in veneration, not only by those, who knew him, but by succeeding generations. He died, August 23, 1723, aged 85. Several discourses were printed upon the occasion; but a more full account of him is in an octavo volume, called "Remarkables of the life of Dr. Increase Mather."

His publications were numerous. In the book above mentioned, we have a catalogue of 85, beside "the learned and useful *prefaces*, which the publishers of many books obtained from him, as a beautiful porch unto them, and which collected would make a considerable volume."

MATHER COTTON, D. D. F. R. S. the eldest son of Dr. Increase Mather, was the most celebrated divine in New England; and if his judgment had been equal to his imagination and memory, he would have ranked with the first scholars of any age. His mother was daughter of the famous John Cotton, teacher of the first church in Boston. He was born in Boston, 1662, graduated at Harvard College, 1678, ordained colleague with his father, May 27, 1684, and died, Feb. 13, 1728. The obituary of the Boston Newsletter describes him, "as the principal ornament of his country, and the greatest scholar that was ever bred in it. Besides his universal learning, his exalted piety and extensive charity, his entertaining wit and singular goodness of temper recommended him to all, who were judges of real and distinguished merit." Oldmixen and Douglass give an account of him very different. One only judges of him from his works; he calls his history a miserable jargon, loaded with many learned quotations, school boy exercises, Romanlike legends, and barbarous rhymes.* The other was prejudiced against him, and descends to every kind of low satire to render the man as well as the writer

* British empire in America.

ridiculous. His own " summary" however is not more elegant, nor are the facts equally correct.

Dr. Mather had his enemies in town and country, and doubtless there were eccentricities in his conduct, as well as weak things in his writings. He wrote too much to write well. He did every thing with amazing rapidity. It is said he could read a folio of many hundred pages, and write a sermon in the course of a forenoon. He became acquainted with every thing by a kind of intuition, and was also a man of prodigious industry. With all his attention to literary pursuits, and his active services, he never neglected any of his parochial duties ; and also allowed himself time for private devotion, spending one day of the week in fasting and prayer. He had less influence in the affairs of the commonwealth than his father, and the events of his life were not so various. The clergy also treated him with less respect, although they were ready to acknowledge, that he had superiour abilities to the old gentleman, and a vast deal more learning. There was a singular gravity in the deportment of Dr. Increase Mather, which qualified him for a patriarch ; Dr. C. Mather discovered often a levity of mind, a strange kind of vanity, a fondness for punning and making remarks inconsistent with the character of that age ; and which sometimes brought him into serious difficulties. He had a great acquaintance with books, but did not understand human nature ; yet he imagined he had a claim to all that reverence from his brethren and the people, which his father's age as well as prudence gave him.

His literary distinctions were chiefly from abroad. The university of Glasgow presented him with a diploma of doctor of divinity ; and his name is on the list of the fellows of the royal society in London. He is styled a fellow of Harvard College in the catalogue ; but he was only chosen among those, who were to be fellows, if the college charter were enlarged.

Twice he thought himself a candidate for the president's chair, and kept days of fasting, that he might be directed how to act upon the occasion ; but he was disappointed. Gov. Dudley persuaded his friend Leverett to accept the place in 1707 ; and when that great man died, in 1726, and the voice of the people cried aloud for Dr. Mather, and it was declared even in the general court that he ought to be president, it was decided otherwise by the members of the corporation. The chair was first offered to Dr. Colman, and Dr. Sewall, and afterwards to Mr. Wadsworth, who accepted it. In a private account of this transaction, Dr. M. says, " this day Dr. Sewall was chosen for his piety." In a publick speech made in the general assembly a member of the Boston seat declared, after Dr. Colman's election, that he was a man of no learning compared with Dr. Mather.*

One of the most elegant compositions of those times, was a funeral sermon upon Dr. Cotton Mather, by this very Dr. Benjamin Colman, who therein declares him to be by far the greatest man he ever was acquainted with.

In the account of the funeral of Dr. Mather, in the newspapers, it seems, that great respect was paid to his remains. After the relatives, proceeded the lieut. governour, Mr. Dummer, his majesty's council, and house of representatives, a large train of ministers, justices, merchants, scholars and other principal inhabitants both of men and women. The streets were crowded with people, and the windows filled with sorrowful spectators all the way to the burying place.

He was a most voluminous writer ; his works amount to more than 300 tracts, histories, biographical sketches, &c. besides the Magnalia, a folio volume. The " biblia Americana," in several volumes, ms. is deposited in the historical library.

It would require more pages to give a just view

* Letters and mss. in the cabinet of historical library.

of his writings, than we can allow to an article of our biography. A volume of memoirs was published by his son and successor, Dr. Samuel Mather, which also contains every remarkable occurrence in his life, a minute view of his studies, and of all his publications. His son was called to the office of pastor of the old north church, 1732, and in 1742 a separation took place by mutual agreement. The people who withdrew built another meeting house, where he was fixed till he ended his labours. He was a man of very extensive reading, and the author of several tracts. He received a diploma of doctor of divinity from Harvard College, 1773. He died, June 27, 1785.*

MAVERICK JOHN, one of the fathers of Massachusetts, and first minister of the church in Dorchester, came over with Ludlow, Rossiter, and others, from the counties of Devon, Dorset and Somersetshire. In the beginning of the year 1630, a congregational church was gathered in the new hospital at Plymouth by those, who intended to come to North America for the purpose of enjoying greater civil and religious privileges. They observed a day of fasting and prayer to seek for the divine approbation and assistance. In the after part of the day they chose and called those godly ministers, rev. John Warham and rev. John Maverick, who lived 40 miles from Exeter, to be their spiritual guides ; who expressed their acceptance, and were separated to the especial care of the intended emigrants. Rev. John White of Dorchester, in Dorset, who was an active instrument in promoting the settlement of New England, and had been the means of procuring the charter, being present, preached in the forepart of the day ; and, in the latter part, the

* The other works of Dr. Samuel Mather are, an essay on gratitude, 1732 ; artillery election sermon, 1739 ; convention sermon, 1762 ; three funeral sermons ; dissertation on the Lord's prayer ; dissertation on the venerable name of Jehovah, 1760 ; a poem, the sacred minister, 1772 ; America known to the ancients, 1774 ; a reply to a pamphlet entitled, salvation for all men, 1780, &c.

new installed pastors performed. They set sail on
the 30th March, and arrived at Nantasket, May 30,
where the master put them on shore, notwithstanding the engagement was to bring them up Charles
river. Here they were left in a forlorn wilderness,
destitute of any habitation, and most of the necessaries of life.* Mr. Maverick died in Boston, 1636,
Feb. 30. A large part of his church had removed
to Windsor, Connecticut, and it was his intention
to follow them. He was 60 years of age. He was
a man " of a very humble spirit, and faithful in fur-
thering the work of the Lord here, both in the
churches and civil state." *Winthrop*.

MAVERICK SAMUEL had planted himself, at
Noddle's island, when gov. Winthrop and his company formed the settlement of Boston. " We went
to Massachusetts," says he, " to find out a place
for our sitting down. We went up Mystick river
about 6 miles. We lay at Mr. Maverick's, and returned home on Saturday." He seemed to have in
view trading with the Indians more than any thing
else, but was a very hospitable, kind and benevolent
man. His name is mentioned by some writers, as
one of the west country people, who came over to
Dorchester ; by other accounts, he was here before,
and he certainly was different from that company in
his religious principles and prejudices. His habits
of life were also different. Josselyn relates several
visits he made to him, and, from his account, he was
a gentleman, in very independent circumstances,
and lived in a very handsome style.† He was a

* Topographical and chronological account of Dorchester, by
the rev. T. M. Harris.

† October 2d, 1639, about 9 o'clock in the morning, Mr. Maverick's negro woman came to my chamber window, and in her
own country language and tune sang loud and shrill, going out to
her, she used a great deal of respect to me, and willingly would
have expressed her grief in English ; but I apprehended it by her
countenance and deportment, whereupon I repaired to my host,
to learn of him the cause, and resolved to intreat him in her behalf, for that I understood before, that she had been a queen ·in

member of the church of England, but was made a freeman before the law was enacted, that every freeman should be a member of a congregational church, but never was chosen into any office. He afterwards complained of the rigid discipline, and oppressive bigotry of the government.

His son, Samuel Maverick, esq. was in 1664 appointed one of the commissioners to inquire into the state of the New England provinces, and settling the peace and security of the country, and discovered peculiar enmity to Massachusetts. In the petition which the general court sent over to the king, after these commissioners were appointed, they say, that their adversaries had obtained this commission to injure them, and that one of the four was their professed enemy, meaning this Mr. Maverick. In 1666, he delivered from the king a letter to the governour, wherein he required five persons to be sent to England to answer for the conduct of the colony. He could not however overcome the prejudices, or defeat the policy of the New England government. On the other hand, the revolution put them upon a foundation, which was not to be shaken by those, who sought their ruin.

MAYHEW THOMAS, of Watertown, was appointed governour of Nantucket, Martha's Vineyard, and the adjacent islands. The earl of Sterling claimed all the islands between Cape Cod and Hudson's river, and it is evident that they were not included in the New England government. The grant is made by his lordship to Thomas Mayhew, and his son Thomas, Oct. 10, 1641. And he grant-

---

her own country, and observed a very humble and dutiful garb used towards her by another negro, who was her maid. Mr. M. was desirous to have a breed of negroes, and seeing she would not yield by persuasion to company with a young negro man he had in his house, he commanded him will'd she nill'd she to go to bed to her, which was no sooner done than she kicked him out again, this she took in high disdain beyond her slavery and this was the cause of her grief.

ed the same powers of government which the Massachusetts people enjoyed by their charter. Mr. Hutchinson says, that the grants of the soil of these islands could not vacate the rights of the Indian sachems and proprietors; and supposes most of the inhabitants or proprietors derive their titles from Indian grants posterior to the grants to lord Sterling, or to that made by his agent to Mr. Mayhew and son. The worthy governour of these islands bent his mind to the business of instructing the Indians. He had talents to make a figure in the civil line; but the name of Mayhew is mostly known in our ecclesiastical annals. If any of the human race ever enjoyed the luxury of doing good; if any christian ever could declare what it is to have peace, not as the world gives, but which passes the conceptions of those who look not beyond this world, we may believe this was the happiness of the Mayhews.

The first Indian, who gave any good evidence of being a christian, was under the instruction of Mr. Mayhew. It was in the year 1643, at Martha's Vineyard. The name of this pagan was Hiacoomes. He became a preacher to his own people. The worthy magistrates made further exertions, and " converted many from the error of their ways." The younger Mr. Mayhew became himself a preacher, and this good work has been carried on by one and another of the name and family from that day to this. In 1657, many hundreds were added to the christian societies in that part of the country of such as might be said, were "holy in their conversation," and that did not need to be taught " the first principles of knowledge," besides many others, who were superficial professors.

MAYHEW JOHN, had under his care, in the year 1689, the Indian church, and they consisted of a hundred communicants, walking according to the rules of the gospel.

MAYHEW EXPERIENCE, son of John, was a gentleman of such superior endowments, according to

the late Dr. Chauncy, who was his intimate friend,
" that he would, had he been favoured with common advantages of education, have ranked among
the first worthies of New England." He spent a
life protracted several years beyond fourscore in
the service of the aboriginals. He had a character
for veracity and judgment, and in his book entitled, " Indian Converts," an octavo volume, published in 1727, he gives an account of more than
30 Indian ministers, and about 80 Indian men,
women, and young persons, within the limits of one
island, Martha's Vineyard. The same writer published another book, in 1744, which will give him a
name among great divines in any part of christendom. It is entitled " grace defended," wherein
the doctrines of " original sin, regeneration, the difference between common and special grace, are considered and cleared." He received an honourary
degree of A. M. at Harvard College, 1720.

MAYHEW ZACCHEUS, son of Experience, was
employed by " the Massachusetts society for propagating the gospel among the Indians and others,
in North America," till his death, in 1803.

MAYHEW JOSEPH, was also a son of Experience,
graduated at Harvard College, 1730, and was chos-
en tutor in 1739, and one of the fellows of the corporation. He was a man of superiour abilities and
scholarship.

MAYHEW JONATHAN, son of the rev. Experience Mayhew, was born at Martha's Vineyard, 1720,
was educated at Harvard College, and received the
honours of that seminary, in 1744. While he was
a youth he exhibited marks of an original genius,
and such strength of mind, as was very uncommon.
He wrote several essays in prose and verse, which
were supposed to be the productions of riper years,
before he finished his studies at Cambridge. In
1747, he was called to take charge of the west
church in Boston, and was ordained, June 17th; Mr.
Gay, of Hingham, preached the sermon upon the

occasion, Mr. Prescott, of Salem village, gave the fellowship of the churches, and the charge came from the lips of old Mr. Mayhew. He soon discovered a liberality of sentiment, and boldness of spirit, which excited surprise in some, and drew observations from others. He spake with glowing sensibility against every priestly usurpation over the consciences of men, and with peculiar earnestness in favour of truth and religion. He was a steady and able advocate for religious and civil liberty, and refused to preach for doctrines the commandments of men. In 1749, he published several sermons upon "the difference between truth and falsehood, right and wrong; the natural abilities of men for discerning these differences," &c. which gave him a name among the best preachers, and which manifest very uncommon talents with a zeal according to knowledge. It is the opinion of many, that the doctor never exceeded these early productions, and it is certain that very few theological compositions ever came near them. In 1750, he preached a sermon on the 30th of January, which contained "reflections on the resistance made to king Charles." This discourse not only gave offence to episcopalians, but to many sober minded dissenters, who thought it discovered more playfulness of fancy and severity of satire than is consistent with the gravity of a clergyman, or the gentle spirit of christianity. It was however much admired, and passed through several editions in England. It abounds in lively and pointed remarks, and is certainly less exceptionable than many sermons preached 30th January by episcopal ministers of high church opinions, who have abused all denominations of dissenters, while they have talked about the saintship, and angelick qualities, and divinity, of Charles, a frail mortal like themselves. The university of Aberdeen presented Mr. Mayhew with a diploma of doctor of divinity the year after this sermon was published. In the year 1754, the doctor was chosen to preach the election sermon, in which he speaks of the origin of civil government, and its end, in the style of a friend to liberty and the British constitution, as settled at the revolution. He was a whig of the first magnitude. "Having been initiated in youth," said he, in another discourse upon a different subject, "in the doctrines of civil liberty, as they were taught by such men as Plato, Demosthenes, Cicero, and other renowned persons, among the ancients; and such as Sydney and Milton, Locke and Hoadley, among the moderns, I liked them; they seemed rational. And having learnt from the holy scriptures, that wise, brave, and virtuous men were always friends to liberty; that God gave the Israelites a king in his anger, because they had not sense and virtue enough to like a free commonwealth, and that where 'the spirit of the Lord is there is liberty,' this made me conclude that freedom was a great blessing," &c.*

In 1755, the doctor published two solemn and pathetick sermons, after the earthquake, Nov. 23, with an "appendix, giving a very particular account of the time, duration, process, extent and effects of the great earthquake."

The same year he printed a large volume, containing fourteen sermons, "on hearing the word, receiving it with meekness," &c. In this book he inculcated the doctrines of grace, as he thought them delivered by Jesus Christ and his apostles. Moderate Calvinists have spoken well of several of these discourses, which are written in a very evangelical style, although it is evident the author had learnt some lessons in the school of Episcopius, Arminius and Locke. At the end of this volume is a sermon upon the shortness of life, in which are two marginal notes on the doctrines of the Trinity and Solomon's song, that excited some severe remarks from Trinitarians, and which all who agree with the doctor in sentiment, must wish were express-

* Sermon on the repeal of the stamp act, 1766.

ed differently. Such subjects ought not to be treated in a ludicrous manner. The doctor himself "declared his wish that they had not been written;" and sent to England to prevent their being inserted in the London edition. They were, however, printed. Probably, his mind was not known at the time the book was emitted from the press.

In 1763, Mr. East Apthorp published his "considerations on the institution and conduct of the society for propagating the gospel." This provoked a controversy in which several famous men engaged, and in which the brilliant abilities of Dr. Mayhew were fully displayed. He wrote a book entitled, "observations on the charter and conduct of the society for propagating the gospel in foreign parts," &c. To this, a reply was made by several members of the society in America; and by Dr. Secker, archbishop of Canterbury. The doctor replied to the book entitled, a "candid examination of his observations," supposed to be the joint production of Mr. Caner and Dr. Johnson, and declares the title page to be false; he endeavours to shew the work to be destitute equally of candour and of truth. His second defence, or "remarks upon an anonymous tract entitled, an answer to Dr. Mayhew's observations on the charter," &c. is written with a more gentle spirit; though we are frequently struck with the poignancy of his wit, it is evident that he avoided severe strokes of satire. The doctor wrote no more in the episcopal controversy; but having printed two discourses "upon the goodness of God," he was attacked, for certain sentiments there delivered, with some severity, by Mr. Cleveland, a minister in the county of Essex; to whom he sent "a letter of reproof," which discovered too much warmth of temper in a minister of the gospel. It must be acknowledged, that the charge of Mr. C. was unfair and groundless; but it was easy to write a defence of his sermons without such bitter sarcasms, and personal reflections.

Mr. Hopkins of Great Barrington, afterwards of Newport, had a desire to engage Dr. Mayhew in a controversy. He wrote a book, " upon the promises of the gospel," in which he makes remarks upon two sermons published by the doctor on Luke xiii. 24. These sermons speak of " promises to the unregenerate." Many Calvinists thought the sentiments advanced by Dr. Hopkins were contrary to truth, and of a very bad tendency, and wrote against his book; but Dr. M. made no reply to him.

In the year 1765, Dr. Mayhew preached the Dudleian lecture, upon " Popish idolatry," and the succeeding year a particular discourse " upon the repeal of the stamp act." These were his last publications. He died, July 8, 1766, in the 46th year of his age. No American author ever obtained higher reputation. He would have done honour to any country by his character, or by his writings.*

MINOT GEORGE RICHARDS was a descendant from one of the most ancient families of Massachusetts. The first of the name died at Dorchester, 1671, in the 78th year of his age. He was a man of respectability, and a ruling elder of the church. The subject of this article was born in Boston, received the rudiments of his education at the south latin school, and was admitted a student of Harvard College in 1774. . He was there distinguished for decorum of behaviour, a most amiable disposition, and close attention to his studies. He excelled in history and the belles lettres, and was, upon several

* Besides the publications above mentioned, he printed two volumes of sermons, 8vo, one addressed to the youth of his congregation, the other upon the 119th psalm, 59th and 60th verses. These are not the doctor's best performances, nor have they a high rank among sermons printed in New England. They are written in a very careless and diffuse style, and might be compressed into a book of small size. Many of his friends wondered that he published them. He printed also thanksgiving sermons, 1758, 59, 60 ; also a sermon, occasioned by the great fire, which happened, March 20, 1760 ; and a funeral sermon after the death of that upright magistrate, judge Sewall, who died the same year.

occasions, the publick orator of his class. Beside the orations usually delivered at that seminary, he was chosen to speak upon a melancholy occasion, when the university was deprived of Mr. Wadsworth, one of the most useful men in the government and instruction of the society.* No funeral oration was ever more interesting to the hearers, or better adapted to the occasion. It gained him great credit among gentleman of taste and learning, and "his classmates were eager to confer on him every honour which it was in their power to bestow." This class received the honours of the college in 1778, by a general diploma. For several years there was no publick commencement, the country being then involved in the calamities of the revolutionary war. Mr. Minot entered upon the study of the law in Boston, with a gentleman of distinction in his profession, and had for his fellow student the late Fisher Ames, esq. The intimate friendship

* John Wadsworth, who taught logick, metaphysicks and ethicks, was graduated, 1762, and elected tutor in 1770. He was distinguished for fine talents more than extensive erudition. No tutor was ever more calculated for the branch of instruction which fell to his share. As an acute logician, he made accurate distinctions, was fluent in speech, and copious in ideas. He could make the worse appear the better reason, which, from love of disputation, he frequently did; or defend truth in the most lively and ingenious manner. He was as fond of politicks as metaphysicks, and being on the side of the loyalists at the commencement of the war, would have lost his tutorship, had it not been for the great affection of the students, and the exertions of some friends in the corporation, who urged in his favour this attachment of his pupils, and his admirable faculty of communicating his ideas, so very necessary in an instructor, and so very seldom found. It was suggested likewise that his political errors were more in appearance than reality. His fondness for talking had led him to express himself imprudently sometimes; but it was no more in his heart than in his power to do any thing injurious to the commonwealth. He had, however, many political enemies, and obtained the vote only by one, though he was of the body, who made the election. He was a member of the corporation from the year 1774 to 1778, the year of his death. Mr. W. was a collateral branch of the same family with president Wadsworth, who died, 1737.

formed at this juvenile age was strengthened by mutual expressions of good will, and tokens of esteem, until death divided them. At the funeral of Judge Minot, Mr. Ames was one of the pall bearers. In the year 1781, when the commonwealth of Massachusetts was blessed with a new constitution of government, Mr. M. was appointed clerk of the house of representatives. He was in this office during the insurrections, which distracted the publick concerns of the year 1786. By his office he was led to a minute acquaintance with the causes of the disturbance, the proceedings of the government, and the conduct of the army raised upon that occasion. These troubles of our country he reviewed in an historical narrative of the rebellion, which gave him high reputation as a writer; it was read with great interest and pleasure by the inhabitants of Massachusetts. He was afterwards persuaded by his friends, to write a continuation of Hutchinson's history of Massachusetts bay, which excited less attention, but is a very valuable book; and will frequently be in the hands of persons, who wish to know the affairs of their own country. The period he describes exhibits the most tranquil state of things. It was not prolifick of great events, like succeeding years of violence and rage, when politicians had their influence, and excited the tumult of the people; when we beheld the traces of war in our own fields, or heard the cry of human distress in our houses, as well as the high way. Histories of such times are eagerly sought after, while many take up a book with frigid indifference, which only tells of peaceful regions, and seasons of publick felicity.

Mr. Minot was twice elected by the people of Boston to deliver publick orations, which he performed to great acceptance. In 1782, he pronounced the annual oration, 5th of March. And in 1800, he spake the funeral eulogy upon Washington, which has been highly praised in other places besides his native town. In 1787, Mr. M. was chosen clerk of the convention which adopted the constitution of the United States. In 1792, the governour and council appointed him judge of probate for the county of Suffolk. He was exactly fitted to fill this station. Soft, pleasant, and affable, he could speak peace to the troubled bosom, whilst he performed all the duties of his office with the purest integrity. The deep sensibilities of those who knew him in this station, when they heard of his death, afforded affecting evidence of his worth.

Judge Minot was never fond of the hurry and bustle of the world, and therefore did not make that figure at the bar, which some of his friends expected from his talents and elocution. He was not bold in his conceptions, nor had he that discursive manner of reasoning, or pathos of expresssion, which are requisite for a first rate pleader. The legal knowledge he possessed, gave him advantage in other pursuits which were connected with his professional business; and he cultivated his mind by a variety of studies. Among his companions his opinion was valued, and the publick opinion was such, as to gratify every feeling of an ambitious man, especially a man whose principles of virtue guided the path to honour.

Besides his office of judge of probate, he was judge of the municipal court in the town of Boston. He was also president of the Massachusetts charitable fire society. Of this institution he was one of the founders, and also of the Massachusetts historical society. He was also a fellow of the American academy of arts and sciences.

The character of judge Minot was delineated in the newspapers by several, who spake the language of truth, while they felt the sympathy of friendship. Justice was also done him by John Quincy Adams, esq. in an admirable oration before the charitable fire society. But the most interesting, full, and accurate memoir is in the 8th volume of the collections of the Massachusetts historical society. It was written by one whose compositions always show the hand of an elegant writer, and who in a relation to judge Minot was as the friend nearer than a brother. Whoever would wish for more minute occurrences in the life of Mr. Minot than can be expected in a sketch for this work, is referred to that valuable paper.* Judge Minot died in the midst of his life and usefulness, Jan. 3d, 1802.

His other publications are fugitive pieces in the magazines and newspapers; also an oration delivered before the charitable fire society.

MOODEY JOSHUA, was the son of William Moodey of Newbury, and graduated at Harvard College, 1653 : he was a preacher in the town of Portsmouth, New Hampshire, 1658. A vote for his establishment there passed in 1660, though a church was not properly organized till 1671. "An account of the gathering of this church" is preserved in his own hand writing, and is a valuable document of our early history. While Cranfield was governour of New Hampshire, Mr. Moodey was the subject of persecution. Whenever a petty tyrant indulges his malignant humour, he renders himself ridiculous, as well as causes mischief to others. He imprisoned this faithful pastor of the church in Portsmouth, because he did not administer the Lord's supper after the way of the church of England. After being in prison 13 weeks, he was dismissed with a charge to preach no more. He was invited, however, to Boston, and preached to the people of the first or old church from the year 1684, the time of his banishment, to 1693, and then, by advice of council, returned to his old charge at Portsmouth.

Before he accepted the invitation of the Boston church, he was chosen president of the college, which place he declined to accept; but acted as one of the fellows of the corporation. The people of Boston were very much attached to him, and much

* Vol. 8th, pages 86, 7, 8, 9, &c.

disappointed when he went to Portsmouth. He often visited them after he left the town ; and during a visit, in the year 1697, was taken ill, and died on the 4th July, etat. 65. Dr. Cotton Mather preached his funeral sermon, and preserved his name in the Magnalia.

The only publication of Mr. Moodey is in the library of the Massachusetts historical society. It is a small volume containing the substance of several sermons upon the " benefit of communion with God in his house."*

* A letter from Mr. Bentley of Salem to Mr. Alden, the present librarian of the Massachusetts historical society, represents the character of Mr. Moodey to great advantage ; he certainly was one of the most judicious and worthy men of those times.

" In the times of the witchcraft in Salem village, no person, distinguished for property, and known in the commercial world, was accused but Philip English. He came young into America from the island of Jersey, lived in the family of Mr. Hollingworth, a rich inhabitant of Salem, and afterwards married his only daughter and child, Susanna. The wife had received a better education, than is common even at this day, as proofs, I hold, sufficiently discover.

" From some prejudices, as early as April 21, 1692, she was accused of witchcraft, examined, and committed to prison in Salem. Her firmness is memorable. Six weeks she was confined ; but, being visited by a fond husband, her husband was also accused, and confined in the same prison. By the intercession of friends, and by a plea that the prison was crowded, they were removed to Arnold's gaol in Boston till the time of trial.

" In Boston, upon giving bail, they had the liberty of the town, only lodging in prison. Upon their arrival Messrs. Willard and Moodey visited them, and discovered every disposition to console them in their distress. On the day before they were to return to Salem for trial, Mr. Moodey waited upon them in the prison, and invited them to the publick worship. On the occasion he chose for the text, IF THEY PERSECUTE YOU IN ONE CITY, FLEE TO ANOTHER. In the discourse with a manly freedom he justified every attempt to escape from the forms of justice, when justice was violated in them. After service Mr. Moodey visited the prisoners in the gaol, and asked Mr. English, whether he took notice of his discourse ? Mr. English said he did not know whether he had applied it as he ought, and wished some conversation upon the subject. Mr. Moodey then frankly told him that his life was in danger, and he ought by all means to provide for an escape. Many, said he, have suffered. Mr. English then replied, God will not suffer them to hurt me. Upon this reply, Mrs.

Morton Charles, minister of the church in Charlestown, was the son of Nicholas Morton, minister of St. Mary Overy's, in Southwack. The family descended from a respectable stock ; among the ancient branches we find Thomas Morton, secretary to king Edward III. Charles, the eldest son of Nicholas, was born A. D. 1626, was sent to Wadham College, Oxford, and had the character of a studious and pious youth. He was, at the same time, zealous for the rites and ceremonies of the

English said to her husband, do you not think that they, who have suffered already, are innocent ? He said, yes. Why then may not we suffer also ? Take Mr. Moodey's advice. Mr. Moodey then told Mr. English that, if he would not carry his wife away, he would. He then informed him that he had persuaded several worthy persons in Boston to make provision for their conveyance out of the colony, and that a conveyance had been obtained, encouraged by the governour, gaoler, &c. which would come at midnight, and that proper recommendations had been obtained to gov. Fletcher of New York, so that he might give himself no concern about any one circumstance of the journey ; that all things were amply provided. The governour also gave letters to gov. Fletcher, and, at the time appointed, Mr. English, his wife, and daughter were taken and conveyed to New York. He found before his arrival, that Mr. Moodey had dispatched letters, and the governour, with many private gentlemen, came out to meet him ; and the governour entertained him at his own house, and paid him every attention while he remained in the city. On the next year he returned.

" In all this business, Mr. Moodey openly justified Mr. English, and, in defiance of all the prejudices which prevailed, expressed his abhorrence of the measures, which had obliged a useful citizen to flee from the executioners. Mr. Moodey was commended by all discerning men ; but he felt the angry resentment of the deluded multitude of his own times, among whom some of high rank were included. He soon after left Boston and returned to Portsmouth.

" Mrs. English died in 1694, at 42 years of age, in consequence of the ungenerous treatment she had received. Her husband died at 84 years of age, in 1734.

" This is the substance of the communications made to me at different times from madam Susanna Harthorne, his great-granddaughter, who died in Salem, 28 August, 1802, at the age of 80 years, who received the account from the descendants of Mr. English, who dwelt upon his obligations to Mr. Moodey with great pleasure."

T t

church of England. He was afterwards chosen fellow of the college, being an eminent scholar. He excelled in various branches of science, but was peculiarly fond of mathematicks. On this account, he drew the attention, and experienced the friendship, of Dr. Wilkins then warden at the university, and afterwards celebrated among the literati of Europe. Mr. Morton was one of the ejected ministers, in 1668. Being unable to carry on the work of the ministry, he set up an academy at Newington Green. For this business he was very well qualified, and many excellent scholars were educated under his care. He had a peculiar talent of winning youth to the love of virtue and learning, both by his pleasant conversation, and a familiar way of making difficult subjects easily intelligible. He came to New England in 1685, and was chosen pastor of the church at Charlestown, and vice president of Harvard College. He died, April, 1697, in the 80th year of his age.

In Dr. Calamy's " account of ejected ministers by the act of uniformity," is a vindication of himself, written by this Charles Morton, from a charge brought against him for teaching at a private academy, contrary to the rules of the university, and thereby breaking his oath. This takes up more than 20 pages, 8vo. Besides this manuscript, which was transcribed by most of Mr. Morton's pupils, he drew up several systems of the arts and sciences, which he explained in his lectures. The doctor has also preserved another paper of his, which is entitled, " advice to candidates for the ministry under the present discouraging circumstances." This was written during the oppressive, as well as licentious reign of Charles II. It is a paper of about 15 pages, containing excellent rules of conduct, and some of them will apply to other times. Mr. Morton being vice president of Harvard College, while in this office, composed a system of logick, which was copied by the students every year as they became members of that society. It was afterwards laid aside for one on a more improved plan, by Mr. Brattle. A copy of each is in the cabinet of the historical society, among the rare specimens of American literature.*

MORTON NATHANIEL, one of the first planters of New Plymouth, should have an honourable mention among those, who have deserved well of their country. He is more celebrated as an author than for any remarkable events of his life. He was doubtless highly esteemed by his fellow planters, as they made him a magistrate, and he was secretary of the court for the jurisdiction of New Plymouth. Probably facts are preserved concerning him in the old colony, and some account of his active services, but these we have not been able to obtain. As a writer of the original events of the plantations he is known to all, who turn their attention to the affairs of New England. No book has been oftener quoted than " Morton's memorial." In this book are precious documents for the use of future historians, who recur to early times, or " remember New England in the day of her smallest things." The work was printed in 1669. It is dedicated to gov. Prince, and has in its favour the testimony of two of the greatest and best divines of New England, Mr. Higginson of Salem, and Mr. Thacher of Weymouth, afterwards minister of the Old South, Boston. They say the " author is an approved godly man ; and that the work is compiled with modesty of spirit, simplicity of style, and truth of matter, containing the annals of New Eng-

* His other works are, the little peacemaker, on Prov. xiii. 10 ; foolish pride, the Make-bate, 8vo, 1674 ; debts discharge, Rom. xiii. 8 ; the gaming humour considered and reproved ; the way of good men, for wise men to walk in, 1684 ; season birds, Jeremy viii. 7 ; meditations on the first chapters of Exodus, and beginning of Samuel. Other treatises are also mentioned by his biographer, viz. the spirit of man, 1. Thess. v. 23 ; the stork in the heavens. Jer. viii. 7 ; several pieces in the philosophical transactions, 1675. He was generally brief and compendious, being a declared enemy to large volumes.

land for the space of 47 years, with special refer-
ence to Plymouth colony, where the author made
his constant abode."

This memorial has gone through many editions.
A gentleman, every way qualified, indulged the expectations of his friends a few years since, that he
would give an improved edition of this work. Nothing but the busy scenes of his active and useful
life could have diverted him from finishing it.

From some documents which have lately appeared, it is evident that Mr. Morton had his prejudices, and suffered them to operate too powerfully
against the sectaries, which had disturbed the church
and commonwealth. A letter from Gorton to the
author of the memorial, preserved in Hutchinson's
collection of papers, is well worthy of perusal. Nor
was he impartial in all respects in describing the
character of Roger Williams, as may be seen from
comparing his account with Winthrop's journal,
Callender's century sermon, or Backus's history.

He doubtless thought his remarks were just, but
excellent men frequently know not the spirit they
are of. Men biassed by religious zeal, in pointing
out the heresies of those, who differ from them,
should frequently pause for the sake of this inquiry,
Who can understand his errors? possibly we ourselves may be in the wrong.

This worthy magistrate of New Plymouth died
in a good old age, but the exact time we are unable
to tell.

NELSON JOHN, made a conspicuous figure at the
time of the Massachusetts revolution, when the sovereign people put down sir Edmund Andross, and
appointed a different governour and council. He
was at the head of the soldiers, who went and demanded the fort, and to whom sir Edmund surrendered himself. He was a near relation to sir Thomas Temple, and attached to the cause of freedom,
though he was an episcopalion. His conduct shews
him to be a man of virtue and principle. He

might have been highly in favour with Randolph, but he detested the arbitrary measures of the government. On the other hand, had he conformed to the manners of the people, and left the church of England, he would have been, not only highly esteemed, but exalted to honour after the revolution. On account of his being an episcopalian, Hutchinson tells us, he was not allowed any share in the administration after it was settled.

He went upon a trading voyage to Nova Scotia, and was taken prisoner. When he was at Quebec he sent a letter to the court of Massachusetts, which gave particular intimations of the designs of the French, and which he wrote at the risque of his life. It is dated, August 26, 1692. Mr. Hutchinson took it from the Massachusetts files, and published it to do honour to his memory. He also acquaints us that, in consequence of writing this letter, he was ordered to be carried upon the field where two Frenchmen were shot, who were concerned with him in giving the intelligence; he expected the same fate, but was sent to France, where he remained in prison two years. " A gentleman who had taken notice of the person who carried the victuals from day to day, had the curiosity to inquire what prisoner was there, and to speak to him at the grate, and to ask, if he could do him any service. Mr. Nelson desired only to have a letter sent to England, to inform sir Purbeck Temple of his condition, which was done, and soon after, a demand was made of his release or exchange. He was then looked upon as a person of some importance. He was sent to the Bastile, and, just before the peace at Ryswick, was allowed to go to England, upon his parole, and security given by a French gentleman for his return. The peace being concluded, he intending to return, was forbad to do it by king William; yet, to prevent any trouble he went and surrendered himself. Being discharged, he was brought into trouble upon his return to England, for going contrary to the

king's order, but at length returned to his family after ten or eleven years absence." *Hutchinson.*

NEWMAN FRANCIS, esq. was secretary of the
colony of New Haven when the commissioners of
the united colonies agreed to make war upon the
Dutch, at Manhadoes, A. D. 1653. In their records
we find, that agents were appointed, who were to examine the whole affair in a conference with gov.
Stuyvesant, and require satisfaction. These agents
were Francis Newman, one of the magistrates of
New Haven, capt. John Leverett, afterwards governour of Massachusetts, and Mr. William Davis.
The Dutch governour avoided the examination,
and the agents returned without obtaining satisfaction. The commissioners of the united colonies
immediately decided for war ; several of the colonies raised troops, but the general court of Massachusetts put a stop to their proceedings ; nothing
could induce them to act offensively upon this occasion. " In direct violation of the articles of the
confederation, they resolved, that no determination
of the commissioners, should they all agree, should
bind the general court to act in an offensive war,
which should appear to such general court to be unjust." This declaration caused great disturbance
to the sister colonies ; they expressed their grief and
resentment, and it almost effected a dissolution of
the union. Another evil was consequential upon
this. The towns bordering upon the Dutch settlements determined they would carry on the war, and
there were insurrections in divers places. Mr.
Newman was elected by the magistrates of New
Haven, with Mr. Goodyear, the deputy governour,
to visit the towns, and compose their minds.

Mr. Newman was the next year chosen commissioner of the united colonies. At the election at
New Haven, 1658, he was chosen governour. Their
excellent chief magistrate, Mr. Eaton, died the year
before ; Mr. Goodyear, the deputy governour, died
also about the same time in London. Trumbull

says, " he was a worthy man of a very respectable family." We find his name often among the commissioners of the united colonies.

Mr. Newman continued in the chief seat of government until the year 1661. He died that year greatly lamented. He was secretary for many years, under the administration of gov. Eaton, and was well acquainted with the affairs of the colony. He is represented, as " a gentleman of piety and unblemished morals, happily imitating his predecessor both in publick and private life." *Records of the united colonies. Trumbull.*

Newman Samuel, author of the Cambridge concordance, was educated at the university of Oxford, and was an able and faithful minister of the gospel many years in his own country. In the year 1638, he came to New England, and spent some time at Dorchester ; then removed to Weymouth, and resided there about 5 years. His next remove was to a place bordering on Providence plantations, which he named Rehoboth, according to the quaint style of that day, but which retains its name to the present times. He lived nineteen years with his people, was a very lively preacher. a hard student, and a pastor well beloved by his flock. The manner of his death was peculiar. He had a certain premonition of it, and seemed to triumph in the prospect of its being near. He was apparently in perfect health, and preached a sermon upon these words, Job xiv. 14, " all the days of my appointed time will I wait till my change come." In the afternoon of the following Lord's day, he asked the deacon to pray with him saying, he had not long to live. As soon as he had finished his prayer, he said the time was come that he must leave this world. But his friends seeing no immediate signs of dissolution, thought it was the influence of imagination. But he turned round saying, angels do your office, immediately expired. This may appear like other marvellous circumstances related in the Magnalia, but it is handed down by persons not connected with that author, and was as much confirmed as any report depending upon tradition, and it is said that accounts of the death of Mr. Newman were written at the time, and sent to England, as well as propagated through the towns of New England. He died, July 5, 1663, in the 63d year of his age. Mr. Norton of Boston and Mr. Stone of Hartford died the same year.

His *concordance* of the bible, was superiour to any that ever had been published. It was a very elaborate work ; but the edition, which was called the Cambridge concordance, was much improved in England, where it received this title.

NEWTON THOMAS, attorney general of Massachusetts Bay, died in Boston, 1721, May 28. He was educated in England, was much beloved in his native country, and highly esteemed here for his virtue, integrity and honour, while he was comptroller of the customs, which was his first appointment ; and in his profession as counsellor of law. " He was affable, courteous, circumspect, devout, exemplary for family government, and all the duties of humanity."

NORRIS EDWARD, teacher of the church in Salem, was ordained, March 18, 1640. After Mr. Peters left the church he had the sole charge of it for 18 years, and, by his prudence and moderation, it grew and flourished : it was preserved in a state of general tranquillity while other towns were agitated by fanaticks, and the commonwealth swarmed with sectaries. He was more liberal in his ideas of toleration than most ministers in New England, and was never active in any of the proceedings against the Gortonists or Anabaptists. So little did he interfere in the affairs of other churches, that when the platform of church discipline was adopted in 1648,* he persevered in a platform of his own church, and preserved not only the love of his peo-

* Bentley.

ple, but the respect of his neighbours unto his death, which happened, April 10, 1659.*

In an account of eminent men by father Barnard, of Marblehead, Mr. Norris's name appears with the first class. He was celebrated as a political writer, as well as a great divine. In 1642, a book was written, by Mr. Saltonstall, one of the assistants, wherein " the standing council was declared to be a sinful innovation." A reply to it was made, by Mr. Dudley. But we learn from gov. Winthrop, that another answer was given by " Mr. Norris, a grave and judicious elder, teacher of the church at Salem, who, not suspecting the author, handled him somewhat sharply according to the merit of the matter."

In 1653, Mr. Norris again appeared as a writer on the politicks of the day. The other colonies were disposed to declare war against the Dutch settlements. The commissioners of the united colonies, with the exception of Simon Bradstreet, had agreed upon this measure as absolutely necessary. The general court of Massachusetts would not consent to the decree of the commissioners, but Mr. Norris wrote in favour of them. He represented such a war as just and proper : " that the spending so much time in parlies and treaties, after all the injuries they had received, and while the enemy was insulting them, would make them appear contemptible to the Indians ; that it was dishonouring God, in whom they professed to trust, and bringing a scandal upon themselves. He insisted that they ought not to leave their brethren at New Haven to bear all the evils which the enemies of New England were disposed, and ready to bring upon them : and that if they did not engage in this business, they deserved the curse which the angel of the lord utter.

* Another thing has been mentioned concerning the Salem people, which implies a peculiar setness in their own way. When all the churches in Massachusetts Bay used the New England psalms, they continued to use Ainsworth. These were sung in this town till the year 1675, so afraid were they of the spirit of innovation, or else fond of singularity in their mode of worship.

ed against Meroz. This, he said, he presented in the name of many pensive hearts."

Mr. Norris left a son, who was preceptor of the grammar school in Salem from 1640 to 1684. He died this year, aged 70 years.

NORTON JOHN, was born May 6, 1606, at Starford in Hertfordshire. At 14 years of age he entered Peter house, Cambridge, but was obliged to leave the university, after he had taken his first degree, on account of some domestick misfortunes, whereby his father's estate suffered. He obtained a curacy of the church in his native town, and was at the same time teacher of the school. His talents were such as would enable him to make a figure in any situation. He might have obtained preferment in the episcopal church, and he was solicited to accept a fellowship in the university ; but his dislike of the ceremonies prevented him from accepting a considerable benefice. He also had an antipathy to Arminianism, which was the prevailing sentiment of the ministers of the church of England. In the year 1634, he was coming to America in the same ship with Mr. Thomas Shepherd, but a storm drove them back again, and he did not accomplish his purpose till the next year. It is said, in Winthrop's journal, that he arrived at Plymouth, October 10, 1635, the vessel being driven into that harbour by contrary winds, but it appears from other accounts that Mr. Winslow, the agent for New Plymouth at the court of Great Britain, had made overtures to him to take the charge of that ancient church. He passed the winter with them, and they were so fond of his preaching, that they set aside Mr. Ralph Smith, their pastor, a man of less gifts, and pressed Mr. Norton's continuance ; yet he left them, and came to Massachusetts. He was immediately invited to settle with the church at Ipswich, where he continued till the death of Mr. Cotton. The old church in Boston, had a very high opinion of his accomplishments. When the synod met at Cambridge, 1647, the Boston church would send no messengers till they heard Mr. N. preach a lecture upon the nature of councils, the power of the civil magistrate to call such councils, and the duty of the churches in regarding their advice ; they then chose 3 delegates to accompany their elders, who had taken their seats at the synod. Upon the death of Mr. Cotton their eyes were turned to him, therefore, as the most proper person to supply the place of that great man. Our ecclesiastical annals, compiled by Cotton Mather, relate the difficulties in obtaining him, and mention also Mr. Cotton's dream, that " he saw Mr. Norton coming into Boston upon a white horse, which actually took place afterwards ;" but it may suffice for this account to say, that Mr. Norton left Ipswich by the advice of council, and that having accepted the invitation of the Boston people, it pleased the great head of the church to add lustre to his character, and give success to his ministry. Had he confined himself to his spiritual concerns, his sun would have set without a cloud ; but he meddled with the affairs of government, and mingled the character of the politician with the divine, which gave a sudden blaze to his reputation, but thick darkness succeeded. Cotton Mather says, "that New England, being a country whose interests were remarkably enwrapped in ecclesiastical circumstances, ministers ought to concern themselves in politicks ;" and he was a lively example of his own advice. He says, likewise, that had Mr. Norton done nothing more than to prevent hostilities between the English people and the Dutch, at Manhadoes, it had been worth his coming into the station he held in Boston. Norris of Salem, as good a man, was of a different opinion ; and Dr. Trumbull, a modern historian of excellent parts and character, has represented the conduct of Massachusetts in not assisting the other colonies at the time, as most base and treacherous. Mr. Norton rendered himself so popular by his interference in this business, that the general court afterwards chose him joint agent with Simon Bradstreet to present the address to his majesty, Charles II. It was a most delicate and difficult business to transact. It required so much art and dissimulation, that a minister of the gospel ought not to have been concerned in it. Cromwell was the friend of New England. Our clergy had justified every circumstance of the usurpation, and publickly announced the piety, as well as justice of the court, which had brought their monarch to the scaffold. Men who had grown grey in practising political devises would have been puzzled to make an address to his son and successor, and conceal their own hypocrisy. The conduct of our agents, the unkind treatment they received from those in whom they trusted, especially the resentment of the fierce republican spirit of this new world, which may be compared to Hercules in his cradle, have been related in the histories of Massachusetts. Mr. Hutchinson gives the most particular account. They all agree that Mr. Norton's death was the consequence. This, however, is always said of a man, who dies suddenly, after meeting with trouble. But often the cause is taken for the effect. A man has bodily complaints from the melancholy disposition of his mind, but it more frequently is the case, that a man becomes melancholy and wretched from diseases of the body. Mr. N. was of a sickly constitution, and died of an apoplexy. It was imputed to chagrin and grief on account of the treatment he received. The other agent lived to be 95 years old. He was more unpopular, for the blame was imputed mostly to him. He was, however, always conversant with state affairs, and could calculate upon the fickleness of the people, and the vexation of office. We have only then to learn this lesson, that every man should mind his own business. He died, April 5, 1663. He was preparing the afternoon exercises when he was taken out of the world. Many, who had enjoyed the benefit of his labours, bewailed his departure.

Their honest hearts were wounded, and they moistened his grave with their tears.

Mr. Norton was distinguished as a writer as much as he excelled in preaching. When a youth he was one of the finest scholars at the university. While he cultivated his master's vineyard, he studied every branch of divinity. In his retired situation, when he was teacher of the church of Ipswich, he was unanimously chosen to answer the questions concerning church government, which Apollonius, by request of the divines of Zealand, had sent over to the divines of New England. This was written in pure elegant latin, A. D. 1645. To judge of its merit we may quote the words of Mr. Fuller in his church history ; " of all the authors I have perused concerning those opinions, none to me was more informative than John Norton, one of no less learning than modesty, in his answer to Apollonius, pastor of the church in Middleburgh." Mr. Norton also advised, modelled, and recommended the Cambridge platform, 1647.

Another book he wrote by desire of the general court in answer to one entitled, " the meritorious price of man's redemption." He was likewise the author of a famous work, " the orthodox evangelist," highly recommended by Mr. Cotton.

After he came to Boston he wrote the life of his predecessor Mr. Cotton, which was reprinted in England. He also wrote, at the desire of the general court, " a tract, on the doctrines of the Quakers."

He preached the election sermon in 1661, Jer. xxx. 17, this was published after his death, with two other sermons, one on John xiv. 3, the last sermon he ever preached. The other was a sermon he preached at Thursday lecture.

To these sermons was annexed, a translation of the famous letter he wrote in latin to Mr. Dury,*

---

* John Dury makes some figure in the early annals of Massachusetts on account of the famous letter, written to the divines of

who began about the year 1635 to labour in a work which none were ever able to accomplish, viz. the pacification of all the reformed churches. Mr. Norton's letter was signed by more than 40 ministers of New England.

NOWEL INCREASE was appointed a magistrate of the province of Massachusstts Bay, in the year 1629; and came over with gov. Winthrop in the Arabella.

He was nephew to Alexander Nowel, dean of St.

New England. This makes part of a large plan he had in view of reconciling the different sects of protestants. The same thing had been attempted by the early reformers of Germany. But those who adhered to the Ausburgh confession and the Calvinists could never agree. When men of liberal minds endeavoured to form a union, the spirit of bigotry operated upon some, who would throw firebrands in the way; and the fire being kindled they separated in anger, and wrote with zeal. Sometimes the princes of Europe discovered their schemes of policy; and the virtue of priests yielded to the pride of opinion. It is said, that Dury shewed more activity and perseverance in the work of charity, than any man of that, or the preceding age. Amidst many vexations, and opposition that required the most intrepid and invincible patience, he wrote, exhorted, prayed and disputed. He employed all the means which human wisdom could suggest to put an end to the dissentions and animosities, which were excited among christians of different denominations. He travelled in all the countries of Europe, and endeavoured to accommodate himself to the prejudices of the several parties. He addressed magistrates and ministers, sovereigns and princes; painted in lively colours the advantages, the utility, and importance of the scheme he had formed, hoping to interest the wise and good in his cause; but his hopes and expectations were all frustrated.

Though many commended his design, and admired his candour, he found few disposed to assist him. And he was often deceived by those, who soothed him with their smiles, without any view of aiding him by their credit and their counsels.

He had enemies, who ascribed wrong motives to his zeal, and the Lutherans returned invectives often to his kind advice. He was at last beat from his labours and oppressed with injurious treatment, and was obliged to acknowledge, that he had undertaken what was impracticable. He ended his days in repose and retirement at Cassel.

He was a native of Scotland.

The letter of the ministers of New England was penned by Mr. Norton. It contains high commendations, without any pledge or promises of their aid in the coalition.

Paul's, in queen Elizabeth's reign, or else the dean was his great uncle. This we learn from Mr. Hutchinson, who says, that he was a worthy, pious man. When our fathers planted their church in Charlestown, they chose him ruling elder. He acted in this capacity, until a difference of opinion arose among the people, and a question was agitated, " whether an officer of the church could act as a civil magistrate ?" It was decided that the offices were inconsistent. He resigned the eldership, therefore, and was a very active and useful person in the civil affairs of the province. For many years he was employed in publick life, and succeeded Mr. Bradstreet, as secretary of the colony. For many years he was assistant. His name with Endicott, Dudley, and other magistrates, appears in an association, 1649, against wearing the hair long, as a thing which tended to corrupt good manners. He also joined, with several other counsellors, in calling a special meeting of the commissioners of the united colonies, April, 1653, when the country was so much alarmed by the machinations of the Dutch with the Indians. He was one of the magistrates who put the question to Ninnegret, Pessicus and Mixam, sachems of the Narragansetts. The result of this meeting has been considered in another place.*

NOWEL SAMUEL, supposed to be the son of secretary Nowel, was employed in several publick offices. He was one of the assistants in 1681 ; of the high republican party, who adhered to the old

* The names of our magistrates for the year 1629 were, John Winthrop, governour, Thomas Dudley, deputy governour, Matthew Cradock, Thomas Goff, sir Richard Saltonstall, Isaac Johnson, Samuel Aldersley, John Venn, John Humphrey, Simon Whercomb, Increase Nowel, Richard Percy, Nathaniel Wright, Samuel Vassal, Theophilus Eaton, Thomas Adams, Thomas Hutchins, George Foxcroft, William Pinchon, John Pocock, Christopher Corolson, William Coddington, Simon Bradstreet, Thomas Sharp ; 1730, were added, Roger Ludlow, Edward Rossiter, John Endicot ; 1632, John Winthrop, jun.

charter; and one of the magistrates against whom
Randolph exhibited to the lords of the council articles of high misdemeanour.* When Mr. agent
Mather was in England, two of the assistants joined with him in an address to the king, Samuel Nowel and Elisha Hutchinson, but they did not succeed
in their object. The name of Mr. Nowel is not
among the counsellors under the new charter of William and Mary.

NOYES JAMES, teacher of the first church in
Newbury, was born, 1608, at a town in Wiltshire.
He came to New England, in 1634. He had an invitation to settle at Watertown, but preferred to settle with his friend, Mr. Parker, at Newbury. These
men taught in one school at Newbury in England.
They came to America in the same ship, were pastor and teacher of the same church, and lived together in one house till death divided them. They
agreed together about the doctrine and discipline of
the churches more than with the inhabitants of the
country in general. In a memoir of Mr. Noyes,
written by his nephew, one of the ministers of Salem, it is said that, at the desire of Mr. Wilson and
others, he preached upon a particular occasion
against the Antimonian principles then prevailing,
which he did with good success, and to the satisfaction of those, who invited him. Mr. Wilson dearly
loved him. There must indeed have been something very sweet and amiable in the disposition of
the man, for he was much loved and honoured in
Newbury; he had his friends in every part of Massachusetts, and met with no disturbance from the
bigotry of the people in any part of the government,
though he spoke and wrote against the prevailing
sentiments of the magistrates and ministers. He
was no more a republican in politicks than in church

* This faction of the general court, as he calls them, were
Danforth, Gookin, Saltonstall, Nowel, Richards, Davy, Gedney
and Appleton, magistrates; and Fisher, Cooke, Brattle, Stoddard, Bathurst, Wait, Hathorne, Johnson, Hutchinson, Sprague,
Oakes, Holbroke, Cushing, Hammond and Pike, deputies.

discipline. He bitterly lamented the death of Charles I. Both Mr. Parker and he had high expectations of good times if Charles II. should ascend the throne. He did not live to have his expectations frustrated ; but his colleague lived to see that his restoration brought unhappy times to New England. He might say, perhaps, the evil arose not from the kingly government, but having such a king as Charles to reign over them. In church government Mr. Noyes had peculiar sentiments, that were neither presbyterian or congregational; the " brethren could act in certain matters, and join in church censures, but the pastor might take the power from their hands." He no way approved of a governing vote in the fraternity, being afraid equally of schism, and of ceremonies. He was in opinion for episcopus, præses ; but not episcopus princeps. He died in the 48th year of his ministry, October 22, 1656.*

OAKES URIAN was the son of a plain man " who dwelt in tents," to use the language of Dr. Mather, but " deserving of everlasting remembrance." He tells us likewise that, when Mr. O. was a child, he was in danger of being drowned, and " that his life was saved by a kind of miracle, that he might be the Moses of his people." He came to New England with his parents about the year 1634, and was graduated at Harvard College, 1649. He excelled as a scholar ; but his mind was bent especially to theological studies. His first sermon he preached at Roxbury, and soon after returned to his native country. He was settled at Titchfield, till the Bartholomew act in 1662, which deprived so many worthy men of

* His works are, " a catechism for children," which continued in use many years. " The temple measured ;" this is the book alluded to by Mr. Baxter when he said he was a lover of the New England churches according to the New England model, as Mr. Noyes had explained it. A copy of this rare book is in the library of the historical society. He also wrote a work entitled, " Moses and Aaron," which was afterwards printed in England, and dedicated to Charles II.

their livings. Mr. Oakes at this time was noticed by a gentleman in whose family he had once been chaplain, and received competent provision for his maintenance; but having received an invitation from the church at Cambridge, he left the old country in 1671, and succeeded Mr. Mitchel in his pastoral church. To come after such a man, who was a star of the first magnitude in this American hemisphere, it was necessary to give diligence to his studies, and all the duties of his office.* If the powers of his mind were not equal to his predecessor's, they were superiour to most other men. He was an excellent preacher, and was esteemed as highly for his knowledge as for his pulpit talents. He was the man to whom the government of the college turned their attention to fill the chair, when president Hoar resigned his office. He would not accept it without he could combine his pastoral duties with the duties of his station in the college. He was allowed to hold both offices, and was able to give universal satisfaction. His days, however, were short, except they be measured with his usefulness. He died suddenly, July 25, 1681, in the 50th year of his age, and 10th of his ministry.

* Mr. Mitchel, pastor of the church at Cambridge, was highly celebrated for his learning, but more for the native vigour of his mind. Dr. Mather calls him, the "matchless Mitchel." He died young, hence the greater eclat to his reputation. He ought to have been the subject of a particular article in this biographical work, but the notices which were prepared were mislaid. There is the less need to make an apology, as the publick have been gratified by a very excellent memoir from Dr. Holmes, in his history of Cambridge. (Historical collections, vol. vii.)—Mr. M. died in 1668, in the 43d year of his age. His writings were few. He printed the election sermon, 1667; a discourse upon "the glory of believers," first printed at London. Several editions of it have been printed in America. Mr. Mitchel also wrote in defence of the Synod, 1662, in opposition to Increase Mather, who surrendered himself "a captive to his victorious arguments," says Dr. Cotton Mather. The same author tells us what the great Mr. Baxter said: "That if there could be convened an œcumenical council of the whole christian world, Mr. Mitchel would be worthy to be the moderator of it."

His publications are, a set of astronomical calculations with this motto,

" Parvum parva decent, sed inest sua gratia parvis."

an elegy on Mr. Shephard of Charlestown ; the
artillery election sermon, 1672 ; the election sermon, 1673. These were all printed by Mr. Samuel Green, Cambridge.

OLIVER DANIEL was the son of capt. Peter Oliver, a gentleman of property and reputation, and
one of the principal founders of the old south church
in Boston, in May, 1669. Capt. Oliver had 3 sons ;
Nathaniel, a merchant, and James, a celebrated physician, at Cambridge, who died young, and Daniel,
the subject of the present article. This gentleman
was one of the first merchants of the place ; and
was employed in many publick offices, all of which
he discharged with fidelity, and to universal acceptance. He was one of the selectmen, overseer of the
poor, a justice of the peace, representative, and one
of his majesty's council. He died suddenly in the
month of July, 1732, in the 69th year of his age.
" In his will, among other legacies, he bestowed a
large house, called the *spinning* school, for which
use he first designed it, and which cost him 600
pounds, for the benefit of poor children, that may
learn to read the scriptures."*

Mr. Oliver married the second daughter of the

* Mr. Prince preached upon the death of Mr. Daniel Oliver,
senior, Mr. Oliver, jun. and Mrs. Elizabeth Oliver, sister of gov.
Belcher, who was then in the chair. She died in 1735. These
sermons were printed, and are three very excellent discourses.
Mr. Mather Byles also published a poem after the death of
Mr. O. in 1732. It was inscribed to gov. Belcher, the brother in
law, at whose desire it was written. Mr. Byles the minister of the
church in Hollis street, Boston, printed a little volume of poems.
He corresponded with Pope, who sent him a copy of his works.
He also printed a number of sermons, and received a diploma of
D. D. from Aberdeen. He was a florid preacher, with a very fine
voice. Notices of him were prepared for this work, but with
many other lives were suppressed, lest the volume should be of
too large a size. Whoever wishes to see a particular account of
him is referred to a memoir handsomely written in the 4th volume
of the Polyanthos, a periodical paper, lately printed in Boston.

honourable Andrew Belcher, esq. by whom he had
several children, all of whom were graduated at
Harvard College, and made a considerable figure in
the world.

OLIVER DANIEL, the eldest son of the honourable Daniel Oliver, commenced bachelor of arts in
1722, and proceeded master in 1725. He applied
himself to merchandize, for which he had an excellent genius and ability. He went to London in
1726, travelled over a great part of Europe, was
preparing to come home, but was taken sick of the
small pox, at London, and died July 5th, 1727, in
the 24th year of his age. He was buried under the
church, in Fenchurch street.

" His short life," says Mr. Prince, " was a worthy
example of a wise and virtuous conduct, to the youth
of his native country, both at home and abroad ;
and his premature death an affecting instance of the
uncertainty of their earthly prospects and expectations."

OLIVER ANDREW, lieut. governour of Massachusetts, the second son of the hon. Daniel Oliver, was
graduated 1724, and was distinguished more for his
solid learning, and sobriety of conduct, than brilliant parts. He was highly respectable in his character for his piety, integrity and knowledge of the
affairs of the province, until the latter years of his
civil and political life, when he was held up to public view, as one destitute of patriotick virtues, and
inimical to the true interests of his country. The
early part of his life was devoted to business, for
which he was not so well qualified as many, who
make no figure upon the publick theatre. He rather diminished than increased his patrimony by any
successful speculations. He was very soon employed in publick stations ; was representative
for Boston at the general. court, and one of

The present generation recollect Dr. Byles more as a man given
to punning, than any other kind of wit. His works, some of
which are valuable, are seldom met with.

his majesty's council.   Upon the death of the venerable secretary Willard, he was appointed secretary of the province, and held the office till 1771; then he succeeded Mr. Hutchinson in the place of lieut. governour.   When the stamp act passed the British parliament, he was made *distrib-uter*, which would have been a lucrative office, and which he reluctantly resigned, being compelled to do it by the loud voice of the multitude.   The riots this act occasioned have been frequently alluded to.   Mr. Oliver's house was among those which were injured, for which the general court made him sufficient compensation.

His political principles, and propensity to acquire wealth and power, stimulated him to act a similar part in publick life with Mr. Hutchinson, to whom he was nearly related.   It was supposed that he was influenced by that gentleman; but his own views led to the same object, and his own letters betrayed the spirit by which he had been actuated for some years.   In the same petition, therefore, which the general court presented to his majesty for the removal of gov. H. they begged that Mr. Oliver might also be removed from the place of lieut. governour.   He was then in very ill health, and soon after descended to the grave with all his imperfections upon his head.   He died, March 3d, 1774, during the session of the general court, who voted to attend his funeral, but all left the procession, on account of some improper management, which implied a want of respect to the legislature of the province.

Had the politicks of the lieut. governour been different, his character would have been very respectable.   The family had been greatly beloved, and his abilities were connected with indefatigable industry.   He was a friend to the college, and to the interests of religion.   He wrote well upon theological and political subjects.   Some of them were adapted to the times, and are scattered, with other ephemeral productions; but some remain, and discover a cultivated mind, and considerable acquaintance with the subject.

Mr. O. left a number of sons, to whom he gave a liberal education. The eldest,

OLIVER ANDREW, esq. of Salem, was graduated at Cambridge, 1749, was judge of the court of common pleas for the county of Essex before the revolution; one of the original members of the American academy of arts and sciences; also a member of the philosophical society of Philadelphia. He possessed fine talents, and was reckoned among our best scholars. He never was fond of publick life, but loved his friend and his books, and was much beloved by all that knew him. Several valuable communications of his are in the first volume of the transactions of the American academy. He was also the author of a work much celebrated entitled, an "essay on comets," printed in the year 1772. He died in 1799, aged 68.

OLIVER PETER, chief justice of Massachusetts, the younger son of the hon. Daniel Oliver, was graduated at Harvard College, 1730. He lived on a family estate in the town of Middleborough, and for many years was highly respected for his talents, his virtues, and his knowledge of the affairs of the commonwealth. He had the true spirit of an old colony man. Every relick, or document, which related to the settlement of the country, or was curious, had a value stamped upon it. He collected many papers and records, and even transcribed all William Hubbard's ms. history with his own hand. All these, except such as Hutchinson made use off, were carried away with him when he went to England. He filled several offices in the county of Plymouth, which he executed with ability and faithfulness, and when he was raised to the supreme bench, it was a very popular appointment, though he had not that knowledge of the law, which others had, who were of the profession, and looked up to

the place. He expected to have succeeded Mr.
Hutchinson, as chief justice. But he did not obtain
the station at that time. Judge Lynde was appointed, who resigned as soon as an alteration was made
in the method of the judges receiving their salaries.
Mr. Oliver was then made chief justice, with a salary of 400*l.* sterling, which was to be fixed, and paid
without any dependence upon the legislature of the
province. This rendered him completely odious.
And for this he was impeached by the house of
representatives. His prejudices were strong against
the country during the war. He went away with
the other loyalists, when the British troops abandon-
ed the town, and lived in England some years upon his salary, or the pension he received from the
crown. A diploma of L L. D. from the university
of Oxford, was presented to him. In his own country, he was not distinguished with this literary honour. He was, however, a handsome writer in poetry and prose. Several specimens of his talents are
preserved. He wrote many political pieces in the
publick papers, especially in the *Censor*, a paper
which the tories patronized, and which was devoted
altogether to the party. Several of the best political speculations in that paper were written by judge
Oliver, and his brother the lieut. governour.

OLIVER THOMAS, was the last lieut. governour,
under the crown. He was of a different family from
the gentlemen above mentioned. He was in no
publick office till the charter of Massachusetts was
changed, and his name was then at the head of the
mandamus council, with a commission, as lieut.
governour of the province. It was a matter of so
much surprise, that it was the current conversation,
that the name of Thomas Oliver had been accidentally inserted for Peter, the chief justice. But it
appeared afterwards, this very gentleman was appointed, by the particular advice of Mr. Hutchinson. With what views time perhaps will not discover.
On other occasions he had preferred his own rela-

tions.   Politicians always have some design, and
never act from disinterested motives.   Doubtless
the debt of gratitude was to be paid.   Mr. Oliver
would have rejoiced to exchange his publick honours for his private station.   He was a man of letters and possessed much good nature and good
breeding; was affable, courteous. a complete gentleman in his manners, and the delight of his acquaintance.   He was graduated at Harvard College, 1753.
He built an elegant mansion house in Cambridge,
and enjoyed a plentiful fortune.   When he left
America, it was with extreme regret.   He lived in
the shades of retirement while he was in Europe,
and very lately his death was announced in the
publick papers.

OSBORN JOHN, physician, was born, 1713, in
Sandwich, Barnstable county, and was graduated at
Harvard College, 1735.

The first entrance of a young student on the
world, whose future prospects depend upon his profession, and that profession on his own choice, is
frequently marked by indecision and inactivity.
This was the case with Osborn.   After leaving college, he repaired to his father's house at Eastham,
and spent some time in a state of irresolution.   To
while away this awkward interval, and to gratify the
wishes of his father, he paid some attention to divinity.   At an association of the neighbouring clergy
in Chatham, he delivered a sermon of his own composition.   The ingenuity of this discourse, though
not perfectly orthodox, commanded the approbation
of his reverend hearers.

After this exhibition we hear no more of him in
the desk ; but being duly qualified, he afterwards
became a physician, and removed to Middletown,
Connecticut.   He married about this time; and in
1753 wrote to a sister, then living at Plymouth, the
following account of himself and family.

" We are all in usual plight, except myself.   I
am confined chiefly to the house ; am weak, lame,

and uneasy; and never expect to be hearty and strong again. I have lingered along almost two years a life not worth having, and how much longer it will last, I cannot tell. We have six children; the eldest fourteen years old last November; the youngest two years last January; the eldest a daughter, the next a son, and so on to the end of the chapter."

The illness he mentions was the effect of a fever from which he never recovered. The life, which he thought *not worth having*, lasted but a short time after he wrote the above mentioned letter. He died at the age of 40.

He certainly possessed a fine poetick genius, which appears from his whaling song, which has been highly celebrated, and which no whaleman ever sings or speaks of but with rapture. He also wrote a very beautiful elegiack epistle addressed to one sister on the death of another.*

OTIS JOHN, one of the council for Massachusetts, was born at Hingham, A. D. 1657. His parents were very respectable among the early settlers of that town. He removed to the town of Barnstable when he was a young man, and was an ornament to that part of the country. He very soon trod the path to honour, and was employed in a variety of trusts, which he discharged with fidelity and skill. For 20 years he was representative of Barnstable to the general court. In 1706 he was chosen one of his majesty's council, and sat at that honourable board 21 years, till death gave him a discharge from every labour, and laid his earthly honours in the dust.

Above 18 years he was at the head of the militia in the county of Barnstable; chief judge of the court of common pleas 13 years; and judge of the probate of wills. Such was his sagacity and prudence, that he often composed differences both in church

* These poems were printed in the Boston Mirror, January, of the present year. The biographical sketch, written by a literary friend, appears in this Dictionary with his consent.

and state. He had fine talents for conversation. His pleasantness and affability made him agreeable; his wit and humour often enlivened the company, which was improved by his wisdom. A gentleman who converses with people of various classes ought to make the best use of rustick simplicity; he must bear with the ignorance of some, and check the pride and ill manners of others; for such as speak their minds with vulgar freedom, often affect to be something beyond their neighbours. Col. Otis had this requisite knowledge of mankind, and preserved his popularity at the same time " he was known in the gates" for his uprightness. He was strict and exemplary in attending upon religious duties, and was as remarkable for his humility and modest worth among christians, as for his intellectual powers and active services among his fellow men. He died, Nov. 30th, 1727, aged 70, the age of man, but very old, if he lives " the longest, who lives the most usefully."

OTIS JOHN, son of the gentleman before mentioned, was representative for the town of Barnstable a number of years. He was chosen a counsellor in the year 1747, and every year successively till 1756, the year of his death.

OTIS JAMES, was also an honourable man in his generation. He had a superiour genius, and great accomplishments, acquired by the strength and application of his natural powers. Having turned his attention to the study of law, he became the most eminent pleader in the county of Barnstable. His reputation was so high in his profession, that he was a candidate for the office of judge in the superiour court. When judge Sewall died, in 1770, it was supposed one of the judges would take his place as chief justice, and Mr. Otis be advanced to the bench. Mr. Hutchinson, however, obtained the place of chief justice. This caused great surprise, frustrated expectations, and provoked resentment. It kindled party spirit and spread the flames over the province. Many persons became inimical to the lieut. governour, who perhaps would have stood his friends in those troublesome times when his patriotism was tired. Mr. O. had great influence in the general court, and had lately been chosen one his majesty's council ; he was also colonel of the militia, which in those days was not only held in great honour, but gave a man as much influence as respect. There was, however, something like a coalition of parties, in 1763. Col. Otis was appointed justice of the court of common pleas, and judge of probate for the county of Barnstable. The controversy with the parent country soon succeeded the peace, which had been established among the nations of Europe. In 1764, the British parliament passed an act for raising a revenue in the colonies. This roused the spirit of New England, and all the brilliant abilities of the Otis family were exerted on the side of opposition. The younger Mr. O. was in the house of representatives. He blazed in the cause of liberty, like the genius of the times, and powerfully counteracted the schemes of the ministry. In 1766, gov. Bernard negatived several counsellors, because the lieut. governour, secretary, and attorney general were not chosen, who had been honoured with a seat at that board during sundry years. Mr. Otis was one of five leading whig characters, who had this mark of royal displeasure. The town of Barnstable again chose him representative. He was elected into the counsel every succeeding year, and was negatived while Bernard continued in the administration of government. When he left the province, Mr. Hutchinson approbated the choice, and he was at the board during the first years of the revolutionary war. He died in the month of November, 1778, having lived long enough to see his country glorious in her struggles for freedom, with a prospect full in view, that her mighty efforts to secure independence, would be crowned with success.

OTIS JAMES, of Boston, son of col. Otis of Barn-stable, was born in that town, and received every advantage of education it was in his father's power to bestow. The old gentleman was a friend to learning, and learned men, and often lamented his want of academical improvement. The son enter-ed Harvard College, in 1739, and received his de-grees at the usual time. After he left college, his object was the study of law ; but previously to entering his name in any office, he spent several years in furnishing his mind with various kinds of knowledge, and cultivating a classical taste. He then studied law with Mr. Gridley, and soon appear-ed with distinguished lustre in his profession. No one at the bar was supposed to possess more exten-sive information. He first began the practice of the law at Plymouth ; but he soon came to Boston, where he had a better opportunity to display his talents, and increase his business. He was con-stantly employed ; and obtained such celebrity, that application was made to him in the most important causes from other counties in Massachusetts, from neighbouring colonies, and even from Nova Sco-tia.* There are persons now living, who can recol-lect how successfully he managed certain law cases of magnitude and importance. He was appointed advocate general at the court of admiralty, which place he resigned in the year 1761, and openly pro-tested against the officers of the customs, and expos-ed the treacherous conduct of Charles Paxton, who from this time became his personal enemy, though it was not in the power of such a man to do him great injury.

Mr. Otis was now the idol of the people of Bos-ton. At the election of May, 1761, he was sent to the general court as one of their four representa-tives. He was considered by the inhabitants of the town, as the best orator who spake in Faneuil hall, and, upon one occasion, when he was moderator, he addressed them in a long speech, which was afterwards published. The whigs praised it highly, but on the other side were found persons, who made the most sarcastick remarks. The observation of a great statesman, whose opinion, and knowledge of facts, claim every kind of respect, was just, who said of Mr. Otis, that " he was a senator, whose parts, literature, eloquence and integrity, were equal to any in the times when he lived ; yet no man was ever more abused by the tory writers, who ceased not to throw their vile aspersions on his character as well as on his writings."* They viewed him as the leading character among the whigs in the general court ; for he delivered his sentiments with the same manly freedom, and commanding eloquence, in the house of representatives which had given him such eclat in other assemblies. His hatred to Bernard and Hutchinson, combined with his zeal for his country's cause, gave ardour to his spirits, a glow to his imagination, and energy to his expressions. His wit was often keen ; his sarcasms always severe.

The house of representatives manifested their high respect for his character by choosing him their speaker in the year 1766 : but he was negatived by the authority of the governour. About this time his fame reached the old country. Several of his political essays on the " rights of the colonies ;" and " vindication of the measures of the general court," were reprinted in England. These were circulated among the members of the opposition in the British parliament. With some of their leading men he corresponded.† It was currently reported that a motion was made in parlia-

* Novanglus—the Boston Gazette, Feb. 1775.

† Extracts from a letter of James Otis, esq. of Boston, to a noble lord, dated July 18, 1769. " I embrace the opportunity with all humility and gratitude to acknowledge the honour I have received in a letter from your lordship. At a time when so heavy a cloud seems to be impending over North America, it gives singular pleasure to find a nobleman of your lordship's rank, genius, and learning, so clearly avowing the cause of liberty and injured

ment " to send for him, and try him for high treason." Such a motion does not appear in their debates. It is not likely it ever was made. Letters
came from London, which suggested that such a
motion was either made or to be made ; and people
on this side the water have generally supposed, that
this was actually proposed by lord North. It is
true, however, that a handsome compliment was
paid Mr. Otis by Mr. Edmund Burke, the British
Cicero, in one of their debates on American affairs.

After the repeal of the stamp act, the famous
" act laying a duty upon tea, painter's oil and colours," &c. passed the British parliament. It was
introduced by Charles Townsend who, in 1766, was
appointed chancellor of the exchequer. His purpose was, " to raise a revenue in America ;" and,
" to make the governours, judges and attorney generals free and independent of the humours and ca-
prices of the people." This act, with its direful
consequences, put our politicians in a phrenzy.
The agitation of the publick mind was increased by
the arbitrary and ridiculous conduct of the commissioners. Beside their parade of high life and

innocence. Your lordship's sentiments are a full proof, that the
love of virtue and truth are the best and securest basis of nobility.

The cause of America is, in my humble opinion, the cause of
the whole British empire. An empire which, from my earliest
youth, I have been taught to love and revere, as founded in the
principles of natural reason and justice ; and upon the whole the
best calculated for general happiness of any, yet risen to view, in
the world. In this view of the British empire, my lord, I incessantly pray for its prosperity, and sincerely lament all adverse
circumstances.

The hon. Thomas Cushing, speaker of the house of representatives, Mr. Samuel Adams, John Hancock, esq. and the hon.
James Otis, of Barnstable, desire to present their respectful
thanks to your lordship, for putting it in my power to gratify
those you have distinguished, as of the same principles and sentiments of civil and religious liberty with yourself.

Situated as we are, my lord, in the wilderness of America, a
thousand leagues distant from the fountains of honour and justice, in all our distresses we pride ourselves in our loyalty to the
king, and our affection to the mother country."

their contempt for the good and wholesome laws of this province, they wrote letters against the country ; and represented some worthy characters as guilty of political crimes which existed only in their pregnant fancies.   Mr. Otis was one upon whom their malignity vented its poison.   He called upon the commissioners individually, and as a board, for an explanation of some things which they had written against him.   He used perhaps unguarded expressions in the heat of his resentment, upon which Mr. Robinson one ot the commissioners threatened to chastise him.   They met at the coffee-house in state street, in the month of Sept. 1770, and an affray took place, which caused serious consequences. The whole account may be seen in the papers of the times.   The friends of one took oath, that Mr. Otis was attacked by numbers.   On the other side, men swore that no man struck him but Mr. R.   It was likewise said, that " it was a plan to kill him, contrived in Mr. Paxton's room."   This was never brought forward at the trial : there it appeared that the attack of Mr. R. was base and cowardly ; but the other part of the story served to make the commissioners more odious.

Mr. Otis prosecuted Robinson, and recovered 2000 pounds, which sum he generously remitted upon his making an acknowledgment of his offence.

He was subject to fits of insanity after this, and found it necessary to retire from publick business. At the election of representatives the ensuing season the town of Boston sent him a letter of thanks for his publick services.   They lamented his ill state of health, and earnestly prayed for his recovery. They publickly declared that his services were such as ought to be remembered with gratitude, and distinguish him among the patriots of America.   Mr. Bowdoin, one of the counsellors, who had been negatived by gov. Bernard, was chosen in his place. The next year Mr. Otis recovered his health, and was again chosen representative.   Whenever he en-

gaged in business, he was one of those, who gave
his whole soul to the object, and, like other great
men, lost his health by "being overplied with publick energies." He lived a number of years, and
frequently rendered himself useful to the community. When his health would not permit him to engage in publick concerns, he retired into the country. In one of these seasons of retirement, May
29, 1783, as he was standing at the door of Mr.
Osgood's house, in Andover, he was instantaneous-
ly deprived of life by lightning.*

OVERING JOHN, attorney general, came into this
country with gov. Burnet. He was remarkable for
his fluency of expression and agreeable manner of
speaking at the bar. He exercised his abilities in
the law with great success, and acquired considerable fortune and influence. He held the office of attorney general from the time of his appointment, in
1728, to the administration of gov. Shirley. He
died about the year 1745, and was succeeded in his
office by Mr. Trowbridge.

OXENBRIDGE JOHN, one of the ministers of the
old church, in Boston, was born in Daventry, a
town in Northamptonshire. He received the de-

---

* The following lines are extracted from a poem, written by a
gentleman of eminent character and worth, in Boston :
　　"Blest with a native strength and fire of thought,
　　With Greek and Roman learning richly fraught,
　　Up to the fountain head he push'd his view,
　　And from first principles his maxims drew.
　　Spite of the times, this truth he blaz'd abroad,
　　The people's safety is the law of God."
His works are, "the rudiments of latin prosody, with a dissertation on letters, and the principles of harmony, in poetick and
prosaick composition, collected from some of the best writers,"
pp. 72, 1760 ; it is said to be a most clear and masterly treatise
by the reviewers in the Monthly Anthology ; "A vindication of
the house of representatives of Massachusetts," 1762 ; "remarks
on the Halifax libel," 1763 ; "rights of the British colonies,"
1764 : "considerations on behalf of the colonists," 1765. He
wrote many political speculations in the Boston Gazette, which
had a high reputation among the writings of those times.

gree of master of arts, at Cambridge, A. D. 1631, where he finished his education, though at first he was sent to Oxford. He soon became a preacher of the gospel, and made several voyages to the West Indies. In the year 1644, he was ordained pastor of a church in Beverly, and was chosen fellow of Eton College. He is in the list of ejected ministers in 1662, published by Dr. Calamy, who tells us, that he was settled at Berwick on the Tweed, where he was silenced. He sailed again for the West Indies; went first to Surrinam, and, in 1667, he was at Barbadoes. In 1669 he fixed at Boston, as colleague with Mr. Allen, after the death of Mr. Davenport. His name was *John*, "a man sent from God." Dr. Mather thinks it remarkable that he should succeed four of this name. He was one of the most popular preachers in Massachusetts.* In all his compositions he seems to breathe an evangelical spirit. He died, Dec. 28. 1674. Towards the close of a sermon, which he was preaching at the Boston lecture, he was taken with an apoplexy, and continued only two days.

His works are, "the duty of watchfulness," in a number of discourses; the election sermon, 1671; a sermon entitled, "seasonable seeking of God." He also published "a proposition for propagating the gospel by christian colonies, in the continent of Guiana, being some gleanings of a large discourse." That large discourse was preserved some years. We know not where it can be obtained. Dr. Mather says, he had read it, and found a grateful variety of entertainment.

PARKER THOMAS, pastor of the church at Newbury, was the son of Robert Parker, a famous controversial writer against the form and ceremonies of the church of England. He wrote a very learned book, "de Politia ecclesiastica." The son became also a very excellent scholar. He was educated at Dublin, under the care of the famous archbishop

* Chalmer's annals.

Usher.   He afterwards studied with Dr. Ames, or received advice and assistance from him, while he continued his studies at Leyden.   He received the degree of master of arts, when he was 22 years old, and the particular esteem of several divines, celebrated in the Belgick universities.   In the diploma they gave him they testified, " Illum non sine admiratione audiverimus ;" and, " se philosophiæ artiumq ; liberalium peritissimum declaraverit."   After leaving Holland, he resided at Newbury, in England.   He came into New England, in 1634, with many of his people, and settled in a spot on Merrimack river, which was called Newbury, according to their desire.   He applied himself to the study of the prophecies, and wrote several volumes, mostly in Latin.   He was a man of the most extensive charity and liberal principles.   He thought too much satire was mingled in the fathers' writings against the bishops ;   and because he expressed this in a preface to a book, president Chauncy entered into a controversy with him, calling him " Urijah the priest, who would set up the altar of Damascus to thrust out the brazen altar of the Lord's institution." Mr. Parker died in the month of April, 1677, in the 82d year of his age.*

PARKER SAMUEL, D. D. minister of Trinity church, Boston, and bishop of the protestant episcopal church in Massachusetts, was born in Ports-

---

* The works of Mr. Parker upon the prophecies were never printed, except a commentary on Daniel, which he wrote in English, and which is not according to the common opinion of expositors.   When he was a young man, he composed theses " de tractuetione peccatoris ad vitam " which have been bound up with Dr. Ames's smaller works.   He did not choose to appear as the author at the time.

Mr. Popkins, his successor in the pastoral office, mentions some facts not recorded in the Magnalia.   He instructed a school, and took no pay.   The pupils must be designed for the church or he would not admit them   When he was blind he could teach Latin, Greek and Hebrew. He could talk in these languages, and even speak his mind upon occasions in arabick.—See appendix to the sermon of rev. J. S. Popkins, preached at quitting the old and building the new meeting house, Newbury, 1806.

mouth, New Hampshire. His father, judge Parker, was an eminent lawyer, a man of great integrity and benevolence, and for many years deacon of the first church in that town. The son was graduated at Harvard College, 1764, with a view of being a minister of one of the congregational churches. He soon manifested a preference for the church of England, and, in 1773, received orders from Dr. Ternch, bishop of London, as an episcopal clergyman. He was chosen assistant minister of Trinity church, where he officiated above 30 years. His moderation and prudence were manifested upon some very important occasions. Prejudices against episcopal clergymen were strong during the revolutionary war, because their political principles were on the side of government. He maintained the esteem of the people, and of ministers of other denominations, whose opinions were entirely different. Among them his reputation was high as a clergyman, and he was looked up to, as the head of the episcopal church in New England. The university at Philadelphia presented him with a diploma of doctor in divinity. After the decease of bishop Bass, by an unanimous vote of their convention, he was elected to succeed him in his office. He was consecrated but a few months before he was seized with the disorder of which, after a second return, he died.

His death was lamented by a numerous acquaintance. To many of these he was a very sincere friend : some of whom received his advice, others his bounty. He was an active and useful officer of several institutions for pious and humane purposes, capable of transacting a variety of business, and faithful in whatever he engaged. The several societies attended his funeral, Dec. 9, 1804, and an elegant discourse, well adapted to the occasion, was preached by his colleague, Mr. Gardiner, which was afterwards published.

PARTRIDGE RALPH came into this country among the early planters, and was settled at Dux-

bury. He was one of the synod, who met at Cambridge, 1647, to compose the platform of church discipline. Three gentlemen were appointed to draw a
model of church government, according to the word
of God. Each made a separate draft, and the synod
collected from the whole, as they judged proper to
complete their system of ecclesiastical government.
The other gentlemen were Mr. Cotton and Mr.
Mather, whose names rank with the great men of
New England. When most of the ministers in the
colony of Plymouth left their parishes, on account
of the "paucity and poverty of their congregations,"
he remained with his people. They highly respected him, and he died in a good old age about the
year 1658. For more than 40 years he was a preacher of the gospel, and was not interrupted by any
bodily sickness.

PARSONS MOSES, pastor of the church at Byfield,
was graduated at Harvard College, 1736 ; ordained
June 20, 1744 ; and died, Dec. 14, 1784, in the 68th
year of his age. He was an excellent and judicious
practical theologian ; conversant in the most substantial parts of divinity, and could speak handsomely upon these subjects, as occasion required. His
sermons were calculated to improve the mind, and
affect the heart. His grand object was to establish
essential points in religion, and the rest he left to
the disputers of this world. He attended very particularly to the circumstances of his flock, was very
amiable in his domestick character, and much beloved by his brethren in the ministry.

An oration was pronounced at his funeral by the
rev. Levi Frisbie, which is a handsome composition.
The next Lord's day, Mr. Tappan of Newbury, afterwards professor of divinity at the university at
Cambridge, preached a funeral sermon, which is
one of the best discourses that worthy man ever
printed.

Mr. Parsons preached the election sermon, 1772 ;
it was well received and excited more than common

attention by the free manner in which he spake of the British nation. He was a whig from principle. He loved his country, but his zeal for its welfare and honour was tempered with great charity and moderation towards those whose politicks were different.

He left a number of children ; to several of his sons he gave a university education, one of whom is now chief justice of the state of Massachusetts ; another, who was graduated in 1773, was first a student in divinity, and then turned his attention to physick.

" Mihi, post——nullos sodales."

The powers of his mind were great, his application to his studies very uncommon, and his conduct exemplary, but his death was immature, just as he had entered upon the duties of his profession. He sailed from Newburyport, as surgeon of a vessel, during the revolutionary war, which foundered at sea.

" Huic neque defungi visumest, nec vivere pulchrum ?
Cura fuit recte vivere, sicque mori."

PAYSON PHILLIPS, son of the rev. Phillips Payson of Walpole, Massachusetts, was educated at Harvard College, and in the year 1754, received the honours of that university.

He was ordained the minister of Chelsea, Oct. 26, 1757, and continued to preach and perform all the duties of the ministry till a few weeks before his death.

In the line of his profession he had a distinguished reputation. His imagination was lively and vigorous. His memory retentive. His discourses were well composed and evangelical. Like a wise master builder he looked at the foundation, while reasoning upon the moral duties, or describing, with a glowing pencil, the triumphs of the christian's hope.

The diploma of doctor in divinity was presented him by the seminary where he received his education, a real testimony of his wisdom and worth, which gave pleasure to the friends of religion and learning.

He had much classical erudition, and a fondness for the study of natural philosophy and mathematics.

When the American academy of arts was instituted, he was one of the first members. He always shewed a zeal to promote the cause of science and every useful institution.

He was a member of the society for propagating the gospel among the Indians and others in North America; and also one of the Scotch commissioners for the like benevolent purpose, being named in the commission, when the board in Scotland established a corresponding board in this country.

Dr. Payson was frank and open in his disposition, and had a ready utterance in conversation. With uncommon energy of expression he pourtrayed vice and meanness, tore the garb of the hypocrite, and exposed fanaticism in every shape.

In his domestic and social relations he appeared with dignity and tenderness. As a companion was agreeable, and as a neighbour obliging; warm in his friendship, hospitable in his house. He was a condescending and instructive parent; the kind, attentive, and affectionate husband.

He was ready to every good work for the benefit of his people, mixing with them and interesting himself in their concerns : he encouraged the spirit of industry in the town, and, upon proper occasions, administered the consolations of religion. Their attachment increased with his years. But while they were indulging hopes of returning health, and days of further usefulness, they beheld him, with grief and sorrow, among the trophies of the grave. He died Jan. 11, 1801, aged 65.

PELHAM HERBERT, was one of the assistants in Massachusetts, and highly valued by the people. He was of the same family with the duke of Newcastle. He tarried but a few years in New England.

In 1646, he was one of the commissioners of the united colonies. In 1650 he lived upon his estate in England. He was intrusted by the colony of Massachusetts with some of their most important affairs, and was a great promoter of the society for propagating the gospel among the Indians. Among the sixteen of whom the corporation first consisted, Herbert Pelham stands the second on the list. *Hutchinson. Records United Colonies.*

PEMBERTON EBENEZER, pastor of the old south church, was born in Boston, A. D. 1672, and graduated at Harvard College, 1691. After some years residence at Cambridge, he was chosen fellow of the house, and, on the 28th of August, 1700, ordained assistant to the venerable Samuel Willard. He was greatly valued and beloved while he lived, and had the reputation of as an accomplished a preacher as this country ever produced. He died Feb. 13, 1717, in the meridian of his gifts, usefulness, and age.

Dr. Colman, in a sermon preached after his death, says, " that he was a hard student from his childhood, and being blessed with brightness of mind, fervour of spirit, and strength of memory, he made wonderful dispatch. The college never had a more accomplished tutor, nor one that more applied himself to teach and watch over the morals of it. His conspicuous learning and piety soon fixed the eyes of Mr. Willard upon him to be the colleague of his age, and successor at his death. He was master of logick and oratory in great perfection. His delivery was lively and vigorous, being strongly convinced of the reality of things invisible and eternal. His warm and passionate temper (which was sometimes his great infirmity) seemed here to set the greater edge, and give a further energy to his admirable discourses."

He says, likewise, " that he had a superiour soul, formed for great things, and was ever framing them, but that it was lodged in a distempered body."

Mr. Barnard thus describes Mr. Pemberton : "a man of strong genius, extensive learning, a possessor of raised thoughts, and a masculine style, of flaming zeal in the cause of God and religion, violent in his passions, and as soft as you would wish for out of them, a good christian, and a faithful pastor."*

A volume of sermons was printed after Mr. Pemberton's decease. They contain those he published ; and several which were added because they were much celebrated. There is among them a most masterly defence of the " validity of Presbyterian ordination." These discourses are written in the best style, and would do honour to any preacher of the present age. They are wonderful compositions for the period. When he prepared a sermon for the press, he was slow in correcting it ; every sentence he framed with deliberation and care. Hence he published very little. " He carried the mighty stores and treasures of his laborious studies in his own vast mind, and for the most part wrote only hints for himself to be enlarged upon in the pulpit." This may appear the language of an eulogist; but if there be any truth in tradition, it agrees with the opinion which was universally received of this eminent character.

PEMBERTON EBENEZER, D. D. son of the rev. gentleman pastor of the Old South church, was deprived of his father's care and instruction at a tender age, but was blessed with a surviving parent, a woman of a most excellent spirit, and adorned with all the virtues of a christian. Her son has done due honour to her memory in the account he has published of her life and character.

His friends intended him for a secular employment; but his inclination to a studious life prevailed, and he was educated at our publick university, at Cambridge, where he distinguished himself as a scholar,

* Historical collections, vol. x.

and made those improvements in useful knowledge, which qualified him for the work of the ministry.

Soon after he entered on publick preaching, he was appointed chaplain at castle William, by Mr. Dummer, the commander in chief of the province. In this pleasant and retired situation, he had a happy opportunity of cultivating and improving his own mind, and at the same time do good to others.

There was one circumstance, which rendered the situation peculiarly desirable. The castle was the usual residence of the lieut. governour, in whom were united the gentleman and christian, and under whose wise and just administration the province, for some years, enjoyed great quiet and prosperity. This honourable person condescended to admit Mr. Pemberton to an acquaintance, that was both agreeable and useful, and which continued with mutual esteem till Mr. Dummer was admitted to the world of spirits.

His services in the fortress were only preparatory to a larger scene of action. He was soon invited to take the charge of the Presbyterian church in the city of New York, and was publickly set apart to that important trust by the ministers of this town. The late Dr. Colman preached the ordination sermon. In this conspicuous orb he moved for twenty two years. At length a spirit of discord broke loose in the society. Though the pastors had no part in the dispute, yet the contention ran so high, that Mr. Pemberton, and his worthy colleague, the rev. Mr. Cumming, thought themselves obliged to apply to the presbytery for a dismission. Just at this time, the church in Middle street, Boston, was deprived of their pastors, Mr. Welsteed and Mr. Gray, two excellent men, " pleasant in their lives, in their deaths not divided." This christian society unanimously chose Mr. P. to be their pastor, and he was introduced to the pastoral charge, 1753.

While at New York, he had been præses of the board of correspondents, commissioned by the society in Scotland, for propagating christian knowledge among the Indians in New England and parts adjacent.

While he was pastor of the church in Boston, the honourable and reverend trustees of the college in New Jersey, to which board he formerly belonged, presented him with a diploma of doctor in divinity. It was the first occasion of their exercising this privilege.

His piety was of that fervent kind for which his father was remarkable. He had not his superiour powers of mind, and in his old age grew unpopular in his delivery, though in former times he drew crowded assemblies by his manner. His reading, however, was extensive, and his sermons correct in diction and style. He was a calvinist, according to the principles of our fathers, and zealous against arminianism, so as to provoke the satire of writers, " who worshipped the God of their fathers after the way, which is called heresy ;" but in the latter years of his life, those who were conversant with him observed a candour and charity to such as entertained different sentiments on some points of doctrine upon which great stress has been laid. He vehemently aspired after the spirit of the gospel, and had the consolations of it during a long and trying sickness. Instead of suffering from the fear of death, he seemed to possess the peace, which passeth all understanding.

Dr. P. died, Sept. 15, 1777, aged 73, and in the 51st year of his ministry. He published, a few years before his death, a volume of sermons upon " salvation by grace." While he was minister of New York he printed several occasional sermons ; and a small volume on " the wonderful propagation of the gospel, and the coming of Christ." He preached the election sermon in 1756 ; the Dudleian lecture in 1766. He also printed a sermon, preached at the Thursday lecture, after the death of Mr. Whitefield, in 1770. *Character of Dr. Pemberton, ms. by a friend.*

PEPPERELL SIR WILLIAM, was a merchant, distinguished for his opulence, integrity and politeness. He was early in life chosen a representative to the general court, and sat at the council board 32 years. He had a martial turn of mind, which was increased by living in a part of the country the most exposed to the ravages of the French and Indians. From being a subaltern officer in the militia, he rose to the highest military rank, and was equally qualified to command a large army, and to adorn his civil station by his virtue and wisdom. When the plan was formed to attack Louisburg, it gave animation to the troops, and to the people in general, that such a man was to lead them. Nothing but a zeal for his country's good could have carried him from the scenes of domestick enjoyment, and from the head of his majesty's council, the highest honour his native country could bestow upon him, to the fatigues of a camp, and uncertain victory. Indeed, many of our most judicious people thought the expedition romantick, and had it not been successful, no braven or prudent conduct of the commander would have saved his reputation; nor would the loss to the publick have been ever brought into any calculation. It ended much to the honour of New England, and was certainly the most glorious event of the war. " The illustrious undertaking being so well accomplished, it caused the name of sir William Pepperell to spread far and wide, and to be remembered with gratitude and respect by succeeding generations." The king bestowed upon him the title and dignity of a baronet of Great Britain, an honour never before conferred on a native of these North American provinces. He had also a commission of colonel of a regiment which was then to be raised for the preservation of Cape Breton. Many would have appeared vain, and been bloated with an idea of their own consequence with a small part of the honours conferred upon this gentleman. He received the thanks of the ministry, congratulatory addresses were made to him, peculiar tokens of respect and affection were shown him by several branches of the Royal family; but his manners did not change by his exaltation to honour. His affability gained him friends among all classes of people, and he conciliated, still more the affections of his former acquaintance. He had a deep sense of the providence of the Supreme Being, which seemed to influence every action of his life, and made him modest and humble. He made an open profession of religion, and exhibited the christian virtues to the credit of his religious sentiments; he died at his seat in Kittery, July 6, 1759, aged 63; and exhibited the Christian hero on his death bed, meeting the conflicts of the last enemy with fortitude and putting entire confidence in the Captain of his salvation.*

PETERS HUGH, minister of the church of Salem, was born, 1599, in Foy, Cornwall. He was educated at the university of Cambridge, where he received his master's degree, 1622. He was licensed to preach by Dr. Mountain, bishop of London, and preached with such success, that he converted multitudes every week. According to his own account an auditory of 7000 assembled at one time at Sepulchre church A general remark may be made upon preachers at certain times. They will draw the multitude, if they have a great deal of zeal, and a strong voice. It often happens, that they have zeal without knowledge, and faith without charity. Such a preacher was Hugh Peters; but active and enterprising, one who would push himself forward, as the head of a party, and overcome every difficulty by his bold adventurous spirit. He left England

* Notices of the life of sir William Pepperell may be found in a most excellent discourse which his minister and friend Dr. Stevens published after his death. Also in the first volume of the Collections of the Massachusetts Historical Society. The actions of this illustrious American officer are related likewise by the English writers in the histories of the French war which ended with the peace of Aix la Chapelle.

because he had scruples about conforming to the ceremonies of the episcopal church; or, because the ruling power "persecuted the saints." He went first to Holland, and he was pastor of a church in Rotterdam. The celebrated Dr. Ames was his colleague, and died in his arms. He arrived in New England, A. D. 1635. Sir Ferdinando Gorges says, "this year came that famous servant of Christ, Hugh Peters, whose courage was not inferior to any." He was invited to the pastoral office at Salem, Dec. 21, 1636, and was very respectable among the fathers of the country, for his piety, as well as the lively interest he took in the concerns of the plantation. During five years that he was minister the town flourished; and he was the instrument of its prosperity. He stimulated his people to engage in commerce. "He formed the plan of the fishery, of the coasting voyages, of the foreign voyages; and among many other vessels, one of 300 tons was undertaken by his influence. He provided the carpenters, and entered largely into trade, with great success." He received from his church 200 acres of land in what is now called Northfield, and several other spots of ground, which were considered as a reward for his services. His farm still bears the name of Peter's neck.

As a politician he took very decided ground. The country was then divided between Winthrop and Vane. Each had his party. The ostensible cause was a religious controversy about the covenant of grace and a covenant of works, but it had a great influence upon the politicks of the day. Vane was a rigid Antimonian. The old church of which Wheelwright and Cotton were ministers were zeal on the same side. The pastor, Mr. Wilson, and gov. Winthrop, and the elders of other towns, were for those principles, which agreed with most churches of the reformation. Hugh Peters was strenuous to support them. He exerted every nerve to help the interest of gov. Winthrop, who was again chosen governour in 1637; and " paid a just tribute to Mr. Peter's activity and publick spirit."

In 1641, Mr. Peters was sent to England, as agent for Massachusetts. It was supposed a man, so active in commercial pursuits, could represent the colony upon the laws of excise and trade. The persons designed to this business, according to Winthrop, "were, Mr. Peters of Salem, Mr. Weld of Roxbury, and Mr. Hibbins of Boston. When it was proposed to the church of Salem, Mr. Endicot opposed it. Some reasons were offered, as that officers should not be taken from their churches for civil occasions, that the voyage would be long and dangerous, &c." But in the true style of New England, something was added about the reformation of the churches, which made the business of the agency more palatable to those who were against sending clergymen to negociate regulations of trade. Mr. Peters and Mr. Weld would, however, have been more serviceable to the souls of men in their own country, than they were in managing their temporal interests in Great Britain. There Mr. Peters was duped by the creatures of Oliver Cromwell to serve the views of his policy. He was exactly suited to act the extravagant part he did, because he could be wrought up to a political or religious phrenzy adapted to the circumstances of the times, or the madness of the nation. He would either fight or pray, as his services were thought necessary. He, who had his flock in the American wilderness, was slaying and killing his fellow creatures amidst the armies of Europe. For it is certain he led a brigade into Ireland, and came off victorious. He was also very famous as a political preacher. His discourses before the king were abominable for the severity of their sarcasms, and evil tendency of the sentiments delivered. Doubtless things were exaggerated by the other party; but his own expressions were not only vulgar, calculated not only to give pain to fallen majesty, but to increase the prejudices of those, whose anger was fierce, and their wrath cruel. If falsehoods were spread to make Mr. Peters' character odious or ridiculous, what gave rise to these stories, but certain eccentricities or extravagancies of which no other man was guilty?

His friends bring testimonies of his kind attention to Charles. He says himself, " I had access to the king. He used me civilly. I, in requital, offered my poor thoughts three times for his safety. I never had a hand in contriving or acting his death, as I am scandalised, but the contrary to my main power."

It is easy to reconcile the different accounts given, by supposing every thing true, which is related, concerning the preaching and coarse declamation of Hugh Peters before the king's condemnation. And yet he might be moved with compassion when he saw him struggling with adversity, and returning civilities for the rude treatment, which had been given. Is it not natural for tenderness of spirit to succeed the ebullition of violent passions? We learn nothing very exceptionable in Peters' conduct after this. Cromwell appointed him one of the " triers for the ministry," and a " commissioner for amending the laws," but he speaks humbly of his qualifications. " When I was a trier of others, I went to hear, and gain experience, rather than to judge, when I was called about weighing laws, I rather was there to pray, then to amend laws. But in these things I confess I might as well have been spared."

He was, however, the only one, of all the Independent ministers, condemned to the scaffold. Others were equally guilty, and doubtless as obnoxious to Charles. It is probable, he had offended some by his rudeness and ill manners, who exerted the influence they had, after the restoration, to wreak their vengeance upon him. And his own friends were all out of the way.

The manner of his death was shocking. Such fortitude as he discovered would have made another man called a hero. Ludlow relates, that chief justice Cooke and Mr. Peters were ordered to be executed the same day. They were carried to the place of execution on two sleds, the head of major general Harrison being placed on that which carried the chief justice and directed towards him, which, instead of producing the designed effect, tended only to animate him. Before he died, he received other marks of insult. To which he replied, "that it had not been the custom in the most barbarous nations much less in England to insult over a dying man." When he was cut down, and ordered to be quartered, a col. Turner called to the sheriff's men to bring Peters' to see what was doing; which, being done, the executioner came to him, and rubbing his bloody hands together, asked him, How he liked this work ? He told him he was not at all terrified, and that he might do his worst. And when he was upon the ladder, he said, "Sir, you have butchered one of the servants of God before my eyes, and have forced me to see it, in order to terrify and discourage me, but God has permitted it for my support and encouragement."

To make Mr. Peters more odious, a story was propagated of his being the very man who, in disguise, cut off the king's head. This was never believed by the persons who spread the report.

His ministerial conduct while he was in England has been the subject of animadversion. He was more respectable among his brother clergymen, as a preacher, than he appeared before Cromwell, and the army, when he beat the pulpit drum to carry on their warfare. It is said, he was not friendly to the charities for propagating the gospel among the Indians. This is a fact. He, perhaps, had little hopes of success. Allowing the prospect fair, he spake with contempt of the management of their friends, and of their *parsimonious* treatment of

Mr. Eliot, of which that good man complains. The president of the society, Mr. Steel, thus writes to the commissioners of the united colonies in a letter, dated 18th Feb. 1653 : " Mr. Peters who but 14 days before told Mr. Winslow in plain terms he heard the work was only a cheat, and that there was no such thing as gospel conversion among them presently after charged the same man, upon a letter he received from Mr. Weld, that you, the commissioners of the united colonies, forbad the work in that you would not allow competent maintenance to Mr. Eliot and others that laboured therein ; and however we have otherwise charitable thoughts of Mr. Peters ; yet he has been all along a bad instrument towards this work who though of a committee of the army for the advance of it amongst them yet protested against contributing a penny towards it in his person ; and indeed some of us have been fain to intreat the rest of the gentlemen not to trouble him any further in the business : nor know we any cause unless it be that the work is coming to such perfection and he hath not had the least hand, or finger in it."* *Records United Colonies, vol. ii. page 313. Bentley's History of Salem. Critical Life of Hugh Peters.*

PHILLIPS GEORGE, pastor of the church at Watertown, is called, by Dr. Cotton Mather, " one of the first saints in New England." He was born at Raymund in Great Britain, and had an university education, but the name of the college is not

---

* The publications of Mr. Peters are, a sermon preached before both houses of parliament, the lord mayor and aldermen of London, and assembly of divines, 4to. 1646; Peters's last report of the English wars, occasioned by the importunity of a friend, pressing an answer to some queries, printed the same year, 4to. ; a word for the army, and two words to the kingdom, to clear the one, and cure the other, forced in much plainness and brevity, from their faithful servant Hugh Peters, 1647 ; he also wrote good work for a good magistrate, or a short cut to great quiet ; and the legacy to his daughter, which was published after his execution.

mentioned. He was eminent for his memory and invention, and his diligent reading of the fathers. He was settled at Boxford, in Essex, before he came to New England, with gov. Winthrop, in 1630. His wife died at Salem, upon their arrival, and she was buried near the lady Arabella Johnson. When the company chose their settlements about Charles River, he fixed upon a pleasant spot, which has ever since been called Watertown ; and, upon a day set apart for solemn fasting and prayer, they entered into a covenant.* It was signed by sir Richard Saltonstall at the head of 40 names. He continued pastor of the flock 14 years, and died greatly lamented, July 1, 1644.

In Winthrop's journal, among the events of the year, it is written, " July 2d, George Phillips was buried, he was the first pastor of the church at Watertown, a godly man, specially gifted, and very peaceful in his place, much lamented of his own people, and others."

He left a son, Samuel, who was afterwards minister of the church in Rowley.

He published " a vindication of infant baptism ; and of the church." It was recommended by the London ministers. Mr. Shepard of Cambridge wrote a preface to it. He also wrote letters in answer to Mr. Shepard, who differed from him upon some points of church discipline. Neither his or Mr. Shepard's arguments were printed.

PHILLIPS SAMUEL, lieut. governour of Massachusetts, was the son of Samuel Phillips, esq. of Andover. He was educated at Harvard College, where his conduct was peculiarly correct and exemplary. He was much esteemed by his fellow students, as well as by officers of the society. Among the ingenuous youth of the university were certain associations for practical improvement and usefulness. They consisted generally of good scholars, who combined good principles and pure

* This writing is preserved in the Magnalia.

morals with an ambition to shine as sons of knowledge. At the head of these, and among the most
active, was Phillips, whose name and character were
often mentioned to stimulate others to adorn their
own lives. He was graduated in 1771. When he
left college it was supposed he would enter one of
the professions ; but he turned his attention to other pursuits. He was, however, persuaded to go into
publick life, and though he never neglected his private concerns, but was a diligent promoter of every
good thing in the small circle of those, who " rose
up and called him blessed," yet was he as assiduous and unwearied in his attention to his publick
duties of the general court. He seemed to make it
a part of religious principle to be punctual to his
engagements, that he might redeem time in every
way possible. Hence he was able to accomplish so
much business, besides alluring others to diligence
by his example. He was representative from his
native town in the year 1775, a year remarkable in
our annals, and was then called one of the best
speakers in the assembly. For a number of years
he was in the lower house ; but as soon as the
constitution was formed for the state, he was chos-
en a senator from the county of Essex. It was
during the winter of 1779, 80, the draught of the
committee, which was presented to the convention, became the subject of discussion. Mr. Phillips was of the committee that made the draught,
and supported the main questions in it in the larger
assembly. In 1785, he was chosen president of the
senate, and continued to be elected till he was honoured with the second place in the government. In
1781, he was also appointed justice of the court of
common pleas, and held the office till the year 1797.

During the whole period of his publick life, he
was very friendly to the interests of literature. It
was a rare thing to find him absent from the board
of overseers of the University. He was often on

committees, and improved the opportunities to render essential services to the place of his education. He was one of the founders and original members of the academy of arts and sciences.

In 1793, he received a diploma of doctor of laws, which, in the opinion of our first lawyers, was bestowed with great judgment.

He was a professor of religion from his youth, and possessed a very evangelical spirit. This was manifested in fruits of piety, virtue and benevolence. By his will, we find he employed his last days in exhibitions of the law of kindness which should yield their fragrance after his body was laid in the dust. The first object of his legacies was, to serve the rising generation, that they might early know, that, without being good, they could never be happy. He also left a considerable sum towards promoting the cause of religion and learning, which is not included in the charity for the benefit of district schools. He supported years of ill health and bodily infirmities, until he breathed his last, Feb. 10, 1802, in the 50th year of his age.*

* Other gentlemen of the name of Phillips have made a considerable figure in New England,either as magistrates, or divines. Rev. Samuel Phillips of Rowley, and the rev. Samuel Phillips, grandfather to the lieut. governour, and pastor of the first church in Andover, were gentlemen highly respectable in their profession.

The hon. John Phillips, of Charlestown, who died in 1709. He was for many years one of his majesty's council.

John Phillips, esq. of Boston, colonel of the Boston regiment, and representative for the town at the general court.

William Phillips, esq. of Boston, son of the rev. Mr. P. of Andover, was highly distinguished among the patriots of 1775. At that time he was one of the Boston representatives, and was afterwards of the senate of Massachusetts. He was one of the most opulent merchants in the town, and his name is worthy of respect for his many benevolent exertions to promote useful institutions. Mr Phillips was a member of the convention which formed the state constitution; and also a member of the convention which adopted the constitution of the United States.

Samuel Phillips, the father of the lieut. governour, was a per-

PHIPS SIR WILLIAM, was born at Pemaquid, Feb. 2 1650. His mother had 26 children. Of these, 21 were sons, and William one of the youngest, who lived with his mother until he was 18 years old. The father died when he was a child. He then bound himself to a ship carpenter, and afterwards set up his trade at Boston. He was so illiterate that he could not read nor write, but discovered talents, and a remarkable spirit of enterprise. He soon acquired learning sufficient for all the purposes of common life, and address enough to recommend himself to a young widow of a respectable family, with whom he became connected by marriage. When he became master of his trade, he built a ship at Sheepscot river ; but was soon driven off by the Indians. Afterwards he followed the sea, and hearing of a Spanish wreck near the Bahamas, he went to England, and offered to go in search of it. They sent him upon this business in the Algier and Rose frigates, but he failed of success. This was in 1683. But instead of being discouraged he importuned to be sent once more with a

son of note in the town and country where he lived. He was graduated at Cambridge, 1734, was justice of the peace, representative and counsellor. He founded the academy at Andover, in 1778, with the assistance of his brother William Phillips, esq. and his other brother John Phillips, esq. of Exeter in New Hampshire. The gentleman last mentioned was graduated at Harvard College, 1735 ; had a degree of doctor of laws from Dartmouth University, and rendered himself very conspicuous, while he lived, for his benevolent deeds. He founded and liberally endowed an academy at Exeter, and at his death left large sums for pious and literary institutions.

In the " retrospect of the eighteenth century" by the rev. Dr. Miller of New York, that excellent writer observes, " The family of Phillips in Massachusetts and New Hampshire, has been long distinguished for its great wealth, and also for its love of religion and literature. A complete history of the munificence towards publick institutions at different times, by the members of this family, would probably furnish an amount of benefactions seldom equalled in this country."

He also observes, " that in furnishing instances of individual liberality to publick institutions it is believed that Massachusetts exceeds all other states."

kind of romantick assurance which might strike adventurers, but would never succeed with men of
calculation.   The duke of Albemarle fitted him out
for a second voyage, and he brought from the wreck
300,000 pounds, his own share being only about
16,000.   For this success he was much applauded,
and the king knighted him.   He also appointed him
high sheriff of New England, but not falling in with
the measures of Andross and Randolph, his place
was not easy to him, and he returned to the old
country.   While he remained in Boston, he built a
large brick house in Charter street, which even at
this day makes an elegant appearance.

He always said that when he was a poor sheep
shearer at Kennebeck river, he dreamt that he should
be captain of a ship, and build a brick house in
Boston.   This is related by C. Mather, with a number of marvellous circumstances.   King James offered him the government of New England, but he
did not accept it.

In 1690, he took Port Royal, but was not so successful in the expedition against Quebec.   The
accounts of these military enterprises are recorded
in the annals of those times.   At the anniversary
election, 1690, May 30, sir William Phips was
chosen by the freemen a magistrate of the colony.
He did not stay long in Boston, however, but embarked again for England, to solicit an expedition to
Canada, being fully assured that it was in his power to reduce the province to the subjection of the
British government.   At this time the agents of
Massachusetts were making application to king
William for a restoration of their old charter.
When this could not be obtained, and the charter of
William and Mary was accepted, sir William Phips
was invested with a commission to be " captain gen-
eral and governour in chief over the province of
Massachusetts Bay in New England."   He arrived
at Boston, May 14, 1690.

Different opinions will always be held of men in

public stations. Sir William Phips sought the good of the country, according to his own apprehension. " Palest envy must allow this," says Dr. Mather, who devotes nearly 40 pages of the Magnalia to the biography of this gentleman. He says it is not enough to call him " father of the province, but he should be called the angel, assigned to the special care of it, by a singular deputation from heaven." In another place, he speaks of his " being dropped from the machine of heaven." It seems, however, that sir William had the passions of men, and discovered strong corporeal qualities ; for he would quarrel, sometimes, with the officers of government, and use his fists upon certain occasions to bring them to his own views of a proper conduct. Instances of this sort with a captain of a man of war, and a collector, occasioned complaints against him, which he was sent for to answer. He had an opportunity there to justify himself, according to Mr. Hutchinson, and was about returning to his government, but was taken sick and died in London about the middle of February, 1694. He was buried in the church of St. Mary Wolnoth. The character of sir William Phips which others give, setting aside the life of him by Dr. Cotton Mather, which is rather an eulogy upon one of the pious members of his church, is, that he was a blunt honest man, who had a lively confidence in every thing he undertook, open hearted and generous, but vulgar in speech and manners. His talents were considerable, otherwise he never could have done so much, or obtained such promotion. This, however, has been attributed to fortunate circumstances rather than to superiour abilities. *Histories of New England, by Mather, Douglass, Hutchinson.*

PHIPS SPENCER, lieut. governour of Massachusetts, was nephew, and adopted son, of sir William. He was a man of respectability rather than influence in the province, and was more indebted to his wealth and connections for his rising to office, than any thing very splendid in his abilities, or patriotick in his character. He was of his majesty's council a number of years before he was appointed lieut. governour. Mr. Adam Winthrop was a candidate for this office when Mr. Tailer died in 1732. He was the friend of Belcher, who solicited in his favour; but the friends of Mr. Phips were more powerful, and obtained the place for him. He was lieut. governour from 1732 to the year of his death. While Shirley was in the chair, he expressed an opinion that the lieut. governour was not a counsellor ex officio. It was supposed he was. He had been always so considered, and therefore he was not chosen by the legislature. The conduct of Shirley gave great disgust to the lieut. governour, and led him to much retirement. He is represented as a very prudent and upright magistrate. He was several times in the chair of government, and was in this office, as commander in chief of the province, when he died. This event took place, April 4, 1757.

PIERSON ABRAHAM was from Yorkshire. He came into New England, and joined the Boston church. Afterwards he went to Long Island, with a number of families, who removed from Lynn in Massachusetts, to this new plantation. They incorporated themselves into a church state before they went, and also entered into a civil combination, for the maintaining government among themselves. This was about the year 1640. The town they settled was called Southampton, east end of Long Island. Part of this church afterwards divided, and went over upon the main, and settled Brainford. By advice of the council, Mr. P. went with them. The year of his death is not mentioned, only that he died, leaving the name of a prudent and pious man.*

* Dr. Mather mentions three worthy divines of New Haven colony, who were famous in their day. Mr Blackman. Mr. Pierson, and Mr. Denton, the first minister of Stamford, who was

In the records of the united colonies, there is frequent mention made of his services to the Indians,
for which he had a fixed salary. When Mr. Eliot
was allowed 40*l*. Mr. Pierson had 15*l*. He was
a missionary,whose services are mentioned with respect by the corporation in England. They ordered
1500 copies of a catechism which he wrote in the
Indian language to be printed and dispersed. *Magnalia. Records of U. C.*

PIERSON ABRAHAM, rector of Yale College, son
of the minister of Brainford, was graduated at Harvard College, 1668. He was soon after ordained
over the church at Killingsworth. In the year
1700, he was appointed one of the fellows of Yale
College, and the succeeding year chosen to preside
over that seminary, with the title of rector. His
character was high as a scholar and divine. While
he held this office, he composed a system of natural philosophy, which was used by the students for
many years. He was a very zealous calvinist, and
strongly attached to the form and discipline of the
New England churches. It was the general wish
of the people of Connecticut to remove the College
from Saybrook ; but they were not able to accomplish it during the rectorship of Mr. Pierson. The
people of Killingsworth opposed it, who enjoyed
the excellent preaching of their pastor ; the expense
of the removal also, was more than could be allowed from their funds. This took place after his
death. The rector died in April, 1707, and was
greatly lamented. *Private mss. Holmes' account
of Yale College.*

POWNALL THOMAS, governour of Massachusetts
Bay, was descended from a respectable family in
England. His mother was daughter of John Burnis-
ton, governour of Bombay ; his brother, John Pownall, esq. was secretary to the lords of trade, &c.

also a Yorkshire man, and first settled at Halifax, in England.
" Though he was a little man, says he, his well accomplished
mind was as an ' Iliad in a nut shell."

and was more acquainted with the affairs of these
plantations than any man in England. By his attention to the business, many thousand papers relating to the history of the colonies are now regularly filed, and preserved for future use, which had
been neglected and scattered, and in a few years
would have been entirely destroyed. What precious documents they are may be known by any one,
who has read Chambers's political annals!

In 1757, Mr. Pownall was appointed governour
of Massachusetts, in the room of Shirley. He arrived in Boston the beginning of August, and immediately received to his confidence those gentlemen, who were styled friends to liberty and the
constitution of the province. These had opposed
the late administration, which had been strongly supported by most who held offices in the state, at the
head of whom were Hutchinson, Oliver, Paxton,
&c. A lawyer of very eminent abilities, Mr. Pratt,
who was afterwards chief justice of New York, and
a popular clergyman, the rev. Dr. Cooper, were
always considered as the principal friends and ad-
visers of gov. Pownall. They were men of talents;
but talents, wit and satire were more conspicuous
on the other side, and he was deeply wounded by
the shafts of ridicule, or by serious attacks upon
his conduct. When he found his intrigues exposed,
by a pamphlet written at New York,* and so large
a part of the government of Massachusetts in favour
of those whom he had injured; his great pretensions to learning of no avail with the literary societies; his own manners, light and debonnaire, so inconsistent with the grave and sober habits of New
England, he solicited a recall from this government,
and was appointed successor to gov. Littleton of
South Carolina. He sailed from Boston to London
the 3d. of May, 1760. After his arrival in England
he obtained offices, which he preferred to a government in North America. He was chosen a mem-

* Historical Collections, vol. vii.

ber of the British parliament, and, in 1762, appointed general of controul, with the rank of lieut. colonel, to the combined army in Germany, a short
time previous to the peace of 1763.

During the time of his being in the parliament he
was in the opposition ; of consequence, a friend to
the colonies.   His speeches and writings against
the measures employed to bring them into subjection, were read in our house of representatives, and
reprinted with lively demonstrations of gratitude
and joy.   The patriotick exertions of this governour were contrasted with the wicked designs of
the tory administration which succeeded.   Pownall
was as much the idol of the whigs as Bernard and
Hutchinson were odious to them.*

Mr. Pownall had no small influence in the house
of commons from his knowledge and experience in
American affairs.   While those who knew nothing
of the colonies represented them as turbulent, ungrateful, and without any merit in the conduct of
the war which secured Canada and the West Indies
to the British crown, he pointed out " the aid they
afforded the British arms whenever they were em-

* A town in the district of Maine, was named Pownalborough.
Part of the lands before they were located, were granted to the
governour.   In his latter days he desired these might be sold, or
leased in such a manner, as a fund might be raised for the establishment of a professorship of law in Harvard College.   This
town is now divided ; part of it is called Wiscasset, and the other
part Dresden.   The reason given for the alteration was, that
Wiscasset was the Indian name, and the name by which it was
known.   It is right to preserve the Indian name ; but why
change that of Pownal for Dresden ?   It was supposed to be a
prettier sound ; but ought any thing less than a weighty consideration to make wise men change the name of a place ?   Especially when a town has been so called out of respect to a benefactor
to the country.   Pownall was a great friend to this province, and
the friends of the revolution loved him.   Why should his name
or services be forgotten ?   Besides the injustice of the thing, it is
bad policy.   Who is secure of the honours given him by one generation, if the next, from the whim of the occasion, will take it
away ?   Shall the name be lost before the mould gathers on the
sepulchral monument, or the letters grow illegible on the grave
stone ?   How will this lessen the stimulus to patriotick exertions !

ployed from the year 1755 to the peace of Paris, 1763 ;" he censured the measures in operation against the colonies; he urged the expediency of repealing the revenue acts, and redressing every grievance, not merely as an act of justice to them, but for the honour and true interest of Great Britain.

He lived long enough to see many things take place which he predicted. The pride of opinion was gratified; but doubtless he lamented the dividing of the nation. He enjoyed much leisure in old age, and employed himself in writing books, which manifest great political knowledge, some scientifick research, but cannot be recommended for an easy and correct style.* He died, Feb. 1, 1785.

PRATT BENJAMIN, a celebrated lawyer in Boston, and afterwards chief justice of New York, was descended from poor parents, and bred to a mechanical employment. But the misfortune of losing a limb, and a long confinement by sickness, led him to study. The powers of his mind were uncommonly strong, and he had made some progress in scientifick researches before he determined to give himself a college education. He was without resources, without friends, and somewhat advanced in years, yet he knew human life enough to believe that every thing may be done by perseverance. He had also that opinion of himself, that he believed he should not only gain a subsistence by his learning, but make a shining figure among his contemporaries. When he entered college he was admitted into one of the higher classes, was better informed as well as older than any of his classmates, and was graduated in 1737. His name is the lowest, because the students were then placed according to their parentage. Upon leaving college, he entered Mr. Auchmuty's office, as a student of law. From that

* His works are, rights of the colonies stated and defended, 4to. speech in favour of America, 1769; administration of British colonies, 1774.

gentleman he derived great assistance; and he afterwards married his daughter. At the bar he was distinguished for legal knowledge, and a philosophical arrangement of his ideas. He was also an able reasoner in the house of representatives, where he was a member for Boston a number of years. His politicks were in opposition to Shirley, and hence he was a favourite of Pownall. This also made him popular in Boston, where his splendid abilities might excite admiration, but would not have gained him votes. The inhabitants of that town could never love a man who had no complacency in his disposition, nor urbanity in his manners; a man who emerged from low life to a high station, and despised those who formerly knew him, even those from whom he had received favours. When Pownall left the province, Pratt lost entirely the regard of the people. The merchants and mechanicks in the town were very indignant at his conduct in the general court in supporting a motion to send away the province ship. This ship, though owned by the government, was designed to protect the trade, and the merchants had subscribed liberally towards building her. Yet, in the midst of the war, it was proposed by Pownall's friends, that this ship should leave the station, and the trade suffer merely for his personal honour or safety. The clamour was so great, that the governour found it necessary to take his passage in a private vessel. But the spirit of the people was not suddenly calmed. A larger town meeting than ever had assembled at Faneuil hall, discovered their displeasure by leaving out Pratt and Tyng from the list of their representatives. Pownall, however, remembered Mr. Pratt, and by his recommendation he was made chief justice of New York. He died soon after this promotion.

What talents judge Pratt possessed as a fine writer we cannot learn from any publication with his name. The verses found in his study, and published in the Royal American magazine, April, 1774, discover a strong vigour of fancy. If these were his own compositions, he ought to have exercised a fine genius for poetry.

PRINCE THOMAS, governour of the colony of Plymouth, was first elected into this office in the year 1634; afterwards, in 1638. When gov. Bradford died, in 1657, he was chosen to succeed him, and continued to be chosen as long as he lived. For many years he was one of the assistants, and commissioner to the united colonies. He was one of this respectable body when the disputes happened between Massachusetts and the other colonies about the war with the Dutch, and joined heartily in the letter of reproof which the colony of Plymouth sent to our general court. Mr. Morton gives him the character " of a very worthy, pious gentleman, capable of the office of government." He was a man of great integrity, a just man in private life, and so steady to his trust, as never to betray the publick confidence reposed in him. Douglass says, he had " strong natural powers, but no learning." He was a friend to learning and religion, whatever his own acquirements might be, according to the account we have " that the most able men in the colony thought no method would be more effectual in preventing the churches being overwhelmed with ignorance, than the election of Mr. Prince to the office of governour; and this point being gained, the adverse party from that time sunk into confusion."* He also procured revenues for the support of grammar schools. It was this gentleman, with six others, who first settled the town of Eastham. He removed there, in 1644, and returned to Plymouth, when he was fixed in the chair of government.

Gov. Prince died, March 29, 1673, in the 73d. year of his age. Having lived in New England from the year 1621. *Morton's Memorial. Prince's Annals, &c. &c.*

* Historical collections, vol. viii. page 167.

PRINCE THOMAS, was born at Middleborough, and graduated at Harvard College, 1707. He passed several years in travelling, but with no particular object. He says, "that when he made reflections upon that part of his life, he never could see with satisfaction the reasonableness and consistency of it." While he was in England he was invited to settle as a minister in several places, but his love to his native country induced him to return. He arrived at Boston in 1717, having been absent about seven years. He was ordained pastor of the Old South church, Oct. 1, 1718, and was one of the most learned and useful men of the age. He would deserve this character if he had never published any thing but the chronology.

The worth of this book was not known at the time he wrote it. He enlarged his method from what the proposals stated, and the first part of the work was so unacceptable to the publick, that he could not get subscribers to the second volume. He did, however, publish several numbers which bring the New England annals down to 1633, and which are so valuable for the precious documents they contain, that all who look into the affairs of their own country lament the work was not continued. Concerning this book one of the first men of that generation, Mr. Callender writes, in a letter, dated Newport, April 4, 1739, " It gives me great concern, that Mr. *Prince's chronology* has been so ill received. I look on it as an honour to the country as well as to the author, and doubt not but posterity will do him justice. But that you will say is too late. Some of the very best books have had the same fate in other places and other ages. I need not tell you of Milton, Rawleigh, &c. I wish for *his sake* he had taken less pains to serve an ungrateful and injudicious age, lest it should discourage his going on with his design. I hope it will not, and hope you will encourage him, for sooner or later the country will see the advantage of his work and their obligation to him."

That Mr. Prince was a great scholar is evident from the opinion given of him by the most learned men among us. Dr. Chauncy says, " he may be justly characterised as one of our great men, that his learning was very extensive, but that he was very credulous. He could easily be imposed upon. Another imperfection hurtful to him, was a strange disposition to regard more the circumstances of things, and sometimes minute and trifling ones, than the things themselves." He says, from his own acquaintance with him, he could relate many instances of this ; yet with all these weaknesses he possessed intellectual powers far beyond what is common.

As a preacher Mr. Prince was excellent, if we may judge from the sermons he published. It is said his delivery was bad. Objections have been made, that he frequently rendered his common discourses too learned for common people. He printed the discourse at his own ordination, which no ordinary man could write ; several funeral discourses, which are as remarkable for their pathetick effusions, as judicious observations, and are valuable on account of the information concerning the worthies of Boston, many of whom belonged to that church ; the election sermon, 1730 ; several fast and thanksgiving sermons; and also published some philosophical essays. His revisal of the New England psalms in metre discover his acquaintance with the oriental languages, but not any glow of fancy, nor the least glimmering of genius. A man may be a good historian and no poet.

The friends of Mr. Prince observed his declining health with anxiety. The means used to restore it failed, and he died, October 22, 1758.*

* The father of Mr. Prince was Samuel Prince, esq. of Middleborough, who was born in Boston, 1649, and died 1728, aged 80. He was justice of the peace for Plymouth county, and a very respectable man. His son wrote an account of the family with the character given in the New England Journal, July 15, of that year. He tells us that he was the fourth son of Mr. John Prince,

PRUDDEN PETER, was minister of the church in Milford, Connecticut. He came with his church to New Haven, but removed to Milford. There he lived many years an example of piety, gravity and zeal, against the evils of the times, which our pious ancestors complained of, in the same manner, as those who talk about the great degeneracy of the present age. He died, A. D. 1656, in the 56th year of his age. Dr. Mather says, " that his death was felt as a pillar, which made the whole fabrick to shake."

Dr. Trumbull says, that his estate in this country was appraised at 924*l*. 18*s*. 6*d*. He left a landed interest in England, at Edgton, in Yorkshire, valued at 1300 pounds sterling, which is still enjoyed by some of his heirs. He had two sons. One of them, John Prudden, was graduated, after his father's decease, at Harvard College, in 1668. He settled in the ministry at Newark, in New Jersey. The other inherited the paternal estate. Their descendants are numerous in Connecticut and New Jersey.

PUTNAM ISRAEL, major general in the army of the United States, was born at Salem, Essex county, Jan. 7. 1718. His parents were respectable, and his ancestors among the early settlers of Massachu-

ruling elder of the church in Hull, New England, who was the eldest son of the rev. John Prince, rector of East Strafford, in Berkshire, England, in the reign of James and Charles I. Elder Prince came to Massachusetts when archbishop Laud persecuted the non-conformists. He was two or three years at the university of Oxford, but did not think himself sufficiently learned to enter into the ministry, and therefore applied himself to husbandry. He died, August 6, 1676, in the 66th year of his age. His second wife was the daughter of Thomas Hinckley, esq. governour of Plymouth. She was the mother of the rev. Mr. Prince of Boston, and of Nathan Prince, a distinguished character in our literary annals. A man of superiour genius to his brother, and in mathematicks and natural philosophy superiour to any man in New England. He was fellow of Harvard College many years, and a candidate for the professor's chair. He wrote a book upon the laws and constitution of that seminary. This was after he was dismissed from the government and instruction of the college on account of his intemperate habits, which destroyed his usefulness.

setts. In the year 1739, he removed from Salem to Pomfret, in Connecticut. He there applied himself to husbandry, and, being very industrious, with a firm constitution, acquired a good estate. In the French war, which commenced on our frontiers, in 1755, Mr. Putnam had the command of a company in Lyman's regiment of provincials. He was highly distinguished at the head of a party of rangers, who were the most bold, active and enterprising men in the army. Amidst his hazardous undertakings, and valourous feats, he was taken prisoner, and suffered every hardship which Indians, in their sportive cruelty, could invent; or in their savage passion execute. He returned to the army as soon as there was an exchange of prisoners In 1762, he was lieut. colonel of a regiment of provincials, which were sent to Cuba. After the city of Havannah was taken, he returned to New England, with a few of his regiment who had escaped the dangers which surrounded them. Some had fallen in battle, many fell a prey to the diseases of the climate. In 1763 peace was proclaimed between the English and French nations; but the savages of the American wilderness were not yet tamed. Gen. Bradstreet was sent to the western frontiers, in 1764; col. Putnam was with him, having the command of a regiment. The Indians were, however, brought into complete subjection without much fighting, and col. Putnam returned to the tranquillity of domestick life. Like other great characters we read of, he went from the field of battle to the plough.

At the commencement of the revolutionary war, when the spirit of patriotism, like a fire bursting from its enclosures, spread over the country, the name and actions of Putnam were on every tongue. His soul was on fire upon the news of Lexington battle, and he immediately left all his private concerns for the field of action. It is impossible to express the confidence placed in him. He was equal to a host. It was the language of many, that the

British troops would not dare to come out of Boston, when they knew they would have such a hero to oppose. On the other hand the loyalists within the lines attempted to expose to ridicule those very things which excited the admiration of the patriots. They called him the "wolf catcher," a mere Indian hunter, who was hardly equal to command a company of grenadiers. They acknowledged his courage, and several of the higher officers of the army, who had served with him, gave a just tribute to his other good qualities, as well as his valour.

He commanded a wing of the army during several campaigns; was an active, useful officer, more brave than prudent, and frequently wanted dignity in his style of conduct; but always generous, humane, the soldier's friend. It was unfortunate for the country, as well as himself, that he was taken off from all active service by a paralysis in the winter of 1779. He lived, however, to enjoy the blessings of peace, to see his country in prosperity, his friends contented and happy. He died, May 29, 1790.*

* "Among the many worthy and meritorious characters with whom I have had the happiness to be connected in the service through the course of the war, and from whose cheerful assistance in the various and trying vicissitudes of a complicated contest, the name of a Putnam is not forgotten ; nor will it be but with that stroke of time which shall obliterate from my mind the remembrance of all those toils and fatigues through which we have struggled for the preservation and establishment of the rights, liberties and independence of our country." *Gen. Washington's letter to gen. Putnam, April* 2, 1783.

For this letter, and several facts we are indebted to col. Humphreys, late American minister to the court of Madrid. His life of Putnam is a very interesting piece of biography. It will be read with repeated pleasure. It would greatly increase our stock of information, if other gentlemen of sentiment and observation would give memoirs of our revolutionary characters. Many incidents of the war would be mingled with the narrative of their lives. Many anecdotes also might be furnished by those who knew them, intimately, which we shall doubtless lose, as those who relate them are dropping off the stage. We love to see men in all their various attitudes, whom we admire for the distinguishing features of their character.

PYNCHON WILLIAM, one of the first planters of Massachusetts, was a gentleman very respectable for his learning, as well as his piety. He laid the foundation of the town of Roxbury. With this company Mr. John Eliot preferred to settle, when the first church in Boston were very desirous to have him for their pastor. Many of them had been his friends and neighbours in England. In the year 1636 the settlements at Connecticut river began. Those who settled Windsor went from Dorchester. Mr. Pynchon, and those who went from Roxbury, settled higher up the river. The place was called Agawam, by the Indians, which doubtless means a river, in their language; several other places were so called. This was certainly the original name of Ipswich. Mr. Pynchon may be considered as the father of two principal towns in Massachusetts, Roxbury and Springfield. He lived to old age, and grew rich trading with the Indians. It is said, that some of his landed property is in the possession of his posterity to the present day. It is a fact, that the town of Springfield, had always had one of the name and family among their magistrates. A late appointment of a justice of peace, since Mr. Gore has been in the chair of government, is an evidence, that the family is still worthy of respect, as it always has been, if we view the line from their first ancestor.

PYNCHON JOHN, who had been a magistrate 50 years, died at Springfield, June 16, 1702.

PYNCHON JOSEPH, one of the descendants, was a magistrate for the county of Suffolk; for many years of his majesty's council, and died at Newtown, previous to the revolution.

QUINCY EDMUND, agent for Massachusetts at the court of Great Britain, was born at Braintree, Oct. 21, 1681. He was descended from worthy ancestors, who were esteemed highly by the fathers of our country. The first Mr. Edmund Quincy was a member of the Boston church, which then included Braintree, in the year 1633. He died at the age of thirty three. His son, Edmund Quincy, married the daughter of major general Gookin, a man of renown in that generation, and whose memory is still precious. Mr. Q. was also distinguished by his honours and his virtue. He fixed his residence upon the spot now called Quincy ; was lieut. col. of the Suffolk regiment, and a magistrate of the county. It was his desire, that his son, the subject of this article, might have every advantage of a liberal education, and he sent him to Harvard College, where he was graduated, 1699. The father died while the son was a student, in the month of January, 1697.

Deprived of his care at this tender age, the youth improved the opportunity he had to acquire knowledge. The example of an excellent father was before him, and his conduct manifested the influence of those sentiments with which his mind was early imbued. His mind was active, his genius brilliant, and he laid up wisdom for future years. He was soon honoured with the confidence of the publick, and he never frustrated the fond hopes of those who loved him, nor the expectations of those who had a high opinion of his accomplishments. In the year 1713, he had a commission from gov. Dudley to be colonel of the first regiment, previously to which he had shown himself to be a very active and skilful military officer.

In 1718, he was appointed one of the judges of the superiour court, and he always maintained the dignity of this honourable bench by his excellent deportment, his attention to duty, his wisdom and integrity. In the legislature, he was a very eloquent and graceful speaker. He was chosen a representative in 1713, 14 ; and one of his majesty's council the year succeeding. In the year 1733, he had an additional commission of justice through the province. " He sought not these honours, but several of them he was solicited to accept," as we are assured by persons intimately acquainted with him.

In the year 1737, a serious controversy took place between Massachusetts and New Hampshire about settling the boundary line. Commissioners were appointed by the crown to bring the dispute to a termination. Mr. Q. was one of the agents of this province, before the commissioners, and was afterwards chosen to represent the whole business before the court of Great Britain. Hutchinson says the Massachusetts were sure of their cause. "They thought it safest, however, to send a special agent, who was joined with Mr. Wilks the former agent; to whom was added Mr. Richard Partridge, whose chief merit was, that he was a relation of gov. Belcher. Mr. Q. died of the small pox, by inoculation, soon after his arrival in London, and the other two knew little or nothing of the controversy." Mr. Q's. death was on the 23d of Feb. 1737.

The loss to the country was great, as he was one of the most useful and accomplished gentlemen in the province. He loved his country; and understood the laws and constitution of this government equal to any man in it, and was very popular, as well as wise and judicious. "He walked in his uprightness," says an affectionate friend, "and led us in the way to heaven by a shining example of piety and goodness. His memory ought to be always dear and precious with us, and his great name mentioned with peculiar honour in the annals of New England. Semper honos, nomenque tuum, laudesque manebunt."* *Hancock's funeral sermon. Mss. penesme.*

* The province were at the expence of the funeral, and the general court gave orders to erect a handsome monument in Bunhill Fields, London, with an elegant latin inscription englished as follows :

Here are deposited the remains of Edmund Quincy, esq. native of Massachusetts bay, in New England ; a gentleman of distinguished piety, prudence and learning, who early merited praise for discharging with the greatest ability and improved integrity the various employments both in the civil and military affairs with which his country entrusted him : these especially as one of his majesty's council, a justice of the supreme court of judicature, and colonel of a regiment of foot. The publick affairs of his coun-

QUINCY JOSIAH, jun. an eminent lawyer, orator, and patriot, was the son of Josiah Quincy, esq.
merchant in Boston, who acquired a handsome fortune in trade, and in his latter years retired to Braintree, the seat of his ancestors.   His son was born
in Boston, 1743, entered Harvard College, 1759 ;
where he was distinguished for the vivacity of his
genius, and his application to study.   In 1763, he
received the honours of that seminary.   Three
years after, when he proceeded master of arts, he
pronounced an English oration, by which he obtained great eclat.   Except in one instance, there had
been no English performance since the foundation
of the college, and in no instance could an orator
have been brought forward, to obtain more universal applause.

At the bar he discovered much legal information ;
he was energetick, and fluent, and seldom failed
of impressing his sentiments upon the jury in the
most pointed and perspicuous manner. His political character, however, gave him the greatest claim
to publick favour.   As a friend to liberty the people regarded him with admiration bordering on enthusiasm.   Those who have heard him speak will
never forget his voice and manner, when the great
body of the people assembled in Faneuil Hall, or in
the Old South meeting house, to express their abhorrence of the acts of the British parliament, and
their determination to live and die like freemen.
Mr. Q. had a tongue to speak, and a pen to write,
which have not been exceeded in this country. The
controversy between Great Britain and the colonies
was the general topick of conversation.   The revenue acts had been passed.   The Boston port bill

try so requiring, he embarked their agent to the court of Great
Britain in order to secure their rights and privileges. Being seized with the small pox, he died a premature death, and with him
the advantages expected from the agency, with the greatest prospect of success.   He departed the delight of his own people but
of none more than the senate, who, as a testimony of their love
and gratitude, have ordered this epitaph to be inscribed on his
monument.

soon after arrested the attention of the people, and Mr. Q. had a fine opportunity to display his talents and patriotism. His publication, in 1774, entitled, " Thoughts on the Boston port bill, &c. addressed to the freeholders and yeomanry of Massachusetts," was a seasonable work, fraught with much information, written with becoming energy, and it stimulated the body of the people to manly and decent exertions in defence of their natural and constitutional rights. He received an anonymous letter, May 17, 1774, from the British coffee house in Boston, which warned him of the imminent danger of his life, and hazard of confiscation of his property. To which he made the following reply, in the Massachusetts Gazette, No. 3685 : " The dangers and wrongs of my country are equally apparent. In all publick concerns I feel a sense of right and duty, that not only satisfies my conscience, but inspires my zeal. While I have this sentiment *I shall persevere*, till my understanding is convinced of its error. A consideration, that will not be warped by the arm of power, or the hand of an assassin. Threats of impending danger communicated by persons who conceal their name and character, ought never to deter from the path of duty ; but exciting contempt rather than fear, will determine a man of spirit to proceed with new vigour and energy in his publick conduct."

The health of Mr. Q. had been sometime declining. Amidst his vigourous exertions for the publick good, he thought too little of himself. His friends, therefore, persuaded him to take a voyage across the Atlantick, which might also give him an opportunity, from his own knowledge and experience, to explain many things to the friends of the colonies, and thus contribute to the service of his country. He embarked at Boston, Sept. 28, 1774, and the very day on which he arrived in the harbour of Cape Ann, April 27, 1775, he departed this life. His remains were interred in that town with every mark of respect. Few, however, compared with those who felt the loss, could attend the funeral. The multitude of the people were his mourners. The death of such a man was a heavy stroke upon the community, as well as his family, friends and acquaintance. The effect it had upon various classes of people is still remembered. Many knew, or had heard of his patriotick zeal; also, with what eloquence he had plead the cause of his country. A great deal was expected from the communications he would make of what he had learned abroad. The news of his death, therefore, when a general gloom was spread over our publick affairs made every eye look down with concern, and every heart throb with sensations of grief.

It was a subject of conversation, likewise, very natural, that two of the same family, two men of sterling eloquence, who had the love and confidence of the publick, should both die, when the country was waiting for their communications. High hopes seemed to be raised only to be blasted.*

* The grandfather died in England; the young gentleman before he reached these western shores.

In a letter from a gentleman of some distinction in the literary world is the following passage: " I think it worthy of observation, that the Quincy's have been friends to liberty and the rights of the people from the most ancient times. When the English barons made that noble stand in the beginning of the 13th century, that obliged king John to grant the Magna Charta, sieur de Quincy was one of them. Although more than five centuries have rolled away since that great event, yet the spirit has not been lost. Josiah Quincy, esq. in the most trying times of our revolution, exerted his great abilities with success in favour of the rights of the people," &c.

The family is certainly one of the most ancient in Massachusetts: many have been distinguished in publick offices, several for their abilities, learning and patriotism. Two sons, Edmund and Josiah, were magistrates in the county of Suffolk. Josiah had a commission of colonel of the regiment. His three sons, Edmund, Samuel and Josiah, were men of letters. The youngest of the three made the greatest figure in life, and he died in the morning of his days. Edmund died abroad. He was a zealous whig, and a political writer in those times. Samuel was a poet, and an elegant writer in prose. His politicks were different from the rest of the family. He was ap-

RANDOLPH EDWARD, in the year 1676, was sent over to inquire into the state of the colonies. He was an active and implacable adversary to New England. He brought with him copies of the petitions of Mason and Gorges relative to their patent of New Hampshire, the limits of which interfered with the grants made to Massachusetts.

While he was in Boston, he represented that the province was refractory, and disobedient to the requisitions of the crown. He was zealous to promote the cause of episcopacy, and to destroy the New England churches ; and he was the principal instrument of depriving the inhabitants of Massachusetts of their charter privileges, the people against whom he had conceived a most violent antipathy.

When the charter was taken away, and James II. succeeded to the crown, the king appointed a council to govern the province, of which Dudley was president, and Randolph was one named in the commission. The next year sir E. Andross arrived with a commission to be governour of New England. Randolph was a conspicuous character during his short administration; and involved in his fate. How much the people were exasperated against him appears, by their refusing him bail when he applied, and when it was granted to others. The house of representatives, June 25, 1689, voted,

pointed solicitor general when Jonathan Sewall, esq. who married his cousin, was attorney general. He left his country with the loyalists, and died in the West Indies, after the peace.

The hon. John Quincy, esq. who was speaker of the house of representatives in 1737, and afterwards of his majesty's council, was a nephew of the celebrated judge Edmund Quincy. His son, Norton Quincy, esq. was chosen a counsellor in 1774, and was one of the eleven whom gov. Gage negatived. One of his daughters married the rev. William Smith of Weymouth, a worthy divine, much beloved by those who knew him. The late president of the United States, his excellency John Adams, esq. married a daughter of Mr. Smith.

The lady of the late gov. Hancock was also a grand-daughter of judge Quincy.

" that Mr. E. Randolph is not bailable, he having broken a capital law of this colony in endeavouring and accomplishing the subversion of our government, and having been an evil counsellor."

Mr. Randolph died in the West Indies. It was said, that he always retained his prejudices against the churches and people of Massachusetts. On the other hand the inhabitants of this province who once held him in abhorrence, regarded him and his reproaches with the utmost contempt.

RATCLIFFE ROBERT, was the first episcopal minister who ever formed a church in New England. The church was formed in the year 1686, though a house of worship was not built for some years. It has since been called the king's chapel, or the first episcopal church, Tremont-street. Randolph says, " the congregation consisted of 400 souls." He is not an authority, where his prejudices are concerned. This society grew respectable after the charter of William and Mary, being the place of resort of the crown officers. But when Ratcliffe was rector, they met in his house, or the library room in the town house. We hear nothing of Mr. Ratcliffe after the year 1686.

RAWSON EDWARD, secretary of the colony above 40 years, under the old charter, was graduated at Harvard College, 1653. He was a respectable character, as we may judge from his having this office so long, while there was an annual election. He was also appointed treasurer of the corporation for propagating the gospel. In this office, he did not give so much satisfaction as in the other. The praying Indians complained to Ratcliffe and Randolph, that they could not get cloaths, &c. which were allowed them. The letters also that came from England to the commissioners here, give some reproofs which amount to a charge of negligence. He lost his office of secretary when the government was changed, being succeeded by Randolph, and afterwards by Mr. Addington. We do not learn from Mr. Hutchinson when secretary Rawson died, nor has he even given his name in his index.

READ JOHN, a gentleman of very brilliant talents, of sterling integrity, a friend of the people, of the laws and government. For his superiour abilities he was considered as one of the greatest lawyers in this country. The succeeding generation indulged a pride in quoting his legal opinions, and his sayings, in common conversation. He died, at an advanced age, Feb. 7, 1749, having been graduated at Harvard College at the commencement of 1697.

He had served as a representative of this town for many years; and afterwards was elected into the council. While he sat at that board, he was their oracle, and was eminently useful to the country.

REVEL JOHN, was one of the five original undertakers of these New England plantations. There are five who are thus distinguished by Mr. Prince. Their venerable names are Winthrop, Dudley, Johnson, Saltonstall and Revel. He was chosen assistant, October 20, 1629, 30, and was therefore the 10th of this board. He returned to England, with Mr. William Vassal, the succeeding summer.

ROBIE THOMAS, fellow of Harvard College, was graduated, A. D. 1708; instructed a class from 1714 to 1723; he then studied physick. He was eminent as a mathematician, and a handsome writer; specimens of his scientifick abilities, and his manner of composing, may be found scattered in the magazines and newspapers during 20 years of the 18th century, particularly a letter to the publick, concerning a very remarkable eclipse of the sun, Nov. 27, 1722. He also published a theological treatise, or a discourse upon "the knowledge of Christ superiour to all other knowledge." It was delivered in the college chapel to the students, and dedicated to president Leverett.

ROBINSON JOHN, pastor of the English church at Leyden, will be had in everlasting remembrance. Though he never set his foot on this American strand, yet it was his determination to follow his flock into this wilderness; and the planters of New Plymouth looked up to him, as the father and friend of the colony. He had a name to live, if these regions had never been settled. His abilities, accomplishments and sufferings give him a claim to distinction with the worthies of the christian church, but it is as the pastor of the Leyden church that he becomes the object of our biographical notice. When he first separated from the church of England, he was reckoned a Brownist, and hence the first planters of New Plymouth have been called Brownists, by European historians, in which they have been imitated by American writers who ought to know better, or seek accounts from the right sources of information. Mr. R. was early in life among the straitest sect of them who were called puritans. But with a mind open to conviction he altered his sentiments when the celebrated Amesius controverted his opinion. He was ready to embrace the truth of the gospel in its simplicity. Decked in all the meritricious ornaments of the episcopal churches, he lost sight of her beauties, and would not allow the church of England could be a true church. But afterwards he allowed, that many churches were founded on the apostles' doctrine and fellowship, which only needed greater purity in their forms of worship. The church of Leyden, so far from being Brownists, were considered by that sect as inimical to them. Gov. Winslow, a principal member of Mr. Robinson's church, says, " The Brownists in Holland would not hold communion with the church at Leyden. The rev. Mr. Prince, whose account of the Plymouth settlers is very accurate, quotes a passage from Bailie, the bitter enemy of rigid separatists, which says, that Mr. Robinson was a man of excellent parts, and the most learned, polished and modest spirit that ever separated from the church of England ; that the apologies he wrote were very handsome ; that by Dr. Ames and Mr.

Parker he was brought to a greater moderation than
he at first expressed ; that he ruined the rigid separation, *allowing* the lawfulness of communing with
the church of England in the word and prayer,
though not in the sacraments and discipline."

It would have been happy for Plymouth church
if Mr. R. had come over.   Elder Brewster would
never take the office.   The gifted brethren gained
so much influence, as to make every preacher's situation uneasy.   If he had not the *ready* talent of explaining the scriptures, he was put down as a man
of low gifts ; if he were superiour, he found his talents in more demand in Massachusetts.   Our old
historians give this account of the church at Plymouth, and since that day many instances confirm
their opinion, that whenever parishes are long without a minister, they find it more difficult to settle one.
In expectation of Mr. Robinson's coming over the
church grew and flourished ; but when these expectations of seeing him were most highly raised, they
heard the sad news of his death, 1625. "It has pleased
the Lord to take out of this vale of tears, your and
our loving pastor, Mr. Robinson. He fell sick, Saturday morning, Feb. 22, next day taught us twice,
on the week grew weaker every day, feeling little or
no sensible pain to the last.   Departed this life, the
1st of March.   Had a continual ague.   All his
friends came freely to him.   And if prayers, tears
or means could have saved his life, he had not gone
hence.   We will still hold close in peace, wishing
that you and we were together,"* &c.

The parting address of Mr. Robinson, when his
people embarked for this new region, has been frequently printed and quoted, and no speech ever discovered more candour and excellent spirit.   It
shows a mind above vulgar prejudices, the dignity
of reason, and the meekness of a christian. "Words,
says Mr. Prince, almost astonishing in that age of low
and universal bigotry, which then prevailed in the

---

* Letter from Leyden, quoted by Mr. Prince.

English nation ; wherein this great and learned man seems to be almost the only divine, who was capable of rising into a noble freedom of thinking and practising in religious matters, and even urging such an equal liberty on his own people. He labours to take them off from their attachment to him, that they might be more entirely free to search and follow the scriptures."

ROGERS EZEKIEL, was born in England, 1590. He was the son of Richard Rogers, an author of some repute, who wrote a book entitled, the seven treatises, which passed through several editions in London, and has been read a great deal in New England. Ezekiel came to this country in 1638, with a number of people from Yorkshire. He was urged to go with them to New Haven ; but he chose a pleasant spot in the county of Essex, where he could enjoy the society of Mr. Nathaniel Rogers, the first minister of the church in Ipswich. It was called Rowley, because he was minister of Rowley in Great Britain. He preached the election sermon in 1643. The first twelve years of his ministry were attended with great success. He was in labours more abundant, so that a young man was settled with him as a colleague. This caused jealousies and divisions in the parish, and his life was unhappy. He also met with domestick affliction. He buried two wives and all his children ; his house and furniture were consumed by fire ; he lost the use of his right arm, and was obliged to learn to write with his left hand, after he was advanced in years.

Though sometimes cast down by the discouragements of the world he was, however, patient under many tribulations. He believed that, after making the voyage of life over a troubled sea, he should reach the haven of eternal rest. His last sickness was of a lingering nature, and he died, Jan. 22, 1668, in the 79th year of his age.

ROGERS NATHANIEL, was the second son of John Rogers of Dedham, and born in 1598. He was educated at Emanuel College, Cambridge, and settled with Dr. Barkam, in a parish called Bocking, in Essex county. He had no scruples about conforming to the forms and ceremonies of the church of England till he became acquainted with Mr. Hooker, and he then began to show his dissatisfaction, by leaving off the surplice, which gave offence to the rector, and occasioned a removal. After this the bishop of Norwich suffered him to live quietly, and preach at Assington, where he continued five years. He obtained great celebrity as a preacher with the most wise and judicious people. Though he had not the loud voice of his father, yet he was a lively, florid and animated speaker. He, came to New England in the year 1636 in the same ship with Mr. Partridge, and was invited to settle with the church at Dorchester; but for the sake of those who came with him, and could be accommodated better at Ipswich, he preferred that place, and was ordained Feb. 20, 1638. His ordination sermon was 2. Cor. ii. 16. " A sermon so copious, judicious, accurate and elegant," says Dr. Mather, " that it struck the hearers with admiration." He gives also, a very particular account of his preaching upon certain parts of the scriptures, to the acceptation of the people, but says, that he printed none of his discourses. One reason was, that his disposition to be accurate was such, as would injure his health. He was also a remarkably modest man, though one of the greatest men in his profession. " He might be compared with the very best of the true ministers, which made the best days of New England." The biographer says, he was equal to Norton in his greatest excellencies. Such a man, though worthy of respect, is not always sure of it. The *wild notes* of illiterate preachers are frequently read, while the best compositions are neglected. Mr. Rogers suffered many trials. He was subject to hypochondriack complaints, and was often a prey to melancholy humours. At the time Mr. Norton was called from Ipswich to Boston, he was much afflicted, and he gave displeasure to others. He did not live long afterwards, though he grew better of his bodily complaints. In 1655, an epidemic cough prevailed in the country. He had the complaint; but with no symptoms of danger, till the morning previous to his death. He then blessed his family, spake cheerfully of heavenly things, and when he had uttered these words, as his last, " My times are in thine hands," died in peace, July 3d, in the afternoon.*

Dr. Mather says, that although no composures of this worthy man came from the press, except a letter, which he wrote in 1643, to a member of the house of commons, " concerning reformation ;" yet he had in his hands, a manuscript, written in a neat latin style, whereof he was an incomparable master. It is entitled, " a vindication of the congregational church government." From the specimen given in the Magnalia, it must be a desideratum to obtain the whole.

Rogers John, president of Harvard College, son of the rev. N. Rogers of Ipswich, was born in England, before his father left Assington, and came over with him to America. He was graduated at Harvard College, 1649, and was, for some time, a preacher of the gospel; but he either did not meet with success in the ministry, or was more attached to the theory and practice of physick; for he left one profession for the other.

He is described as a man of piety and excellent temper. " So sweet was his disposition that the title of *deliciæ humani generis* might have been given him, and his real piety, set off with the accomplishments of a gentleman, was like a gem set in gold." He was chosen to succeed Mr. Oakes, as president

* In 1655, a distemper went through the plantations of New England like to that in 1647. It was so epidemical that few were able to visit their friends at any distance to perform the last offices to them. It was attended with a faint cough. Mr. N. Rogers minister of Ipswich died of it, July 2d. *Hutchinson*.

of the college, and installed, August 12, 1683.
The next year he died, July 2d, the day after commencement.

An epitaph was engraved on his tomb, written by
one of the students, supposed to be Dr. Cotton
Mather. It is no very elegant specimen of classical style.

ROGERS NATHANIEL, pastor of the church in
Portsmouth, was the son of president Rogers, and was
educated at Harvard College, 1687, and ordained,
May 3d, 1699. He was a very pious minister, a
strict disciple of the Geneva school, had a very
agreeable manner of preaching, and was very elegant in his person and deportment. With all his
wisdom and affability he could not prevent a division in the parish which arose upon building the
new meeting house.* The majority moved from
the old spot to the north section of the town, and
have preserved the name of the first church to the
present time. The inhabitants of the south end
were filled with resentment at their conduct. They
organized themselves as a distinct society. In this
they acted with the advice and assistance o. Dr.
Mather of Boston. An ecclesiastical council was
called, which only widened their dfference. Mr.
Rogers was much disgusted with the conduct of
the ministers, who gave their advice to the people
of the old church. Dr. Mather, on the other hand,
blamed Mr. Rogers, and wondered how so good a
man could discover so much ill humour. The result of the council is not exactly known ; but the
most just inference to be drawn per mss. handed
down, is, that the societies separated, and did not
walk in love " till that generation dropped off the
stage. Mr. Rogers died, October 3d, 1723. The
inscription on his monument was written by a gentleman of classical purity and taste. It is preserved in the collections of the Massachusetts Historical Society. He left a number of children.

* See Alden's account of Portsmouth.

The oldest was the hon. Nathaniel Rogers, esq. father of the present judge Rogers of Exeter. His youngest son was the hon. Daniel Rogers, esq. who for a number of years was one of the king's council, when New Hampshire was a royal government. He resigned this honourable station on account of the *acts* of the British parliament, which prepared this country for the revolution. He was a whig in principle, a man of a strong mind, extensive reading, and strongly attached to the principles of our fathers. His lady was the daughter of the hon. John Ringe, agent at the court of Great Britain, a sister of Mrs. Wentworth, the mother of sir John Wentworth, governour of Nova Scotia.

ROGERS JOHN, minister of the church in Ipswich, was the son of president Rogers. He was graduated at Harvard College, in 1684, and a few years after he received academical honours, he was ordained pastor of the church, where he continued his publick labours fifty six years. He died December 28, 1745, in the eightieth year of his age. An eminent divine, Mr. Wigglesworth, of the same town, preached his funeral sermon, and thus delinates his character : " As to natural endowments, he was blessed with a clear apprehension and sound judgment ; was of a thoughtful and inquisitive temper of mind ; in the diligent improvement of which advantages, through the blessing of God, he acquired much valuable knowledge ; especially much of that knowledge the lips are to keep, and the pastors after God's own heart to feed his flock with. His private conversation was edifying and pleasant. He had a conspicuous degree of prudence, which is so necessary to the well managing and administering the affairs of Christ's household. He was robust, useful and active in old age, being enabled to labour in word and doctrine to the last, and quit the stage in action."

ROGERS NATHANIEL, son of the rev. John Rogers, was settled as his colleague in the ministry. He was graduated in the year 1724, and died in May, 1775, having been in the pastoral office near fifty years. Concerning this venerable man, as one speaks who was well acquainted with him, it is hard to say, whether the great or good was his predominant character. But it must be admitted by all, that there was in him an uncommon measure and a rare combination of both. He had a very discerning mind, and was blest with advantages for acquaintance with men and things. He exhibited generally something superiour in turn of thought and manner of conversation. He could be entertaining and instructive, so that young men took great pleasure in his company. The great things of the gospel were to be sure his favourite subjects. As a preacher he avoided vain philosophy, and subtle disputings. When his heart was most moved, there appeared an energy of address, which is rarely to be met with.

In his latter days he was taken off from his labours, and his mental faculties impaired ; but there were lucid intervals when he conversed like himself. The people of his charge, and the neighbouring churches, lamented his departure with expressions of condolence, that were lively and expressive.* *Dr. Dana's mss.*

* The church of Ipswich was supplied with a pastor by the name of Rogers above 100 years. The first Mr. R. was with them about 17 years ; Mr. J. Rogers 56 ; and Nathaniel between 40 and 50. The family descended from Mr. J. Rogers, who was a martyr to the cause of the reformation. He was burnt at Smithfield, 1555. Mr. Rogers of Dedham was his grandson, whose son Nathaniel came over to New England. The branches of the family are numerous. No one name has been more conspicuous among the divines of Massachusetts. There are preachers in succession for a number of generations. Several have been famous beside those we have mentioned. Mr. Rogers, of Littleton, who was graduated in 1725, with whom the compiler of this work once served as an assistant, possessed very superiour talents, was a very rational and learned divine, a man of scientifick researches, and a complete gentleman in his manners. He died Nov. 25, 1782.
There is nothing published with his name, and it is something

ROSSITER EDWARD, came from the west of England, and was chosen one of the assistants for the government of Massachusetts, October 20, 1629, and died October 23, of the succeeding year. He was grave and pious, and possessed considerable property. His death was felt as a loss to the colony, as we learn from Dudley's letter to the countess of Lincoln. He was present at the court of assistants held at Charlestown, Sept. 28, when 50*l.* was to be levied for a military purpose. This was the third session held at Charlestown, although the majority of the people dwelt on the south side ; for Boston was taxed 11*l.* and Charlestown 7*l.*

SALTONSTALL SIR RICHARD, one of the fathers of Massachusetts colony, was the son of sir R. Saltonstall, who was lord mayor of London, in 1597. He was the first associate of the six original patentees mentioned in the charter of Charles I. March 4, 1628, and the fourth assistant named therein. He came over their *first* assistant, as appears from a record in Prince's annals, who tells us the first general court met at Boston, Oct. 30, 1630. Present, the governour, deputy governour, secretary, R. Saltonstall, Mr. Ludlow, Capt. Endicot, Mr. Nowell, Pynchon, Bradstreet. He was a worthy puritan, the first founder of the church at Watertown, and a great friend to the plantation. He stayed only a short time in New England; but his heart was engaged in their interest. Two of his sons came over here afterwards, and his posterity have made a respectable figure even to the present time. He died in England, about the year 1658, and in his *will* left a legacy to Harvard College.

remarkable that none of the name have appeared as authors, though so many of them have been celebrated for their abilities, as well as pulpit talents. In 1706, the rev. J. Rogers of Ipswich preached the election sermon. This, and one or two occasional sermons of his son, and three sermons by Mr. R. of Leominster, are the only publications we have met with of the name in New England.

SALTONSTALL RICHARD, esq. son to the worthy knight of the same name, came over here in the year 1635, and was chosen one of the assistants in 1637. He continued a number of years to help on the affairs of this little commonwealth. Johnson says, that father and son ought to be remembered, and celebrates their worth with some of his poetical effusions. If the lines would not immortalize their deeds, or the genius of the writer, they have the New England spirit to recommend them :

" His father gon, young Richard on, here valiantly doth war,
For Christ his truth, to their great Ruth, heathens opposed are."

Accrding to Mr. Hutchinson, Mr. Saltonstall continued in the magistracy till the year 1680, except the time he was in England. He had made a vow, when he first came over, that he never would leave the country, while the ordinances continued in their purity. His wife was very sick, and advice was given by the physician, that she should take a voyage to England. He consulted Mr. Cotton whether it would be breaking his vow, if he went. He decided that it would not, because the marriage vow was the most binding. M. C. was doubtless a greater divine than a casuist! In 1672, Mr. S. again went to England, and made a present to Whaley and Goffe of 50l. before he sailed, which they acknowledged in their mss. We suppose this to be the Mr. Saltonstall, mentioned by gov. Winthrop, who wrote a book in 1642, " against the standing council," which was censured by the court, and answered by Mr. Norris of Salem. This gentleman returned to Boston in 1680, and was again chosen the first assistant, and also two years succeeding. In 1683, he went back to England, and died at Hulme, April 29, 1694. He was a relation to the famous J. Hampden, was opposite to the court, and attached to the principles of New England government and churches.*

* *The first form of their government, was that of governour, deputy governour, and assistants ; the patentees with their heirs.

SALTONSTALL HENRY, grandson of sir Richard, was in the first class of graduates of Harvard College. He received a degree of doctor of medicine from Oxford, and was fellow of New College in that university.

SALTONSTALL NATHANIEL, grandson of sir Richard, was graduated at Harvard College, 1659, chosen assistant 1679, under the old charter, and was appointed one of the council of which Dudley was president in 1686. He refused to serve, because he had taken the oath as assistant. He was a firm friend to the old charter, hence his name is enrolled among those whom Randolph marked in his letters, and who were called a faction by that spy of the British court. We read also that in August, 1680, the deputy governour, Mr. Saltonstall, Nowel, &c. sailed from Boston with 60 soldiers in a ship and sloop, to still the people at Casço Bay, and prevent Andross's usurpation.

Mr. Saltonstall was appointed one of his majesty's council in the charter of William and Mary. He left two sons, Nathaniel and Gurdon, who made a figure in publick life.

SALTONSTALL GURDON, governour of Connecticut, was the great grandson of sir Richard Saltonstall, first assistant of Massachusetts, and son of Nathaniel, one of his majesty's council. He discovered genius and an excellent mind, and was sent to the seminary where his father was graduated, to complete his education. He received the honours of Harvard College, 1684. Having a mind disposed unto serious things, he made divinity his study,

assigns and associates, being freemen, &c. But, in this general court, they agreed on a 2d form as follows : The freemen to have the power of choosing assistants, when they are to be chosen ; and the assistants from among themselves to choose the governor and deputy governour, who with the assistants were to have the power of making laws, and choosing officers to execute the same. This was fully assented to by the voice of the people. A list of freemen amounting to 108, desired to be made freemen, Samuel Mavericke, Edward Johnson, &c.

became a very accomplished preacher, and was ordained pastor of the church at New London, 1691.
In this conspicuous orb he shone with a most engaging lustre. He did good to the souls of men,
and was frequently consulted by the magistrates of
Connecticut upon their most important affairs. He
was an oracle of wisdom to literary men of all professions. Upon the death of Fitz John Winthrop,
esq. in 1707, Mr. Saltonstall was elected governour of the state. So great was the respect of the
people for him, " that the assembly repealed the law
which required that the governour should be chos-
en from among the magistrates in nomination, and
gave liberty to the people to elect him from themselves at large." A letter was addressed to him by
the assembly, requesting him to accept the trust ;
another was addressed to the church and society,
begging them to give their consent that he should
leave the pastoral office. They gratified the wishes of the colony. The first of January, 1708, gov.
Saltonstall accepted the office, and took the oaths
appointed by law. He was elected by the freemen
the succeeding year. In 1709, chosen agent to the
court of Great Britain to present an address to his
majesty, " praying for an armament to reduce the
French in N. America to her majesty's obedience,"
&c. The governour did not accept of the appointment. The assistance was granted, and several expeditions carried on against Port Royal and Canada, as we read in the chronicles of those years.
Gov. Saltonstall was continued in office as long as he
lived, maintained the dignity of his station, and was
accepted by the multitude of his brethren. He died, Sept. 20, 1724, aged 59, leaving a widow, who
has been celebrated in New England for her fine
accomplishments, and munificence to literary and
pious societies, and her charity to the poor.* The
governour is also reckoned among the benefactors
of Harvard College.

* The character of Madame Saltonstall, in the New England

SEWALL SAMUEL, chief justice of Massachu‑
setts Bay, was the son of Henry Sewall who came
into this country in 1634, and made a plantation in
Newbury. His father soon followed, whose name
was also Henry : he was the son of Henry Sewall,
esq. a linen draper of Coventry in Great Britain.
That gentleman possessed an ample fortune, and
was mayor of the city. The father of Judge Sewall

journal, Jan. 26, 1729,30, I suppose to be drawn by Mr. Prince : It
carries intrinsic marks of his pen ; and the lady attended his minis‑
try. She descended from the rev. William Whittingham, a fa‑
mous puritan, who, in the reign of queen Mary I. left an estate
in England worth 1100 a year sterling, and fled to Geneva to
preserve his conscience and religion. There he gathered a
church in the congregational way, which seems to be the first
instance of it in these latter ages, and was chosen their pastor.
Upon queen Elizabeth's accession, he returned to England, and
was created dean of Durham, and assisted Mr. Sternhold in the
old England version of the psalms of David, being the author of
those composures prefixed with W. W. and compiled such a trea‑
tise against the ecclesiastical constitutions, as the learned Mr.
Lee used to say never was, and never could be answered. His
estate chiefly lay at Southerton about 6 miles south of Boston in
Lincolnshire. His only son Baruch was the principal builder of
the church there, having his name distinguished in almost every
window, to be seen many years after. He designed to visit New
England, but was taken sick and died. His widow came over and
had a son, who was the heir of the family, named John. He mar‑
ried a daughter of the rev. William Hubbard of Ipswich, and
lived and died in the town. He left three sons, John and Rich‑
ard, who went to England, and died there unmarried. The third
son was named William, and he was the father of Madame Sal‑
tonstall. He took his degree at Harvard College, 1660, and set‑
tled at Boston, married a daughter of John Lawrence, (formerly
of Ipswich, afterwards alderman of the city of New York) applied
himself to merchandize, and going over to London, to take care
of the estate falling to him, died of the small pox. He left five
children, 1. Richard, who took his degree at Harvard College in
1689. 2. William, a merchant, who went to the West Indies,
and died. 3. Mary, Mrs. Salstonstall. 4. Elizabeth, wife of the
hon. S. Appleton of Ipswich. 5. Martha, married to rev. John
Rogers of the same town. Mary, now deceased, first married
William Clark, esq. merchant of Boston, in 1683. He died in
1710. She was then married to gov. Saltonstall, and upon his
death returned to Boston. As for her character, she was univer‑
sally known to be a gentlewoman of bright intellectual powers,
and to have made a good improvement of them. Full of spirit,

married the daughter of Mr. Stephen Dummer. They were members of the first church in Newbury, where Messrs. Parker and Noyes officiated. Mr. Dummer being in a poor state of health, they all returned to England. They dwelt at Warwick, and then removed to Bishop Stoke, in Hampshire. In this place Mr. Sewall lived some time. His eldest son Samuel was born, March 28, 1652, and was baptised the Sunday following in Stoke church, by Mr. Rashly, who was once a member of the old church in Boston ; then went to England ; was one of the subscribers to the truths of the gospel, 1648, with the London ministers, and ejected by the Bartholomew act, in 1662.

In the year 1661, Mr. Sewall returned to New England, with his family. The subject of this article was 9 years old. He was sent to the school of Mr. Parker, and made great proficiency for one of his age. He was admitted a student of Harvard College, in August, 1667, and received his first degree from the hands of president Chauncy ; the degree of master of arts he received, from president Hoar, in 1674. He was fellow of Harvard College a number of years, and his name is recorded with the benefactors of that seminary. In 1684, his name is among the magistrates of the colony. For several years succeeding, all was confusion and disorder in Massachusetts. Mr. S. went to England

much inclined to reading, and the most instructive company. At the head of the neighbouring colony, she shone in every accomplishment and virtue that became her exalted station. And wherever she went, she was admired for her superiour knowledge, wit, good sense and wisdom. Above all was adorned with exemplary piety. Before gov. S. died, she gave 100 pounds a piece to the two New England Colleges, and by her will 1000 pounds more to this at Cambridge, to be appropriated to two students of bright parts, sober lives, designed for the ministry. She has also left a very large silver bason to the south church in Boston, of which she had been a long while a great ornament ; ten pounds to each pastor, and a hundred pounds to the poor of the town, besides several other noble bequeathments and legacies to others ; and her will was all written by her own hand.

in 1688, the year of the glorious revolution. He very soon returned to America. He was one of the first counsellors after the charter of William and Mary, and continued to be chosen till 1728, when he resigned, having outlived all who were first appointed with himself. In 1692, he was appointed judge of the superiour court, and, in 1718, promot. to the place of chief justice. He resigned his seat upon the bench in 1728, and also his office as judge of probate, to which he was appointed in 1715. His character is delineated by Mr. Prince in a funeral sermon, who says, that " he was universally reverenc. ed and esteemed and beloved for his eminent pie. ty, learning and wisdom ; and that he was one of the most shining lights and honours of the age and land where he lived, and worthy of a very distin. guishing regard in the New England histories."

He printed a work which has been much read in this country, though now the copies are scarce : " Some outlines towards a description of the new heavens and new earth," 4to. A 2d edition of which was printed in 1727.

SEWALL STEPHEN, brother of judge Sewall was one of the worthies of that generation. He was universally respected by his acquaintance for his excellent generous temper, and obliging manners ; and by all his fellow citizens for his prudence, knowledge and patriotism. He had a good school education, and entered college ; but was unable to stay the years necessary for obtaining a degree. He always indulged an attachment to this seat of the muses, and mingled with the friends of virtue and literature. The ministers of religion lost a very particular friend when he bid adieu to these earthly mansions. While he lived, he was useful, as well as amiable. He was employed in several publick offices, in the county of Essex. He was clerk of the court, and register of the county, which places he filled with the approbation of all his constituents. In 1682, he married the daughter of the rev. Mr.

Mitchel of Cambridge, and they were blessed with 17 children; the larger number of these survived their parents. The good man died in Salem, October, 1725, and was buried the 21st day of this month with peculiar honours. The guns of the fort of which he was commander were discharged; also many through the town, by order of col. Brown, who then commanded the Essex regiment. A great concourse of people, with the magistrates and ministers of the neighbouring towns attended, and every mark of esteem and regard was manifested; for all that knew him, lamented his death.

SEWALL STEPHEN, son of Stephen Sewall, esq. was born in Salem, in December, 1702. He was graduated at Harvard College, 1721, and then took the charge of a school at Marblehead. The office of a grammar master ought to be accounted honourable. It is the most useful employment, and some of the greatest men in this country have thus begun their publick course. Mr. Sewall was chosen tutor in 1628, and continued in that office till the year 1739, when he was elevated to a seat on the bench of judges. His character was very eminent as a scholar. Dr. Chauncy, who was his classmate, and whose judgment none will dispute, speaks of him, as a man of first rate talents. "Quickness of apprehension," says he, " and a capacity to look thoroughly into a subject, were united to him in the highest degree I ever saw in any of my acquaintance. One could scarcely begin to mention a train of thought, but he would at once perceive the whole of what was going to be said; and if it was a disputable point, had in readiness what was proper to be said in answer." He studied divinity, and was an excellent preacher, but did not incline to settle in the ministry. Having turned his attention to law, his wisdom and knowledge were so conspicuous, that he was recommended by the first gentlemen of the profession, as the most proper person for a vacant place of the superiour court. Judge Dudley was then chief justice ; and, upon his death, he was appointed his successor, though he was not the senior of the surviving judges. His reputation was high when he first went upon the bench, but in this superiour station he gained more applause. " He preserved a great decorum in the court. He moderated the debates with a becoming calmness and dignity, in conjunction with a strict impartiality ; shewing himself at once the man of honour and spirit, the knowing lawyer, and upright judge."*

This great and good man was taken off in the midst of his usefulness. The powers of his mind were in full vigour ; as a judge, he was held in admiration, and one of the most learned and useful members of his majesty's council. To this office he was elected when he was chief justice. He would have been chosen some years before, but could not be persuaded to accept the place. He departed this life, Sept. 10, 1760, aged 58.

No one's death ever excited a more general sympathy. He was as much beloved for his good qualities, as admired for his superiour wisdom. His polite and elegant manners gave a charm to the virtues of his life. It was remembered, likewise, how much he had dispersed and given to the poor ! He was so kind to his relations and friends, and all who applied to him for help, " that he outdid his proper capacity." Two orphan children of his brother, Mitchel Sewall, esq. were under his immediate care.† It was his intention to give them every advantage of education. The loss to them was irreparable.

Judge Sewall died a bachelor. He was a member of Dr. Mayhew's church. The Dr. printed the sermon he preached after his death, which may appear too much in the strain of eulogy ; but he ob-

* Dr. Mayhew's funeral sermon.
† One of these was the late Mitchel Sewall, esq. of Portsmouth, who once made a figure at the bar, and was celebrated as a poet.

serves, that the memory of wise and just men ought to be praised with all ardour of expression. "It seems but just and equitable," the Dr. adds, "that *he*, who never spoke evil of any one, but honoured all men, and delighted to give all their due share of praise, should, at least, when he is dead and gone, be praised by all in his turn ; and so much the rather because he would not willingly suffer any to commend him while living, which was the truth concerning this excellent person."

SEWALL JOSEPH, D. D. was the son of the hon. Samuel Sewall, esq. chief justice of the province. He was graduated at Harvard College, 1707, and was ordained as colleague with the rev. Mr. Pemberton, pastor of the old south church, Sept. 16, 1713. For many years he continued to preach to this people, who were edified, instructed and comforted by his labours. He was a man who seemed to breathe the air of heaven, while he was here upon earth ; he delighted in the work of the ministry ; and when he grew venerable for his age, as well as his piety, he was regarded as the father of the clergy. The rising generation looked upon him with reverence, and all classes of people felt a respect for his name. He was a genuine disciple of the famous John Calvin. He dwelt upon the great articles of the christian faith in preaching and conversation ; and dreaded the propagation of any opinions in this country, which were contrary to the principles of our fathers. Hence he was no friend to free inquiries, or to any discussion of theological opinions, which were held true by the first reformers. His advice to students in divinity was, to read the Bible always with a comment, such as Mr. Henry's, or archbishop Usher's, and to make themselves acquainted with the work of his great predecessor, Mr. Willard, whose body of divinity was then in great repute. Though he so often preached the doctrines of the gospel, yet he never entered into any curious speculations ; his object was to impress upon people what they should believe, and how they must live to be eternally happy. His sermons were pathetick, and the pious strains of his prayers, as well as preaching, excited serious attention, and made a devout assembly. His character was uniform, and the observation has often been made, if he entered into company something serious or good dropt from his lips. " His very presence banished away every thing of levity, and solemnized the minds of all those who were with him." He received the degree of doctor of divinity from the university of Glasgow, in the year 1731; and was appointed a corresponding member of " the society in Scotland for promoting christian knowledge." He was also appointed one of the commissioners, by the hon. corporation in London, " for the propagation of the gospel in New England, and parts adjacent."

Although Dr. Sewall was more remarkable for his piety than his learning, yet he was a friend to literature, and endeavoured all in his power to promote the interest and reputation of the college. He was a very good classical scholar. He could write handsomely in latin when he was an old man, and had read many authors in that language. Most of the works of the great divines of the preceding century were written in latin, as it was a kind of universal language among the literati of Europe. In the year 1724, upon the decease of Mr. Leveret, Dr. Sewall was chosen to succeed him as president of Harvard College, which honourable station he did not see fit to accept. In 1728, upon Dr. Colman's resignation, he was chosen a fellow of the corporation, and he faithfully discharged the duties of this office, till the year 1765.

His donation to the college of money to be appropriated to indigent scholars, has been of considerable use. He gave this during his life, and was among the first to repair the loss of the library, when Harvard Hall was consumed by fire, by making a present of many valuable books. This devout man also gave much alms to the people. He possessed an estate beyond any of his brethren ; but he always devoted a tenth part of his income to pious and charitable uses.

It pleased the Lord of life to bless him with health, as well as other means of enjoyment. He lived to a good old age ; and preached to his people the evening he had arrived at fourscore years. The next Sabbath he was seized with a paralytical complaint, which confined him some months, and he died, June 27th, 1769, in the 81st year of his age.

The Dr. published a number of funeral sermons. One on the death of Wait Winthrop, esq. 1717 ; king George 1st, 1727 ; on pres. Wadsworth, 1737 ; on sec'y. Willard, 1756. He printed likewise the election sermon, 1724 ; and a discourse on Rev. v. 11, 12, 1745.

SHARPE THOMAS, one of the first planters, was chosen assistant, Oct. 20, 1629, and is the sixth member who joined in forming the congregational church of Boston and Charlestown. He could not reside long in New England, as we do not find his name among the assistants, who held their court in Boston, October, in the year 1630. He was present at the first court held on board the brig Arabella, August 23, when the question was decided how the minister should be maintained ? And also the second court, held at Charlestown, Sept. 7th.

SHEPARD THOMAS, pastor of the church in Cambridge, New England, was educated at Emanuel College, university of Cambridge, Great Britain, and was one of the nonconforming ministers who were silenced by the arbitrary measures of archbishop Laud. He came over to New England in 1635 ; and succeeded Mr. Hooker, who exchanged his place of abode from Newton as it was then called, to Hartford, a settlement upon Connecticut river.

Mr. S. died in 1649, in the 44th year of his age.

He was a pattern of piety, industry and evangelical preaching. He was esteemed by his cotemporaries among the first divines in New England, and his works are now read with sacred delight by many serious people. His publications were both doctrinal and practical. His treatise upon " the morality of the sabbath" is very learned and judicious. It is a rare book, but still preserved in some libraries ; he also wrote a book upon " the matter of the visible church," and another upon " the church membership of little children." He printed, besides these, a letter under the title of " New England's lamentation for Old England's errors." His practical treatises are a sermon " upon drunkenness ;" a sermon on " subjection to Christ ;" on " ineffectual hearing of the word." " The sincere convert," a larger treatise, which passed through four editions in London ; " the sound believer," a book often printed in America, to these we add, an explanation of " the parable of the ten virgins," which work he prepared, and it was printed after his death. The great president Edwards makes free use of this book in his " treatise on the affections."

SHEPARD THOMAS, minister of the church in Charlestown, was the eldest son of Mr. Shepard of Cambridge, was graduated 1653, at Harvard College, was a fellow of the college, and died Dec. 22, 1677, of the small pox, etat. 43.

To give posterity the knowledge of him Dr. Mather brings the engravings on his tomb-stone, also the testimony of president Oakes who delivered an elegant latin oration the ensuing commencement, in which he says, Amisimus, Amisimus, memoratisimum illum virum, reverendissimum Thomam Shepardam : republica civem optimum, Ecclesia, theologum clarissimum, academia non filium tantùm, et alumnum charissimum, sed curatorem etiam vigilantissimum ; municipium scholasticum, socium suum primarium, amiserunt."

The third testimony of his fame, is his own e-
lection sermon, 1672, where the reader will see so
much wisdom, learning, and faithfulness "constel-
lated," that he will pronounce the author to be a
man of first rate talents.

SHEPARD SAMUEL, pastor of the church in
Rowley, was the second son of Mr. S. of Cambridge.   He was graduated at Harvard College,
1658, ordained about 1662, and died 1668, etat 27.

The celebrated Mr. Mitchell wrote his character
in these words.   He was a precious, holy, meditat-
ing, able, choice young man. *One of the first three.*
He was an excellent preacher, most dearly beloved-
ed at Rowley.   The people would have plucked out
their eyes to have saved his life.   But he was ripe
for heaven, and God took him thither."

SHEPARD JEREMIAH, pastor of the church at
Lynn, was the third son of Mr. S. of Cambridge.
He was graduated at Harvard College, 1669, and
ordained in 1679.   He lived to be much older than
his brothers : was a minister at Lynn, 41 years, and
died June 2, 1720, etat. 72.   The three brothers
are recorded in the Magnalia, as three excellent
ministers, which the author thinks to be something
better " than to have three orators like the Curii at
Rome."

SHEPARD THOMAS, the only son of Mr. Shepard of Charlestown, and his successor in the ministry, was graduated at Harvard College, 1676.   The
people of Charlestown invited him to the place of
his father, as he resembled him in all his virtues,
" nullum unquam monumentum clarius, relinque-
re potuit, quam effigiem, morum suarum, virtutis,
constantiæ, pietatis ingenii filium."   These lines
which Tully writes concerning S. Sulpicius, have
been applied to Mr. Shepard of Charlestown.   The
last of the three died younger than his father or
grandfather.   They died when they were turned of
40.   This excellent young man, died when he was
only in the 27th year of his age.   He seemed to

have some premonition of his dissolution, and preached 13 sermons on Eccles. xii. 5. " Man goeth to his long home." He did not publish any of his writings, but he left for the benefit of others the perfume of his name, and the lustre of his example.

SHERMAN JOHN, a great divine and eminent mathematician, was born at Dedham, Dec. 26, 1613, and received his first impressions of religion under the ministry of the famous John Rogers. At school he discovered uncommon industry and ingenuity, and at an early age went to the university of Cambridge. He did not receive his degree, because he could not subscribe the articles required, preferring the name of puritan to the literary honours he might have by conforming to the church of England. He came to America in the year 1634, and preached his first sermon at Watertown, as an assistant to Mr. Phillips. Having continued some time with this people, he then removed to New Haven, and preached occasionally as he was invited by people in their several towns. Mr. Hooker and Mr. Stone once declared in an assembly of divines, " Brethren, we must take heed to ourselves and our ministry, or this young man will outdo us all." He declined settling at Milford where he had a call, and went into civil life. For some time he was a magistrate of the colony. He was persuaded, however, to put off his robes of office, when the people of Watertown, after the death of Mr. Phillips, gave him an invitation to be his successor. At the same time one of the Boston churches expressed a desire that he would settle with them, and he received a letter from London making a similar request. He accepted the call from Watertown, and for many years they rejoiced in his light. He was also a great blessing to the college. He was chosen fellow of the corporation, and delivered lectures which most of the students attended. Being a first rate scholar, an accomplished preacher, they were willing once a fortnight to walk a few miles to hear him. For 30 years he continued these lectures and drew many hearers from other towns in the vicinity. He improved his great intellectual abilities by a close attention to his studies. Dr. Mather says he was undoubtedly " one of the greatest mathematicians that ever lived in this hemisphere of the world." He left many astronomical calculations in mss. For some years he published an almanack, and always added pious reflections. This is one of them. " Let me entreat one thing of thee and I will adventure to promise thee a good year : the request is in itself reasonable, and may be to thee eternally profitable. Its only this : duly to prize, and diligently improve time, for obtaining the blessed end it was given for, and is yet graciously continued to thee, by the eternal God. Of 365 days, allowed by the making up of this year, which shall be thy last, thou knowest not ; but that any of them may be it, then oughtest thou to know, and so consider, that thou mayest pass the time of thy sojourning here with fear."

Mr. Sherman married twice, and had 26 children, twenty by the last, she lived his widow some years. The last sermon he preached was at Sudbury—He was there taken sick and died at Watertown, Aug. 8, 1685, aged 72. *Magnalia.*

SHERMAN ROGER, was born at Newtown, April 19, 1721. His first ancestor in this country was John Sherman, who came from Dedham in England, and settled at Watertown, 1635. His son John was the father of William, who was the father of the gentleman, the present subject of our notice. R. Sherman removed from Massachusetts to Milford, Connecticut, about the year 1741. He was admitted to the bar, as a counsellor of law in 1754, and made a figure in his profession, though he had never been bred to the law, or had the advantages of an academical education. The resources of his own mind were very great, and he pursued his stu-

dies with wonderful diligence. He was a representative for the town of New Milford, and afterwards of New Haven. In 1765, he was appointed
a justice of the court of common pleas. He received an honorary degree of A. M. from Yale College,
and was treasurer of the college many years. In
1776, he was elevated to a seat on the supreme
bench, and elected one of the assistants of the colony. When the law was enacted making these offices inconsistent, he resigned his place, as counsellor or asssistant and continued on the bench of
judges. He was the same year present in congress,
and signed the glorious act of independence. He
not only was delegate but one of the committee
which drew up the declaration. In 1787, he was
appointed a delegate to the convention which formed the federal constitution ; and afterwards in the
state convention which adopted it. He was then
elected a representative to the first congress under
the new constitution, and when a vacancy for Connecticut happened in the United States senate, he
was elected to fill it, and in this office he continued
till his death which took place at New Haven, July
20, 1793.

SHIRLEY WILLIAM, governour of Massachusetts from 1740 to 1757, was an English gentleman who practised law, in Boston. At the time
he was appointed, his lady was in England. She
had been soliciting a post of profit for Mr. S. in the
province, and by the assistance of her own friends,
and the intrigues of Belcher's enemies, obtained the
government. He was a man of address, knew how
to manage the several parties, and conducted so well
as to gain the affection of the people, and continue
on the side of the prerogative.

The court did more for him than they were willing to do for any of his predecessors ; for they advanced the governour's salary to 1000 pounds sterling per annum.

The principal events in his administration were

these. In 1745, the expedition to Louisburg. Of
this he was not the projector, nor as some have
supposed, even an adviser, though after the success of it, he was desirous of being considered
as the main spring of the whole business. Mr.
Auchmuty laid the plan in his study, says Smol-
let. Neither Hutchinson, nor Belknap mention
Auchmuty's name. The plan is given by Vaughan,
and pressed upon Shirley, who was gratified with
the enterprise, but was afraid to be responsible,
and therefore contrived to have the general court
patronise it ; so that if it had not succeeded, he
should be free from blame. Hence he always spake
" your expedition gentlemen"—till the capture,
and then it was " our expedition."

The year succeeding the capture of Cape Breton,
the famous expedition against the colonies was
frustrated. The duke d'Anville's fleet was completely destroyed.

A body of provincials stationed at Minas, was
surprised by a party of French and Indians, and the
whole number, amounting to about 160, slain or
made prisoners. In 1747, an uncommon tumult
happened at Boston, in which the governour was
accidentally involved. Commodore Knowles impressed a number of men from the vessels and
wharves. The governour's house was surrounded
by the enraged multitude, and he fled to the castle,
which was considered by many, the high sons of
liberty, as an abdication of the government. In
1749, an act was passed calling in the bills of credit, and exchanging them for silver, and the province
was enabled to do it, by the reimbursement for
the Louisburg expedition.

In 1754, the governour refusing his assent to the
excise bill, became very popular. It is to be reckoned
among the strange events of our political assembly,
that the excise bill, so unfriendly to the liberties of
the people, was supported in the house by men who
had been whigs hitherto. And that it met its death

blow by those who have ever been styled the tory administration. Hutchinson opposed it. Shirley negatived it. From this period the governour left the management of civil affairs, for which he was very capable, for the military department which he knew very little about. Upon the conquest of Louisburgh, he was appointed to be the col. of a regiment on the British establishment to be raised in America. Afterwards he had a higher military command, and went to dispossess the French of Niagara in which he was unsuccessful.

When gov. Shirley was in Europe, with a commission, to settle an important business, for which he was supposed to be qualified, as it related to the French claims in America, he there formed a matrimonial connexion with a lady of the Catholick religion. This was disgusting to the province, as the people at that time detested the French, and all popish connections. It had such an effect upon his administration, that he felt the weight of the opposition, and soon lost his place. He was superceded in his government by Thomas Pownal, esq. without losing the favour of the crown. He afterwards received an appointment as governour of the Bahama Islands. In 1770 he, returned to Boston, and for the short space he lived he resided in his house at Roxbury, which had been kept in the family. It was indeed a spacious mansion, well situated, and capable of great improvement around it. This house was made a barrack for our soldiers in 1775, and much injured. He died in April, 1771, a poor man, but was honourably interred.

SHUTE SAMUEL, esq. arrived in Boston, 4th of October, 1716, with his commission, as governour of Massachusetts. He had been colonel of a British regiment, and served under the duke of Marlborough. He was of a family eminent among the dissenters. A similarity of religious principles rendered him very agreeable to the inhabitants of the province, and they felt the more satisfied, as they had some reason to think that a warm episcopalian, and a man of arbitrary notions, was to be put into the chair. His administration, however, of a few years, was rendered irksome to himself, and not grateful to the people. This was owing to party spirit, or the peculiar increase of it, among the popular leaders by his instructions to have a salary fixed. These instructions he adhered to, and to these the friends of the old charter were violently opposed. There had been parties ever since the new charter. Dudley's adherents had been styled enemies of charter privileges. But in Shute's time there was another cause of division; they who were called the bank party, were in the opposition to government. The prudence rather than the interest of the governour led him to prevent such accumulation of ideal property in the hands of colonists; especially as it was a serious evil to the inhabitants of the colony. Hence so sedate and acceptable a man as Mr. Shute could not please the generality, and his friends were unable to resist the tide that set against him. The discordant sound was heard when he negatived Mr. Cooke who was then considered as the man of the people. The controversy, which had been excited, was managed with zeal by the house of representatives; and continued during his whole administration. The council was not so much engaged, and were often on the side of the governour, which displeased the leaders of the other house.

The conduct of Mr. Shute displeased some of the more precise adherents to the garb of religion. He sometimes indulged himself in amusements and parties of pleasure, which these *grave censors* of human manners supposed incompatible with the dignity of his station, and inconsistent with that godliness which should characterise a christian commonwealth. In 1723, Jan. 1, the governour left Boston and sailed for England, he embarked suddenly, acquainting only his particular friends with his design.

The memorials he exhibited after his arrival caused the proceedings of the house of representatives to be censured by the king and council. Whether he was to be justified or blamed must be learned from the history of those transactions published by those of different opinions.

He had a pension in England settled upon him for life, where he could indulge his natural love of ease, free from the tumults of a people who were disposed to vex him. There he died full of days, having lived to the age of fourscore years. His character was, in and out of the province of Massachusetts, when men were not engaged in the violence of dispute, a man of an open, generous, humane disposition, a friend to liberty, and if not endued with great abilities as a governour, yet just and upright in his private affairs, and with the best intentions of regulating the affairs of his government.

Skelton Samuel, pastor of the church in Salem, was a minister of Lincolnshire, Great Britain, a pious man, whose abilities and character were respected by the puritans. He was associated with Mr. Higginson as a minister of the new plantation; for we learn that at a meeting of the Massachusetts company in London, April 8, 1629, Mr. Francis Higginson, Mr. Samuel Skelton, &c. are entertained, and engage to labour among the Indians and English. Their names are put into the council, next to Mr. Endicot's, where the style runs, "governour and council of London's plantation."* The vessels in which they sailed arrived at Naumkeak in the month of June; the 20th of July was set

* April 10, at a general court of Massachusetts company in London, they elected Mr. Endicot, governour, Mr. Higginson, Skelton, Bright, John and Samuel Brown, Thomas Graves, and Samuel Sharpe to be of the council. The governour and council to choose three others : the planters two more ; of which twelve counsellors the major part may choose a deputy and secretary, that they continue a year, &c. *Prince's chronology.*

apart for prayer and fasting, and the trial and choice
of a pastor and teacher; and August 6, for the
choice of elders and deacons. Their office was then
defined, the delegates from Plymouth being present.
Mr. Skelton, being further advanced in years, was
constituted pastor of Salem church, Mr. Higginson
teacher. The elder was Mr. Houghton, who died
the next year. Mr. Higginson likewise died before a year elapsed from his installation. Mr. Skelton was the particular friend of Mr. Endicot. He
was the more regarded by that gentleman, because
he received his first religious impressions under his
preaching. He was ready to support Mr. Endicot,
likewise in the strict discipline which he thought
necessary for the churches, and fell in with all his
superstitious notions about veils, &c. His colleague, Mr. Williams, who came over in 1631, confirmed him in his prejudices against the church of
England. They also acted in concert against the
ministers of the bay, whom they accused of seeking
power and influence, and of forming themselves
upon the model of a presbytery, because they met
together in a body once a fortnight, although it was
more for the enjoyment of social propensities, than
any religious purposes. There was a want of friendship between the ministers of Boston with its neighbourhood, and the ministers of Salem. Every
thing which one party did, was found fault with by
the other. It is remarkable that no kind of notices
of the character of Mr. Skelton, a man so distinguished among the first planters, should be given
by the writers of that, or the succeeding generation.
Governour Winthrop just mentions his death, August 2, 1634. Dr. Mather mentions very little
about him, though so apt to introduce the lives of
men in his history. In an account of Salem by the
rev. Mr. Bentley, we are told that he died when
Mr. Endicot, his benefactor, was out of favour.
" No particular records of his services was kept.
His opinions made him no personal enemies; but

as he never acted alone, he yielded to others all the praise of his best actions."

STANDISH MILES, first military officer in New Plymouth, came over with the pilgrims in 1620. He was a man brave, enterprising, whose perseverance was equal to the boldest resolutions formed upon the impulse of the mind. As success always attended him, the first settlers placed the greatest confidence in the man. When the town of Plymouth was fortified, he had the care of it committed to him, and with a very few men he was able to defend it. He made several bold excursions in the neighbourhood of Plymouth in 1723, and also went to Mr. Weston's plantation which he saved from destruction. He certainly delivered the people from the death which the Indians threatened, and were ready to execute. He also went to Cape Ann in 1624, where the fishermen of Plymouth had been abused by a company from the west of England. The captain was disposed to finish this business by some warlike achievement, but it was settled by men of more prudence and moderation. The particulars of these expeditions are related by Hubbard and Hutchinson, and make part of an excellent memoir in "Belknap's American Biography." This narrative of the affair at Cape Ann is given in Hubbard's mss. as follows, " capt. Standish was bred a soldier in the low countries, and never entered into the school of Christ, or of John the Baptist ; or if ever he was there, he forgot his first lessons, to offer violence to no man, and to part with the cloak, rather than needlessly contend for the coat, though taken away without order. A little chimney is soon fired ; so was the Plymouth captain, a man of small stature, yet of a very hot and angry temper. The fire of his passion soon kindled, and blown up into a flame by hot words, might easily have consumed all, had it not been seasonably quenched." In other parts of his writing he speaks of capt. Standish with more respect.

He not only gives him a good character as a soldier, but says he performed his duty well as a civil officer. "He was improved to good acceptance," says he, and success in affairs of the greatest moment to the colony ; to whose interest he continued firm and stedfast to the last, and always managed his trust with great integrity and faithfulness."

In the year 1625, he went to England as agent for the colony. He did every thing to serve his constituents, which a skilful and prudent man could do, but the plague raged in London, and had carried off 40,000 persons, and those who otherwise would have turned their eyes to this infant settlement, were engaged in more interesting matters, the saving themselves as well as their property from the dangers which hung over them. He returned to Plymouth in 1626, with a small supply of goods, which was of great advantage to the poor pilgrims, but their souls were filled with grief by the sorrowful intelligence which he brought them of the death of their pastor Mr. Robinson, and their faithful friend Mr. Robert Cushman.

After this voyage capt. Standish retired to his farm, and lived in rural tranquillity, though not in the shadows of obscurity. He was magistrate of the Plymouth colony as long as he lived. He died a man full of years, and honoured by his generation, in 1656, at Duxbury. The spot in that town which is called Captain's hill, belonged to him, and took its name from this circumstance.

STEVENS BENJAMIN, D. D. minister of the church at Kittery point, was the son of the rev. Joseph Stevens, minister of Charlestown, who had been tutor and fellow of the college when he was a young man ; and was again chosen fellow of the corporation 1712, in which office he continued till his death in 1722. His son was graduated at Harvard College in 1740. Having lost his father when he was a child, he was deprived of the advantages of his instruction, but was an object of the tender contern of others, and his own exertions and excellent disposition lessened the care of his friends, as well as gratified their fond and lively expectations. He was ordained at Kittery some years after he left the place of his education. When he settled with this people, they were in fair and flourishing circumstances. Several merchants of large property resided in the town ; navigation was carried on in various branches ; elegant houses were built ; and strangers were allured to the spot where they might visit sir William Pepperell, and be entertained by the various branches of his family in their hospitable mansions. Mr. S. lived to see vast alterations made in the place, and to bury his old friends with whom he enjoyed religious fellowship, as well as the friendship which gives a charm to social life. Of late we should not select this place for a minister of the first talents in his profession, or one as remarkable for social qualities, as his wisdom. Mr. Stevens was distinguished for his piety and learning. His intellectual powers were strong, and he engaged with ardor, and great diligence in the pursuits of science. He shone in conversation, and in the pulpit. Possessing a great stock of religious knowledge he introduced maxims, useful and pious, with great pertinence, which rendered him an instructive and entertaining companion. In his publick discourses he reasoned well. These were happily diversified. He was methodical and ingenious, pathetick and scriptural. His voice was rather strong, but not clear or musical ; otherwise the perspicuity of his manner would have rendered him popular. But he wanted the graces of delivery.

He did not print many discourses, but those he did publish are among the very best American sermons. The election sermon 1761, was much celebrated, as likewise a sermon delivered before a convention of ministers at Portsmouth ; the funeral discourses, one upon the death of Andrew Pepperell, 1752 ; and the sermon upon sir William Pepperell, 1759. He preached the Dudleian lecture, 1772, upon the evidences in favour of christianity. No man was better acquainted with the deistical controversy. The corporation and overseers presented him with a diploma of doctor in divinity in the year 1785. We do not find any publication of his in latter years. But many have wished to have a volume of his sermons published. He died, May 18, 1798, etat. 70.

STILES EZRA, president of Yale College, was the son of the rev. Isaac Stiles of North Haven, Connecticut. He entered college in 1742, and was distinguished among the students for his bright genius, his intellectual accomplishments, his moral virtues, and the suavity of his manners. When he received the honours of the seminary in New Haven in 1746, he was esteemed one of the greatest scholars it had ever produced. He first commenced his course of life with the study and practice of the law, he afterwards thought it his duty to preach the gospel; and settled at Newport, as pastor of the second church, where he continued from 1755, to the year 1776. During this, and several succeeding years, the enemy were in possession of Newport; and the inhabitants of the town scattered. Dr. Stiles was solicited to preach in several places, but he accepted the invitation from the church at Portsmouth to remove and settle with them. In this place he was universally admired. He has left acknowledgments of the kind attention of this people; they indulged a pride in the relation which subsisted between them. They thought him the most learned man of the age, were willing to hear very long sermons, some of them very critical disquisitions; because they flowed from the lips of Dr. Stiles. There were many polite families in the place. The doctor was a gentleman in his manners. His mildness, condescension, fluency in conversation, entertaining and instructive mode of giving his opinion, endeared him to those who felt a reverence for his character. He had a kind of familiar intercourse which was very pleasing to all classes of people especially the rising generation. He would excite their emulation and make them think favourably of themselves. Hence some have called him a flatterer, which was not the case. His candid spirit and a disposition to view every person in the best light, and to put the best construction upon every action, made him speak and act, as though he coveted the good opinion of others, by addresses to their vanity. But his acquaintance knew where to trace the cause. They had as high an opinion of his integrity, as of his charity and affability. His private diary discovers his sincerity. In this he celebrates the virtues and accomplishments of persons who could make no return. He might betray want of judgment, in some instances, but cannot be accused of paying empty compliments; he certainly had a greater knowledge of books, than of mankind.

In 1778, he was chosen president of Yale College, to the great disappointment of the Portsmouth church. They wished to fix him as their pastor. But this election gave pleasure to the friends of science. The plain language of Dr. Chauncy expressed the wish of the publick, while it declared the opinion of the Boston association. "I know of none," said he, "but who rejoice at the election to the presidency, and unite in the opinion that you are loudly called to accept the appointment." On the 8th of July, 1778, he was inducted into the office. In this conspicuous orb he shone with uncommon lustre a number of years, was an honour to the college and his country, and left a name worthy of everlasting remembrance. He died on the 12th of May, 1795, etat. 68.

His character is delineated in the publick papers, and in several sermons; memoirs have been also printed by Dr. Holmes, in an octavo volume, entitled "life of president Stiles," which is a very in-

teresting and very useful work, containing many entertaining anecdotes, biographical sketches and
much literary information, besides a minute and very just account of the president. Dr. Stiles had
every literary honour which his country could bestow upon him, was a member of many learned societies abroad, and was the intimate friend and correspondent of the first characters in Europe and
America.   His publications are not numerous.
They are known in the learned world, and consist
of philosophical essays, and historical narratives,*
but chiefly sermons, and theological tracts.

STODDARD SOLOMON, pastor of the church of
Northampton, has always been considered as one of
the greatest divines of New England.   His sermons, his theological essays, and controversial
writings have given him uncommon distinction.
He was born at Boston, 1643, Antony Stoddard,
esq. was his father; his mother was the sister of
sir George Downing.   He received the elements of
his education under the famous master Corlet at
Cambridge ; and was graduated at Harvard College
1662.   He was afterwards one of the fellows of the
house.   Close application to his studies having injured his health he sailed to Barbadoes, as chaplain
to gov. Serle, and preached to the dissenters in that
island.   When he returned to his native country
he was invited to the pastoral office at Northampton,
to succeed the rev. Eleazer Mather, who was the
first minister of the town and died young.   He was
ordained, 1672, and preached without any interruption 56 years.   " His sermons were plain and powerful, experimental and spiritual, close and search-
ing, yet rational and argumentative.   He preached
for many years the publick lecture in Boston the
day after commencement, and crowds of pious people assembled to hear."† He was strictly calvinisti-
cal in his opinions upon doctrinal points but more

* See Dr. Holmes's book.
† Dr. Colman's funeral sermon.

liberal than other divines of this country upon
points of church discipline and government.   In
the year 1700, he wrote an answer to Dr. Increase
Mather's book, entitled the "order of the gospel,"
which excited a very alarming controversy.   The
preface to this book contains these words, "The
reader is desired to take notice that the press in Boston is so much under the influence of the rev. author we answer, and his friends, that we could not
obtain of the printer there to print the following
sheets," &c. The book was patronised by the founders of Brattle street church, and when Mr. Green
denied the assertion in the preface, and said "that
neither president Mather, nor his son Cotton ever
discouraged the printing any book."   Mr. Brattle, Mr. Mico, Mr. Tuthil, declared upon oath that
such conversation as this took place, "It was a
shame so worthy a minister as Mr. Stoddard must
send so far as England to have his book printed,
when young Mr. M. had the press at his pleasure.
To which he replied that he hoped Mr. Mather was
another guess man than Mr. Stoddard."   Some
years after this Mr. Stoddard and Dr. Increase Mather had another controversy.   Mr. S. printed a
sermon concerning qualifications for the Lord's
supper.   Dr. M. wrote a dissertation, wherein the
strange doctrine, lately published in a sermon,
"the tendency of which is to encourage unsanctifi-
ed persons to approach the table of the Lord," is
confuted.   This was answered by Mr. S. in a
book of 100 pages, entitled an "appeal to the learned, in vindication of the rights of visible saints to
the Lord's supper."   A small anonymous pamphlet, "the appeal of some of the unlearned,"
followed this, but the question was handled in
such a masterly manner by Mr. Stoddard that most
of the churches in Connecticut or upon the river
were guided by his sentiments.   This controversy
was about the year 1708.   It was revived in 1749
by the grandson of Mr. Stoddard Mr. Jonathan Ed-

wards, who was settled a colleague with the old gentleman, and for some years was of the same opinion. He altered his sentiments afterwards and publickly defended them. The controversy ended in his dismissal from Northampton, but his writings had a wonderful effect. Many of the churches, who thought Mr. Stoddard could not be in an error, were convinced by the arguments of Mr. Edwards. Mr. Stoddard, however great he was considered while he lived, was surpassed by his grandson, in the opinion of the succeeding generation.

That great divine, who is considered by many, the light of these New England churches, as John Calvin was of the reformation, wrote his " inquiry concerning the qualifications for a complete standing in the visible church" about the year 1749.

The works of Mr. Stoddard are numerous, and several theological treatises of his, have passed through several editions.

He died February 11, 1729, etat. 86, and left an aged widow, the daughter of Mr. Warham who came over to Dorchester in 1630, and afterwards settled at Windsor in Connecticut. She was first married to Mr. Eleazer Mather. His eldest son, Anthony Stoddard, was settled at Woodbury, as pastor of the church. The second son, col. John Stoddard, was for many years one of his majesty's council. But few men, according to Hutchinson, were more universally esteemed. The several governours intrusted to his direction the military affairs of the county of Hampshire, which in the time of war was peculiarly exposed. He died June 12, 1748.

STONE SAMUEL, teacher of the church in Hartford, Connecticut, came over to New England in the same vessel which brought Mr. Cotton, and Mr. Hooker. He went with the company that settled the town on Connecticut river, which they called Hartford, this being the name of the place where Mr. Stone was born in the old country. He continued his labours with this people about 30 years, fourteen with Mr. Hooker, and sixteen after the death of that great and worthy divine. The latter years of his life were rendered very uncomfortable by a schism in his own church, which caused the fire of contention to spread over the colony. It originated between him, and the ruling elder, in a speculative opinion ; and it is not the only instance where disputes have soured the disposition which were founded in the pride of the understanding. The towns in the neighbourhood entered warmly into the quarrel, and most of them, as Dr. Mather says, "did not know what the quarrel was." Mr. Stone had a logical head, and perhaps would hold arguments where a little common sense would answer better. The elder was doubtless a gifted brother, and knew more from the light within, than his minister, who was only a master of reason. Mr. Stone has the name of a great disputant. In the pulpit, he would introduce propositions to discuss, before he came to any application. The heart is more apt to be affected, however, by evangelical sentiments delivered in an impressive manner ; and truth, like other beauties, appears best in a plain dress. The church at Hartford, sent for council after council, who were all under the influence of party zeal. To bring the matter to an issue, they at last sent to Boston where the ministers or delegates could have no particular bias, but all they could do, did not prevent a division of the church. There was a removal of part of the church farther up the river, and those friends who once had dwelt in unity, never were reconciled after this unhappy difference.

Mr. S. was very exact in his church discipline. Being once asked what a *congregational* church was ? He said, it was a " speaking aristocracy in the face of a silent democracy."* He printed a discourse " upon the logical notion of a congregational

* Magnalia, book iii. chap 16.

church." He also wrote a book " against antinomianism," which the famous Baxter wished to see
published. His greatest work, was a " body of divinity." This was never printed. But, says the
author of the Magnalia, " this rich treasure has
often been transcribed by the vast pains of our candidates for the ministry, and it has made some of
our most considerable divines ; but all attempts to
print it have proved abortive."

STOUGHTON WILLIAM, lieut. governour of
Massachusetts, was born at Dorchester, 1632. He
was the son of Israel Stoughton, who was chosen
assistant in 1637, and the same year commanded the
Massachusetts forces in the Pequod war. He
died, 1645. William was graduated at Harvard
College, 1650. Having turned his mind to the study of divinity, he became one of the most eminent
preachers of those times. His election sermon
1668, is certainly one of the best that was printed
during this century. He was never settled in the
ministry but in the year 1671 was chosen a magistrate. In 1677, he was appointed agent to the court
of Great Britain, with Mr. Bulkley, speaker of the
house of representatives to answer the complaints
of Gorges and Mason concerning the patent line.
He afterwards grew unpopular in the colony, on account of his connexion with Dudley and Andross.
He was on the moderate side of politicks. Such
men though pure in their principles, are supposed
to be wrong by violent men who must run to ex-
tremes. They however very frequently save the
vessel, when tossed by the waves and billows of the
tempestuous sea. Afterwards, he obtained the
friendship of Dr. Mather, on account of his piety,
and became a favourite with all classes of people.
Being recommended by him to king William, he
was appointed lieut. governour under the new charter of William and Mary. He was also chief justice of the province. Unfortunately for the country,
the governour, lieut, governour, and the judges of

the court believed in witchcraft. Stoughton's great abilities were combined with so much weakness, and he was more obstinate in his error than others on the bench. Sewall humbled himself on account of the calamity to which he had been instrumental. The chief justice felt no remorse of conscience, though his opinion had caused innocent beings to suffer the most ignominous punishment inflicted on the guilty. In 1694, when Phips left the government, he was the commander in chief, and under his administration, the affairs of the province were conducted with great wisdom. When lord Bellamont died in 1700, he again took the chair, but he did it with reluctance. His age and infirmities required him to leave publick business. He did not live through two years. He died, May, 1702. His estate was large, and being a bachelor, he was enabled to assist literary and pious institutions. He built a college at Cambridge, which had the name of Stoughton hall inscribed upon it. The foundation stone was laid May 9th, 1698. It stood almost a century. A new college has been raised since, near the spot, and bears his name.

"The inscription upon his monument in Dorchester burial place is now very legible. It was published in the collections of the historical society, vol. ii."

SULLIVAN JOHN, major general in the American army, was the eldest son of a Mr. Sullivan who came from Ireland, and settled in the district of Maine. The father having some knowledge of the latin language, kept a school in several parts of the eastern country and passed his latter years at Berwick, where he died at the age of 105. It has been said that he could speak French and latin fluently when he was 100 years old. His sons possessed talents, which being united with uncommon industry, they, without the advantage of academical education, emerged from their obscure situation to the most conspicuous stations, and the highest honours their coun-

try could bestow.   For several years before the revolution, Mr. John Sullivan practised law in New
Hampshire.   He was a bold, energetick pleader at
the bar, his business increased rapidly, and had he
been governed by avarice, he would have acquired
a fortune in his business.   But ambition was his
predominant passion, and he preferred military glory to every other kind of reputation.   He first accepted a commission as major of a regiment in the
militia in 1772.   There was then no immediate
prospect of war, and he might only receive it as a
mark of distinction.   But as soon as hostilities
commenced he appeared among the most ardent
patriots and intrepid warriors.   With a party of
men in 1774 he went to the fort, and by a manœuvre obtained possession of it.   This was attended
with no great danger had he made the attack, but
the consequence might have been ruinous to him,
if the independence of America had not taken place.
In 1775, he was appointed brigadier general of the
American army, and during that campaign commanded on Winter hill.   The next year he went to
Canada, and after the death of gen. Thomas,* took
the command of the troops, no longer destined to
conquest.   In making his retreat from this province of the British empire, he discovered great
military prudence as well as courage.   His conduct
gained him credit, and he was a favourite of the soldiers.   In a skirmish on Long Island, August 27
of this year, he was taken prisoner.   He had liberty

* Major general John Thomas of Kingston in the old colony
of Plymouth, was an officer who acquired reputation in the
French war which ended with the peace of Paris in 1763.   He
was one of the best officers of our army in 1775, and commanded the division nearest the British lines in Roxbury.   When
Boston was evacuated he was sent to Canada, to take the command of the troops which Montgomery and Arnold led into that
province.   A more brave, beloved and distinguished character
did not go into the field, nor was there a man that made a greater
sacrifice of his own ease, health and social enjoyments.   He died
of the small pox, June 30, 1776.

to go upon his parole to Congress, and deliver a message from lord Howe. In October he was exchanged for gen. Prescott and returned to the camp. At the battle of Trenton he commanded the right division, and gen. Greene the left ; also at the battles of Brandywine and Germantown, in the fall of 1777. He was chief in command of the troops which went on an expedition to Rhode Island, August, 1777, when count D'Estaing blocked up the port. The marquis de la Fayette and gen. Greene served as volunteers. Gov. Hancock went from Massachusetts at the head of the militia. The particulars of the failure are related in the histories of the war. Sullivan and the regular troops did every thing to support the credit of the army. In 1779, an expedition was planned by gen. Washington to attack the indians in their own settlements. A well chosen army was prepared, and gen, Sullivan put at the head. They penetrated above 90 miles through a wilderness, where they passed horrid swamps, and barren mountainous desarts. All the occurrences are related in a letter to the president of congress, Sept. 30, 1779. After the peace with Great Britain, Mr. S. resumed his practice at the bar, he was one of the convention which formed the state constitution for New Hampshire, and chosen into the first council. When president Langdon accepted the place of senator of the United States, he was chosen president, and continued in the office till his death. He was succeeded in this office by col. Bartlett in 1790.

Gen Sullivan has a high rank among the officers of the revolutionary army, and has an equal claim to distinction among the statesmen, politicians and patriots of 1775, his name appears with some splendour among the literati of America. He acquired an extensive knowledge of men and things. He read more than any could suppose consistent with the active scenes of his life. Harvard University received him among her sons, as master of arts, and he was presented with a degree of doctor of laws by the university of Dartmouth. It ought to be noticed that gen. Sullivan was a member of the first congress in 1774. He resigned this office for the sake of going into the army.

SMIBERT NATHANIEL, a celebrated painter, died in the prime of life, and his death excited universal sorrow. He was a most amiable and accomplished youth, but like a fair flower just opening to the view, he was soon cut down. It is the general opinion of those who knew him, that, had he lived, he would have obtained a reputation equal to that of West, and Copely, or any other American genius, who has done honour to his country in the imitating art. They have had laurels heaped upon them. The myrtle grew upon his grave. His father was a painter of some eminence in the line of his profession, and designed his son should be a scholar. For this purpose sent him to the school of which the famous Mr. Lovell was preceptor. One of the first and best pieces of Smibert's pencil was " the portrait of his old master while the terrifick impressions vibrated on his nerves." Smibert was a fine classical scholar, but did not incline to pass the number of years necessary for obtaining the honours of college. He was passionately fond of his father's business, and their room was often visited by connoisseurs, for the sake of the pictures, many years after their heads were laid in the dust. One of the most prominent of this exhibition was a groupe, and dean Berkeley the principal character. We have been told of a portrait, once having a place there, of John Checkley, the famous scholar, and droll, with lines under it written by young Smibert, that discovered talents for poetry.

The year of his death is not recollected exactly by his friends, had he been graduated at college, it would have been in the year 1757. He died about this time.

SYMMES ZACHARIAH, pastor of the church in Charlestown, was born at Canterbury, April 5, 1599.

His father's name was William. He was minister
of Sandwich in 1587; and also the son of William, a man who was a protestant in the reign of
Queen Mary. Zechariah was educated at the university of Cambridge. He came into New England
in 1635, and was invited to settle in Charlestown,
as their teaching elder, Mr. James, being pastor of
the church. Johnson speaks highly of the wife of
this Mr. Symmes. He belonged to Charlestown,
and was doubtless acquainted with her. "Among
all the godly women," says he, "that came through
the perilous seas, Mrs. Sarah Symmes ought not
to be omitted, her courage exceeded her stature,
she bore every difficulty with cheerfulness, and
raised up ten children to people this American wilderness." Mr. Symmes had several children added after Johnson wrote, according to his epitaph,
which gives him 5 sons and 8 daughters. He died
Feb. 4, 1676.

SYMMES ZACHARIAH, minister of Bradford, was
the son of Mr. S. of Charlestown, and was graduated
at Harvard College, 1657. He was one of the fellows of the college, was ordained at Bradford about
the year 1660, and died, March 22, 1708.

SYMMES THOMAS, son of the minister of Bradford, was graduated at Harvard College, 1698,
and settled first at Boxford. After he had left
that people, he was invited to succeed his father
in the church at Bradford. He had very popular
talents in the pulpit, and made considerable of a
figure in his profession, but he wanted prudence in
the economy of his family, and a kind, winning
manner of address with his parishioners. With a
better salary than his neighbours he lived and died
poor; and he likewise kindled a party spirit in both
parishes where he was settled. One matter of dispute was concerning church musick. The people
were not used to regular singing, and he was determined to introduce it in opposition to their prejudices. He was a singer himself, and could not

bear jargon. He wrote an anonymous pamphlet upon this subject; this was followed by "a joco-serious dialogue concerning regular singing," by Thomas Symmes, philomusicus, 1722. There was much ingenious satire, mingled with his argument, and he gave great offence. He died Oct. 22, 1725. His death was much lamented by ministers and the publick. That he was a fine speaker we may judge from the compliment of Dr. Colman in the preface to the artillery election sermon which Mr. Symmes preached and printed, 1720, "may it be as profita-ble in the reading of it as it was pleasant in the hearing. The preacher was unto us, as a very lovely song of one that has a pleasant voice and can play well on an instrument," &c. Mr. Symmes al-so published in 1725, "historical memoirs of the fight at Pigwacket, and a sermon on the death of capt. Lovwell."

TAILER WILLIAM, lieut. governour of Massa-chusetts, came over with his commission from the queen in 1711. He was a very facetious, pleasant man, and agreeable to the people in his manners, though in his politicks on the side of the preroga-tive, and in his religious principles an episcopalian. In 1722 Mr. Dummer was promoted to his place, and he had another office given to him, which he preferred, because the income was better and surer. But when Belcher was advanced to the chair of gov-ernment, he had promised a place to a gentleman, whom the agent, Mr. Wilkes, had recommended. On this account, it was settled that Mr. Tailer should again be lieut. governour, and Mr. Dummer a man every way qualified for his station, should be set aside. He died, March 1, 1732, aged 55 years. From a sermon preached at Thursday lecture, printed with a dedication to Mrs. Tailer, it seems he mar-ried a relation of gov. Stoughton, and possessed his estate at Dorchester. The preacher also tells the lady, "her husband was no bigot, for he often at-tended worship with her at Dorchester meeting."

This is not complete demonstration, considering what influence ladies have : to balance it we might produce his name to a complaint of the episcopalians against the dissenters from their mode of worship.* He was doubtless a very respectable character, and his principles catholick for those times, and he was attached to the country. He was also a man of sense and information. His funeral was splendid, the bells in Boston all tolled from 11 until 5 o'clock, though he was buried at Dorchester, and a greater number of carriages had never been exhibited. His excellency, gov. Belcher, the hon. Mr. Dummer, Addington Davenport, Thomas Hutchinson, Elisha Cooke, and Adam Winthrop, supported the pall.

THACHER THOMAS, first minister of the Old South church in Boston, was born in England, May 1, 1620. His father was the rev. Peter Thacher, minister at Sarum, who intended to come over to these new regions, but was prevented by the state of his family. Thomas had a good school education, and it was his father's desire to send him to the university of Oxford or Cambridge ; but he declined, and came over to New England, A. D. 1635. In a letter published by his uncle, Antony Thacher, we learn how remarkably he was preserved from shipwreck. His friends sailed from Ipswich in the month of August for Marblehead, where Mr. John Avery, a worthy divine, was to settle. A terrible storm threw the vessel upon the rocks, most of the people perished, and Mr. Thacher was cast ashore on a desolate island. It bears his name to this day, as also a place is called *Avery's fall,* where this good man perished. Thomas Thacher preferred to go by land, and escaped these dangers. He received his education from Mr. Chauncy, who was afterwards president of the college. He studied not only what is common for youth to acquire, but also

* Funeral sermon, by rev. Mr. Cooper, and Historical Collections.

the oriental languages. He afterwards composed a Hebrew lexicon, and we learn from Dr. Stiles, that he was a scholar in Arabick, the best the country afforded. This is not mentioned in our ecclesiastical annals. Dr. Mather tells us, that he was a great logician; that he understood mechanics in theory and practice, that he would do all kinds of clock work to admiration. He was eminent in two professions. He was pastor of a church; ordained at Weymouth, June 2, 1644. After some years marrying a second wife, who belonged to Boston, he left his parish at Weymouth, where he practised physick as well as preached, and was an eminent physician in this town. He was still looked upon as a great divine, and when a third church was founded, he was chosen their minister. Over this church he was installed, Feb. 16, 1669, and in this station he continued till he died. The last sermon he preached, was for Dr. I. Mather, 1. Peter, 4, 18. He afterwards visited a sick person, and was himself seized with a fever, and expired Oct. 15, 1678.

He left two sons, who were by his first wife, the daughter of the rev. Ralph Partridge of Duxborough. The eldest, Peter, was a famous minister in the neighbourhood of Boston. And Ralph, who was settled at Martha's vineyard.* *Magnalia.*

THACHER PETER, son of the rev. T. Thacher, of Boston, was graduated at Harvard College, in 1671. He was an excellent scholar, and an object of esteem and affection with the ingenuous youth of the university. An attachment to one of his classmates, Mr. Samuel Danforth, son of the deputy governour, Thomas Danforth, led him to cross the Atlantick for the sake of enjoying his company in his travels. They had been tutors at the same time,

* He printed very few of his productions. Except his Hebrew Lexicon, and his catechism, each of which was on a sheet of paper; and some account of the small pox in a few pages, there is nothing to be found, but " a fast sermon, 1674 ;" and this was transcribed from the minutes of those who heard it.

and were unwilling to be separated, but death, the
destroyer of every hope, who levels our most pleasing prospects with the dust, cut short the days of
Mr. Danforth; upon which event, Mr. Thacher returned to his native country.   He was invited to
take charge of the church, at Milton, and ordained
September, 1681.

He married the daughter of the rev. Mr. Oxenbridge, pastor of the old church in Boston.   She
was the mother of the children which survived him.

He was pastor of the church at Milton above 46
years, and was very much distinguished among his
brethren.   He preached the election sermon, 1711;
Artillery election sermon, 1705; the convention
sermon, 1724.   The first of these was printed, the
last is preserved in mss. being among the the valuable treasures of the Historical society.   He died,
December 17, 1727.

His character was delineated by an able hand in
the Boston Weekly Newsletter.   From which it
appears that he had " a great deal of vivacity, tempered with grace and wisdom ; that he was very engaging in conversation, and in his publick performances; that he was a zealous assertor of the purity
and liberty of the congregational churches, but catholick to those who embraced other opinions ; and
that his advice was often solicited in ecclesiastical
councils."

He did not outlive his usefulness, his intellectual vigour remaining at the last sabbath of his life.
He then preached in a lively and affectionate manner.   The next day he was seized with a complaint,
which in 36 hours finished his course.

THACHER OXENBRIDGE, was the son of Mr.
Thacher of Milton ; was graduated at Harvard College, 1698 ; was a preacher for several years, and
then fixed in Boston in a different line of business.
He was selectman and representative, and was left
out of the general court, with the other friends of
gov. Belcher in 1739.   Soon after this, he retired to

Milton, where he passed the rest of his days. He lived longer than any of the generation with whom he sat out in the journey of life. He was 93 years old, when he died, in 1772.

THACHER OXENBRIDGE, an eminent lawyer, son of Oxenbridge Thacher of Milton, was graduated, 1738. He, also, was a preacher, but with a small voice, and slender state of health, did not meet with success equal to some who have only the sounding brass to give them a reputation. Mr. Thacher was sensible, learned, pious, a calvinist, beloved by his friends, and respected by the numerous friends of a family distinguished from the first settlement of the country ; yet with all these advantages, found it necessary to leave his profession, and go into a line of life, which required no abilities but a vast deal of drudgery to transact. He soon failed, and was persuaded to study law ; for which he had no great inclination at first, but afterwards made a shining figure at the bar, and upon the theatre where politicians act their parts. He was representative for Boston when the first acts were made to raise a revenue. Being a genuine whig he opposed every measure of the British parliament against the constitution of his country. He also wrote a pamphlet, entitled "the sentiments of British Americans," which is read with pleasure at the present day. It was particularly levelled against the navigation act, but contains general remarks, and well adapted to the times. Mr. T. also published a pamphlet, "considerations upon reducing the value of the gold coins within the province." It contained the substance of several pieces he wrote in the newpapers in opposition to the opinion of gov. Hutchinson. The controversy is ably discussed in Minot's continuation of the history of Massachusetts. The health of Mr. Thacher declined from the time of his receiving the small pox, in 1764. Pulmonary complaints succeeded, and he died, July 8th, 1765.

He was a man of strict integrity, highly esteemed by his fellow citizens for his moral worth, as well as his legal knowledge. His death was universally lamented as a great loss to the publick. He left two sons who have since made a figure in their profession, rev. Peter Thacher,* who died 1802, pastor of the church in Brattle street, and rev. Thomas Thacher, pastor of a church in Dedham.

THOMSON WILLIAM, pastor of the church in Braintree, is called by Dr. Mather, one of the American pillars. He came from Lancashire into New England. He first went to Virginia, but was too much of a puritan to find his labours acceptable there. He was a very acceptable preacher in these parts, where his sentiments were more congenial to the publick opinion. This good man was unhappy in his mind, a prey to melancholy, and under great temptation to commit suicide. He prayed earnestly to be brought out of darkness, the pastors and brethren of the neighbouring churches poured out their cries and supplications for him, and his end was peace. He died, Dec. 20, 1666. It is said that he was an author of some reputation, but except one or two prefaces to the books of others, none of his publications have come down to us.

TORREY WILLIAM, one of the first settlers of Massachusetts, was one of our earliest authors. The place where he fixed his abode was Weymouth, and he was active in calling the rev. T. Thacher to be pastor of their church. He was appointed a justice of peace, " with a power to marry." He was one of the first military officers in the colony. When he received a commission to be captain of the train band, it was as high a rank as was then known. He was a man of very considerable learning, and wrote a book upon the Millenium. It is entitled, " a discourse concerning futurities to come written by a very old man, in continual expectation of his

* For the details of the character of the rev. Peter Thacher, D. D. see the close of the 8th vol. Historical Collections.

translation into another life and world." It was a 4to. about 60 pages. A second edition was printed in 8vo. in 1757, with a preface by Mr. Prince.

TORREY SAMUEL, son of William Torrey, was an eminent scholar and divine. His school learning he received from his father who understood latin very well. He entered Harvard College, and would have taken his degree in 1650, but left college with a number of others, because a law was made, requiring the students to stay 4 years in order to receive their degrees. He soon preached, and was invited to settle at Weymouth, 1656, where he continued 51 years a faithful, laborious, exemplary minister. He had such a gift in prayer that he was always chosen upon publick occasions, as Mr. Prince tells us " to bring up the rear of their religious exercises." Upon a publick fast in the year 1696, he prayed two hours after all the other exercises were over, and was so pertinent, so regular, so natural, so free, lively and affecting, that towards the end, hinting at some new and agreeable scenes of thought, we could not help wishing him to enlarge upon them. This was the language of that eminent lawyer, Mr. Read, to Mr. Prince. He was a student of college, at the time, and he said his fellow students regretted that he did not pray an hour longer.

Mr. T. was invited to preach the election sermon three times, in 1674, 1683, 1695, and the discourses are excellent. He was a person " of such deep and extensive views that the governour and council would send for him to come 15 miles, to help them with his advice and wise observations. His intimate friends were gov. Stoughton, Judge Sewall, rev. Mr. Moodey, Willard, Hobart of Newtown and Thacher of Milton. His wife was the daughter of secretary Rawson. Although he never had the honour of a degree at college, yet upon the death of president Rogers in 1686, he was chosen to succeed him, but excused himself from accepting that honourable station ; but acted a number of years as fellow of the corporation. He died, April 10, 1707, etat. 76.

Mr. Prince says his father was " an instance of what eminent men of the civil order once adorned our New England churches." We may observe, that the son was an instance of what our divines were a century ago, when the first gentleman of the civil order so highly respected them ; Mr. Pemberton likewise alludes to the death of Mr. Torrey, when he says " we had not dried our eyes for the loss of our *Samuel*, when Providence opens anew the fountain of our tears by afflicting us with the news of another."*

TREADWELL DANIEL, an eminent mathematician, was born at Portsmouth, New Hampshire, his parents came from Ipswich, Massachusetts. He was graduated at Harvard College, 1754. He was elected professor of mathematicks in King's College, New York, the same year he took his degree at Cambridge, to which place he was recommended by Mr. professor Winthrop. He died a few years after greatly lamented. In Chandler's life of president Johnson, after speaking of their obtaining this excellent young man to be professor, he says, " in the year 1759, there was a private commencement on account of the small pox. The president spent the winter at Stratford, but under great anxiety of mind, for he left Mr. Treadwell, the mathematical professor in a declining state of health, which soon turned to a consumption, and put a period to his life early in the spring."

TRUMBULL JONATHAN, governour of Connecticut, was a descendant from the early settlers of New England. Two brothers, of the name, came from the west of England into the Massachusetts colony. The one fixed at Charlestown, the other at Ipswich. The father of gov. Trumbull was a substantial farmer in the town of Lebanon in Connecticut. When he was a young man he went to this place, and was

* Sermon upon Mr. Willard.

one of the first settlers in the year 1700. He emI-
grated from Westfield in the county of Hampshire,
where his father had removed from Ipswich, who was
among the most respectable of the yeomanry. The
governour was born at Lebanon in 1710. In the
year 1723, he entered Harvard College. He early
discovered fine talents and a most amiable disposition. He was a modest ingenuous youth, very bash-
ful when he first entered college, owing to his tender years, as well as retired situation; but he was
much beloved by his classmates, and when he took
his degree, one of the finest scholars, with such
accomplishments as qualified him to be useful, as
well as to make the most conspicuous figure. He
was fond of the study of divinity, and for some
years was a preacher of the gospel; he then turned
his attention to jurisprudence, and soon became an
eminent civilian. It is an observation of Mr.
Hutchinson " that many of the first characters in
Massachusetts were at first probationers for the
ministry, and afterwards made a figure at the bar,
or in the legislative or executive courts of the province." We recollect the names of Stoughton,
Read, Gridley and judge Stephen Sewall. That gentleman adds, that when persons have been ordained
they ought " to have very special reasons to leave
the profession for a civil employment." We have
seen an instance of this in gov. Saltonstall, where
the publick was much benefitted.

Gov. Trumbull was employed in many civil offices all of which he executed with great fidelity, and
grew in the esteem of the people as he advanced in
years. He was an active man in publick life, 51
years; 15 of which he was governour of Connecticut colony. When he first went into this office it
required a man of prudence, firmness, consistency
and ability to manage affairs. A good pilot is necessary for every bark which sails on the tempestuous sea. In Connecticut the appearance was
more tranquil than the neighbouring province, but

the clouds were gathering which soon darkened the face of the country. Gov. Trumbull saw the storm burst upon Massachusetts in 1775; he lived to see the auspicious day, also, when his country enjoyed the blessings of peace, and the glory of her independence. No man could guide the vessel of state with more care. No man ever loved his country more. During the whole American war, he showed himself the honest and unshaken patriot, the wise and able magistrate. In an excellent speech he made to the general assembly, October, 1783, he thus expresses himself, " I have to request the favour of you, gentlemen, and through you, of all the freemen of the state, that after May next, I may be excused from any further service in publick life, and from this time I may no longer be considered as an object for your suffrages for any publick employment. The reasonableness of the request I am persuaded will be questioned by no one. The length of time I have devoted to their service, with my declining state of vigour and activity, will I please myself form for me a sufficient and unfailing excuse with my fellow citizens."

This excellent man departed this life on the 17th of August, 1785, at his seat in Lebanon in the 75th year of his age. His father had lived the same number of years.

Gov. Trumbull made a great collection of papers, mss. &c. which were presented by the family to the Massachusetts historical society, several of them have been printed in the volumes of their collections. They consider the whole as an invaluable treasure. Among their honorary members, and truly honourable men is the present Jonathan Trumbull, esq. the eldest son of his late excellency, and the present worthy governour of Connecticut.*

* Mons. Chastelleux, who saw gov. Trumbull when he was 70 years old, writes, " He was governour by excellence, for he had been so 15 years, having been rechosen every *two years*, and equally possessing the public esteem, under the British government and that of congress. His whole life is devoted to business,

TUCKER JOHN, D. D. a celebrated divine and
controversial writer, was graduated at Harvard College, 1741, and ordained over the first church at
Newbury in 1745.   He was a man of very superiour abilities, and having pursued his studies with
diligence, he shone with a mild, engaging, as well
as brilliant lustre amidst the stars of our churches.
Being a man of inquiry, like some of his great predecessors, he was subjected to vexations and trials,
on account of his opinions, which differed from
the generality of the neighbourhood.   He had too
fair a mind to disguise his sentiments and too much
honour and liberality to impose them on others. He
never willingly entered into a theological dispute,
but whenever he was called upon to defend his
tenets, did it with boldness and skill, as a reasoner, a man of pious sentiment, a divine filled with
christian candour, and influenced by the love of religion. No man was less opinionated, or discovered
more pleasantness, good humour and good manners in social intercourse.   In his writings, however, upon controverted points, while he treated the
subject with reverence, he indulged a vein of humour and satire, against his antagonist which gave
a keen edge to his style, and made dry arguments
entertaining.   This appears in a work of his, entitled, " a brief account of an ecclesiastical council so
called, convened in the first parish of Newbury,
March 31, 1767."   They had several sessions, and
he printed an account of each session as soon as it
was ended ; and at the conclusion of the whole, a
sermon, Acts xx. 17, 18, " being a minister's appeal to his hearers as to his life and doctrine." Mr.

which he passionately loves, whether important or not, or rather
with respect to him there is none of the latter description.   He
has all the simplicity in his dress, all the importance and even all
the pedantry, becoming the great magistrate of a small republic.
He brought to my mind, the burgomasters of Holland, the Hein-
siuses and the Barneveldts," &c.
    He mentioned several other things mingled with the mistakes
of a traveller.

Aaron Hutchinson one of the council preached, and wrote against him, which he answered very lively, keen and pointed remarks.

Another spiritual adversary of Mr. T. was the rev. Jonathan Parsons of Newburyport. Those who were disaffected to Mr. T. went over to his church, and were aided by him, in making exceptions to their minister's preaching until they become, as thorns in his side. In the year 1757 Mr. T. printed a pamphlet "observations on the doctrines and uncharitableness of the rev. Jonathan Parsons," &c. These were followed by another pamphlet several years after, in which he vindicated the civil government of this province from that gentleman's severe charges of spiritual tyranny and slavery. This was printed 1774, Mr. P. made no reply. Mr. Tucker had another controversy with a gentleman in the neighbourhood, a very respectable clergyman, and zealous calvinist. This was managed with more gravity and respectful attention to the character of a brother in the ministry. In the year 1767, the rev. James Chandler of Rowley, printed a sermon in which was a marginal note aimed at what Mr. T. had written concerning "confessions of faith." Mr. T. addressed a printed letter to Mr. Chandler, in which he spake against making any rule of faith, but the bible. To this Mr. Chandler replied in a sensible sedate manner, but defended, with some zeal, the doctrines of the New England churches, and the propriety of creeds and confessions, &c. This produced a "second letter from Mr. Tucker in reply to Mr. Chandler's vindication," 1768, 54 pages.

The same year Mr. T. was chosen to preach the convention sermon; he also preached the election sermon, 1771; and the Dudleian lecture, 1778.*

* Beside the publications above mentioned, he printed four sermons upon evangelical subjects, and a thanksgiving sermon in 1756. Several ordination sermons and other occasional dicourses. Also a sermon, Mark xvi. 15, 16; on John vi. 44, 1769.

The university of Harvard presented him with his diploma of doctor in divinity.

The latter years of his life he suffered much from ill health, but was not wholly taken off from his labours till within a few months of his death, which event took place on the 22d of March, 1792.

UNDERHILL JOHN, capt. one of the first planters of Massachusetts, was the friend of sir Henry Vane, and sent by him, as commander of the colony troops to Saybrook in 1637. He made the attack with capt. Mason upon their fort at Mistick, where the fierce spirit of that tribe was broken by the loss of so many men as were then destroyed; even Sassacus was discouraged, and fled to the Mohawks, and very soon those Indians, as a tribe, were extinguished. In 1641, Underhill was chosen governour of Exeter and Dover, but his honours did not set well upon him; he was soon in deprest circumstances. Gov. Winthrop tells a long story of his setting upon a stool of repentance in the Boston church, with a white cap upon his head, and making a confession of his sins. His character was very excentrick in many things, and in whatever he did he run to excess. He was a very great enthusiast in religion, but a debauchee in practice. It is surprising, however, that when he was accused of such immoralities, the church censure did not rest wholly upon these. One great crime was that he dated his conversion from a time he was smoking tobacco. Hence they thought it not sincere. It was necessary to be under the " preaching of the word."

After seeing many changes, capt. Underhill left the New England provinces, and died among the Dutch at Manhadoes. *Winthrop.*

USHER JOHN, lieut. governour of New Hampshire, was counsellor of Massachusetts after their charter was taken away, and when Dudley had a commission as president, in 1686. The same year we find his name among the counsellors of sir Edmund Andross. He was also treasurer of this province, and it is said he was of eminent service in purchasing the district of Maine. By some he was held up to public odium, as an enemy to New England, one who was ready to sacrifice their charter rights for the sake of his own aggrandizement. By others he is represented as just and honest, a true lover of the country, though on the side of prerogative. While he was lieut. governour of New Hampshire he was not a popular character, perhaps his own interest led him to act against the interest of the people. He had married the daughter of Samuel Allen, esq. and therefore had every temptation to assist in maintaining the large claims of the family. After he was dismissed from the government, he left that province, and retired to his estate at Medford, near Boston, where he died, Sept. 1st, 1726, etat. 79.

VANE SIR HENRY, was the son of sir H. Vane, who was in king Charles's court. A very pious man, but no fanatick. His son was equally fanatical in politicks and religion. Displeased with the manners of men in his own country, he came into New England. In 1635, on the 3d of March, he was made a freeman of the colony. In 1636, he was chosen governour. The Boston people were very fond of him. The country people did not like him, and the next year exerted themselves to put him out of office. This caused some goads to his earthy nature though his friends pretended that, in his mind, all was heaven. His religion was pure antinomianism. His adherents said that sanctification was no evidence of justification, and that there was no such thing as personal holiness. Many of them settled Rhode Island. Sir Henry went to England, warmly espoused the cause of O. Cromwell, was an hot headed zealot, an enemy to the presbyterians as well as royalists. He was a man tossed about by new opinions, and the mere sport of his feelings worked up to a kind of spiritual ardour. His ideas of Christ's imputation, led him to believe universal salvation, which indeed is very consistent with antinomian principles. And he was as zealous in diffusing his ideas, that all men should be happy, as he had been to prove that none but he and a very few others should be saved.

When the royal party prevailed, and Charles II. ascended the throne, Vane had no idea that he should be excepted from the act of indemnity. He was executed for treason, June 14, 1662. "His enthusiasm," says Mr. Hume, excited by the prospects of glory, embellished the conclusion of a life, which, through the whole course of it, had been so much disfigured by the prevalence of that principle. In all his behaviour, there appeared a firm and animated intrepidity, and he considered his death but as a passage to that eternal felicity, which he believed prepared for him."

Sir Henry left some writings, mostly religious. Men of reason and sentiment may wonder how so great a man could write so weakly, or so crudely. All are not alike unintelligible: " The mystery of godliness, written by sir H. Vane, contains serious and good observations. A copy of it, is in the historical library. Some have thought the father of our governour was the authour.

VASSALL WILLIAM, the 18th associate mentioned in the charter of Massachusetts, came over as the 5th assistant. Mr. Prince says, that although one of the patentees and assistants, yet in the lists of the courts he could not find his name mentioned. He returned to England in the year 1631. A few years afterwards he returned to New England, and settled at Scituate, in Plymouth colony. When Jamaica was taken, he laid the foundation of the great estates which his posterity enjoyed till the revolution. William and his brother Samuel Vassall were less puritanical than those friends on the new plantation, and soon manifested their difference of opinion. When the Browns carried their complaints home against Endicot, and the matter was referred to certain gentlemen, Samuel and William Vassal were two of the referees, chosen by the complainants; Winthrop, Johnson, &c, were chosen by the company. *Hutchinson and Prince.*

WADSWORTH BENJAMIN, president of Harvard College, was the son of capt. Samuel Wadsworth, who was killed at Sudbury in 1676. He was born at Milton in 1669; was graduated 1690, and ordained pastor of the first church in Boston, 1696. In July, 1725, he was installed president of the college. His mind was rather strong than brilliant, as a preacher he was grave, but not animated. He delivered his sermons without notes, and his memory was so tenacious, that on all occasions he could quote any chapter or verse of the bible, without recurring to the pages. Hence he retained all the learning he acquired in his youth, which was of great advantage to him, when he was president. The general opinion, however, was that he was better fitted for the pastor of a church, than to be master of the school of the prophets. He had confined his studies to theology, and was not a man of extensive erudition, or much acquainted with the sciences. He departed this life March 16, 1737, etat. 68.*

WALTER NEHEMIAH, was born in Ireland, December, 1663, where he had the rudiments of his education. When he was 13 years old, he could converse in latin fluently. About the year 1680, his father came into New England, and put his son under the care of the celebrated Cheever, who declared the lad to be completely fitted for college. He was graduated 1684. After leaving college, he went to Nova Scotia, for the sake of learning French, and he was so fond of the lan-

* His works are a discourse on the last judgment, 1709; a small volume of sermons in 12 mo. 1711, Luke 14, 16; an artillery election sermon, 1700; election sermon, 1716; twelve sermons in 1717; and in 1718, an essay for spreading the gospel into ignorant places; three sermons in 1722; one in 1725; also an essay upon the decalogue; and fourteen sermons upon a good conscience; a discourse upon the christian Sabbath.

guage, that he afterwards procured many French authours; and he conversed so much with the protestant refugees, that he could preach to them in their native tongue. In 1688, Oct. 17, he was ordained over the first church in Roxbury. The old apostle, John Eliot, hearing him preach, declared he must have him for his colleague. Mr. Dudley opposed so sudden an invitation, but approved the choice when they had farther proof of his talents. He continued the pastor of this church above 60 years, and died September 17, 1750, aged 87. Mr. Eliot died in 1690, having been minister 58 years. He said of Mr. Walter, that he would be a most brilliant light of the New England churches. He was indeed an admirable preacher, as well as fine scholar. His discourses were always studied, and he delivered them with great animation, though with a feeble voice. He always had a very delicate bodily frame; and was very small of stature. His character and preaching were often the subject of praise to young candidates. When he was very old he preserved the affection of the people, and the esteem of the publick. Being a meek and humble christian, he had his conversation in the simplicity of truth, and sincerity of the gospel. Mr. W. never put himself forward to preach upon publick occasions, and was seldom persuaded to print any of his discourses. He published several, however, which were very acceptable, and are read to the present time.*

---

* A sermon warning unfruitful hearers, which has been reprinted; also, the body of sin anatomised; a discourse upon vain thoughts; the great concern of man; the wonderfulness of Christ; the holiness of heaven; and the convention sermon, 1723. A volume of his sermons was printed after his death, upon the 55 of Isaiah, with an account of him, from which the compiler has taken some facts. Other notices were communicated by those who knew him. To these might be added Dr. Colman's opinion, " when one is hearing Mr. W. it seems as if any man could preach so, yet few can equal him." Mr. Pemberton used to say, " I know no man that, in his preaching, reconciles perspicuity with accuracy, like Mr. Walter."

WALTER THOMAS, son of the minister of Roxbury, was graduated at Harvard College, 1713, was ordained his father's colleague, October 19, 1718, and died January 10, 1724. He possessed a very extraordinary genius, having all his father's vivacity and richness of imagination, with more vigour of intellect. When he was at college he was not a hard student, and was too fond of company. His intimate associate was John Checkley, who had much learning with his wit and humour. This was a grief to his father; and his uncle Dr. Cotton Mather who warned him to beware of that man; but however he might be attached to his friend for his companionable qualities, he soon entered into a publick altercation with him upon theological sentiments. Checkley wrote certain dialogues upon predestination, in which he threw sarcasms upon the religion of our fathers, which Mr. W. answered.* Dr. Chauncy in his account of eminent men, says, " there was no subject but what Mr. Walter was eminently acquainted with, and such was the power he had over his thoughts and words, that he could readily, without any pains, write or speak just as he would; that he made himself master of all Dr. Cotton Mather's learning, by taking frequent opportunities of conversing with him; and that had he not died in the prime of life, he would have been known as one of the first of our great men."

* In the year 1719, 20, an anonymous pamphlet was published, entitled, Choice dialogues between a godly minister, and an honest countryman, concerning election and predestination, detecting the false principles of a certain man, who calls himself a presbyterian of the church of England. By a reverend and laborious pastor in Christ's flock, by one who has been for almost twice thirty years, a faithful and painful labourer in Christ's vineyard.

This was answered in a book of about 80 pages duo. entitled, a choice dialogue between John Faustus, a conjurer, and Jack Tory his friend, occasioned by some choice dialogues lately published concerning predestination, &c. By a young stripling. The author was well known.

He excelled also "in the science of harmony," and printed a book upon the ground work of musick, with the rules which have been generally in use. His book was a standard work in New England, near half a century. The tunes he collected were introduced into our churches when there was regular singing, and his rules taught in the schools. He also published a sermon upon 2 Samuel, xxiii. 1, " The sweet psalmist of Israel." A more beautiful composition does not exist among the occasional sermons handed down to us from our fathers. It discovers much learning as well as pious sentiment. This sermon was preached at the Boston lecture, 1723, and printed at the desire of the ministers. It is dedicated to judge Dudley. The next year he published a " a sermon upon the scriptures, being the only rule of faith and practice." This was also preached at the Boston lecture, and was very acceptable to the publick.

WARD NATHANIEL, an eccentrick genius, and learned divine, was the son of the rev. John Ward of Haverhill, and born 1570. He was educated at the university of Cambridge, and came into this country, 1634. He settled as pastor of the church at Ipswich, then called Agawam. In 1641, he was invited by the freemen to preach the election sermon. This was rather a political than an evangelical discourse, according to Mr. Winthrop, in which he has been imitated by preachers in modern times. It is a good observation, and has been often repeated, " that the election sermon is the pulse by which we can tell the state of the body politick." Mr. W. had been bred a lawyer, was a traveller, and knew so much of the law of nature and nations that he was employed to draw up a code of laws for New England. Though a pious man he was very eccentrick in his conduct. He soon left his charge at Ipswich, was without employment for some time, and returned to England in 1647. He was afterwards a settled minister at Sheffield. The account of his death is in 1653.

His works are curious and scarce. The book entitled the "simple cobler of Agawam," which he wrote at Ipswich, and printed afterwards in his native country, is a medley of wit and humour, original observation in a strange style, and obsolete language; yet interesting the attention, where we cannot approve the remarks. He was an enemy to toleration in every shape, a great bigot to his own opinions, and wonderfully ingenious and satirical against those of a different opinion.

He wrote other books of humour, and some learned treatises, but none have come down to the present age, but the "simple cobler," which has passed through many editions. *Winthrop.*

WARD JOHN, son of the famous Nathaniel Ward, was born in England, 1606, before his father left Haverhill. The place where he settled in this colony, was called Haverhill, a pleasant spot on Merrimack river, where he continued a faithful pastor from 1646 to the year 1694. He preached Nov. 19, of this year, being then in the 88th year of his age, and died of paralytick affections, Dec. 27. *Magnalia.*

WARD ARTEMAS, major general of the American army, deserves a distinction among those patriots who exerted themselves in the cause of liberty, and for the independence of their country. He was a gentleman of liberal education, having received the honours of Harvard College in the year 1748. He was an active and useful member of the general court for several years; and one of the provincial congress in 1774. He had served in the war previous to the peace of Paris. When the revolutionary war commenced, he was the first officer in rank, and commanded the troops at Cambridge till gen. Washington arrived. No man could show more firmness and intrepidity than he did upon some trying occasions. When Washington was generalissimo, he was the first major general, and commanded the division at Roxbury. Gen. Thomas and gen. Heath were brigadier generals. He resigned his commission in 1777, and went into the civil line.   He was chosen one of the council of Massachusetts, and was highly esteemed for his political integrity, his independency of spirit, and steady attention to the duties of his station.   In 1786, he was speaker of the house of representatives; and chief justice of the court of common pleas for the county of Worcester. A lawless mob, with Wheeler and Convers at their head, arose to unhinge the government, and stood at the door of the court house with bayonets fixed to oppose the court. Gen. Ward behaved with coolness and intrepidity, and used every wise method to bring them to consideration.*   After the constitution of the United States was established, he was a member of congress, and then retired to private life, where he lived some years, receiving honour and respect from the people.   He died at Newbury in the year 1800.

WARHAM JOHN, came over with the company from the west of England, who settled the town of Dorchester in Massachusetts, in 1630 He and Mr. Maverick continued together for six years. He then went to Connecticut and laid the foundation of the town of Windsor, and continued with this people till his death, the 1st of April, 1670.   He was the only minister who used notes in his preaching, but was more animated in his delivery than most of his brethren, and was a very excellent divine.   He was subject to hypochondriack complaints, which had such an effect upon him at times, as to fill his mind with spiritual gloom.   He frequently administered the communion without partaking of it, thinking himself unworthy, when no one else doubted his qualifications.   *Magnalia.*

WARREN JOSEPH, major general of the American army, was born at Roxbury. His parents were respectable, and in that place he received the first rudiments of his education.   He entered Harvard College when he was but 15 years old, and receiv-

* Minot's history of the insurrection in Massachusetts.

ed the honours of that seminary in 1759 and 1762. Having turned his attention to medical studies, he was soon qualified for the practice, and in the year 1764, when the small pox spread through Boston, and vast numbers were inoculated, he was among the physicians, who were most eminent in the profession. Had he confined his views to professional business he might have enjoyed the affluence of wealth, with a high reputation. He certainly was happy in the affection of a numerous part of this town, who had the most lively opinion of his humanity and skill. His fine address, as well as his taste for philosophy and the belles lettres, gained him the esteem and regard of the polite and learned, while his frank, open disposition, and obliging attention to persons under various circumstances of human distress, caused him to be greatly beloved by those who tread the humble walks of life. But his mind was too ardent and active to be confined to the duties of a profession, and he was a stranger to the passion of avarice. He soon had an opportunity to show his talents as a fine writer, and also his eloquence and patriotick zeal. These were manifested upon many occasions from the year the *stamp act* was passed, to the time of the war which separated the colonies from the parent country. He was in the class of *bold politicians*, as they were then distinguished from the *moderate whigs*. While some made a distinction between internal and external taxes; while many were sending petition after petition to the foot of the throne; while the generality of the people dreaded a war on account of our want of resources, and the omnipotence of the British nation; he felt superiour to these fears and despised the suppliant tone of children to mother Britain; he was uniform in his opinion that every kind of taxation was complete tyranny; and it was a common expression with him, that we could fight our own battles, if Great Britain sent her armies over the Atlantick. He was persuaded that they never would send large armies, in which he would have found himself mistaken, had he lived a few years longer; but allowing they made ever so great exertions to conquer America, they could only, in his opinion, destroy the seaports; they would not be able to penetrate into the country; and he said that we ought to make any sacrifices rather than submit to arbitrary and oppressive measures; or be so mean and pusillanimous as to tremble at the *rods* which would continually be shaken over our heads.

From the year 1768, a number of politicians met at each other's houses to discuss publick affairs, and to settle upon the best methods of serving the town and country. Many of these filled publick offices. But the meetings were private, and had a silent influence upon the publick body. In 1772 they agreed to increase their number, to meet in a large room, and invite a number of substantial mechanicks to join them, and hold a kind of *caucus, pro bono publico.* They met in a house near the north battery, and more than 60 were present at the first meeting. Their regulations were drawn up by Dr. Warren and another gentleman, and they never did any thing important without consulting him and his particular friends. It answered a good purpose to get such a number of mechanicks together; and though a number of whigs of the first character in the town were present, they always had a mechanick for moderator, generally one who could carry many votes by his influence. It was a matter of policy likewise to assemble at that part of the town. It had the effect to awake the *north wind*, and stir the *waters* of the *troubled sea.* By this body of men the most important matters were decided—they agreed who should be in town offices, in the general court, in the provincial congress, from Boston. Here the committees of publick service were formed, the plan for military companies, and all necessary means of defence. They met about two years steadily at one place. After the destruction of the tea, the place of assembling was known, and they met at the Green Dragon in the spring of 1775, with as many more from the south end, and the records of their proceedings are still preserved. The writer of these memoirs has been assured by some of the most prominent characters of this *caucus*, that they were guided by the prudence and skilful management of Dr. Warren, who, with all his zeal and irritability, was a man calculated to carry on any secret business ; and that no man ever did manifest more vigilance, circumspection and care. In every country there are politicians, who are the mere cymbals of the mob, and answer some good purpose, when they are *not left to themselves*. In this country, through all stages of the revolution, we had many such, who, to their own imagination, appeared to direct the affairs of the publick. Such men were never admitted to be members of the *caucus* here mentioned ; many of them never knew the secret springs, that moved the great wheels, but thought themselves very important characters, because they were sons of liberty, and excelled others in garrulity, or made a louder cry upon the wharves, or at corners of streets.

Dr. Warren was twice chosen the publick orator of the town, and his orations were among the best compositions, as any one will see, who reads the volume containing all the orations, spoken on the 5th of March.

At the battle of Lexington, he was perhaps the most active man in the field. His soul beat to arms, as soon as he learnt the intention of the British troops. It is said, in the memoirs of gen. Heath, that a ball grazed his hair, and took of part of his *ear lock*.

He was ready upon every alarm, from this time, till he was slain. Nothing could be in a more confused state than the army which first hastily assembled at Cambridge. This undisciplined body of men were kept together by a few, who deserved well

3 N

of their country.   Among them gens. Ward and
Putnam were distinguished; the one for his firm,
prudent conduct, and the other for his romantick
courage.   Dr. W. was perhaps the man who had
the most influence, and in whom the people in the
environs of Boston and Cambridge placed their
highest confidence.   He did wonders in preserving
order among the troops.   Four days before the battle of Bunker's Hill he was appointed major general of the American army.   When the entrenchments were made at Breed's Hill, he, to encourage
the men within the lines, went down from Cambridge, and acted as a volunteer.   Col. Pres-
cot commanded the party within the lines, and col.
Starks the men who were without, behind a rail
fence, and did such amazing execution by a well
directed fire.

Gen. Warren fell in the trenches.   A female historian of the war tells us, that he chose to die rather
than be taken prisoner.   We are at a loss to know
how this can be ascertained.   We always understood he was killed outright, and had not at his own
option any of the circumstances of his death.

It is true, however, that at all times he discovered the greatest fortitude and bravery, and, as he lived an ornament to his country, his death reflected a
lustre upon himself, and the cause he so warmly espoused.   No person's fall was ever more regretted,
and yet no one could help feeling the *sentiment*, who
repeated the line

Dulce et decorum est pro patria mori.

Had success attended the Americans, his death
would have been sufficient to damp the joys of victory, and the cypress would be blended with the
laurel.   The loss of such a man, in addition to our
defeat, and at a time when the distracted state of
our affairs greatly needed his advice, threw a gloom
upon the circumstances of the people, and excited
the most sincere lamentation and mourning.   The
elegant, the generous and humane " all mingled the

sympathetick tear," and paid their respects to his memory.

In the spring of 1776, when the British troops left Boston, his body was brought from *Breed's Hill*, where it had lain undistinguished from his fellow soldiers, to be entombed in a Boston burial place. The several lodges of free masons preceded, and multitudes of his fellow citizens followed, the corpse. An eloquent orator, a brother mason, pronounced the funeral eulogy, in the Stone Chapel. The exordium, addressed to the " Illustrious Relicks," had a very strong effect upon the auditory.

Gen. Warren had been grand master of free masons through North America for a number of years, and all the friends *of the craft* now highly respect his memory.

Having said, that in private life gen. Warren was amiable, we repeat it, that in person, mind, and manners he was equally well accomplished. He gained the love of those who lived with him in habits of intimacy, while the publick voice celebrated his virtues. With sensibilities uncommonly strong, and a zeal which blazed in the cause of liberty, he was candid, generous, and ready to do kind offices to those who had different sentiments concerning the controversy. There are persons now living, who recollect his polite attentions, when they were slighted and wounded by others whose minds were less liberal, or more corroded with party spirit.

> ——Cui pudor, et justitiæ soror,
> Incorrupta fides, nudaque veritas.
> Quando ullum invenient parem ?
> Multis ille bonis flebilis occidit.

WEARE MESHECH, president of New Hampshire, was descended from respectable ancestors, who were concerned in most of the publick and political transactions of the province. He himself was engaged above 30 years in publick employments. He was first chosen representative, from the town of Hampton, for the general court. In this place he succeeded his father, and was also a magistrate for the county. For some years he was speaker of the house. In the year 1754, when the American congress assembled in Albany, he was appointed a commissioner. His knowledge of the law qualified him for a place on the bench of judges of the supreme court. In the year 1777, he was appointed chief justice. During the revolutionary war he was an active man in managing the concerns of New Hampshire. He was annually elected president of the body politick, or chief magistrate, from 1776 to 1784, when a constitution was formed for the state. The people paid so much respect to him, as to choose him their first president, though it was evident his age and infirmities required rest from his publick labours. He sought retirement, and resigned the office before another election. The historian of New Hampshire delineates his character, " as a person, not of inventive or original genius, but of clear discernment, extensive knowledge, accurate judgment, a calm temper, a modest deportment, an upright and benevolent heart, and a habit of prudence and diligence in discharging the various duties of publick and private life."*

WELD THOMAS, first pastor of the church in Roxbury, came from a town called Tirling, in Essex. Not being willing to submit to the ceremonies, as the law required, he was obliged to leave the place, and he came over to New England, in the year 1632. He was immediately invited to settle at Roxbury. He was a man of very considerable talents, and a favourite with the magistrates. He distinguished himself at the trial of Mrs. Hutchinson, being one of her principal opposers, and afterwards wrote a book to expose the errors of those sectaries.† In Winthrop's journal continual mention is

* Belknap's history, vol. ii. page 485.
† The book is entitled, " short story of the rise, reign and ruin of the Antinomians, Familists and Libertines, that infested the

made of the calling upon ministers for advice.
Weld was always present; hence we may suppose
him a very prudent and judicious man, as well as
good minister. He was sent agent to Great Britain
with Hugh Peters in 1641, and never returned.
He went to Ireland with lord Forbes, where he stayed for some time, and then returned to his parish,
which was a living, in the bishoprick of Durham,
from which he was ejected in 1662.

WENTWORTH JOHN, lieut. governour of New
Hampshire, was the son of William Wentworth, one
of the first settlers of the country, an amiable, pious,
sensible man, who was a ruling elder, and adorned
his station in the church. The son, a man of
enterprize and spirit, was commander of a ship, in
the early part of his life, and acquired a good estate,
if not the affluence of wealth. He lived in a style
of elegance beyond his neighbours, and was more
of a gentleman in his manners, was popular in his
address, and received continual marks of publick
favour. Having been 5 years a counsellor, he was
appointed lieut. governour. His commission had
annexed to it the name of Joseph Addison, who was
then secretary, 17th Dec. 1717. The people were
satisfied with his administration. They thought
him more wise and moderate than his predecessors,
and more attached to their interest. The multitude
soon distinguish between men whose object it is to
make the most of an office, and such as love their
country, or have an eye to the publick good, while
they are willing in some measure to serve themselves. Selfish men are not fit for publick stations;
yet few men are so patriotick as to sacrifice their

churches of New England." There is an edition of it in 4to.
1692, in the library of Harvard College. His other works were,
an "answer to W. R. his narration of opinions and practices of the
New England churches," 4to. 1644; "the perfect Pharisee under monkish holiness." This he and three other ministers
wrote in 1654. It was levelled against the Quakers; and afterwards they wrote "the false Jew detected," &c. against a man,
who pretended to be first a Jew, and then an Anabaptist.

own concerns entirely. The general asssembly made frequent grants to their lieut. governour, believing him to be upright, and that he made every exertion to serve the province. He received tokens of affection from them; but an alienation happened in the year 1728. The general assembly had continued 5 years. It was dissolved of course when king George I. died. A new assembly being called, the lieut. governour, not satisfied with their proceedings, dissolved them by his authority, which was legal, as gov. Burnet had not yet arrived; but it excited acrimonious feelings. These were increased when the next assembly met, and he negatived their speaker, Mr. Nathaniel Weare. Nothing happened in this dispute, however, to make him fearful of losing his office. Their opinions varied, and they debated with some temper. His conduct was approved by Burnet when he was governour of New Hampshire as well as Massachusetts. Mr. W. had the misfortune to offend gov. Belcher, who was very unreasonable in the degree of his resentment. The lieut. governour had written letters of friendship to Mr. Shute and Mr. Belcher while they were in England. Belcher received his letter, and returned his attentions when he came to New Hampshire. But upon learning that he made the same kind of address to Shute, was very angry, and not only refused common civilities, but made use of his authority to lessen the importance of his station. He said that Wentworth was guilty of deception. It was only that kind of artifice which politicians make use of to preserve their places. It was what Belcher himself had practised in some measure to get the government of Massachusetts, and what his enemies used to some purpose, when they effected his dismissal from his government. It was also bad policy on this account; he put all Wentworth's friends in opposition to him, who might have been of great assistance in his political trials. Mr. Wentworth lived not long after Belcher entered on his government. He died, Dec. 12, 1730, in the 59th year of his age.* *Belknap's history of New Hampshire.*

WENTWORTH BENNING, governour of New Hampshire, was the son of lieut. governour Wentworth, and was educated at Harvard College, where he was graduated, in 1716. He turned his attention to business, and was an eminent merchant in Portsmouth. He was sent to the general assembly, as one of the representatives, and advanced to a seat at the council board. He was always in opposition to Belcher, during his whole administration. When New Hampshire was made a distinct government, he was promoted to the chair in the year 1741. He did many things to render himself popular, and to promote the honour of the station, and the prosperity of the province. A ruler in a popular government may always expect opposition. If he act from the purest motives, he will meet with some who envy his situation, and with others who have claims that can never be satisfied. Belcher had also friends in New Hampshire, who could feel no very great attachment to a man who had uniformly found fault with his measures. The enemies of gov. Shirley were scattered through the New England provinces. Wentworth was a great friend to him, and this excited an opinion, that he approved his arbitrary measures. He was a zealous episcopalian, likewise, which caused jealousies among those who were attached to the form and discipline of the New England churches. With all the opposition from political or religious prejudices, he continued his administration longer than any of the other governours. This office he resigned in the year 1766, and was succeeded by his nephew, whose talents added lustre to a family which for many years had been the most brilliant in New Hampshire, and

* A very good portrait of lieut. governour Wentworth is in the room of the historical society. It was presented by his grandson, sir John Wentworth.

whose amiable qualities gained him the love as well as applause of all classes of people.

Gov. B. Wentworth found his situation very unpleasant and his seat very uneasy, the latter part of his administration.   Such mortifications he only shared in common with all who have held high and important stations in this or perhaps any country. Dr. Belknap observes, that " notwithstanding some instances, in which a want of magnanimity was conspicuous, his administration, in other respects, was beneficial.   Though he was highly censured for granting the best lands of the province to the people of Massachusetts and Connecticut, with views of pecuniary reward, yet, the true interest of the country was certainly promoted ; because the grantees, in general, were better husbandmen than the people of New Hampshire.

WEST SAMUEL, D. D. an eminent divine, metaphysical, theological and controversial writer, was graduated at Harvard College in the year 1754. Some years after he left Cambridge, he was invited to take charge of the church at Dartmouth.   The part of the town in which he settled has since taken the name of New Bedford.   He was a very extraordinary person in his way, and his name certainly ought to be recorded in every book of American biography.   His mind was very capacious and strong, his reading extensive, and being very communicative, he frequently instructed and entertained those who desired information ; his company was also solicited by men of literary taste from all parts of the commonwealth.   He was peculiarly fond of associating with those who maintained the cause of rational religion and christian liberty.   His pulpit talents alone would not have given him celebrity. He had a commanding voice, but knew not how to modulate it ; his attitude and manner were very uncouth, and he would never attempt to touch the passions.   His common discourses were carelessly written, but, upon publick occasions, when he took pains in composing them, were very excellent. He was great as a biblical critick, and it has been well observed, that with the same advantages he "had fallen little short of Buxtorf, Mede, Pool, Kenicott," &c.* In politicks he was a zealous whig, and had considerable influence in the section of the province where he dwelt. During the first year of the American war he was brought into general notice by a particular circumstance. There were certain letters intercepted which were supposed to contain a secret and criminal correspondence with the enemy. He, being a curious and philosophical man, was employed to decipher them. It was acknowledged by the writer, that he did the business correctly. He was chosen to preach the election sermon, in 1776. The next year, 1777, he preached at Plymouth, on the 22d of December. He took a passage from the lxvi. of Isaiah, "Shall a nation be born at once?" and applied it to the independence of America. Whether the novelty of the sentiment, or the truth of the prophecy had the most effect, it is certain, that no sermon was ever more the subject of praise. No person, who reads the discourse at the present day, can conceive the impressions which were then made. To some, however, it appeared a playfulness of fancy; but to him every thing delivered was a solemn reality. He was so tenacious of his opinion, that he was hurt if any man expressed a doubt upon the subject. When the convention met at Cambridge and Boston, to form a constitution for the state, he was a leader in several of the debates; and during the whole session was a very influential and important member. He was also a member of the Massachusetts convention which adopted the constitution of the United States. He preached the Dudleian lecture upon the validity of Presbyterian ordination, 1782. The university presented him with a diploma of doctor in divinity,

* Anthology for March, 1808.

1793. He was one of the original members of the American academy of arts and sciences, and an honorary member of the philosophical society in Philadelphia. The oddities of this good man have been frequently the subject of remark, and have excited the mirth of humourists. In his days of health and vigour such things were lost amidst the excellencies of his character, or absorbed in the splendour of his reputation; but in his latter days all his foibles were spread and exaggerated. His old age was full of infirmities, and his friends could only look with pity upon the relicks of a mind which was once so superiour as to command admiration. He departed this life, Sept. 24, 1807.*

WHEELOCK ELEAZER, D. D president of Dartmouth College, was educated at Yale College, and received the honours of that seminary, 1733. He was ordained pastor of a church in the town of Lebanon; was a minister of extraordinary zeal and pious sentiment, and his ministry was blessed with uncommon success. His active views were not confined to christian churches, although great revivals of religion took place during the course of his ministry, but his ardent mind was employed in the conversion of the aboriginals of the land. For this purpose he opened an Indian charity school in which a number of children of the natives might be educated, and become missionaries among their several tribes. This scheme originated with Mr. John Sargeant at Stockbridge, who begun a school, and procured assistance from many well disposed and liberal gentlemen. He died in 1749, before his plan was accomplished. Mr. Wheelock revived the business, and called it Moore's school, in honour to the name of its greatest benefactor. This

* His other publications were, beside occasional sermons, a letter upon infant baptism; essays on liberty and necessity. To these Dr. Edwards replied in a volume very ably written. Dr. West thought he had mistaken his meaning in some passages, and had prepared further illustrations of the subject, but did not live to finish the work.

school was kept at Lebanon a number of years. In 1770, Dr. Wheelock removed it to New Hampshire. There he had to subdue the wilderness, and to instruct Indian youth. Other scholars were added, until a greater number of missionaries were prepared from the English than the Indians. From this institution grew a flourishing college, where learned, orthodox ministers were qualified to fill vacant churches. It is now a university in high reputation. The funds, however, are kept separate. The money raised in Scotland is appropriated, and at this time several Indian youths are instructed agreeably to what was expressed in the foundation. The first commencement at Dartmouth College, was held in 1771. The rev. Dr. Wheelock died in 1779, aged 69. His son, the hon. John Wheelock, is his worthy successor, and also professor of history.

WHEELWRIGHT JOHN, one of the most famous men in the beginning of the plantations, was brother in law to Mrs. Hutchinson, and of the same mind concerning justification, though he did not pretend to have such peculiar revelations. He had a more correct judgment, but not much greater stability. He was much attached to her, and was involved in her sufferings. In 1637, he was banished the colony, having preached a sermon the year before at Boston which gave great offence. It was pleasing to several members of the Boston church of which he was a member, and one of the preachers.* A complaint however was made to the general court of some things he delivered, as tending

* Mr. Wheelwright, minister to a branch of that church, at a place since called Braintree (where the town had some lands) was eager and zealous against a covenant of works ; and was banished by the court for what was called sedition, by the same rule which will make every dissent from, or opposition to, a majority in any religious affairs to be sedition, and an iniquity to be punished by the judge. The minor part must always be seditious, if it be sedition to defend their own opinions, &c. *Callender's century sermon, page* 27.

to sedition, and disturbance of the plantation. Mr.
W. put forth a reply to the complaints against him,
in which he endeavoured to clear the doctrine of the
sermon from sedition, and declared he only meant
to explain the doctrine of grace.   Hubbard says,
" that in this he differed from the sermon, and was
confuted by some of the ministers with strong arguments."   But it seems Mr. Cotton replied to
their answer, and Mr. Wheelwright could not be
prevailed upon to make any recantation ; which
might have saved him many difficulties, and prevented the division of the colony.   Some of the
magistrates signed a petition in favour of their minister.   He was the peculiar friend of Mr. Coddington, also of Aspinwall and Coggeshall, members of
the general court from Boston, who were expelled
the house for signing the petition.   Hence a civil
strife was consequent upon religious contentions.
It was this which gave rise to a new settlement, and
a new government, at Rhode Island. Mr. W. after
his banishment went to New Hampshire, and laid
the foundation of the town and church at Exeter.
He afterwards went to Hampton, and thence to
Salisbury.   In the year 1644, he wrote to the governour of Massachusetts, made an acknowledgment
of his offence, and was restored to the favour of the
people. It has always seemed very strange, that he
did not go with his friends to Rhode Island instead
of removing to New Hampshire.   His conduct in
New Hampshire discovered an ambitious turn, a
desire to be chief, and to have that influence over
the people which his learning and abilities gave him
some claim to expect.   Hence he might prefer being where none could appear in competition with
him.   The gentlemen who went to Rhode Island
were shrewd, sensible men ; some of them gifted
brethren, who thought themselves superiour to their
teachers.   In 1758, Mr. Wheelwright was in England, a great favourite with Cromwell ; he then corresponded with his friends in New England.   A

letter to the church of Hampton is preserved. When he returned to America is not mentioned ; but he lived to be the oldest minister in New England. He died in 1680, leaving children who were highly respectable for their character and stations. His son, grandson, and great grandson were counsellors of Massachusetts.

WIGGLESWORTH EDWARD, D. D. Hollis professor of divinity at Harvard College, was the son of Michael Wigglesworth, pastor of the church at Malden, who was graduated in 1651, and was also a fellow of the corporation. He died June 10, 1705, aged 74. Among his publications was a poem, called the "Day of Doom," which has been celebrated by good people in New England. It is a curious and scarce book. His son Edward was graduated in 1710, and deserves a place in the highest class of his contemporaries. To an extensive knowledge in his profession, he added the ornaments of classical literature. He was also as remarkable for his piety as his learning. As a minister of a particular church he might not have shone among the popular preachers ; but he was completely accomplished for the chair of divinity professor. As soon as the benevolent and pious Mr. Hollis of London laid a founddation for such a professorship in New England, the eyes of the clergy were turned towards Mr. Wigglesworth. Dr. Colman, in a letter to Mr. Hollis, speaks of him, "as a man of known and exemplary piety, literature, modesty, meekness, and other christian ornaments." He was publickly inducted into his office, in the college hall, Oct. 24, 1722, and in 1724, elected a member of the corporation. The university of Edinburgh presented him with a diploma of doctor in divinity in the year 1730. He was elected rector of Yale College, but declined on account of his deafness which also unfitted him to shine in conversation, for which he had fine talents. On this account, however, he paid more attention to his studies, and his lectures were filled with arguments, excellent thoughts, liberal views of the christian doctrines, and just discrimination of the contested points. His polemical pieces gave him a high reputation abroad, as well as in New England. The Whitefieldian controversy employed the pens of several divines, some of whom exposed his vanity and enthusiasm, which he had enough of when he was a young man, as he afterwards confessed ; none wrote in such an engaging and interesting manner as professor Wigglesworth. He wrote in an animated and nervous style, and mingled the glow of resentment with a delicate, satirical mode of reproving a man who had endeavoured to blast the reputation of an institution, which he knew nothing about. Dr. Wigglesworth wrote his answer to Mr. Whitefield's reply to the college testimony, in 1745. In 1754, he preached two lectures upon " the distinguishing characters of the ordinary and extraordinary ministers of Christ." These were occasioned by Mr. Whitefield's preaching at Cambridge, and were printed at the request of the students.*

The latter years of Dr. Wigglesworth's life were years of infirmity and pain. He was patient and submissive, an example to those who highly estimated his character. He died, January 19, 1765, in the 73d year of his age.

WIGGLESWORTH EDWARD, D. D. son of the first Hollis professor of divinity, was graduated at Harvard College, 1749 ; was tutor when his father died, and chosen to succeed him in the professorship. He was a learned man, and very much attached to the interests of the college. Upon the death of Dr. Winthrop, in 1779, he was elected fellow of the corporation. When the society in Scotland for propagating the gospel among the Indians

---

* Other printed works of Dr. W. are, lectures upon the punishment of the wicked ; on the imputation of Adam's guilt ; upon reprobation ; inspiration of the O. T. trial of the spirits ; Dudleian lecture, upon the infallibility of the church of Rome ; also a sermon on the death of president Wadsworth.

in North America, established a corresponding board in Boston, he was chosen secretary. He received a diploma of doctor of divinity from the university of Harvard in the year 1786.

Dr. Wigglesworth was one of the original members of the American academy of arts and sciences.

Being unable to attend his professional duties by reason of paralytical affections, which greatly debilitated his mind and body, he resigned his professorship in 1791. But the legislature of the college continued him as professor *emeritus* till his death, in 1794.

He published, in the year 1775, "calculations on American population, with a table for estimating the *annual* increase," &c. He printed two sermons, one "upon the death of Dr. Winthrop;" the other was the Dudleian lecture "against the errors of the church of Rome," 1786.

Willard Samuel, pastor of the Old South church in Boston, and vice president of Harvard College, was one of the most celebrated divines of Massachusetts. His descent was honourable. His father was a member of the council, and at the head of the militia.* He sent his son to Harvard College, that he might receive a liberal education. His genius was uncommon, and he made such progress in his studies, as gave lively hopes of future useful-

* In 1654, major Simon Willard commanded the army sent against the Narragansetts. The commissioners of the united colonies agreed to raise 270 foot and 40 horse. The Indians, with Ninigret their sachem, retired into a swamp. Willard did not think it prudent to attack them in that situation, and the forces returned with no other success, than taking a few Pequods who had been with the other Indians after the destruction of their tribe. The commissioners were displeased with this retreat, and charged Willard with neglecting an opportunity of humbling the pride of Ninigret, which had always been insufferable, and would now be increased. Hutchinson observes, that major Willard, being a Massachusetts man, might comply with the views of the colony. They were averse from a war with the Indians, or Dutch. It was the second time of their preventing an open war, contrary to the minds of six commissioners. The court acted with more policy, than honour and justice.

ness. He was settled in the first place at Groton, an obscure situation for a man of such great abilities, who was not only a profound scholar, but an eloquent speaker, possessing every qualification necessary to give a great man a splendid reputation. The place where he dwelt being destroyed by the Indians, and the flock of which he was pastor scattered in the wilderness, he was invited to fix his station in the metropolis, where he became a great blessing to the churches, and of eminent service to the college. "The providence that occasioned his removal to this place," says his eulogist, "was an awful judgment upon the whole land; yet was eventually a mercy in this respect, that it made way for the translation of this bright star to a more conspicuous orb, where his influence was more extensive and beneficial; and in this it was a great blessing to this congregation, to this town, and to all New England. His common sermons might have been pronounced with applause, before an assembly of the greatest divines."* But as a writer he has been more known to the succeeding generations. He was fond of publishing his works, and was called upon on all great occasions to deliver his sentiments from the pulpit. No divine, except Dr. Cotton Mather, in this country prepared more works for the press; and they were all calculated to do honour to the author, and edify pious people. He died in the 68th year of his age, Sept. 12, 1707, having been minister of the third church in Boston from April 10, 1678.†

* Pemberton's discourses, page 137.

† His works are numerous. In 1673, he published three sermons, containing useful instruction for a professing people; the artillery election sermon, 1676; a funeral sermon on gov. Leverett, 1679; animadversions upon the Baptists, 1681. From this time to 1690, about 20 sermons, or tracts. In 1682, miscellaneous observations on witchcraft, in a dialogue between S. and B.; in 1693, the covenant of redemption, and rules for discerning the times; in 1694, the election sermon; and artillery election sermon in 1699. The same year, a course of sermons upon spiritual devotions; in 1700, a volume of sermons on the blessed man,

WILLARD JOSIAH, secretary of the province of Massachusetts bay, son of that famous divine, Mr. Samuel Willard, was born in Boston. He was graduated at Harvard College, 1698. The next year he was chosen tutor, and continued in that office till he entered on his travels. Having visited several parts of the West Indies, and Europe, he returned to his own country, improved in mind and manners. His piety gave a lustre to his moral character, and he appeared with the dignity, grace and politeness of the gentleman in his private walk, and in every publick station. In 1717 he was appointed secretary of the province; in 1731, judge of probate; in 1734 he was elected one of his majesty's council. He resigned most of his publick offices as he grew into the vale of years; but continued to do his duty as secretary till his death. He departed this life, Dec. 6, 1756, in the 76th year of his age. Dr. Sewall, and Mr. Prince, each printed a funeral sermon upon the occasion, in which his character is fully delineated. These gentlemen were intimately acquainted with him; Mr. Prince had been his pupil.

WILLIAMS ROGER, minister of the gospel, and governour of the Providence plantations, was born in Wales, and educated at the university of Oxford. He was a minister of the church of England before he came to Boston, but disliking the form and government of the episcopal church, he left his native country, and came into this American wilderness. Here he expected to enjoy liberty of thinking, and

and a number of single sermons on particular texts of scripture, for particular occasions; in 1701, a number of sermons upon Satan's temptations; two upon brotherly love, &c.; in 1703, a brief reply to George Keith; in 1704, a sermon, Romans viii. 31; in 1706, the just man's prerogative, a sermon, Prov. xii, 21.

His posthumous works are, a thanksgiving sermon upon the return of a young gentleman from his travels, 1709; sacramental meditations, a volume, 1711; in 1726, the body of divinity, being 250 lectures upon the assembly's shorter catechism, which is a very complete view of the doctrine of the New England churches.

3 P

acting, without any peculiar restraint from the civil power. He was then a young man, singular in his notions, and fond of manifesting his singularities. He arrived at Boston, Feb. 1631, and from this place went to Plymouth, where he resided two years, and spake freely his sentiments upon religion, without offending the brethren of that church. He was peculiarly gifted as a preacher, and was willing that they should speak at publick and private meetings; hence they were always attached to him, and were ready to help him in the time of his greatest necessities. He was not willing to settle with the church at Plymouth, but went to Salem, while Mr. Skelton was living, in whose pulpit he *prophecied*, according to the language of the times, when a man preached who had not been inducted into the office of pastor or teacher. The church of Salem invited him to be their pastor when Mr. Skelton died. This gave offence to the government of the colony. It was the opinion of the ministers of the bay, that if Mr. W. was allowed to propagate his opinions, the churches might run into heresy and apostacy, and the people defy the civil magistrate. The church of Salem was censured, as well as their teacher. When the court met, he was ordered to appear before them. He was charged with writing two letters. One to the churches, complaining of *the magistrates* for *injustice and extreme oppression*, &c. the other to his own church, persuading them to *renounce communion with all the churches in the bay*, because they were filled with antichristian pollution, &c. He justified these letters, maintained his opinions, and offered to defend them in a publick dispute. Mr. Hooker was chosen to confer with him, but could not convince him of his errors. He was ordered to depart from the jurisdiction in six weeks. The church at Salem acknowledged their fault in joining their voice with Mr. W. in the letter he sent to the churches. The banishment of Mr. W. was in 1635. He went to Secunke, now called Rehoboth.

He afterwards fixed upon Mooshausick, which he named Providence, which is now one of the most flourishing places in New England. Strangers often seek the spot where Roger Williams fixed his humble dwelling, and drink at the spring, which ran before his door, where he slacked his thirst during his weariness and perils. A very odd way of shewing respect to the memory of this uncommon man, who was poor, and altogether spiritual in his views, is now discovered by the people of that town. One of the Providence banks is named " Roger Williams' bank." In 1637, Mr. Williams was employed by the government of Massachusetts to be their agent in the business they transacted with the Indian tribes. His conduct was marked with fidelity, disinterestedness and wisdom.* Gov. Winthrop was a friend to him after this. His former associates respected his talents and integrity, though they still blamed him for his bigotry, pride and singularity. He had the entire confidence of the Indian sachems.

From this time we are to view Mr. W. as a different character from what he was when teacher of a particular congregation in Salem; or would have been, had he continued in Massachusetts among the pastors of the churches. His sphere of usefulness was very extensive, and, where religious opinions had no influence, he conducted wisely, and beyond what could be expected from a man, who had shown such strange prejudices, and whose education gave him but little knowledge of the world. We are to view him, as the father of one of the provinces, and a writer in favour of civil and religious freedom, more bold, just, and liberal, than any other, who appeared in that generation.

Many would smile at seeing the name of Roger Williams enrolled with the legislators of ancient times, or with the statesmen of modern Europe, or

* For the details of Mr. Williams's life, see historical collections, vol. x. pages 17, 18, 19, 20, &c.

with such a man as Penn, the proprietor of Pennsylvania, whose steps were more majestick upon
the theatre of the great world. But this man was
equal to conducting the affairs of this infant colony
as well as if a complete system of legislation was
formed ; and, as a mediator between the aboriginals
and the English inhabitants, if he were the instrument of preserving peace, of teaching the Indians
some of the arts of life, and of illuminating the
minds of the heathen with the *light* of christianity,
he is certainly worthy of more credit, than some
mighty hunters of the earth, or those sages, whose
maxims have made men fierce and revengeful, and
caused human blood to flow in streams.

He was very instrumental in settling Rhode-
Island, or procuring the grant of land, which Mr.
Coddington and others had chosen for their plantation, when they left Boston. The historian of that
colony has favoured us with a ms. of his, which he
says is in *perpetuam rei memoriam.*

In 1643, Mr. Williams went to England as agent,
and it was there, by the assistance of Vane, he obtained " *a charter of civil incorporation by the name
of Providence plantations in the Narraganset bay of
New England.*" It was dated 7th of March ; which
form of government subsisted till 1651. Then upon differences, they sent their former agent, and
joined Mr. Clarke with him, who transacted the business to the advantage of the colony, and the satisfaction of a large majority of the people.

Roger Williams lived to a great age. He died,
1682, 48 years after his banishment. The various
scenes of his life did not make him alter his sentiments on religious freedom ; and his latitudinarian
principles had no ill effect in plantations where there
was no church rule or authority.*

---

* The first of Mr. Williams's publications was a dialogue between *Truth* and *Peace*, a book of 247 pages, printed in London,
1644.
It required great boldness of thinking, and uncommon abilities,

WILLIAMS JOHN, pastor of the church at Deerfield, was the son of Mr. Samuel Williams of
Roxbury. He was born 1664, was graduated
1683, and ordained in 1686. The town being
among the frontier settlements, was continually
exposed to the incursions of the French and Indians. In 1704 a party of savages destroyed the
place, and carried Mr. Williams and his family
through a wilderness of 300 miles. They killed

to write this work. Here are disclosed sentiments which have
been admired in the writings of Milton and Furneaux. His ideas
of toleration he carried further than Mr. Locke, but not beyond
the generality of dissenters in England. The book was answered
by Mr. Cotton, whose zeal and knowledge would give him a name
among christian worthies in any age of the church, and who was
the most distinguished of the clergy in Massachusetts. But so
far from supposing himself confuted, Mr. Williams replied with
great spirit and argument, which reply has been since published,
together with Mr. Cotton's attack upon him, which he called the
Bloody Tenent, washed in the blood of the Lamb, in allusion to the
first writing of Mr. Williams, which he styled *The Bloody Tenent,
or Dialogue between Truth and Peace,* meaning that the idea of the
interference of the magistracy, in matters of religion, is a bloody tenent.

The title of another book is, *George Fox digged out of his bur-
rows, &c.* by Roger Williams. The answer, a New England
fire-brand quenched, being an answer to a lying, slanderous book,
&c. by one Roger Williams, confuting his blasphemous asser-
tions, by George Fox and John Burnyeat. These controversial
pieces were printed about the years 1676—1678, and the contents of a large volume are similar to the title pages.

Many tracts are ascribed to Mr. Williams as a writer. He
wrote letters to individuals of his acquaintance, and to gentlemen
in office, which are among the most valuable antiquarian stores ;
some of them very curious and rare.

It is a desirable object to collect the mss. of Mr. Williams. He
mentions receiving scores of letters from his excellent friend gov.
Winthrop. Doubtless there are many letters of his writing, as
well as his correspondents, which would be accounted precious
by those who desire to know the history of their own country.

A most valuable book was published by the subject of this memoir, upon the language of *sauvage* America. It is called a *Key*
to the language of the *Indians of New England.* It was printed
in 1643, in a small duodecimo volume. The original is in the library of the historical society ; and most of the contents have
been published in their collections.

his wife, two children, and two servants. He was sent first to Montreal, then to Quebec, and in 1706, returned home, with other captives, to the number of 57. Mr. Williams was again settled at Deerfield, where he lived till the year 1729. He died suddenly of the apoplexy, in the month of June, aged 65. He was a pious and worthy man. His natural vivacity of temper, his vigourous mind, and firm constitution, fitted him for his situation, where he had to endure trials of the heart, as well as those trials which are common to men, and ministers. One of his children was brought up among the Indians, and never could be persuaded to leave her wandering life. She married and passed her days in Canada. He left 3 sons who were favoured with a college education, and settled in the ministry.* His wife, who was killed by the Indians, was the daughter of E. Mather, the first minister of Northampton, and grand-daughter of the famous John Warham, who came to Dorchester in 1630.

WILLIAMS NATHANIEL, preceptor of the south grammar school, Boston, was the son of very respectable parents, who gave him a college education with a view of his becoming a minister of the gospel; and to this he was early inclined. He was graduated at Harvard College, 1693; and, in July, 1698, was ordained an evangelist for one of the West India Islands. The climate was unfriendly to his constitution, and he soon returned to his native town. Being an excellent classical scholar, he was chosen successor to the celebrated master Cheever in the publick and free grammar school, " the principal school," says Mr. Prince, " of the British colonies, if not of all America." He continued from the year 1703 to 1734 a very useful instructor, when

---

* His publications were, the redeemed captive returning to Zion, as a history of his captivity, 1706; also a sermon preached the same year at the Boston lecture, Psalm cvii. 13, 14, 15; of these, the fourth edition was printed, 1793; the convention sermon, 1728.

his age and infirmities obliged him to resign his office. His assistant, Mr. Lovell, was then placed in the chair. When he was in the West Indies he applied his mind to the study of physick, and entered into the profession after he came to Boston. Those who employed him, persuaded him not to leave his line of business, when he took the grammar school. He visited many families, and when he gave up the school, passed the latter years of his life in the duties of his profession. He was called " the beloved physician," and was so agreeable in his manners, that, when he entered into the chambers of the sick, " his voice and countenance did good, like a medicine." It revived the spirits, and lightened the maladies. Amidst the multiplicity of his business, as a publick instructor, and a physician in extensive practice, he never left the *ministerial work.* He preached occasionally, and his prayers and sermons were highly acceptable to the pious and judicious.

He was very much attached to the religious principles and manners of New England. " The graces of the gospel seemed to shine in his countenance and conversation, and he was one of the most useful men in the town and land." He died, Jan. 10, 1737, 8, aged 63. There is no publication with his name, except a pamphlet upon " inoculation for the small pox." This was printed when the publick mind was so much agitated about introducing the practice. One of the satirical pamphlets of the times introduced him with Boylston and Douglass in a conversation which brought forward all the arguments for and against it. The book is entitled, " Mundungus, Sawney, Academicus, a debate, 1721." *Prince's sermon.*

WILLIAMS ELISHA, rector of Yale College, was the son of the rev. William Williams of Hatfield. The father, who was one of the most eminent clergymen in the county of Hampshire, was graduated in 1683, and died in 1753. He preached the election ser-

mon in 1719. He also printed a volume of sermons in 12mo. on Heb. ii. 3. The preface was
written by Dr. Colman, who speaks highly of the
writer. Rector Williams was graduated at Harvard College in 1711. He was ordained over a
church in Weathersfield, Connecticut, and introduced to the chair of Yale College, Sept. 1716. He
resigned his office in 1739, on account of his ill
state of health. He reformed the college very much,
and advanced useful and polite literature.

In 1745, he went as chaplain to the Connecticut
forces upon the expedition to Cape Breton. The
next year he had a colonel's commission given to
him, when an expedition to Canada was formed.
He made a conspicuous figure after he went into the
civil line. Being speaker of the house of representatives, he displayed so great talents that he was sent
to Great Britain, as agent for the colony. While he
was in England, he married a most amiable lady
with whom he lived happily till his death, in 1755.
He died at Weathersfield, July 24, etat. 61.*

WILSON JOHN, first pastor of the church in Boston, was the son of Dr. William Wilson, prebend
of Rochester. His mother was niece of Dr. Edmund Grindal, the renowned archbishop of Canterbury. He was born at Windsor, had a pious education, and made considerable progress in classical
learning at school and at college. He was 4 years
at Eaton, and during this time was directed to speak
a latin oration, when the duke de Biron, minister
from Henry IV. visited the schools ; for which the
duke bestowed 3 angels upon him. He was admitted into King's College, Cambridge, 1602. His
prejudices were strong against the Puritans till he

* In 1744, Mr. Williams wrote a pamphlet in 66 pages, 4to.
entitled, " the essential rights and liberties of protestants ; "or, a
letter from a gentleman in Massachusetts to his friend in Connecticut, wherein " some thoughts on the origin, end, and extent
of the civil power, with brief considerations on several late laws
in Connecticut, are humbly offered by a lover of truth and liberty."

read the work of Mr. Richard Rogers, called the *seven treatises*. He afterwards, by the advice of Dr. Ames, joined a pious company at the university, who held conferences upon religious subjects. He studied diligently the controversy between the episcopal church and the puritans, and became convinced, that he ought not to conform to the rites and ceremonies of the church of England. For this he was expelled the university. When his father could not persuade him to alter his views of religion, he advised him to enter the *inns* of the *court*. By the influence of the earl of Northampton, chancellor of the university, he afterwards received his degree at Cambridge. When he began to preach, he had frequent invitations to take the charge of a church; but as frequently was complained of to the spiritual courts, and silenced. The earl of Warwick was his friend, and by his influence he obtained leave to exercise his ministry. In the year 1629, when the plantation of a new colony was begun, Mr. W. was invited to join them, and embarked in the fleet which came here in 1630. When he arrived at Salem he was about 42 years old; but had a large share of health and vigour. He was able to assist his brethren under the difficulties of a new plantation, " the main design of which was, to settle the ordinances of the gospel, and worship Christ according to his own institutions." The next month after their arrival, they organized their church in Charlestown. He was installed teacher of this church, August 27, 1630. Afterwards he was chosen pastor of the church in Boston, and separated to the charge, Nov. 22, 1632. They were careful to mention that, although they used imposition of hands, it was only a sign of election, and not that he renounced the ordination he received in England. In the dispute, which divided the Boston church, Mr. Wilson and gov. Winthrop were on one side. Most of the church, with their teacher, Mr. Cotton, were of a different opinion, and were like-

wise strengthened by the authority, talents and fanatical zeal of sir Henry Vane. Mr. Wilson threw
all his influence in favour of gov. Winthrop at
the next election. He even stood upon a tree, and
spoke to the people. Upon this occasion he discovered much spirit, though his general character was
that of a mild and moderate man. He was very affable in speech, and condescending in his deportment.
He yielded to the superiour and more overbearing
influence of the great Cotton in every thing, except
in this Antinomian controversy, and in giving the
government to Winthrop. He lived to be an old
man, and followed to the grave both Cotton and
Norton.

When Mr. Norton returned from England, good
Mr. Wilson censured him for his conduct. He and
elder Penn, in the name of themselves and others,
acquainted him, that an assistant must be chosen.
Mr. Allen had preached, and the people were much
captivated with him. Mr. Norton, however, had
his friends, and they increased, though the generality of his flock had their prejudices against him.

Mr. Wilson preached his last sermon at Roxbury lecture for his son in law, Mr. Danforth; and
died August 7, 1667, in the 79th year of his age.
His remains were interred with uncommon respect.
Mr. Mather of Dorchester preached his funeral sermon, Zech. i. 5. *Our fathers, where are they?**

• Dr. Cotton Mather printed the life of Mr. Wilson, from
which a number of facts were taken. Some likewise from Prince's
annals, who collected further accounts of him. Mr. Wilson published many poems, anagrams, &c. in Latin and English. None
of his theological tracts have come down to us. A sermon of his
was printed, taken in short hand, by one of his hearers. When
he was young, his preaching was very methodical. Several judicious men in England followed him, on account of his excellent
discourses; and when he first came to New England, Mr. Shepard said, " Methinks I hear an apostle when I hear this man."
In his old age, his sermons were made up of exhortations, and
might be compared " to a good kind of talking." This may be
a reason why he published no more, while his colleagues sent so
many works to the press.

An observation of Dr. Ames, the celebrated professor, deserves to be recorded to the honour of Mr. Wilson, " that if he might have his option of the best condition this side heaven, it would be the teacher of a congregational church of which Mr. Wilson was pastor."

That witty writer, Mr. Ward, author of the simple cobler of Agawam, remarking the hospitality of Mr. Wilson, and knowing that he was fond of anagrams, said, that the anagram of John Wilson was, " I pray come in, you are heartily welcome." This anecdote is better attested, than one lately given to the publick about this same Mr. Ward, concerning his interview with Dr. Mather, who refused him even entrance to his house. Mr. Peters, who relates this, did not recollect that Dr. Mather was not one of the same generation.

WINSLOW EDWARD, governour of Plymouth colony, was born in the year 1694. He was an English gentleman of Worcestershire, who travelled over Europe, and joined Mr. Robinson's church at Leyden. He came over to New England with the first planters, and his name appears conspicuous among those who subscribed " the covenant of incorporation," at Cape Cod. His address and activity made him very useful to the company, and his eminent services are mentioned by every writer who gives an account of the landing of our fathers, or the circumstances of their settlement. Having lost his wife among those who died the first winter, he married the widow of William White, May 12, 1621. This is the first marriage which ever took place in New England. The lady was also the mother of the first child born in this newly discovered region. His name was Peregrine, who lived to the age of 83 years, 8 months, and died, July 20, 1704.

Mr. Winslow several times visited Massasoit, the sachem of the Indians who dwelt nearest the English settlement, of which he gives an account in his own journal, which happily has been preserved.

It makes part of the invaluable collections of Purchase, and is printed by Dr. Belknap, in the appendix to the American biography. Mr. Winslow also made another excursion to the bay of Penobscot,
in 1622, to procure bread from the vessels, fishing
upon the eastern coasts. He obtained a present
supply, and this led to a beneficial traffick with the
natives. The next year he went to England, and,
after an absence of six months, arrived at Plymouth
with provisions, cloathing, and neat cattle. He went
back to Great Britain, and again returned to the
plantation in 1625. He was chosen one of the assistants. In this office he continued till 1633, and
was then elected governour. Mr. Bradford importuned him to take the office. These virtuous men
entered into competition, not like the politicians
of this world, but like the rulers of a christian
commonwealth, " in honour preferring one another." In 1635, Mr. Winslow was employed as
agent for the colonies of Plymouth and Massachusetts at the British court. He transacted the business much to their satisfaction, but subjected himself to peculiar trials and difficulties. By order of
archbishop Laud, that archfiend to the puritans, he was
committed to prison. A complaint was made against
him by Thomas Morton of " Merry mount," who
gave information, that Mr. Winslow preached to the
people at Plymouth, and married without license.
Mr. W. acknowledged, " that sometimes, when the
church was destitute of a minister, he exercised his
gift for the edification of the brethren." He also
acknowledged the fact of his marrying people ; but
he considered marriage " as a civil contract, and
had been himself married by a Dutch magistrate in
Holland." He was confined several months in the
Fleet prison. When he returned to Plymouth,
1636, he was elected governour ; but the year succeeding took his place among the magistrates. In
1643, he was appointed a commissioner of the
united colonies. In 1646, he was persuaded to go

once more to England, to answer to the complaints of Gorton and others against the colony. While he was in England, his pious and benevolent mind was bent to an object which has since been pursued by christians of various denominations, " the propagation of the gospel among the Indians." This corporation, under the name of " the London society," was continued till the American revolution.

In 1655, Mr. Winslow was appointed one of the three commissioners to superintend the operations of the fleet sent to the West Indies. Admiral Penn and gen. Venables made an attack on St. Domingo, but were defeated. They took Jamaica; but in their passage from one island to the other, Mr. Winslow fell a sacrifice to the diseases of the climate. His body was committed to the deep, with the honours of war, 42 guns being fired, May 8, 1655. *Morton. Prince. Belknap.*

WINSLOW JOSIAH, son of that illustrious man, Edward Winslow, had all his father's great and good qualities. He was the first governour who was born in New England. Having been a magistrate several years, he succeeded Mr. Prince in the government, 1673, and was annually chosen, till 1680. He had what may be called a liberal education for this country, and discovered much good sense in his management of publick affairs. As a military officer he possessed skill, address and bravery. In 1656, when Alexander, the eldest son of Massasoit, was suspected of plotting against the English with the Narragansetts, Mr. Winslow, with several armed men, took him by surprise, which put an end to his machination ; but his breast swelled with rage, and his passion brought on a fever, which was fatal. In 1675, Philip, the youngest son, stirred up all the natives against the English. Mr. Winslow wrote to the governour of Massachusetts, " that he could not learn that Philip pretended any wrong done to him by the English, but suspected that he should be made to answer for the murder of John Sausaman," a christian Indian, whom the Indians of Mount Hope hated on this very account. Sensible of the prowess of gov. Winslow, the enemy tried every way to cut him off; but he was not to be moved with their threats. In the month of December he commanded the forces that attacked the Indians in their strong holds, and slew 1100 of them. This gave him a high reputation among his countrymen, and made the savages dread him. Gov. Winslow died at Marshfield, Dec. 18, 1680, in the 52d year of his age.

WINSLOW ISAAC, son of gov. Winslow, was president of the provincial council, and the chief military officer in the colony. He died, 1738.

WINSLOW JOHN, major general, was also a distinguished character in the colony; nor was his celebrity confined to New England. He commanded a company in the regiment, that was sent to Cuba in 1740. He had a commission in the line of the British troops, and rose to the rank of major general. He was the chief in command in several expeditions to Kennebeck. He was brave as a soldier, and an excellent military officer. His son, Dr. Isaac Winslow, is now living in Marshfield upon the family estate. The general died, 1774, aged 71. *Morton. Hutchinson. Belknap.*

WINTHROP JOHN, governour of Massachusetts, was the son of Adam Winthrop, esq. of Groton, in Suffolk. He was born June 12, 1587. When he was 18 years old he had such a knowledge of jurisprudence, as to be appointed a justice of the peace. The family estate was large; but he converted it into different property, that he might come over to America. So pious a man would prefer an uncultivated country where he could enjoy his religion to ease and affluence amidst those who were of a persecuting spirit. In 1630 he brought over the charter, and arrived at Salem, June 12. He was chosen governour several years successively ; but for the sake of a rotine among the magistrates, Mr. Dudley was put into his place, and Ludlow, a west countryman of fine abilities and great intrigue, was chosen deputy. The next year Mr. Ludlow tried for the chief place, but was disappointed of both. He therefore went to Connecticut, as related in the sketch of his life. In 1636, Mr. W. being deputy governour, had need of all his wisdom and integrity to prevent the consequences of sir H. Vane's rash proceedings, and to calm the religious commotions, which made confusion in the metropolis. He met with other troubles, which affected his ingenuous mind, because his intentions were pure, and his aim was to serve the people. To be injured by those we love, and exert ourselves to serve, is a severe trial of the heart; but he bore even these trials with meekness, and benevolent wishes to the country. He was conscious of rectitude ; and whenever the people had time for consideration, they found him to be a most faithful magistrate, and wise and prudent man, who always sought their interest to the sacrifice of his own. When he left England he possessed a very catholic spirit. He was more of a puritan in New England from his acquaintance with Dudley, Endicot and others, who thought toleration a crime, and that no kind of religious sentiments should be suffered to prevail, except what they had imbibed : before his death, he expressed a wish that more moderation had been used towards persons accounted hereticks. He suffered great losses of a pecuniary nature by the bad management of his steward; such depredations were made on his property as excited the compassion of the people, who exerted themselves to assist him by publick and private contributions. This great and good man also met with domestick affliction in a more tender part, in the breaches that were made upon his family. Ill health of body affected his mind, and he died, 26th of March, 1649, in the 63d year of his age.

He left a journal of events from the settlement of

the colony to his death. An island in the harbour of Boston bears his name, and is still in the posses-sion of one of his descendants. His picture is pre-served in the council chamber. Several of his pos-terity have exhibited the image of their illustrious ancestor, and his family have been more eminent for their talents, learning and honours than any other in New England.*

WINTHROP JOHN, governour of Connecticut, eldest son of the first governour of Massachusetts, was born in England, 1605, was educated at the university of Cambridge, and travelled over the greatest part of Europe. In 1633, he came over to this country, and was chosen a magistrate of the col-ony of Massachusetts. The spot which he preferred for a dwelling, was Agawam, where he went with 12 men, to begin a plantation. They called it Ipswich. There his first son was born. He went back to England; but in the same year came over to Ameri-ca with a commission from lord Say and Seal, lord Brook and others, to be governour of their plan-tation, at Connecticut. A fort was built at the mouth of the river, and the spot called Saybrook, in compliment to the noble lords who owned the land. In 1651 he was chosen a magistrate of this people, and then deputy governour, and after-wards governour. In 1662 he was agent at the court of Charles II. and obtained a charter for the colony of Connecticut. An account of this agency is cel-ebrated in poetick strains, by one of his successors, Roger Wolcott, esq.† He was annually chosen chief magistrate to the time of his death. In the spring of 1676, upon a visit to Boston, he was taken sick, and expired April 5th, and was buried in the same tomb with his father. He was one of the greatest philosophers of the age ; and his name is among the founders of the royal society of Lon-

* A very interesting and particular part of Belknap's American Biography, is the life of gov. Winthrop.
　　　　† Historical collections, vol. iv.

don. The great Mr. Boyle, bishop Wilkins, with several other learned men, had proposed to leave England, and establish *a society for promoting natural knowledge* in the new colony of which Mr. Winthrop, their intimate friend and associate, was appointed governour. Such men were too valuable to lose from Great Britain, and Charles II. having taken them under his protection, the society was there established, and obtained the title of the *royal society of London.* It was soon considered as the most learned society in Europe. Mr. Winthrop sent over many specimens of the productions of this country, with his remarks upon them, " and, by an order of the royal society, he was in a particular manner invited to take upon himself the charge of being the chief correspondent in the West, as sir Philiberto Vernatti was in the East Indies." "His name," says the same writer, who was secretary to this society in 1741, "had he put it to his writings, would have been as universally known, as the Boyles', the Wilkins', and Oldenburghs', and been handed down to us with similar applause." *Dedication of the 40th volume of philosophical transactions, &c.*

WINTHROP FITZ JOHN, son of John Winthrop, esq. first governour of Connecticut, was born at Ipswich, 1638. He was a magistrate of the colony, and major general. In 1693 he was appointed agent of the colony to present a petition to king William to secure their charter rights; and when he returned, at the election, May, 1698, he was chosen governour. He resembled his father in fine accomplishments, had an excellent moral character, was famous for his philosophical knowledge, and was elected a fellow of the royal society : he was also famous for his skill in politicks. This he manifested when he was at the court of Great Britain : his conduct there was so pleasing to the people of Connecticut, that they not only voted him thanks for his successful agency, but, as a further testimony of their esteem, presented him with 500 pounds for the services rendered,

3 R

The colony sustained a great loss by his death. He died at Boston, of the stone, Nov. 27, 1707. *Harris's mss. Trumbull's history of Connecticut.*

WINTHROP JOHN, F. R. S. grandson of the first governour of Connecticut, was graduated at Harvard College, 1700. He was a magistrate in the colony of Connecticut; but left this country, went to England, and there passed the rest of his days. He died in the year 1747. To this gentleman the " 40th volume of the transactions of the royal society" was dedicated by Dr. Cromwell Mortimer their secretary. It seems he left America on account of some contention between his family and the government of Connecticut.* He was elected a fellow of the royal society, and was distinguished as one of the most conspicuous members of that learned body. He was also esteemed and courted by learned and good men for his " extraordinary skill in the deep mysteries of the hermetic science."

WINTHROP JOHN, L L. D. F. R. S. was the son of the honourable Adam Winthrop, esq. one of his majesty's council in Massachusetts. The grandfather and great grandfather were also honourable men, each named Adam, and the eldest a son of the first governour. The subject of the present article was graduated at Harvard College, 1732. He was then an amiable youth, and one of the first scho-

* " When the injustice and ingratitude of a reigning party in power among that very people, whereof the Winthrops have been always in the most strict sense the fathers, the patres patriæ, had most cruelly driven you from your family and native soil, to seek justice and security in your natural rights from the hands of our most gracious sovereign ; amidst the vexations of the greatest abuses, and the hurries of the most sudden departure, you were not unmindful of the royal society ; for soon after your being chosen a fellow, you increased the riches of their repository with more than 600 curious specimens, chiefly in the mineral kingdom, accompanied with an accurate account of each particular ; thereby shewing your great skill in natural philosophy, and at the same time intimating to England the vast riches which lie hidden in the lap of her principal daughter. Since Mr. Colwell, the founder of the museum of the royal society, you have been the benefactor who has given the most numerous collection," &c.

lars in his class. In 1738 he succeeded Mr. Greenwood, as Hollis professor of mathematicks and natural philosophy, and was more eminent for his scholarship, than any other man in New England. In mathematical science he was considered as the first in America during the 40 years he continued professor at Cambridge. In the year 1740, he made observations upon the transit of Mercury, which were printed in the transactions of the royal society; in 1755 he printed a lecture upon earthquakes, and 1756 a letter to the rev. Mr. Prince, who made observations upon the professor's opinion; two lectures upon comets in 1759. In the year 1761 there was a transit of Venus over the sun's disk, and, as Newfoundland was the most western part of the earth where the end of the transit could be observed, it was an object with the literati, to have observations made in that place. Mr. W. offered his services to go there, and the general court made provision for his voyage. He took with him two pupils, who had made progress in mathematical studies,* and sailed from Boston, May 9th. The sixth of June was a fine day for observing the transit of the planet, and he gained high reputation when these observations were published. In 1769 he had another opportunity of observing the transit of Venus at Cambridge. As it was the last opportunity that generation could be favoured with, he was desirous to arrest the attention of the people. He read two lectures upon the subject in the college chapel, which the students requested him to publish. The professor put this motto upon the title page, agite mortales! et oculos in spectaculum vertite, quod hucusce spectaverunt perpaucissimi; spectaturi iterum sunt nulli.

He received literary honours from other countries beside his own. The royal society of London elect-

---

* Samuel Williams, who succeeded him in the professorship, and Isaac Rand, who was lately president of the medical society of Massachusetts.

ed him a member ; and the university of Edinburgh
gave him a diploma of L L. D. In 1767, he wrote
Cogitata de cometis, which he dedicated to the royal
society, as a testimony of respect after he was admitted into their body. This was reprinted in London the next year. Professor W. was an excellent
classical scholar, and also a biblical critick. Some
of his criticisms are published in Dr. Chauncy's
book, entitled, " salvation for all men." The Dr.
acknowledges the assistance he received from the
learned professor, and always spake of him, as one
of the greatest theologians he ever met with.

The active services of Dr. Winthrop were not
confined to the duties of his professorship at Cambridge. He was a brilliant star in our political
hemisphere. The family of Winthrops had always
been distinguished for their love of freedom, and the
charter rights of the colonies. When Great Britain
made encroachments upon these, by acts of parliament after the peace of Paris, in 1763, he stepped
forth among those, who boldly opposed the measures of the crown. He had much influence from
his knowledge, and the weight of his character.
He was chosen one of his majesty's council when
Hutchinson was in the chair of government, who
did not negative him ; but in the year 1774, a royal
mandate was issued to negative three gentlemen,
who had been most active in opposing the measures
of the administration. These were Mr. Bowdoin,
Mr. Dexter, and Mr. Winthrop. When the people
took the government into their own hands, he was
again chosen one of the council, and continued in
his publick character till his death.

The best part of Dr. Winthrop's character was, that
he was a christian philosopher. He believed the truths
of christianity from study and conviction, and was
an ornament to his profession. To his numerous
acquaintance, he was a " friend, philosopher and
guide." He had the consolations of our divine religion, during his latter years, when his bodily frame

was subject to pain and infirmities. His mind continued strong, his faith was steadfast, and his views
spiritual and pure. He died, May 3, 1779, aged 65.

WOLCOTT ROGER, governour of Connecticut,
was born in Windsor, 1679. He made his first appearance in publick life, as an officer in the army
that went to Canada in 1711. He was afterwards
colonel of the militia, and was commander of the
Connecticut forces when Cape Breton was taken by
the Americans in 1745. He was employed in many civil offices, which he filled with reputation, and
discharged with fidelity. He was a member of the
general assembly, assistant, deputy governour,
chief judge of the superior court, and, in the year
1751, succeeded Mr. Law in the chair of government.
In 1754, he resigned his publick honours, and passed the rest of his days in the shades of retirement.
The evening of his days was gilded by the reflection of a well spent life. He died May 17, 1767.

Gov. Wolcott had not the advantage even of a
common education; but the resources of his
mind were great. His private affairs he managed
with discretion. He was fond of books, conversed
upon literary subjects with ease, and was highly respected by gentlemen of the first abilities in the colony. He wrote and published several works in
poetry and prose. His account, in poetry, of the
agency of gov. Winthrop, in 1662, was lately reprinted in the 4th volume of the collections of the
Massachusetts historical society; it makes one of
his poetical meditations, published in 1725, in a
small volume. These resemble the jingle of the
early productions of New England rather than
the versification of later days. In 1760 he
engaged in a controversy, which then agitated the
churches of Connecticut. In the year preceding,
Mr. Hobart of Fairfield wrote a book, entitled,
" The principles of the congregational churches
considered, and applied to the ordination at Wallingford." The settlement of Mr. Dana, who now

ranks among the distinguished writers and divines of New England, at Wallingford, gave great offence to the neighbouring clergy. The ordination was contrary to the rules of the Saybrook platform, and Mr. Hobart highly censured the proceedings. Mr. Hart wrote remarks upon Mr. Hobart's book, and Mr. Wolcott also addressed a letter to him, wherein he compares the Cambridge and Saybrook platform; and proves the latter to be inconsistent with the general principles of toleration, and religious freedom. Mr. Hobart replied to Mr. Hart in 1761. We have no answer to the letter of Mr. Wolcott, which is dated April 25, 1760.

WOLCOTT OLIVER, L L. D. governour of Connecticut, was the son of Roger Wolcott, and possessed his father's talents and virtues, with a mind improved by a liberal education. He was educated at Yale College, and received his degree in 1747. He then applied his mind to the study of physick, and had an extensive practice in the town of Litchfield. He had a taste for publick life, and was well versed in the laws and politicks of New England. For a number of years he was high sheriff of the county of Litchfield. He was among the high whigs who resisted the oppressive acts of the mother country. In 1776, we find his name among those who signed the declaration of independence. From that time he was annually chosen a member of congress till the year 1785, when he was appointed deputy governour, and continued in this office till gov. Huntington died in 1796. He was then advanced to the chair; but died the next year in December, 1797.

His character was very respectable in private life, and in every publick station. He was a gentleman and scholar, very liberal in his sentiments, and also a friend to the constitution of the New England churches. By some he might be considered as too liberal, as his ideas of moral agency were different from many of the clergy. He frequently expressed his opinion that necessarian principles ought not to be propagated with theological opinions; that it was an injury to the cause of morality, as people did not distinguish between the doctrine of necessity, and common notions of fate. In this he differed from some excellent characters, and agreed with others, equally wise and good. He had a humble view of himself, though others thought highly of his abilities. Having lived a religious life, he enjoyed the hope of a christian, looking for a reward, as well as rest from his labours.

WOODBRIDGE BENJAMIN, first graduate of Harvard College, in 1642, was an eminent scholar, and an excellent preacher. He left America, and settled at Newbury, Berks, as successor to the great Dr. Twiss. In 1662 he was ejected from the parish; but afterwards preached by a particular indulgence of the king, who had a very favourable opinion of him. He died, 1684.

YALE ELIHU, a friend to learning and religion, was born at New Haven, 1648; and when he was very young, was carried to England. He was brought up to merchandize, and, by his industry and attention to business, grew rich, and also gained publick esteem. At the age of 40 he sailed to the East Indies. He was there appointed commander of fort St. George. When he returned to London he was chosen president of the East India company. He sought opportunities of doing good, and either founded, or encouraged, many literary, pious and useful institutions. In the year 1717, Dr. Cotton Mather wrote to Mr. Yale, and advised him to present a liberal donation to the college at New Haven. They will name the college after you, said he, and that will be better than to have sons and daughters. In a letter to gov. Saltonstall, the Doctor tells him, that the college had better be named Yale, and says something handsome will be given. Hence the name of Yale College was given to one of the most respectable seminaries of New England.

ERRATA ET ADDENDA.

Page 3, line 8, from bottom, for 1701, read 1721 ; p. 4, l. 11, fr. top, dele *in* ; p. 5, l. 2, fr. top, for 1778, read 1775 ; p. 20, l. 3. fr. bot. for 1737, read 1697 ; p. 21. l. 7, fr. top, for proposition, read *propositions* ; p. 24, l. 2, fr. bottom, for year, read *years* ; p. 24, l. 3, fr. bot. for 1771, read 1778 ; p. 31, l. 14. fr. top, for or, read *for* ; p. 47, l. 8, fr. top for composition, read *compositions* ; p. 48, l. 15, fr. top, for preventative, read *preventive* ; p. 51, l. 6, fr, bot. for Mr. B. read *Mr. H.* p. 73, l. 4, fr. bot. for 1740, read 1748 ; p. 75, l. 16. fr. bot. for less. read *more* ; 76, l. 16, fr. top, read *one of the fifteen* ; p. 76, l 22, fr. top, dele *of* ; p 78, l. 24, fr. top, for 1720, read 1721 ; p. 78, l. 3, fr. bot. read *Colman* ; p, 84, l. 4, fr. bot. dele *have* ; p. 86, l. 5, fr. top, C for c ; p. 91, l. 14, fr. bot. add, except a preface to Roger Wolcott's meditations, and an ordination sermon, preached at Colchester, 1729 ; p. 97, l. 18. fr. bot. for 1630, read 1621 ; p. 99, l. 14 fr. bot. for prasidem, read *præsidem* ; p 100, l. 6, fr. top, for imperato, read *imperatore* ; p. 101, l. 9, fr. top, for Intergerrimi, read *Integerrimi* ; p 101, l. 12, fr. top, read *liberali* ; p. 101, l. 16, fr. top, dele *L C* ; p. 106, l. 6, fr. top, after is, read *in* ; p. 107, l. 12, fr. bot. for scriptures, read *scripture* ; p. 110, l 19, fr. bot. dele *to* ; p. 113, l. 7, fr. top, for built, read *gathered* ; p. 119, l. 12, fr. bot. read *everlasting* ; p. 121, l. 4. fr. bot. for to, read *of* ; p 122, l. 20, fr. top, read *continued till he went to England* ; p. 141, l. 3, fr. bot. read *discharged with fidelity* ; p. 148, l. 5, fr. bot. for well wishes, read *well wishers* ; p. 146, l 19 fr. top, for 1771, read 1671 ; p. 146, l. 25. fr. top, for 1134, read 1634 ; p 154, l. 6 fr. bot. read *to make* ; p. 158, l. 13, fr. bot. for White, read *Wight* ; p. 162, l. 2, fr. top, dele *no* ; p. 168, l. 18, fr. bot. for Dr. read *Mr.* Eaton ; p. 179, l. 5, fr. bot. read *loins* ; p. 181, l. 6, fr. top, for character, read *charity* ; p. 185, l. 4, fr. bot for whose, read *whom* ; p. 192, l. 5, fr. top, for 30, read 13 ; p. 213, l. 3, fr. top, for in, read *into* ; p. 230, l. 6, fr. bot. for bills, read *bill* ; p. 236, l. 5, fr top, read *MDCCLXXXVI* ; p. 236, l. 19, fr. top, add, *He died at South Carolina, Oct. 12, 1745* ; p. 246, l. 6, fr bot. read *New England* ; p. 264, l. 4, fr. bot. for 1779, read 1780 ; p. 272, l, 10, from top, dele *to* ; p. 289, l. 5, fr. top, for Dowes, read *Dawes* ; p 301, l. 1, fr. top, read 1776; p. 305 l. 10, fr. bot. for on, read *or* ; p. 313, l. 17, fr. bot. read *magistrate* ; p. 331, l. 9, fr. bot. for discharge, read *discharged* ; p. 354, l. 7, fr. bot. for 1770, read 1760 ; p. 355. l. 4, fr. top, for tired, read *tried* ; p. 354, l. 10, fr. bot. read *council* ; p. 362, l. 1, fr. bot for building, read *entering* ; p 362, ls. 2 and 3, fr. bot. for Popkins, read *Popkin* ; p. 366, l. 19, fr. top, for of, read *off* ; p. 366, l. 22, fr. bot. read, As a companion *he* was, &c. p. 367, l. 17, fr. bot. dele *an* ; p 369, l. 3, fr. top. for do, read *doing* ; page 370 ; l. 5, fr. bot. read 1757, add. artillery election sermon, 1756 ; p 378, l. 7, fr. bot. read *zealous* ; p 379, l 15, fr. bot. dele *It was* ; p 396, l. 19, fr. bot. for had, read *have* ; p. 401. l. 9, fr. top, for plead, read *pleaded* ; p. 401, l. 20. fr. bot. read *Quincys* ; p. 420 l. 21. fr. top, for 1628, read 1728 ; p. 434, l. 2, fr. bot. read *record* ; p. 461, l. 2. fr top, read, which he answered *with* very lively, &c, p. 473, l. 7, fr. bot. for of, read *off* ; p 487, l. 18, fr. top, for 86 read 77 ; in several places where etat is mentioned, the first letter should be a dipthong.

Every-Name Index

www.ingramcontent.com/pod-product-compliance
Lightning Source LLC
Chambersburg PA
CBHW072038020426
42334CB00017B/1314